PowerShell 7 Workshop

Learn how to program with PowerShell 7 on Windows, Linux, and the Raspberry Pi

Nick Parlow

PowerShell 7 Workshop

Group Product Manager: Pavan Ramchandani

Publishing Product Manager: Khushboo Samkaria

Book Project Manager: Neil D'mello

Senior Editor: Romy Dias

Technical Editor: Rajat Sharma

Copy Editor: Safis Editing

Proofreader: Safis Editing

Indexer: Manju Arasan

Production Designer: Vijay Kamble

DevRel Marketing Coordinator: Marylou De Mello

First published: February 2024

Production reference: 1090224

Published by Packt Publishing Ltd.

Grosvenor House

11 St Paul's Square

Birmingham

B3 1RB, UK

ISBN 978-1-80181-298-6

www.packtpub.com

For Chris, Megan, Tom, Bryn, and Mam and Dad. I love you all more than I can say.

Contributors

About the author

Nick Parlow is a Fujitsu Fellow and has been an email specialist for the last 20 years. He's a Microsoft Certified Master in Exchange, a VMware Certified Advanced Professional, and a Microsoft Certified Trainer. He's got master's degrees in network engineering from Sheffield Hallam and software engineering from Northumbria. Best of all, he's a Raspberry Pi Certified Educator.

Before IT, he worked as a metallurgist, including at the Joint European Torus, and also worked as a deckhand and a tree surgeon's mate. It's all good.

He works with schools in Hertfordshire, teaching programming and physical computing. In his spare time, he likes to play with chainsaws, watch Welsh rugby, listen to punk music, and drink cider.

It takes a village to raise an idiot. I name (some of) the guilty: Jon Funiciello and all my PTSG colleagues; Dave Snelling, Joseph Reger, and the FDEs; Beth Rowlands and Zara Brooke; Romy, Neil, Sean, and Khushboo at Packt; Craig, Steve, and Farah, the technical reviewers; Mark and Helen Kerr; Mark and Sue Custerson; Tim Parlow; Uncle Bob and Auntie Gill; Mam and Dad; Megan, Tom, and Bryn; and above all, my amazing wife, Chris.

Thank you, all. I owe you everything, but you'll have to settle for beer.

About the reviewers

Stephen Atherton (Steve) "fell into" IT in the late 1980s, when, as a civil servant, he was provided with a sparkling new PC and told to "get on with it!". Very soon he was hooked, creating databases and batch jobs, and soon moved on to PC and Novell NetWare support. He later moved into network design when outsourced to Fujitsu (then ICL) in 1995 and progressed to CTO on a couple of major government contracts overseeing numerous network migrations and BAU. For the last 8 years, Steve has developed and maintained standard server builds and Ansible and PowerShell automation solutions. Married for nearly 40 years, with 3 children and 4 grandchildren, Steve moved to Blackpool from North Wales in 1982 and enjoys nothing better than a round of golf (over 19 holes!).

My wife, Tracey, has been my rock over the many years we've been together, putting up with my absences for work and many hobbies; my family is the reason I did what I did, and I wouldn't be anything without them! My dear friend and golf buddy, Allan, and his wife, Sue, have always helped me keep it light, get out, enjoy life, and sustain my sanity. I am my father, my mother, and my brother; may they rest in peace. And remember – no rain, no rainbows!

Craig Lloyd is a computer science graduate from the late 1980s with a 34-year timeline in the IT industry. His primary role has always been technical, originally in mainframe digital communications, then later, when the world adopted TCP/IP, moving into pure network infrastructure problem analysis and troubleshooting at the network packet level. More recently, he has carried forward his technical skills into the arena of server hosting, hypervisors, and hybrid infrastructures across multiple vendor cloud platforms. Every day has been an opportunity to learn something new, and PowerShell, which has liberated the Command Prompt, has given Craig a platform to do that.

Table of Contents

Preface   xv

Part 1: PowerShell Fundamentals

1

Introduction to PowerShell 7 – What It Is and How to Get It   3

Technical requirements	3	Running PowerShell with administrator privileges	18
What is PowerShell 7?	4	Autocomplete	19
What is PowerShell 7 used for?	6		
Scripting languages versus system programming languages	6	**Getting help**	**19**
		Get-Command	20
Getting PowerShell 7	**7**	Get-Help	21
Installation from an .msi file	8	Get-Member	23
Installation from the .zip file	12	**Summary**	**25**
Installation with winget	14	**Exercises**	**25**
Other ways to install	15	**Further reading**	**25**
Running PowerShell 7	**16**		

2

Exploring PowerShell Cmdlets and Syntax   27

Technical requirements	27	Understanding cmdlet syntax	30
What are cmdlets?	28	How to find more cmdlets	35
Exploring cmdlet structure	28	Finding modules and cmdlets on your machine	35
The correct use of aliases	29	Finding new modules and cmdlets	39

Working interactively with PowerShell   **43**

Windows Terminal – an alternative terminal emulator   44

Installing Windows Terminal from Microsoft Store   44

Summary   **49**

Exercises   **50**

3

The PowerShell Pipeline – How to String Cmdlets Together   51

How to bring cmdlets together – the pipeline   **52**

What is an object?   54

Selecting and sorting objects   **55**

Using Select-Object   56

Ordering objects with Sort-Object   57

Filtering objects   **60**

Understanding comparison operators   60

Understanding Where-Object advanced syntax   62

Multiple filters in the advanced syntax   63

Filter optimization   66

Enumerating objects   **67**

Parallel enumeration   68

How the pipeline works – parameter binding   **68**

Understanding ByValue parameter binding   69

ByPropertyName parameter binding   71

Troubleshooting the pipeline – pipeline tracing   **72**

Summary   **74**

Exercises   **74**

Further reading   **75**

4

PowerShell Variables and Data Structures   77

Understanding PowerShell variables   **77**

Variables are not their contents   78

Naming variables   80

The three common types of PowerShell variable   81

Exploring object types   **83**

What is an object? – redux   84

Discovering value types   **86**

Booleans   86

Integers   87

Real numbers   87

Char   88

Typing explained   **88**

Dynamic versus static typing   88

Casting variables   89

Navigating reference types   **91**

Arrays   92

Strings   98

Hashtables   102

Splatting – a cool use for hashtables   **106**

Summary	106	Further reading	107
Exercises	107		

5

PowerShell Control Flow – Conditionals and Loops   109

An introduction to IDEs and VS Code	110	The do while and do until loop statements	128
		The while loop	130
Installing VS Code	110	The for loop	130
Configuring VS Code for PowerShell	113	Breaking and continuing	133
Conditional control – if, else, elseif, and switch	117	The break statement	133
		The continue statement	133
The if statement	118	Let's play a game	135
The switch statement	123	Summary	138
Loops – foreach, do while, do until, while, for	126	Exercises	138
		Further reading	139
The foreach loop statement	126		

6

PowerShell and Files – Reading, Writing, and Manipulating Data   141

Understanding formatting	142	A brief note about PSProviders and PSDrives	153
Format-List	143	Item- cmdlets	154
Format-Table	144	Working with files	155
Format-Wide	144	Get-Content	156
Formatting gotchas	144	Import- cmdlets	156
Writing a text file	145	Let's have some fun – measuring the most frequent words in a text file	160
Using ConvertTo- and Export- cmdlets	146		
CSV	147		
XML	149	Summary	163
HTML	150	Exercises	164
Handling files	152	Further reading	164

7

PowerShell and the Web – HTTP, REST, and JSON   165

Working with HTTP	**166**	**Working with JSON**	**180**
Why don't we see Forms information		ConvertFrom-Json	182
in PowerShell 7?	170	ConvertTo-Json	184
Authentication	172	Test-Json	187
Getting to grips with APIs	**174**	**Let's have some fun – who is on**	
RPC APIs	175	**the International Space Station?**	**188**
SOAP APIs	176	**Summary**	**189**
REST APIs	176	**Exercises**	**190**
WebSocket APIs	176	**Further reading**	**191**
Working with REST	**176**		
Invoke-RestMethod	177		

Part 2: Scripting and Toolmaking

8

Writing Our First Script – Turning Simple Cmdlets into Reusable Code   195

Introduction to scripting	**196**	Switch parameters	207
Why do we want to write scripts?	196	**Providing help for our script**	**208**
Getting scripts	197	Comments	208
Running scripts	198	Comment-based help	210
Writing a script	**198**	Write-Verbose	212
Identifying changing values	**200**	Parameter help messages	213
Working with parameters	**201**	**Summary**	**214**
Creating useful parameters	201	**Further reading**	**215**
Specifying type	204	**Exercises**	**215**
Making parameters mandatory	204		
Taking values from the pipeline	205		

9

Don't Repeat Yourself – Functions and Scriptblocks   217

Why do we care about repeating code?	218	Scope modifiers	234
How to turn repeating code into a function	220	Exploring scriptblocks	235
		How to run a scriptblock	235
What makes a function?	222	Lambdas	237
Function parameters	225	Let's do something useful	238
Filters	231	Summary	240
The concept of scope	232	Further reading	241
Parent and child scopes	233	Exercises	242

10

Error Handling – Oh No! It's Gone Wrong!   243

What is an error?	244	Exploring debugging	255
Terminating and non-terminating exceptions and errors	246	Script instrumentation	256
		Debugging cmdlets	259
Understanding error actions	248	Debugging with VS Code	262
The $ErrorActionPreference variable	248	Summary	265
The -ErrorAction parameter	249	Exercises	266
Catching errors	250	Further reading	266
Try/Catch/Finally	250		
Creating errors	253		

11

Creating Our First Module   269

Working with modules	269	Writing a simple module	273
Module locations	270	A word of caution – dot-sourcing	274
Module autoloading	271	Turning a script into a module	276
Importing modules	272	Nested modules	279
PowerShellGet	272	More modules	282

Module manifests   283
Using scaffolding tools
such as Plaster   287

Summary   291
Exercises   291
Further reading   292

12

Securing PowerShell   293

Why is security so important?   293
A PowerShell remoting whistlestop tour   294
Enabling PowerShell remoting   294
Creating a session   295
Joining and leaving a session   296
One-to-many sessions   297

Securing PowerShell against
inadvertent mistakes   297
Execution policy   298
Other features   300

Running PowerShell securely   301
Application control   301
Language modes   301
Security servicing criteria   302
Software Bill of Materials   302

Windows Antimalware
Scan Interface support   302
Secure Shell (SSH) remoting   303
Just Enough Administration   303

PowerShell logging   303
Over the shoulder logging   303
Deep script block logging   305
Module logging   306

Writing secure code   307
Storing passwords securely   307
Signing scripts   308
Parameter security   309

Summary   310
Exercises   311
Further reading   311

Part 3: Using PowerShell

13

Working with PowerShell 7 and Windows   315

Understanding PowerShell 7
and Windows PowerShell   316
Exploring compatibility   316
Which modules are compatible
with PowerShell 7?   316

What doesn't work
with PowerShell 7   324
Managing machines with
CIM and WMI   324
Introduction to CIM and WMI   324
Querying data   328

Making changes 331
Summary 335

Exercises 336
Further reading 336

14

PowerShell 7 for Linux and macOS 339

Technical requirements 340
Installing PowerShell 7 343
Installing PowerShell on Ubuntu 22.04 343
Installing PowerShell on CentOS 8 and 9 346
Installing PowerShell on CentOS 7 347

Installing VS Code 348
Running PowerShell on Linux 350
Remoting with OpenSSH 352
Checking that PowerShell has OpenSSH support 352
Installing OpenSSH on Windows 352

Installing OpenSSH on Linux 354
Running remote sessions 355
Authentication 356

PowerShell for macOS 358
Installing Homebrew on macOS 358
Installing PowerShell on macOS 358
Installing VS Code on macOS 360

Summary 360
Exercises 361
Further reading 361

15

PowerShell 7 and the Raspberry Pi 363

Technical requirements 363
Introduction to the Raspberry Pi 364
Installing PowerShell 7 and VS Code 365
Installing PowerShell 365
Installing VS Code 368

Connecting remotely to the Pi 368
Working with a headless Pi 369
Connecting to the Pi with PowerShell 372

Connecting to the Pi with VS Code 374

Running PowerShell on Raspberry Pi OS 376
Installing the IoT module 376
Exploring the IoT module 377

Simple physical computing 379
Summary 383
Questions 383
Further reading 384

16

Working with PowerShell and .NET   385

Exploring .NET   385
Software frameworks explained   386
Common language infrastructure   386
Common language runtime – CoreCLR   387
Framework Class Library – CoreFX   387
.NET history   387
The uses of .NET   388

The components of .NET   388
Assemblies   388
Types   389
Enumerations   390
Classes   390
Namespaces   390

Members   392
Versioning   393

Working with .NET in PowerShell   393
PowerShell assemblies   394
Dynamic assembly loading   394
Creating instances of types   395

Using .NET   395
An alternative to the Task Scheduler   395
Creating GUI objects   396

Summary   397
Exercises   398
Further reading   398

Answers to Activities and Exercises   401

Index   429

Other Books You May Enjoy   442

Preface

PowerShell is a free, powerful, and easy-to-learn programming language. Originally written as a scripting and administration tool for Windows, it's now available as an open source resource that can be installed on almost all laptops and desktops. I have been teaching PowerShell to my colleagues for the last decade, and in my spare time, I teach coding to kids in local schools, mostly in Python. Why not teach coding with PowerShell?

Many books and courses on PowerShell assume an audience with access to multiple machines, Active Directory domains, and various other enterprise environments. They often also play down the traditional coding elements of PowerShell. This book does neither and attempts to teach coding with PowerShell, in a similar way to how we teach coding with Python. I've been inspired by the incredible work of Dr Chuck Severance of the University of Michigan – if you want to learn Python, his *Python for Everybody* course at `py4e.org` is excellent.

The book is split into three parts. In the first part, we cover traditional coding theory; starting with how PowerShell works as a language, we look at the building blocks of the language and then move on to how we can combine them in a programmatic flow.

In the second part, we start to put together the principles we've learned into scripts and modules that we can share and reuse.

In the final part of the book, we look at how PowerShell works in different environments, before finishing with a chapter on how we can access the underlying framework that PowerShell is built on.

I've included many interesting and varied examples and exercises in the book. To get the most out of it, I encourage you to actually type out the code, rather than just read it; the physical act of typing it drives a much deeper engagement than just scanning it ever will. Try out the questions and activities, and have a good think about the questions before skipping ahead to the answers. You'll get much more out of the exercises if you have to work a little.

I would love to hear what you think and any suggestions you have for how the book might be improved.

Who this book is for

This book is for people who want to learn to write code and want to learn it using PowerShell. That might be school pupils who want to try something different, IT engineers who want to move to the next level, hobbyists, makers… everybody. It's probably not for experienced programmers who want to add PowerShell to their impressive list of competencies; if you can already write in Java, C++, or C#, then you might do better to look at a book such as *Mastering PowerShell Scripting* by Chris Dent, published by Packt.

What this book covers

Chapter 1, Introduction to PowerShell – What It Is and How to Get It, explains what PowerShell 7 is, describes its uses, and how it differs from Windows PowerShell. It describes how to get it, how to install it, and how to run it, explaining the difference between User and Administrator mode. It describes how to run cmdlets and how to get help in PowerShell.

Chapter 2, Exploring PowerShell Cmdlets and Syntax, focuses on how PowerShell cmdlets work, approved verbs, parameters, how to find new cmdlets with the PowerShell Gallery and elsewhere on the internet, and finally, how to work interactively with PowerShell.

Chapter 3, The PowerShell Pipeline – How to String Cmdlets Together, covers how the PowerShell pipeline is one of the most important concepts in PowerShell and is quite different from how pipelines work in Bash and the Command Prompt. This chapter will show you how to successfully chain cmdlets together in a pipeline to produce useful outcomes. It will talk about filtering, output, how the pipeline works, and why it sometimes doesn't!

Chapter 4, PowerShell Variables and Data Structures, is an introduction to variables and the different types they may be, integers, floats, and how these are all objects. We'll explore the object concept and why it is important. We'll look at data structures as collections of objects, then arrays and hash tables, and finish with splatting.

Chapter 5, PowerShell Control Flow – Conditionals and Loops, covers conditional flow (*IF* this, *THEN* that) and loops, including for, each, and while loops. Often, you won't want to process cmdlets in a linear fashion – you'll want to only do something if another thing is true or do something for all the objects in a pipeline. Control flow is how we do this. This chapter will also move us on from running interactive cmdlets to writing very simple scripts in VS Code.

Chapter 6, PowerShell and Files – Reading, Writing, and Manipulating Data, shows you how to take data from common file types such as CSV and TXT files and manipulate it, as well as how to send your output to files, alleviating the tedium of having to read output off a screen and typing loads of it in. We'll also cover how to output to HTML, which is great for creating formatted reports and live data in web-hosted dashboards.

Chapter 7, PowerShell and the Web – HTTP, REST, and JSON, explores PowerShell and the web. Files are all very well, but a lot of cloud administration requires the manipulation of data from the internet; to do this, we'll need to be able to manipulate the most common internet data type, JSON. We'll also want to manipulate cloud services, for which we will need to be able to use REST API calls. This chapter will walk through that.

Chapter 8, Writing Our First Script – Turning Simple Cmdlets into Reusable Code, focuses on how we can turn lines of code into a script that we can save and run over and over again. We've covered how to write a few lines of code in an IDE. How do we turn that into something that we would want to run repeatedly, and make it useful for other people to run?

Chapter 9, Don't Repeat Yourself – Functions and Scriptblocks, introduces you to functions in PowerShell as well as script blocks and lambdas. When writing a script, we will frequently find ourselves running the same few lines of code. Turning them into functions within the script means we only need to write it once, just calling it every time we need it.

Chapter 10, Error Handling – Oh No! It's Gone Wrong!, covers the two main types of errors that we're likely to encounter – problems that our code encounters and problems with our code. In the first part of the chapter, we'll define what an error is, how we can set PowerShell up to handle errors gracefully, and how we can make sense of them. In the second part, we'll look at how we can identify problems with our code and use VS Code for debugging.

Chapter 11, Creating Our First Module, examines how to turn functions and scripts into a module that can be reused, easily distributed, and incorporated into other scripts. Now we have a script, containing a set of functions, the next step is to turn that into a tool that others can use for themselves.

Chapter 12, Securing PowerShell, delves into how to secure our PowerShell scripts and modules and run them in a secure fashion. PowerShell is a very powerful tool, and with great power comes great responsibility. The chapter will cover script execution policies, code signing, AppLocker, and some of the other security features.

Chapter 13, Working with PowerShell 7 and Windows, explores how to use PowerShell 7 on Windows, when we will need to use PowerShell 5.1, how to interact with remote machines using WinRM, how to manage machines with CIM, and basic interaction with Windows features such as storage. PowerShell originated on Windows, and PowerShell 7 is intended to eventually replace Windows PowerShell, but we're not there yet.

Chapter 14, PowerShell 7 for Linux and macOS, explains how to install PowerShell on Linux, how it differs from running PowerShell on Windows, and how to use VS Code on Linux. It explains remoting with OpenSSH, how to run scripts, and some common administration tasks. It finishes with a section on installing and running PowerShell and VS Code on macOS.

Chapter 15, PowerShell 7 and the Raspberry Pi, examines how to get started with PowerShell on Raspberry Pi, allowing us to do home automation, maker projects and more. It covers installing PowerShell and VS Code, connecting to the Pi, and running scripts. Raspberry Pi is everybody's favorite single board computer, and we can transfer our PowerShell skills to our Pi stable.

Chapter 16, Working with PowerShell and .NET, delves into .NET, which is the developer platform that PowerShell 7 is built on; it's free, open source, and works well with VS Code. There are lots of things we can't do easily with PowerShell alone, but we can leverage .NET to achieve them. Familiarity with .NET is an essential skill for every advanced PowerShell coder, and this chapter will help you get there.

To get the most out of this book

This book assumes you have a client machine, either laptop or PC, that is running Windows, Linux, or macOS. However, at a push, you can use Raspberry Pi for pretty much everything. It also assumes you have an internet connection. The majority of exercises will work on Windows, Linux and macOS; where they don't, it's noted. Read the first chapter, which has installation instructions for Windows, and then follow the installation instructions in the chapters on Linux/macOS or Raspberry Pi.

Software/hardware covered in the book	Operating system requirements
PowerShell 7.x	Windows, macOS, or Linux

If you are using the digital version of this book, I advise you to type the code yourself. Errors are part of the fun, and the sense of achievement when I realize what I've done wrong is not something I'd want you to miss out on.

Conventions used

There are a number of text conventions used throughout this book.

`Code in text`: Indicates code words in text, database table names, folder names, filenames, file extensions, pathnames, dummy URLs, user input, and Twitter handles. Here is an example: "The application gets installed by default in `C:\Users\<username>\AppData\Local\Programs\ Microsoft VS Code` and is only available for the user who installed it."

A block of code is set as follows:

```
$x = 5
if ($X -gt 4) {
    Write-Output '$x is bigger than 4'
}
```

When we wish to draw your attention to a particular part of a code block, the relevant lines or items are set in bold:

```
$Array  = 1,2,3,4,5

switch ($Array) {
    1 {Write-Output '$Array contains 1'}
    3 {Write-Output '$Array contains 3'}
    6 {Write-Output '$Array contains 6'}
}
```

Any command-line input or output is written as follows:

```
sudo apt update
sudo apt install ./<filename>.deb
```

Bold: Indicates a new term, an important word, or words that you see on screen. For instance, words in menus or dialog boxes appear in **bold**. Here is an example: "On the **Select Additional Tasks** dialog, decide whether you want a desktop icon and file and directory context menu options, enabling you to open files and folders directly in VS Code."

> **Tips or important notes**
> Appear like this.

Get in touch

Feedback from our readers is always welcome.

General feedback: If you have questions about any aspect of this book, email us at customercare@ packtpub.com and mention the book title in the subject of your message.

Errata: Although we have taken every care to ensure the accuracy of our content, mistakes do happen. If you have found a mistake in this book, we would be grateful if you would report this to us. Please visit www.packtpub.com/support/errata and fill in the form.

Piracy: If you come across any illegal copies of our works in any form on the internet, we would be grateful if you would provide us with the location address or website name. Please contact us at copyright@packt.com with a link to the material.

If you are interested in becoming an author: If there is a topic that you have expertise in and you are interested in either writing or contributing to a book, please visit authors.packtpub.com.

Share your thoughts

Once you've read *PowerShell 7 Workshop*, we'd love to hear your thoughts! Scan the QR code below to go straight to the Amazon review page for this book and share your feedback.

https://packt.link/r/1801812985

Your review is important to us and the tech community and will help us make sure we're delivering excellent quality content.

Download a free PDF copy of this book

Thanks for purchasing this book!

Do you like to read on the go but are unable to carry your print books everywhere?

Is your eBook purchase not compatible with the device of your choice?

Don't worry, now with every Packt book you get a DRM-free PDF version of that book at no cost.

Read anywhere, any place, on any device. Search, copy, and paste code from your favorite technical books directly into your application.

The perks don't stop there, you can get exclusive access to discounts, newsletters, and great free content in your inbox daily

Follow these simple steps to get the benefits:

1. Scan the QR code or visit the link below

https://packt.link/free-ebook/9781801812986

2. Submit your proof of purchase
3. That's it! We'll send your free PDF and other benefits to your email directly

Part 1: PowerShell Fundamentals

In this part, we'll learn about the basics of PowerShell, how the language syntax works, how we can send the results of one operation straight into another with the pipeline, how PowerShell uses objects, variables, and data structures, how we can create branched and looped code, and finally, how we can write to and from stored files.

This part has the following chapters:

- *Chapter 1, Introduction to PowerShell – What It Is and How to Get It*
- *Chapter 2, Exploring PowerShell Cmdlets and Syntax*
- *Chapter 3, The PowerShell Pipeline – How to String Cmdlets Together*
- *Chapter 4, PowerShell Variables and Data Structures*
- *Chapter 5, PowerShell Control Flow – Conditionals and Loops*
- *Chapter 6, PowerShell and Files – Reading, Writing, and Manipulating Data*
- *Chapter 7, PowerShell and the Web – HTTP, REST, and JSON*

1

Introduction to PowerShell 7 – What It Is and How to Get It

Quite simply, PowerShell is a time machine. Not a science-fiction time machine where you get to go back in time and meet your own grandfather, but a real, practical one. If you put in a small amount of time, then PowerShell, like any simple machine, will act as a force multiplier; it will produce very much more time for you. To use a metaphor, it's a time hammer, and the hours you put into learning PowerShell will save you tens or hundreds of times as many hours once you start putting the knowledge to use.

This chapter is a general introduction to PowerShell 7. It's going to give you some context about PowerShell and get you up and running. You're going to learn what you can do with it and some typical use cases. We'll be installing PowerShell, and you'll get to choose one or more ways of doing that. Once we've got it installed, we'll go through how you run commands (called **cmdlets**), and how you can find cmdlets to run. Finally, and quite importantly, we'll work through how to get help, both with cmdlets and with PowerShell topics and concepts.

In this chapter, we're going to cover the following main topics:

- What is PowerShell 7?
- What is PowerShell 7 used for?
- Getting PowerShell 7
- Running PowerShell 7
- Getting help

Technical requirements

To follow along with this chapter, you will need an internet connection and an operating system. If you're using Linux or macOS, the installation instructions can be found in *Chapter 14, PowerShell 7 for Linux and macOS*, so skip the detailed installation instructions in the *How to get PowerShell 7 section*, in this chapter.

This chapter assumes that you will be using Windows 10 (version 1709 or later) running on standard 64-bit x86 architecture. If you're not sure whether that's what you have, don't worry, it probably is. If you are one of life's worriers, go to the Windows search bar and type `msinfo32`, then press *Enter*. The **System Information** application will open, and under **System Summary,** there will be three relevant lines:

- **OS Name**: Hopefully **Microsoft Windows 10** of some flavor; PowerShell 7.3 is available on all currently supported versions of Windows.

- **Version**: You want a build number higher than 16299.

- **System Type**: Probably **x64-based PC**.

The following screenshot shows how it should look under **System Summary**:

Item	Value
OS Name	Microsoft Windows 10 Enterprise
Version	10.0.19042 Build 19042
Other OS Description	Not Available
OS Manufacturer	Microsoft Corporation
System Name	
System Manufacturer	FUJITSU CLIENT COMPUTING LIMITED
System Model	LIFEBOOK U7510
System Type	x64-based PC
System SKU	SK00

Figure 1.1 – Typical information from the System Information application (msinfo32)

If you're using Windows 11, then good for you; you won't need to do some of the things we'll be talking about as Windows 11 comes with some extras.

What is PowerShell 7?

PowerShell is a scripting language and an alternative to the command-line interface. PowerShell is an automation tool consisting of (at least) three parts:

- A shell, like the Command Prompt in Windows or the Terminal in Linux or macOS

- A scripting language

- A configuration management framework called **Desired State Configuration (DSC)**

In practice, when we talk about PowerShell, we're usually talking about the scripting language. Usage of the shell is largely intuitive to the user, as we'll see, and while we'll talk about DSC later, in my experience, most people don't use it as much as they should.

The first version of PowerShell grew out of a project called **Monad**, which was an attempt by Jeffrey Snover to replicate Unix tools on Windows. He realized that one of the fundamental drawbacks of Unix tools is that they output a bytestream (usually text), and so a lot of effort is wasted on searching, formatting, and extracting the output of commands before you can act on that output. Monad was written to output objects that could be input straight into another command. We'll cover this in more detail when we get to *Chapter 4, PowerShell Variables and Data Structures*. PowerShell 1.0 was released in 2006, but in my opinion, it didn't really take off until PowerShell 2.0 was released in 2009, and Microsoft started re-engineering the administrative interfaces of major pieces of software such as Exchange Server 2010 to make use of it. Other opinions are available.

At the time of writing, there are two main *flavors* of PowerShell: **Windows PowerShell**, which comes bundled with both server and desktop versions of Windows, and **PowerShell 7**, which must be downloaded and installed. The latest (and allegedly final) version of Windows PowerShell, v5.1, is built on .NET Framework 4.5, the proprietary software framework that is bundled with Windows and underpins many of Microsoft's products. PowerShell 7.0 was built on .NET Core 3.1, a simplified, open source implementation of .NET. However, since version 7.2, PowerShell has been built on .NET 6.0. This unified version of .NET is a replacement for both .NET Framework and .NET Core, and was released in November 2020.

Because of the fundamental differences between Windows PowerShell 5.1 and PowerShell 7.x, there can be some differences in how they work on the Windows platform. These will be discussed in *Chapter 13, Working With PowerShell 7 and Windows*.

We'll find it useful to summarize some of the key differences in the following table:

Parameters	Windows PowerShell	PowerShell 7.2
Platform	x64, x86 only	x64, x86, arm32, arm64
OS	Windows	Windows, Linux, macOS
.NET Version	.NET Framework 4.5	.NET 6.0
License Type	Proprietary	Open source
No. of Native Commands	1588 (in vanilla Windows 10)	1574 (in vanilla Windows 10) 290 (in Ubuntu 20.04)

Table 1.1 – Some differences between Windows PowerShell and PowerShell 7

In this section, we have covered what PowerShell is, and how it differs from Windows PowerShell. In the next section, we'll look at why PowerShell 7 exists and see what makes it special.

What is PowerShell 7 used for?

PowerShell is for getting things done quickly. It's for when you need a relatively short piece of code for something that you can reuse and repurpose easily to do something else. It's for when you don't want to spend months learning a language, then more months writing thousands of lines of code. The language can be used in at least four ways:

- You can input single lines of code in the shell, as you would at the Windows Command Prompt or the Linux Terminal. This is great if you need to check a value, accomplish a single task such as rebooting a remote computer, or grab a log file.

- You can write a script, such as a Bash script in Linux or a batch file for Windows, that accomplishes multiple subtasks, such as gathering event logs and performance information from several machines and compiling them into a single HTML report.

- If you write a lot of scripts or need to accomplish something more complex, you can use PowerShell as a procedural programming language with multiple packaged scripts that each describe a single function and are called by a master script.

- You can use it as an object-oriented programming language and package a whole application that can be redistributed and run by anyone with PowerShell installed.

We'll be focusing on scripts and procedural programming in this book, as that is how most people use PowerShell. These are very similar; the difference is that in a script, you are using cmdlets that have been written for you, but in procedural programming, you are creating your own cmdlets, either from pre-existing cmdlets or by using the system programming language C#.

Scripting languages versus system programming languages

The PowerShell language is a scripting language. It's for gluing other applications together quickly and easily – sort of a coding version of Lego. It relies on an underlying interpreter: the PowerShell program. Without PowerShell installed, a PowerShell script can't run. This is quite similar to other interpreted languages, such as Python, and sits in contrast to system programming languages, such as C or C++, which are compiled into executable files. When you compile a C++ program, it can theoretically run on any compatible machine. There are other differences as well – here are some of the main ones:

- Interpreted languages are less efficient than compiled languages because each line has to be interpreted before it can run. This means they are slower than compiled programs. There are programming tricks you can use to speed things up, but performing a task in an interpreted language will pretty much always be slower than doing it in a compiled language.

- Interpreted languages are more efficient than compiled languages in development. They accomplish the same tasks with far fewer lines of code. This means that writing them, debugging them, and reusing them is much quicker. They are also much easier to learn.

- Interpreted languages can run on multiple architectures. As we'll see in this book, code written in PowerShell can run on Windows, Linux, or macOS, with minimal tweaking. A program written in C++ for Windows can only run on Windows, or a machine with Windows emulation. It would need to be rewritten and recompiled for a different platform.

- Interpreted languages produce collaborative reusable programs. With PowerShell (or Python), you produce code that is readable and editable by humans. With a compiled language, you produce a binary file that cannot easily be decompiled into source code for reuse. This means other people can reuse your code for their own purposes. Platforms such as GitHub can be used to distribute your code, other people can contribute to it, improve it, reuse it for their programs, and act in a generally communitarian fashion.

It boils down to this: if you want to write a super-fast first-person shooter game with spectacular graphics, then PowerShell is probably not the language for you. If you want to automate some tasks, simple or complex, then PowerShell is a good choice.

Getting PowerShell 7

In this section, we'll look at some of the ways to get PowerShell onto your machine, where it goes and why, and how you can control aspects of your installation. This chapter will only cover installation on Windows; for detailed installation on Linux, macOS, and ARM systems, please have a read of *Chapter 14, PowerShell 7 for Linux and macOS*, or *Chapter 15, PowerShell 7 and the Raspberry Pi*, and come back for the next two sections of this chapter.

It's possible to have more than one version of PowerShell running simultaneously on your machine – I usually have three at once: Windows PowerShell, PowerShell 7 (current version), and PowerShell 7 Preview. This is not just for when I'm writing a book – we need to know that the scripts we write will run in different environments and rewrite them if necessary. It's also useful to be able to control the installation when you're intending to run PowerShell on a remote machine that may not have it installed yet. Windows PowerShell is included in the Windows operating system and is installed in the \Windows\system32 folder; that's where it lives, and you can't move it anywhere else. In contrast, PowerShell 7 can be installed wherever you like, within reason. We're going to cover the three most common methods of installation:

- Installation from an .msi file with Windows installer

- Installation from a .zip file

- Installation with winget

There are two other methods that we will cover briefly: installing from the Microsoft Store, and installing as a .NET Global tool.

If you want to experiment a little, and you have Windows 10 Pro or Enterprise, then you can enable the **Windows Sandbox** feature in **Control Panel | Programs and Features | Turn Windows features on or off**.

This will give you a completely blank, secure Windows environment to play around in. Be careful – when you turn it off, it's gone for good. The next time you turn it on, all your changes will be lost:

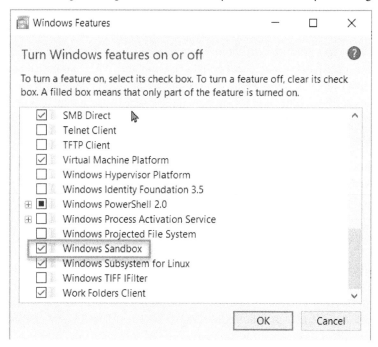

Figure 1.2 – Turning on Windows Sandbox

Full details of the requirements for running Windows Sandbox can be found here: `https://docs.microsoft.com/en-us/Windows/security/threat-protection/Windows-sandbox/Windows-sandbox-overview`.

Let's get started. Make sure you have met the technical requirements listed at the beginning of the chapter.

Installation from an .msi file

All of the official PowerShell distributions can be found on the PowerShell GitHub page at `https://github.com/PowerShell/PowerShell`:

Get PowerShell

You can download and install a PowerShell package for any of the following platforms.

Supported Platform	Download (LTS)	Downloads (stable)	Downloads (preview)	How to Install
Windows (x64)	.msi	.msi	.msi	Instructions
Windows (x86)	.msi	.msi	.msi	Instructions
Ubuntu 20.04	.deb	.deb	.deb	Instructions
Ubuntu 18.04	.deb	.deb	.deb	Instructions
Ubuntu 16.04	.deb	.deb	.deb	Instructions
Debian 9	.deb	.deb	.deb	Instructions

Figure 1.3 – Get PowerShell from the GitHub page

As you can see, for most operating systems and platforms, there are three types of release: **LTS**, **stable**, and **preview**. **LTS** stands for **Long Term Support**. LTS releases come out on a slow cadence, to ensure stability in environments that are risk-averse, and they usually only contain critical security updates and software fixes, not new features. The PowerShell LTS releases are based on the underlying LTS version of .NET. The preview release is the next version of PowerShell. It may have exciting new features, but it will also likely be unstable and have some flaws. Stable releases are updated every month or so and may include new functionality, as well as software fixes and security updates. Each release is supported for six months after the next release.

Let's go ahead and install the most common release, the stable release for Windows x64:

1. Browse to the GitHub Releases page for PowerShell here: `https://github.com/PowerShell/PowerShell`.

2. Click to download the stable `.msi` package for Windows x64.

3. Locate the `.msi` file in your `Downloads` folder and run it. This will start the setup wizard.

4. The first choice you must make is the install location. By default, it will install into a numbered folder under `C:\Program Files\PowerShell`, where the number matches the major version – in our case, 7. If you are installing a preview version, then the folder will have a `-preview` suffix. This is a pretty good location, but you may want to put it somewhere else, for example, if you are running multiple versions of PowerShell side by side. Go ahead and accept the default this time:

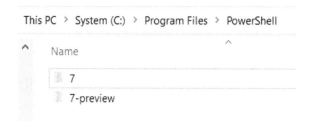

Figure 1.4 – The default install location

5. Now we get to the **Optional Actions** menu:

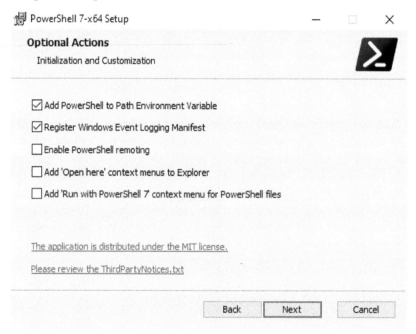

Figure 1.5 – Optional Actions

There are five options here:

- **Add PowerShell to Path Environment Variable**: You will almost certainly want to choose this. With this option enabled, you can start PowerShell from any location. Be aware that if you install a different version side by side, it will overwrite the installation path variable and you will need to manually navigate to the location of pwsh.exe to run this one.

- **Register Windows Event Logging Manifest**: You will want to enable this as well. This will create a new Windows Event log called **PowerShell Core** and start logging PowerShell events to it.

- **Enable PowerShell remoting**: Enabling PowerShell remoting will make the machine listen for incoming connections from PowerShell sessions. This is obviously a bit of a security vulnerability, so you should only enable it if you need it and your machine is on a private network. You don't need to enable it to connect to remote sessions on other machines.

- **Add 'Open here' context menus to Explorer**: This will allow you to open a PowerShell session in a folder in File Explorer – the PowerShell session will open with the path set to the folder you selected.

- **Add 'Run with PowerShell 7' context menu for PowerShell files**: This will allow you to right-click a file and open it with PowerShell 7. For reasons we will see later, this might not always be desirable.

6. After **Optional Actions**, we come to the **Microsoft Update** option. You can use Microsoft Update to keep PowerShell updated; this is highly recommended as it can automatically download security patches for you and apply them according to your existing update schedule. Be aware that this setting can be overridden by group policy if you are working in a domain-joined environment. There are two checkboxes; the first enables updates for PowerShell, while the second enables Microsoft Update on the system. Note that unchecking this box only disables Microsoft Update; if your environment uses a configuration manager such as **Windows Software Update Services (WSUS)** or **System Center Configuration Manager (SCCM)**, then they will still work.

7. Finally, we're ready to install by pressing the **Install** button. This is a short process and should be done in a minute or two. Click **Finish**, and we're all set.

There is an alternative to using the GUI. You can run the `.msi` file from the command line with `msiexec.exe`, as documented here: `https://docs.microsoft.com/en-gb/powershell/scripting/install/installing-powershell-on-Windows?view=powershell-7.2#install-the-msi-package-from-the-command-line`.

To silently install PowerShell on Windows Sandbox as you've just been shown, you can run the following:

```
msiexec.exe /package c:\Users\WDAGUtilityAccount\Downloads\
PowerShell-7.2.1-win-x64.msi /quiet REGISTER_MANIFEST=1 USE_
MU=1 ENABLE_MU=1
```

Notice that there is no property for enabling or disabling **Add PowerShell to Path Environment Variable**. If you run the `.msi` file from the command line, then PowerShell will automatically get added. Because we've used the `/quiet` switch, there is no output to this command, but if it is successful, then you will see PowerShell in your Start menu.

Activity 1

How might you enable the file context menu when installing PowerShell from an `.msi` file using the command line? (Hint: Check the link in the earlier paragraph to find out.)

Installation from the .zip file

Another popular way to install PowerShell is from the .zip file. With this method, we simply extract the binaries and associated files to a suitable folder. The disadvantage is that the prerequisite checking and options that are available with the .msi install are lost; for instance, you can't automatically add PowerShell to the PATH environment variable or enable PowerShell remoting. The advantage is that it is much easier to script the installation of PowerShell as part of a DevOps or Infrastructure as Code pipeline, and you can enable other features as part of the script.

In Windows, there's no native way to install a file from the internet via scripting. You need to either already have PowerShell (which you automatically do in the form of Windows PowerShell on a Windows machine), or install a tool such as **curl**.

Here's how you do it with Windows PowerShell:

```
Invoke-WebRequest https://github.com/PowerShell/PowerShell/
releases/download/v7.2.1/PowerShell-7.2.1-win-x64.zip
```

If you run the preceding cmdlet, then you should see output like this. Notice that it's an HTTP response, and so a StatusCode result of 200 is good:

```
PS C:\Users\PARLOWN> Invoke-WebRequest https://github.com/PowerShell/PowerShell/releases/download/v7.2.1/PowerShell-7.2.
1-win-x64.zip


StatusCode      : 200
StatusDescription : OK
Content         : {80, 75, 3, 4...}
RawContent      : HTTP/1.1 200 OK
                  X-Bst-Request-Id: mpbtDj:6HWc:179187
                  X-Bst-Info: ch=prv,t=1647349707,h=06j,p=194563_13574:1_2510,u=2863269831,c=2339,v=7.11.200100.64
                  Content-MD5: aDTmBCtXN+oesYd6stSsgg==
                  x-ms-req...
Headers         : {[X-Bst-Request-Id, mpbtDj:6HWc:179187], [X-Bst-Info,
                  ch=prv,t=1647349707,h=06j,p=194563_13574:1_2510,u=2863269831,c=2339,v=7.11.200100.64],
                  [Content-MD5, aDTmBCtXN+oesYd6stSsgg==], [x-ms-request-id,
                  5133fd6d-101e-0065-6e6d-388c21000000]...}
RawContentLength : 107754221



PS C:\Users\PARLOWN>
```

Figure 1.6 – Downloading PowerShell 7 with Windows PowerShell

You can run the entire process like this with four lines of code:

```
New-Item -Path c:\scratch\myPowershell\7.2 -ItemType Directory
Invoke-WebRequest https://github.com/PowerShell/PowerShell/
releases/download/v7.2.1/PowerShell-7.2.1-win-x64.zip -OutFile
C:\scratch\myPowershell\7.2\PowerShell-7.2.1-win-x64.zip
Expand-Archive C:\scratch\myPowershell\7.2\PowerShell-7.2.1-
win-x64.zip -DestinationPath C:\scratch\myPowershell\7.2\
Remove-Item C:\scratch\myPowershell\7.2\PowerShell-7.2.1-
win-x64.zip
```

Don't worry too much about the preceding commands – we'll be covering all of them in due course. In summary, the first line creates a new folder. The second line downloads the .zip package from GitHub to your new folder. The third line unzips everything, making it ready for you to run, and the fourth line removes the downloaded package.

There are two errors you may experience with this. Firstly, you may see a red error message:

```
Invoke-WebRequest : The request was aborted: Could not create
SSL/TLS secure channel"
```

This is because, by default, Windows PowerShell will use TLS v1.0, and many websites no longer accept this protocol. If you do see this, run the following .NET code and try again:

```
[Net.ServicePointManager]::SecurityProtocol = "Tls, Tls11,
Tls12, Ssl3"
```

The other error you may see is a message saying this:

```
Invoke-WebRequest : The response content cannot be parsed
because the Internet Explorer engine is not available, or
Internet Explorer's first-launch configuration is not complete.
Specify the UseBasicParsing parameter and try again
```

In this case, run the `Invoke-WebRequest` cmdlet with the `-UseBasicParsing` parameter:

```
Invoke-WebRequest https://github.com/PowerShell/PowerShell/
releases/download/v7.2.1/PowerShell-7.2.1-win-x64.zip
-UseBasicParsing
```

Replace the second line of the script with this line. It's exactly the same but adds the `-UseBasicParsing` parameter.

Installation with winget

winget, also known as the **Windows Package Manager**, is a free, open source package manager from Microsoft for Windows Clients. It is bundled with Windows 11 and may be downloaded for Windows 10 via the Microsoft Store. It is similar in functionality to Linux package managers such as APT, YUM, and DNF. It supports `.exe`, `.msi`, and `.msix` packages – you can't use it to install the `.zip` release. When you run winget, it searches for, downloads, and installs the PowerShell `.msi` release of your choice. You do it like this:

1. First, run a search for PowerShell packages. From the Windows PowerShell Command Prompt, run this line:

    ```
    winget search microsoft.powershell
    ```

    This will return the versions of PowerShell available to winget.

2. You then need to install a package. I'm choosing to install the preview by running the following:

    ```
    winget install --id microsoft.powershell.preview --source
    winget
    ```

And that's it. There are a few things to note here. Firstly, you're installing the `.msi` file, so unless you suppress them, you will see several GUI messages. You can do this with the `--silent` switch. Unless you are happy with the default choices, you will also need a way to pass parameters to the `.msi` file you are calling. You can do this with the `--override` switch, and then by passing the command-line switches for the `.msi` package that we looked at before. Secondly, if you have User Access Control enabled, you will need to give permission for PowerShell to be installed. If you're using the `--silent` switch, then you won't see this prompt. If you want to do a silent install, you'll need to run Windows PowerShell with administrator privileges.

Here's how the whole install looks if you run it from a Windows PowerShell command line with administrator privileges:

```
Windows PowerShell
Copyright (C) Microsoft Corporation. All rights reserved.

Try the new cross-platform PowerShell https://aka.ms/pscore6

PS C:\WINDOWS\system32> winget search microsoft.powershell
Name               Id                        Version Source

PowerShell         Microsoft.PowerShell        7.2.1.0 winget
PowerShell Preview Microsoft.PowerShell.Preview 7.3.0.2 winget
PS C:\WINDOWS\system32> winget install  id microsoft.powershell.preview  source winget  silent
Found PowerShell Preview [Microsoft.PowerShell.Preview] Version 7.3.0.2
This application is licensed to you by its owner.
Microsoft is not responsible for, nor does it grant any licenses to, third-party packages.
Downloading

                            101 MB /  101 MB
Successfully verified installer hash
Starting package install...
Successfully installed
PS C:\WINDOWS\system32>
```

Figure 1.7 – Silently installing PowerShell with winget

The main advantage of winget is that it has its own repository for community-created packages; anyone can bundle an app by writing a manifest and uploading it. The repository is secured with Microsoft SmartScreen to stop malicious code from finding its way into the repository. There's a lot more on winget here:

`https://docs.microsoft.com/en-us/Windows/package-manager/winget/`.

In summary, you're not really doing anything with winget that you didn't do by running `msiexec.exe` previously, but it's a bit newer and cooler, has a useful repository, and is slightly easier to use. In a couple of years, we'll wonder how we ever did without it, especially if they make it available on Windows servers.

Other ways to install

There are two other ways to install PowerShell that we should discuss. Neither is likely to be applicable to us. Firstly, if you have the .NET **Software Development Kit (SDK)** installed, then we can use that to install PowerShell as a global tool. This is only really useful for software developers, and it doesn't make much sense to install the SDK just for PowerShell.

The other way you can install PowerShell on Windows is through the Microsoft Store as an app. The big drawback to this method is that Store apps run in a sandbox environment that restricts access to the application's root folder. This means that several PowerShell features just won't work properly.

> **Note**
>
> A **sandbox** is not necessarily the same as **Windows Sandbox**. The generic term "sandbox" refers to a secure computing environment with separate resources, meaning that whatever is running in there cannot interfere with anything outside the sandbox. Windows Sandbox is a specific example of a generic sandbox.

Running PowerShell 7

The first way everyone runs PowerShell is through the bundled console (remember, PowerShell is not just a language, it's a shell and a configuration management framework as well). Let's assume that you installed using the .msi method from before, and you added PowerShell to the PATH environment variable. If you've done this, then all you need to do to start PowerShell is type pwsh into the Windows search bar and click on the application. Alternatively, you can right-click the *Start* menu and type pwsh in the **Run** box. Or, you could just hold down the *Windows* key and press *R*, which would call up the **Run** box as well.

If you didn't add PowerShell to the path, you will need to type the full path to the executable pwsh, as in C:\program files\PowerShell\7\pwsh.

The first thing you will notice if you've been paying attention to the preceding screenshots or you've followed along is that the console window that comes up has a black background. This differentiates it from Windows PowerShell:

Figure 1.8 – Two different versions of PowerShell

If you have installed PowerShell on Linux or macOS, then open a Terminal and type pwsh – the Terminal will switch to a PowerShell prompt.

It is traditional in most programming books that the first thing you do is coax your application to produce the words "Hello World" onscreen, and there's no reason we should be any different. Type the following into the console and press *Enter*:

```
Write-Host "Hello World"
```

You should get something like this:

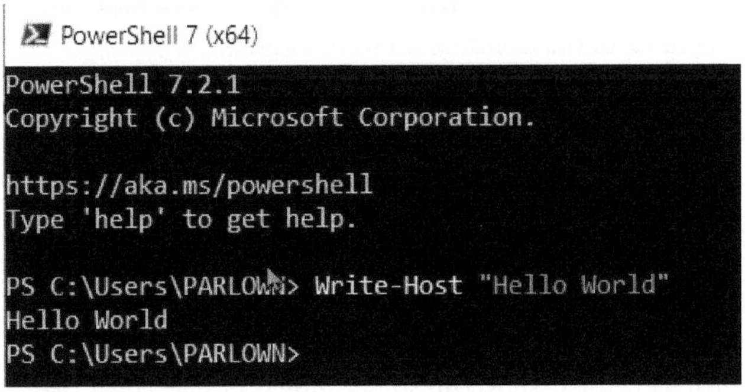

Figure 1.9 – Hello yourself

If you did it, congratulations! You've just run your first PowerShell command, or cmdlet, as they are called.

Notice that the console automatically colors things that it recognizes or expects; cmdlets are yellow, strings are blue. It's also very forgiving – if you had forgotten the inverted commas, then `"Hello World"` would not have been blue, but PowerShell would have interpreted it correctly anyway.

> **Note**
>
> Be careful with this; while PowerShell is quite clever, it won't always interpret input the way you hope. It's best to tell it explicitly what type of input you are giving it. More on this later.

The most likely cause of an error is that you misspelled the cmdlet or didn't close the inverted commas, as illustrated in the next figure. You'll see a helpful red error message telling you what you've done wrong and suggesting ways to fix it. I have come to cherish these error messages:

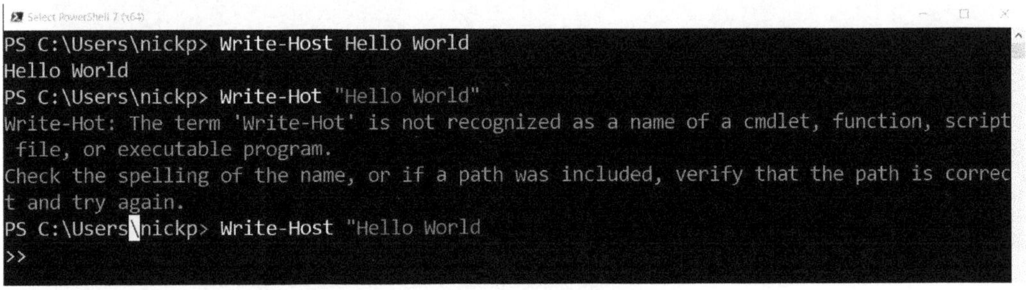

Figure 1.10 – Three ways to be wrong

In the third attempt, I didn't close the inverted commas, so PowerShell was expecting more input. It told us this with >> on the line below. It also told us that it didn't think the cmdlet would run as you have written it by coloring the > in the Command Prompt in red.

Note that unlike in some environments, capitalization here doesn't matter; write-host is functionally the same as Write-Host.

Running PowerShell with administrator privileges

By default, PowerShell will run under the account that launches it, but it will only have standard user privileges. If you need access to your local machine that would normally require administrator privileges, then PowerShell will either fail to run some cmdlets or give you a **User Account Control (UAC)** prompt. To prevent this, you need to start PowerShell with administrator privileges. There are many ways to do this, but here are two of the most common.

Firstly, you can open the search bar, type pwsh, and then right-click on the PowerShell 7 icon and select **Run as administrator**:

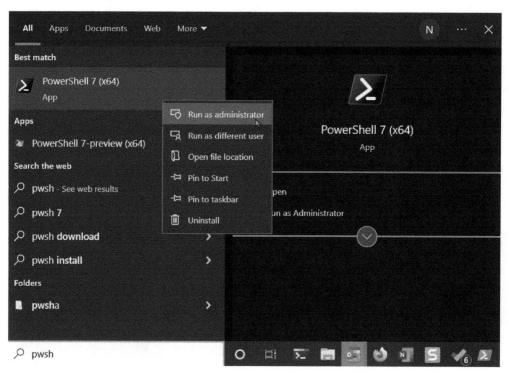

Figure 1.11 – Starting PowerShell as an administrator

The second, slightly more impressive method is to hit the *Windows* key + R to bring up the **Run** box, type pwsh, and then hold down *Ctrl* + *Shift* + *Enter*. This will start PowerShell as an admin.

PowerShell clearly shows whether it is running with admin privileges in the window title. Here are two PowerShell sessions running the same cmdlet. The lower window is running with admin privileges:

Figure 1.12 – Sometimes you have to be an admin

If administrator mode is something you are likely to use a lot, then it's easiest to just right-click the PowerShell icon when it's running and select **Pin to taskbar**. Then you can right-click the pinned icon whenever you need it and select **Run as administrator**.

Autocomplete

By now, you're probably getting a little tired of having to type a lot of long and unfamiliar cmdlets in. Let me show you a great feature of the shell: autocomplete. Try this – in your shell, type the following without pressing *Enter*:

```
Stop-s
```

Now press the *Tab* key. Cool, isn't it? But it's not the cmdlet we want. Press the *Tab* key again. You should now have the `Stop-Service` cmdlet fully typed. Now, add a space, type `-`, and press the *Tab* key again. Keep pressing the *Tab* key until you've gone through all the possible parameters for the `Stop-Service` cmdlet. Press *Esc* when you've done that.

This is a great way to avoid typing out loads of letters, but it's also a really good way of checking that what you are doing will work. If autocomplete doesn't work, then the chances are that the cmdlet, parameter, or option you want isn't available on this machine.

In the next chapter, we'll look at some other ways of starting and using PowerShell, but for now, you're all set with what you need.

Getting help

Now that you've installed PowerShell and can start it, you need to do stuff with it. You're going to need help with that. Happily, PowerShell comes with three useful cmdlets built in: `Get-Command`, `Get-Help`, and `Get-Member`. Each of these cmdlets will tell you useful things and give you guidance. Let's start with `Get-Command`.

Get-Command

`Get-Command` will give you a list of cmdlets. If you type it in just like that, it will give you a list of around 1,500 cmdlets. When you start installing and writing modules, that list will grow significantly. Scrolling through a list of thousands looking for a likely cmdlet is not that efficient. What you need to do is search the list.

Imagine you need to interrogate a particular process that is running on your client. It is likely that a cmdlet for doing that would include the word `process` somewhere. Go ahead and try typing the following into your shell:

```
Get-Command *process
```

You should see something like this:

```
PS C:\Users\PARLOWN> Get-Command *process

CommandType     Name                                    Version     Source
-----------     ----                                    -------     ------
Function        Get-AppvVirtualProcess                  1.0.0.0     AppvClient
Function        Start-AppvVirtualProcess                1.0.0.0     AppvClient
Cmdlet          Debug-Process                           7.0.0.0     Microsoft.PowerShell.Management
Cmdlet          Enter-PSHostProcess                     7.2.1.500   Microsoft.PowerShell.Core
Cmdlet          Exit-PSHostProcess                      7.2.1.500   Microsoft.PowerShell.Core
Cmdlet          Get-Process                             7.0.0.0     Microsoft.PowerShell.Management
Cmdlet          Start-Process                           7.0.0.0     Microsoft.PowerShell.Management
Cmdlet          Stop-Process                            7.0.0.0     Microsoft.PowerShell.Management
Cmdlet          Wait-Process                            7.0.0.0     Microsoft.PowerShell.Management

PS C:\Users\PARLOWN>
```

Figure 1.13 – Searching for relevant cmdlets

The cmdlet interprets `*process` as a string and searches for cmdlets that end in `process`. The `*` is a wildcard character. Try running it like this:

```
Get-Command process
```

You'll probably get an error in red.

Some of those cmdlets look a bit cryptic, but there are a few that really stand out – `Get-Process` especially. Try running that. You should see quite a long list of processes and some information about them. Let's look at a process I know you're currently running: pwsh. Type the following:

```
Get-Process pwsh
```

You should see information for your PowerShell processes:

```
PS C:\Users\PARLOWN> get-process pwsh

NPM(K)    PM(M)    WS(M)    CPU(s)      Id  SI ProcessName
------    -----    -----    ------      --  -- -----------
    76    67.99    53.00     77.33     220   1 pwsh
    71    52.48    51.87     97.45    4052   1 pwsh
   106    85.93    94.57  1,005.44   24972   1 pwsh
    78    59.52   102.11      7.56   28536   1 pwsh
```

Figure 1.14 – My PowerShell processes

That's very nice, but what does it all mean? Let's look at the next of our three helpful cmdlets: Get-Help.

Get-Help

Running the Get-Help cmdlet is easy; type Get-Help followed by the name of the cmdlet you would like help with:

```
Get-Help Get-Process
```

You should then see something like this:

```
PS C:\Users\PARLOWN> get-help get-process

NAME
    Get-Process

SYNTAX
    Get-Process [[-Name] <string[]>] [-Module] [-FileVersionInfo] [<CommonParameters>]

    Get-Process [[-Name] <string[]>] -IncludeUserName [<CommonParameters>]

    Get-Process -Id <int[]> [-Module] [-FileVersionInfo] [<CommonParameters>]

    Get-Process -Id <int[]> -IncludeUserName [<CommonParameters>]

    Get-Process -InputObject <Process[]> [-Module] [-FileVersionInfo] [<CommonParameters>]

    Get-Process -InputObject <Process[]> -IncludeUserName [<CommonParameters>]


ALIASES
    gps
    ps


REMARKS
    Get-Help cannot find the Help files for this cmdlet on this computer. It is displaying only partial help.
        -- To download and install Help files for the module that includes this cmdlet, use Update-Help.
        -- To view the Help topic for this cmdlet online, type: "Get-Help Get-Process -Online" or
           go to https://go.microsoft.com/fwlink/?LinkID=2096814.
```

Figure 1.15 – Running Get-Help for the first time

That doesn't look very helpful. However, if you read the REMARKS section, there's an explanation. PowerShell doesn't ship with full help; you need to download and update it. To update the help files, run the following:

```
Update-Help
```

It will take a little while to run, and if you have installed some modules, help files may not be available online for all of them, so you will see red error messages, but after a minute or two, it should finish, and you can then try getting help for Get-Process again.

Get-Help Get-Process

PowerShell is quite biased toward the *en-US* culture. Culture here refers to a specific meaning within .NET and associated programs such as PowerShell; it's equivalent to **locale** in other systems and refers to the settings specific to a language, number format, and date-time format. If your environment is not set to en-US, then it may not download all of the relevant help files. If you find you're not getting everything, try running this line:

```
Update-Help -UICulture en-US
```

Then, try again. This is something that particularly affects Linux installations.

You should see a lot more information, including a one-line synopsis and a detailed description. If that's not enough, then in the REMARKS section, there will be some other ways of getting even more information about the cmdlet. Try running this:

```
Get-Help Get-Process -Detailed
```

You will see more detailed information, including examples of how to use the cmdlet. To see all the information available, use this:

```
Get-Help Get-Process -Full
```

You will see everything in the help file, including the extremely useful NOTES section, which, for this cmdlet, will tell you how to interpret some of the values in the output.

There is one other useful way to run Get-Help for a cmdlet, using the -online parameter:

```
Get-Help Get-Process -Online
```

This will produce the web page for the cmdlet in your default browser; it gives the same information as when you use the -Full parameter.

About files

`Get-Help` doesn't just help you with cmdlets; you can also get lots of useful information about PowerShell concepts in a special set of files called ABOUT TOPICS. At the time of writing, there are over 140 of them. There's lots of information in these files about programming concepts, constructs, and common queries such as logging for both Windows and non-Windows environments. Have a look yourself by running the following:

```
Get-Help about*
```

Let's have a look at one of the files:

```
Get-Help about_Variables
```

You should see lots of interesting information about how variables are used in PowerShell.

You can also use full-text search with `Get-Help`. If the word you are looking for is not in the help file's name, then the text of the files will be searched. This takes a little longer but can often be worth it. Try entering the following:

```
Get-Help *certificate*
```

Make a mental note of the results you get. Now, try entering `certificates`, plural:

```
Get-Help *certificates*
```

You'll get a different set of results. The first set finds help files with `certificate` in the filename. When `Get-Help` produces the second set, it can't find any files with `certificates` in the name, so it does a full text search. Note that if the search term does occur in a filename, then the full text search won't be carried out.

The only downside I find with these files is that there is some expectation for you to be knowledgeable about everything in PowerShell except the topic in question. For example, ABOUT_VARIABLES mentions the `scope` variable in the first few paragraphs. Nonetheless, if you need to know how something works quickly, then these files are a great resource.

Get-Member

The final helpful cmdlet we're going to look at in this chapter is `Get-Member`. Earlier in the chapter, we discussed how PowerShell produces objects rather than text output like some shells and scripting languages. `Get-Member` allows you to see the members of those objects, their properties, and the methods that may be used on them. It's easier to show rather than tell, so go ahead and type the following into your shell:

```
Get-Process | Get-Member
```

> **Note**
>
> The vertical line between the two cmdlets is called the pipeline character, |. It's not a lower case L – on my en-GB standard PC keyboard, it's on the lower left, next to the Z key, and on a standard en-US keyboard, it's between the *Enter* and *Backspace* keys. If your keyboard doesn't have a solid vertical bar (|), then the broken vertical bar (¦) will work.

What you're doing here is piping the output of the Get-Process cmdlet into the next cmdlet as input, which in this case is Get-Member. We'll be doing plenty of work on the pipeline in later chapters. Get-Member will tell you the type of object you've given it, in this case a System. Diagnostics.Process object, and the methods, properties, alias properties, and events associated with that object, like this:

Figure 1.16 – Some of the members of System.Diagnostics.Process

A few pages earlier, in *Figure 1.14*, we looked at the properties of the pwsh processes running on your machine. These are the properties that were listed: NPM(K), PM(M), WS(M), CPU(s), ID, SI, and ProcessName. As you can now see, that's Non-Paged Memory (K), Paged Memory (M), Working Set (M), and Session ID, which are all aliases, so that they can fit nicely into a table on the screen. The CPU(s) alias is derived in a slightly different way – it's not set on the object. The ID and the process name are not aliases. M and K are abbreviations for **Megabytes** and **Kilobytes**, respectively. That's a really small subset of all the properties available on the object. As you can see, there are also methods available that can be used to perform operations on the object.

> **Activity 2**
>
> Have a look at the methods. What method might you use to forcibly and immediately stop a process? If you get stuck, have a look at the methods here: `https://docs.microsoft.com/en-us/dotnet/api/system.diagnostics.process`.

We'll be returning to `Get-Member` more than once in the rest of the book, as it's such a useful cmdlet.

Summary

We've done a lot in this chapter. We've discussed what PowerShell is and what it's suited for, such as producing short pieces of automation code quickly and easily. We've downloaded and installed it in a few different ways, specifically by installing it from an `.msi` file and extracting it from a `.zip` file.

We've tried some different ways of starting it using the built-in shell, and finally, we've looked at three useful cmdlets: `Get-Command`, for finding cmdlets that we might use, `Get-Help`, for understanding how to use them, and `Get-Member`, to understand what output those cmdlets produce.

In the next chapter, we will explore how cmdlets work, explore parameters and syntax, and look at a useful application for working interactively with PowerShell: Windows Terminal.

Exercises

1.   What cmdlet would you use to generate a random number?
2.   How would you generate a random number between 1 and 10?
3.   What cmdlet would you use to list the contents of a folder?
4.   How would you also get the contents of the subfolders?
5.   What cmdlet would you use to create a new folder?
6.   What cmdlet will tell you how long your computer has been switched on?
7.   What cmdlet might redirect output to a file?
8.   What could you use the `Get-Credential` cmdlet for?
9.   How might you use the `ConvertTo-HTML` cmdlet?

Further reading

- The *Monad Manifesto* by Jeffrey Snover is a great read on the background and philosophy of PowerShell: `https://www.jsnover.com/Docs/MonadManifesto.pdf`.

- John Ousterhout wrote an influential article on the difference between scripting and system programming, and why scripting is important and useful: `https://web.stanford.edu/~ouster/cgi-bin/papers/scripting.pdf`.

2

Exploring PowerShell Cmdlets and Syntax

Now we've got PowerShell installed, it's time to get down to using it. The power of PowerShell lies in the huge number of cmdlets available for it. In this chapter, we're going to learn about these. First, we'll see how the naming conventions work, then we will learn how to control what they do with parameters.

We'll take quite a deep dive into the syntax so that we understand exactly which parameters are available to a cmdlet and what information those parameters need to work. We'll then look at how to get more cmdlets to work with, both from our local machine and from external sources.

Finally, we'll talk about working interactively with PowerShell and will install an exciting new application for Windows that will help us do just that. By the end of the chapter, you will be able to confidently find and use unfamiliar cmdlets and be able to use the versatile Windows Terminal application.

In this chapter, we're going to cover the following main topics:

- What are cmdlets?
- Understanding cmdlet syntax
- How to find more cmdlets
- Working interactively with PowerShell

Technical requirements

This chapter assumes you have a client machine, an internet connection, and have installed the latest stable version of PowerShell 7. The last two sections of this chapter— *Windows Terminal – an alternative terminal emulator* and *Installing Windows Terminal from the Windows Store*—are specifically for Windows users. Those of us on Linux and macOS can feel happy that we don't need to do these parts, as those operating systems already contain multi-tabbed terminals.

What are cmdlets?

Cmdlets (pronounced *command-lets*) are the commands we use in PowerShell. They can either be entered via a terminal application or through a script. They may be **script-based** and constructed from other cmdlets, or they may be **binary** cmdlets written in **C#**. The cmdlets that install by default with PowerShell are binaries. Usually, cmdlets that we write ourselves or download from the internet will be script-based. Cmdlets take an **input object** from the pipeline, perform an action on it, and generally return an object for further processing. We will describe this in detail in *Chapter 3, The PowerShell Pipeline – How to String Cmdlets Together*.

Exploring cmdlet structure

We've already used a few cmdlets, and you may have noticed that they have a common structure: `Get-Help`, `Get-Command`, `Get-Member`. This is a **verb-noun** structure, and it's intended to help us understand what a cmdlet does. The **verb** at the start tells us that in each case, these cmdlets are going to *get* something: help, a list of commands, or a list of members. There is a list of approved verbs here: `https://docs.microsoft.com/en-us/powershell/scripting/developer/cmdlet/approved-verbs-for-windows-powershell-commands?view=powershell-7.2`.

Why do we need a list of approved verbs? For the sake of clarity; one of the primary purposes of PowerShell is to be easily understood. By limiting the number of verbs and clearly defining what each one means and when it should be used, we can tell immediately what a cmdlet will do. For instance, a cmdlet named `Delete-Item` might be just as obvious as `Remove-Item`, but how about `Eliminate-Item`? It's possible this is going to do something unpleasant and terminal. Most well-written cmdlets will conform to this list; hopefully, anything we write will as well.

Notice that not all the verbs in that list are actual verbs in English. `New` is not a verb, but for the purposes of cmdlets, we're going to use it as one.

> **Activity 1**
>
> When should we use `New`, and when should we use `Add`? Check out the preceding link to find out.

The second part of the cmdlet is the **noun**. These are not so tightly defined; the first rule is that they are always singular: `Get-Process`, never `Get-Processes`. The second rule is that they should be descriptive; that is, they should be immediately understandable. This can lead to some long cmdlet names, such as `Get-NetAdapterAdvancedProperty`. This is a bit of a mouthful, but it's easily understood. Autocomplete, which we have already looked at in *Chapter 1, Introduction to PowerShell 7 – What It Is and How to Get It*, makes typing long cmdlets much easier. Type the first part of the noun, hit *Tab*, type the next part, hit *Tab* again, and so on until the cmdlet is complete. Try it with `Get-NetAdapterAdvancedProperty`. We only need to type `Get-NetA`, then press *Tab* twice to arrive at the right cmdlet. Repeatedly pressing *Tab* will cycle through the appropriate cmdlets on a Windows machine, or present you with a list of options on Linux and macOS.

There are also some standards around capitalization; **CamelCase** is preferred, whereby each word in the noun is capitalized. This not only makes it easier for us to read from the screen, but it also means that accessibility tools such as screen readers can handle them correctly.

The correct use of aliases

There is a way around cumbersome cmdlet names: **aliases**. Type `Get-Alias` into the command line. You should see a fairly long list of aliases for common cmdlets. For example, you should see that man is an alias for `Get-Help`. Try it; type in the following code and see what happens:

```
man Get-Command
```

There are two types of aliases, which exist for different reasons. Let's have a closer look at them here:

- **Abbreviations**, such as `gci` for `Get-ChildItem`. These often require you to already know what the correct cmdlet is and can be quite cryptic. They are for people who know PowerShell and want to save time.

- **Synonyms**—We've just used one in the preceding code snippet. man is a Unix command that calls the **manual**. Similarly, `ls` and `dir` are both aliases for `Get-ChildItem` and produce output that looks like the output you might expect if you are familiar with the `ls` Unix command or the `dir` Windows command. These are for old people like me so that years of muscle memory don't have to be relearned.

> **Note**
>
> While we can type `dir` in PowerShell and get relevant output, we are not getting output from the `dir` command. The command switches we may be familiar with in `dir` won't work in PowerShell. We are calling a cmdlet with similar functionality.

We can also define our own aliases for cmdlets we use regularly using the `Set-Alias` cmdlet. We can do it like this:

```
Set-Alias -Name adapters -Value Get-NetAdapter
```

Try it. Type in the preceding cmdlet, and then type in `adapters`. You should see something like this:

```
PS C:\Users\PARLOWN> Set-Alias -Name adapters -Value Get-NetAdapter
PS C:\Users\PARLOWN> adapters

Name                        InterfaceDescription                        ifIndex
----                        --------------------                        -------
Ethernet                    Intel(R) Ethernet Connection (10) I219…          23
vEthernet (Default Switc…   Hyper-V Virtual Ethernet Adapter #5              82
vEthernet (Ethernet)        Hyper-V Virtual Ethernet Adapter                 22
vEthernet (Wi-Fi)           Hyper-V Virtual Ethernet Adapter #2              33
vEthernet (WSL)             Hyper-V Virtual Ethernet Adapter #3              69
Bluetooth Network Connec…   Bluetooth Device (Personal Area Networ…          11
Wi-Fi                       Intel(R) Wi-Fi 6 AX201 160MHz                     5
vEthernet (Fujitsu Europ…   Hyper-V Virtual Ethernet Adapter #4              76
```

Figure 2.1 – Setting an alias

The drawback to doing this is that the alias you set is only available in the current PowerShell session. When you close the window, all your custom aliases are lost. You can save them in your PowerShell profile, but they'll still only be available locally. I avoid using custom aliases and rely on autocomplete instead. It's also poor practice to use them in a script, as this can hinder readability.

Now we have an understanding of what a cmdlet is, let's take a look at the syntax we need to use with them.

Understanding cmdlet syntax

We've already seen that you can pass information to cmdlets for input, or to modify the output. For instance, in the previous section, we typed the following:

```
Set-Alias -Name adapters -Value Get-NetAdapter
```

The cmdlet is called `Set-Alias`, but there are two bits of information after that: `-Name` and `-Value`. These are called **parameters**. They are denoted by the dash character (`-`), which tells PowerShell that the following characters up to the next *space* character represent an instruction, rather than a value. In each of the preceding parameters we've passed a string—we've told `Set-Alias` that the value of `-Name` is `adapters`, and `-Value` is `Get-NetAdapter`. Now, when we type `adapters` at Command Prompt, PowerShell knows to substitute it with `Get-NetAdapter`.

That's great, but how do we know which parameters a cmdlet will take? Well, we're going to go back to our friend `Get-Help` from *Chapter 1*, *Introduction to PowerShell 7 – What It Is and How to Get It*. Open a PowerShell prompt and type the following:

```
Get-Help Get-Random
```

This will call up the Get-Random help file. We are interested in the SYNTAX section, shown next:

```
PS C:\Users\PARLOWN> Get-Help Get-Random

NAME
    Get-Random

SYNOPSIS
    Gets a random number, or selects objects randomly from a collection.


SYNTAX
    Get-Random [[-Maximum] <System.Object>] [-Count <System.Int32>] [-Minimum <System.Object>] [-SetSeed
    <System.Nullable`1[System.Int32]>] [<CommonParameters>]

    Get-Random [-InputObject] <System.Object[]> [-Count <System.Int32>] [-SetSeed <System.Nullable`1[System.Int32]>]
    [<CommonParameters>]

    Get-Random [-InputObject] <System.Object[]> [-SetSeed <System.Nullable`1[System.Int32]>] -Shuffle
    [<CommonParameters>]
```

Figure 2.2 – Get-Random syntax

Well, that's great, but what does it all mean? The help file tells us that Get-Random can operate in three different ways; there is a set of parameters for each. Let's concentrate on the first set. Remember, parameters always start with a dash (-), so we can see there are four parameters in that first set: -Maximum, -Minimum, -Count, and -SetSeed. As it says in the DESCRIPTION section: You can use the parameters of Get-Random to specify the minimum and maximum values, the number of objects returned from a collection, or a seed number. Hopefully, you completed the *Exercises* section in *Chapter 1, Introduction to PowerShell 7 – What It Is and How to Get It*, so you've seen this before. Let's look at the second parameter set. There are three parameters there: -InputObject, -Count, and -SetSeed. Using these parameters makes Get-Random do something different. Instead of returning a random number, now it will return a random object from a list you give it in the first parameter. Let's try it. In a PowerShell prompt, type the following:

```
Get-Random -InputObject "apples", "pears", "bananas"
```

Hopefully, Get-Random will return a random piece of fruit from that list. The comma character tells PowerShell that there are more items to come in the list.

The following screenshot shows some of the ways you can get this wrong:

```
PS C:\Users\PARLOWN> Get-Random -InputObject "apples""pears""bananas"
apples"pears"bananas
PS C:\Users\PARLOWN> Get-Random -InputObject "apples" "pears" "bananas"
Get-Random: A positional parameter cannot be found that accepts argument 'pears'.
PS C:\Users\PARLOWN> Get-Random -InputObject "apples", "pears", "bananas",
>>
```

Figure 2.3 – Passing a list of items the wrong way

In the first example, I've only passed a single item with a lot of double quotes.

In the second one, I've passed a single item to the -InputObject parameter, and PowerShell is interpreting the second string, pears, as input for another parameter and getting confused.

In the third example, PowerShell is waiting for the next item in the list, shown by the >> symbol. If you find yourself with this and you don't know what to type next, press *Ctrl + C* to break out.

But the SYNTAX section tells us a lot more than just the names and sets of the parameters. It also tells us which parameters are mandatory, which ones accept more than one item, which ones need to be explicitly named, and which types of values each parameter will accept. Hold tight—this is going to get a bit complicated. Let's look at the SYNTAX section of the help file for Get-Random again, in the following screenshot. Keep your eyes on the square brackets:

```
SYNTAX
    Get-Random [[-Maximum] <System.Object>] [-Count <System.Int32>] [-Minimum <System.Object>] [-SetSeed
    <System.Nullable`1[System.Int32]>] [<CommonParameters>]

    Get-Random [-InputObject] <System.Object[]> [-Count <System.Int32>] [-SetSeed <System.Nullable`1[System.Int32]>]
    [<CommonParameters>]

    Get-Random [-InputObject] <System.Object[]> [-SetSeed <System.Nullable`1[System.Int32]>] -Shuffle [<CommonParameters>]
```

Figure 2.4 – Get-Random syntax

Our first parameter set starts with [[-Maximum] <System.Object>]. -Maximum is the parameter name, and <System.Object> is the parameter **argument**; that is, the **type** of object that the -Maximum parameter will take as input.

If you type Get-Help Get-Random -Full, then you will see that it only accepts integers, floating-point numbers, or objects that can be interpreted as integers, such as the string two, as shown in *Figure 2.5*. The outer set of square brackets tells us that the -Maximum parameter is optional; we don't need to include it to get a random number. The inner set of square brackets around the parameter name, [-Maximum], tells us that we don't need to include the parameter name to pass a maximum value to the cmdlet. In the following screenshot, we can see that the parameter has a position value of 0—this means that the first unnamed argument will be interpreted as belonging to the -Maximum parameter:

```
-Maximum <System.Object>
    Specifies a maximum value for the random number. `Get-Random` returns a value that is less than the maximum (not
    equal). Enter an integer, a double-precision floating-point number, or an object that can be converted to an integer
    or double, such as a numeric string ("100").

    The value of Maximum must be greater than (not equal to) the value of Minimum . If the value of Maximum or Minimum is
    a floating-point number, `Get-Random` returns a randomly selected floating-point number.

    On a 64-bit computer, if the value of Minimum is a 32-bit integer, the default value of Maximum is Int32.MaxValue .

    If the value of Minimum is a double (a floating-point number), the default value of Maximum is Double.MaxValue .
    Otherwise, the default value is Int32.MaxValue .

    Required?                       false
    Position?                       0
    Default value                   None
    Accept pipeline input?          False
    Accept wildcard characters?     false

-Minimum <System.Object>
    Specifies a minimum value for the random number. Enter an integer, a double-precision floating-point number, or an
    object that can be converted to an integer or double, such as a numeric string ("100"). The default value is 0 (zero).

    The value of Minimum must be less than (not equal to) the value of Maximum . If the value of Maximum or Minimum is a
    floating-point number, `Get-Random` returns a randomly selected floating-point number.

    Required?                       false
    Position?                       named
    Default value                   None
    Accept pipeline input?          False
    Accept wildcard characters?     false
```

Figure 2.5 – Detailed information about the -Maximum and -Minimum parameters

We can see that for the [-Minimum <System.Object>] parameter, there is no inner set of square brackets; this means the -Minimum parameter must always be named if we're going to use it; we actually have to type -Minimum. For both the -Minimum and -Maximum parameters, there are no square brackets around <System.Object>. This means that if we use these parameters, we must pass an argument to them of the type System.Object (specifically in this case an integer, floating-point number, or string that can be interpreted as a number).

Let's look at the second set of parameters. It starts with [-InputObject] <System.Object[]>; this means if we want to use the second set, we must provide some input. The square brackets around [-Input.Object] tell us the name of the parameter is optional, however; PowerShell will interpret the first argument it receives as the input. How is this different from the first set? Look closely at the <System.Object[]> argument—it contains a set of square brackets at the end. This shows that it can contain multiple values, separated by a comma. Try this. Type the following:

```
Get-Random 10, 20, 30
```

Hopefully, you should get one of those values back. PowerShell knows it has received multiple values and knows not to interpret that collection as an argument for -Maximum, because -Maximum can only contain a single value.

> **Activity 2**
>
> How might you provide a single numeric value to the -InputObject parameter?

Let's look now at the third set of parameters. At first glance, they look the same as the second set. They both start the same way, but notice at the end is this parameter: -Shuffle. It's got no square brackets and no argument. This is a switch parameter. If we use it, we are automatically using the third parameter set; this means the -Count parameter is not available to us, as it's not in the third set. It doesn't take any argument because it tells PowerShell to return the entire list in random order.

Each parameter set finishes with [<CommonParameters>]. This is a set of parameters that are available for any PowerShell cmdlet. You can read the about_CommonParameters help file for more information. They include variables to control the action PowerShell will take in the event of an error, or to produce more output from a cmdlet to help with troubleshooting. More on this in *Chapter 10, Error Handling – Oh No! It's Gone Wrong!*.

Let's summarize cmdlet syntax. There are six types of parameters, listed next:

- **Mandatory parameters**: The parameter name and argument have no square brackets. Both the name and an argument must be supplied. For example, Start-Service has a mandatory parameter: -DisplayName.

- **Mandatory positional parameters**: The parameter name is enclosed in square brackets, but the argument is not. The Get-Random parameter -InputObject is an example of this.

- **Optional parameters**: The parameter name and argument are enclosed in square brackets, but there is no second set of brackets enclosing just the parameter name. The Get-Random parameter -Count is an example of this.

- **Optional positional parameters**: -Maximum is an example of this in the Get-Random cmdlet. The whole parameter is enclosed in square brackets, then there is a second set enclosing just the parameter name.

- **Switch parameters**: These parameters take no argument, a bit like my mother. They may be mandatory or optional, but they are never positional. -Shuffle is a good example of a mandatory switch parameter.

- **Common parameters**: These are parameters that are available to all PowerShell cmdlets, and allow you to direct output or control error behavior.

Parameters are organized into **parameter sets** for each cmdlet; which parameters you specify when you type the cmdlet determine which parameter set you use, and this radically alters the behavior of the cmdlet. For example, Get-Random can return a random number, a random item from a list, or the whole list in random order.

Now we understand what cmdlets and parameters are, you're probably wondering where we get them. There are lots included when we download PowerShell, but it's not going to be anything like enough. We'll explore how to get more cmdlets next.

How to find more cmdlets

Cmdlets are usually bundled together into packages called modules. We'll cover module structure in detail in *Chapter 11, Creating Our First Module*, but for now, it is enough to know that a module is a collection of cmdlets with a common theme, such as interacting with a particular application or performing a set of similar functions. Once a module is installed and imported, the cmdlets become available in the shell or to a script.

Finding modules and cmdlets on your machine

We already have a number of modules available to us. Try this; type Get-Module into your shell. Depending on how long PowerShell has been installed, how long the session has been open, and the platform we are working on, we should see a relatively short list—something like this:

```
PS C:\Users\PARLOWN> Get-Module

ModuleType Version   PreRelease Name                              ExportedCommands
---------- -------   ---------- ----                              ----------------
Manifest   7.0.0.0              Microsoft.PowerShell.Management   {Add-Content, Clear-Content, Clear-Item, Clear-ItemPrope…
Manifest   7.0.0.0              Microsoft.PowerShell.Utility      {Add-Member, Add-Type, Clear-Variable, Compare-Object…}
Script     1.4.7               PackageManagement                 {Find-Package, Find-PackageProvider, Get-Package, Get-Pa…
Script     2.1.0               PSReadLine                        {Get-PSReadLineKeyHandler, Get-PSReadLineOption, Remove-…

PS C:\Users\PARLOWN>
```

Figure 2.6 – List of imported modules

That's a list of modules that have been imported into the current session. But that's not all the modules that we can use right now. Try running the cmdlet again, like this:

```
Get-Module -ListAvailable
```

You should see a few more; if you're running on Windows, you'll see a lot more.

The output of the cmdlet will be split according to the directory the modules are in, as shown in the following screenshot:

```
   Directory: C:\program files\powershell\7-preview\Modules

ModuleType Version   PreRelease Name                                 PSEdition ExportedCommands
---------- -------   ---------- ----                                 --------- ----------------
Manifest   7.0.0.0              CimCmdlets                           Core      {Get-CimAssociatedInstance, Get-CimClass, Get-…
Manifest   1.2.5               Microsoft.PowerShell.Archive          Desk      {Compress-Archive, Expand-Archive}
Manifest   7.0.0.0             Microsoft.PowerShell.Diagnostics      Core      {Get-WinEvent, New-WinEvent, Get-Counter}
Manifest   7.0.0.0             Microsoft.PowerShell.Host             Core      {Start-Transcript, Stop-Transcript}
Manifest   7.0.0.0             Microsoft.PowerShell.Management       Core      {Add-Content, Clear-Content, Get-Clipboard, Se…
Manifest   7.0.0.0             Microsoft.PowerShell.Security         Core      {Get-Acl, Set-Acl, Get-PfxCertificate, Get-Cre…
Manifest   7.0.0.0             Microsoft.PowerShell.Utility          Core      {Export-Alias, Get-Alias, Import-Alias, New-Al…
Manifest   7.0.0.0             Microsoft.WSMan.Management            Core      {Disable-WSManCredSSP, Enable-WSManCredSSP, Ge…
Script     1.4.7               PackageManagement                     Desk      {Find-Package, Get-Package, Get-PackageProvide…
Script     2.2.5               PowerShellGet                         Desk      {Find-Command, Find-DSCResource, Find-Module, …
Script     7.0.0.0             PSDiagnostics                         Core      {Disable-PSTrace, Disable-PSWSManCombinedTrace…
Script     2.1.0               PSReadLine                            Desk      {Get-PSReadLineKeyHandler, Set-PSReadLineKeyHa…
Binary     2.0.3               ThreadJob                             Desk      Start-ThreadJob


   Directory: C:\Program Files\WindowsPowerShell\Modules

ModuleType Version   PreRelease Name                                 PSEdition ExportedCommands
---------- -------   ---------- ----                                 --------- ----------------
Script     1.0.1               Microsoft.PowerShell.Operation.Val…   Desk      {Get-OperationValidation, Invoke-OperationVali…
Script     1.4.7               PackageManagement                     Desk      {Find-Package, Get-Package, Get-PackageProvide…
Binary     1.0.0.1             PackageManagement                     Desk      {Find-Package, Get-Package, Get-PackageProvide…
Script     3.4.0               Pester                                Desk      {Describe, Context, It, Should…}
Script     2.2.5               PowerShellGet                         Desk      {Find-Command, Find-DSCResource, Find-Module, …
Script     1.0.0.1             PowerShellGet                         Desk      {Install-Module, Find-Module, Save-Module, Upd…
Script     2.0.0      beta2    PSReadLine                            Desk      {Get-PSReadLineKeyHandler, Set-PSReadLineKeyHa…
```

Figure 2.7 – Modules and their directories

As you can see, on my machine, that cmdlet has found modules from PowerShell 7 Preview and modules from Windows PowerShell, as well as many others. PowerShell uses the PSModulePath environment variable to know where to look for modules in your environment. We can check which locations are in that variable by typing the following:

```
$env:PSModulePath -split ";"
```

You'll need to use a colon if you're working on a Linux or macOS device.

Locations are put in that variable each time PowerShell is started, but they can also be added by applications, or even manually. You can see the results from my machine in the following screenshot. Notice the last entry is for Microsoft Message Analyzer; this was added when I installed that application:

```
PS C:\Users\PARLOWN> $env:PSModulePath -split ";"
C:\Users\PARLOWN\Documents\PowerShell\Modules
C:\Program Files\PowerShell\Modules
c:\program files\powershell\7-preview\Modules
C:\Program Files\WindowsPowerShell\Modules
C:\Windows\system32\WindowsPowerShell\v1.0\Modules
C:\Program Files (x86)\Adaptiva\AdaptivaClient\data\PSModules
C:\Program Files\Microsoft Message Analyzer\PowerShell\
```

Figure 2.8 – The PSModulePath variable

While we can add paths manually, for most purposes it is better to make sure we install modules to the default paths. There's lots more about the PSModulePath variable in the about_PSModulePath help file.

Now we know where to find modules on our machine, how do we know which cmdlets are in them? Notice in *Figure 2.7* that there are properties in the ExportedCommands table; these are the cmdlets that will be available when we import the module. There may be cmdlets that aren't exported and can only be used internally within the module; we won't be able to type these in and use them. We can see just the exported cmdlets by running Get-Command -Module, followed by the name of the module.

Let's try something. In *Chapter 1, Introduction to PowerShell 7 – What It Is and How to Get It*, we used the Get-Command cmdlet to find cmdlets. That cmdlet searches all the available modules for cmdlets, or we can tell it to just search imported ones. Let's say we're interested in cmdlets for manipulating modules. We might type the following to get a list of cmdlets that include the word module in the name:

```
Get-Command *module*
```

However, if we type the following, then we will only get cmdlets from modules that we have already imported into the current session:

```
Get-Command *module* -ListImported
```

This shows how those two cmdlets look on my machine:

```
PS C:\Users\PARLOWN> Get-Command *module* -ListImported

CommandType     Name                              Version    Source
-----------     ----                              -------    ------
Function        InModuleScope                     3.4.0      Pester
Cmdlet          Export-ModuleMember               7.3.0.1    Microsoft.PowerShell.Core
Cmdlet          Get-Module                        7.3.0.1    Microsoft.PowerShell.Core
Cmdlet          Import-Module                     7.3.0.1    Microsoft.PowerShell.Core
Cmdlet          New-Module                        7.3.0.1    Microsoft.PowerShell.Core
Cmdlet          New-ModuleManifest                7.3.0.1    Microsoft.PowerShell.Core
Cmdlet          Remove-Module                     7.3.0.1    Microsoft.PowerShell.Core
Cmdlet          Test-ModuleManifest               7.3.0.1    Microsoft.PowerShell.Core

PS C:\Users\PARLOWN> Get-Command *module*

CommandType     Name                              Version    Source
-----------     ----                              -------    ------
Alias           Import-AzAutomationModule         1.7.3      Az.Automation
Function        Find-Module                       2.2.5      PowerShellGet
Function        Find-Module                       2.2.5      PowerShellGet
Function        Find-Module                       1.0.0.1    PowerShellGet
Function        Get-InstalledModule               2.2.5      PowerShellGet
Function        Get-InstalledModule               2.2.5      PowerShellGet
Function        Get-InstalledModule               1.0.0.1    PowerShellGet
Function        InModuleScope                     3.4.0      Pester
Function        Install-Module                    2.2.5      PowerShellGet
Function        Install-Module                    2.2.5      PowerShellGet
```

Figure 2.9 – Imported and installed cmdlets

How do we use cmdlets from modules that haven't been imported? In two ways, as follows:

- Firstly, we can use the `Import-Module` cmdlet to bring the module into the session, and then use the cmdlet we need.

- Or, we can just use it anyway and allow PowerShell to implicitly import it.

Try it. In *Figure 2.6*, there is a list of imported modules for my current session. It doesn't contain the `PowerShellGet` module. It's probable that your current session hasn't imported that module either, so let's do that now. Type the following:

```
Get-InstalledModule
```

You'll notice a little bit of a pause as PowerShell imports the `PowerShellGet` module, and then you'll see a list of installed modules if any have been installed. That's great, but the clever bit is this: type `Get-Module` again, to get a list of imported modules. You should see `PowerShellGet` has been imported in the background, as follows:

```
PS C:\Users\PARLOWN> Get-Module

ModuleType  Version    PreRelease  Name                              ExportedCommands
----------  -------    ----------  ----                              ----------------
Binary      7.0.0.0                CimCmdlets                        {Get-CimAssociatedInstance, Get-CimClass, Get-CimInstanc…
Manifest    7.0.0.0                Microsoft.PowerShell.Management    {Add-Content, Clear-Content, Clear-Item, Clear-ItemPrope…
Manifest    7.0.0.0                Microsoft.PowerShell.Utility       {Add-Member, Add-Type, Clear-Variable, Compare-Object…}
Script      1.4.7                  PackageManagement                 {Find-Package, Find-PackageProvider, Get-Package, Get-Pa…
Script      3.4.0                  Pester                            {AfterAll, AfterEach, Assert-MockCalled, Assert-Verifiab…
Script      2.2.5                  PowerShellGet                     {Find-Command, Find-DscResource, Find-Module, Find-RoleC…
Script      2.1.0                  PSReadLine                        {Get-PSReadLineKeyHandler, Get-PSReadLineOption, Remove-…
```

Figure 2.10 – As if by magic… the module appears

That leads to two questions. The first one is this: Why bother with importing and installing? Why not make all the cmdlets available every time, right from the start? The short answer is **space**. Each imported module requires a memory space; if we import hundreds of modules and thousands of cmdlets, then every time we start PowerShell, it will get incredibly unwieldy and slow, so we just import the modules and cmdlets we need, as we need them.

The other question is this: Why do we need an `Import-Module` cmdlet if we can get cmdlets implicitly? We need `Import-Module` for two reasons; firstly, you might not install a module into one of the default paths in `PSModulePath`, so implicit importing won't be available. Secondly, you might want to control how the module is imported. For instance, you might not want to import cmdlets from a module that has the same name as cmdlets you have already imported, in which case you would use `Import-Module` with the `-NoClobber` parameter, rather than import implicitly.

> **Activity 3**
>
> How might we import cmdlets, but change their names so that we know which module they are from?

Finding new modules and cmdlets

So far, we've looked at modules that are already on our system, but we have just now imported `PowerShellGet`, and it's really useful because it can help us find modules that are held remotely, in a **repository**. Repositories are storage locations for software packages; usually, it has a table of contents, contains metadata about the packages, and has some form of version control, allowing us to select a particular version of the software it contains. Many applications and operating systems have official repositories; Python has the **Python Package Index (PyPI)**, Docker has Docker Hub, Ubuntu has four repositories, and PowerShell is no different. The official, Microsoft-maintained repository for PowerShell is the PowerShell Gallery, and this is the repository that `PowerShellGet` connects to by default.

The PowerShell Gallery

Let's start by looking at how we might find modules in the gallery that we are interested in. Try running the following:

```
Get-Command -Module PowerShellGet
```

This will give us a list of the cmdlets that are available in the module. We can see they fall into two categories—cmdlets for finding and installing resources such as modules and scripts, and cmdlets for managing repositories. Let's have a look for a module. Try running the following:

```
Find-Module -name *math*
```

My results are shown here:

```
PS C:\Users\WDAGUtilityAccount> Find-Module -Name *math*

Version         Name                    Repository        Description
-------         ----                    ----------        -----------
1.0.7           IPv4Math                PSGallery         IPv4 Math functions, originally from htt...
1.1.0           Math                    PSGallery         Provides a calculator command (Invoke-Ma...
1.4             PokerMath               PSGallery         PokerMath Get-Ratios function calculates...
0.2             ScubaMath               PSGallery         Scuba diving math
1.0             MathLibrary             PSGallery         Math calculator cmdlets
0.1.1           psmath                  PSGallery         PowerShell Math and Statistics Library i...
0.0.2           MathFunctions           PSGallery         Basic module used to demonstate CI/CD us...
```

Figure 2.11 – Math-related modules in the PowerShell Gallery

Some of those look more or less useful—I'm not sure that I need PokerMath, but you may. How do we know which cmdlets are in those modules? We can't use Get-Command, as the modules are not present on our local machine, but PowerShellGet includes the Find-Command cmdlet. If we pass Find-Command the name of a particular module, then it will list out the cmdlets in that module, like this:

```
Find-Command -ModuleName psmath
```

If we run that, we can see that psmath contains a whole range of mathematical functions, from the fairly obvious—such as Get-Math.sqrt—to some more esoteric ones for **artificial intelligence** (**AI**) and statistics. To know how to use the functions, we will need to install the module and examine the help file. We can do this by typing the following:

```
Install-Module psmath
```

You may see a warning that the repository is untrusted, as in the following screenshot. This is expected, as by default, no repositories are trusted. We need to explicitly trust them with the Set-PSrepository cmdlet:

```
PS C:\Users\WDAGUtilityAccount> Install-Module psmath

Untrusted repository
You are installing the modules from an untrusted repository. If you trust this repository, change its
InstallationPolicy value by running the Set-PSRepository cmdlet. Are you sure you want to install the modules from
'PSGallery'?
[Y] Yes  [A] Yes to All  [N] No  [L] No to All  [S] Suspend  [?] Help (default is "N"):
```

Figure 2.12 – Do you trust this repository?

Type Y for yes. After a few seconds of a progress bar, the Command Prompt will reappear. The module is now installed, but not imported. Although we've used PowerShellGet to install the module, it's been installed into a location that isn't in the correct path for implicitly importing it by using one of the cmdlets, but we can explicitly import it using the Import-Module cmdlet, like so:

Import-Module psmath

If we now type the following, we will see one of the disadvantages of community-provided modules:

Get-Help Get-Math.Sqrt

A lot of authors are more excited by writing their software than documenting it, and the help is pretty sparse. However, we can see that Get-Math.Sqrt takes two parameters: either values or an input object. The -Values parameter is positional. Interestingly, it also takes a list of values, not only a single one. You can use the input object to supply the output of another cmdlet or a variable. Try this:

Get-Math.Sqrt -InputObject (Get-Random)

This will generate a random number, and then calculate the square root of it.

Why doesn't PowerShellGet install modules in the right place? This is to do with scope. By default, PowerShellGet will install modules for the current user only, into a path in your Documents folder if you are on Windows, or into your home drive on Linux. We can change this by including the -Scope parameter with the AllUsers argument, but we would need to be running with administrator rights to do so. In the following screenshot, you can see the error message that comes up in this case. The alternative is to add the location to the PATH environment variable:

```
PS C:\Program Files\PowerShell\7> Install-Module psmath -Scope AllUsers
Install-Module: Administrator rights are required to install modules in 'C:\Program Fi
les\PowerShell\Modules'. Log on to the computer with an account that has Administrator
 rights, and then try again, or install 'C:\Users\nickp\Documents\PowerShell\Modules'
by adding "-Scope CurrentUser" to your command. You can also try running the Windows P
owerShell session with elevated rights (Run as Administrator).
```

Figure 2.13 – I'm afraid I can't do that, Dave

We can also view the PowerShell Gallery online at `https://www.powershellgallery.com/`. Searching the website for `math` gives a lot more results, as it will not only search the module name but also any associated tags. We can get similar results by using the `-Filter` parameter with `Find-Module`.

The PowerShell Gallery is not the only repository

While the PowerShell Gallery is great, there are other repositories. You may have an internal repository where you work, or you may decide to build one for yourself later. The advantages of a repository are the version control and the automation it allows. The disadvantages are the maintenance and the potential for exploitation. If you need to use repositories other than the PowerShell Gallery, then `PowerShellGet` includes cmdlets for working with them, such as `Get-PSRepository`, `Set-PSRepository`, and `Register-PSRepository`.

Other sources

The main alternative to the PowerShell Gallery is GitHub, at `https://github.com`, and similar online source code management tools such as GitLab. These platforms are not specific to PowerShell and contain code written in many other languages. The vast majority of the code is open source in one form or another. The GitHub platform is owned by Microsoft but not moderated by Microsoft, and contains everything ranging from the fully official PowerShell repository, with Microsoft's own code, to unmaintained incomplete bits of scripts and malware. Unless you absolutely trust the repository owner always, *ALWAYS* read the code and understand what it does before downloading it.

We can search GitHub for PowerShell modules by entering our search term on the GitHub website and adding `language:PowerShell`, as seen in the following screenshot:

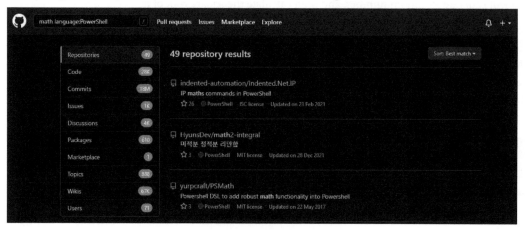

Figure 2.14 – 49 repositories on the GitHub website, some of which may be useful

We can also find plenty of PowerShell scripts on the internet; it's less likely we'll find full modules, but many useful websites publish perfectly usable scripts outside of source-controlled platforms. The caveat still stands, however, only more so. Even if you trust the author, read the code, and understand what it does before using it. Never just blindly run something and hope it's OK. PowerShell is extremely powerful, and you should always run it securely. There'll be plenty more on this in *Chapter 12, Securing PowerShell*

The final way to get cmdlets, modules, and scripts is to write them yourself. This is easier than you might think, and we'll cover it in the second section of the book, starting in *Chapter 8, Writing Our First Script – Turning Simple Cmdlets into Reusable Code.*

We should now have a good idea of the many places where we can find PowerShell resources, and understand their relative value. In the next section, we'll discuss the most basic way to work with PowerShell, and Windows users can have some fun.

Working interactively with PowerShell

PowerShell is, in my experience, unusual for a programming language, in that the huge number of cmdlets available make it particularly suitable for interactive use; open a terminal, type a line of code, and see something exciting happen. It is pretty difficult to do this in other interpreted languages, such as Python, because Python doesn't come with many bundled commands, and it is difficult to import libraries into interactive sessions. Because of this, Python users very quickly move on to writing scripts. In the 10 years I have worked with PowerShell, I've found many of my colleagues never really progress from interactive PowerShell, and that's fine. In the rest of this chapter, we're going to recap how we've been using PowerShell, and Windows users can get to install a really useful utility called Windows Terminal, which will give them the same multi-tabbed terminal experience that Linux and macOS users can get by default.

Each time we've entered a line of code, we've called a cmdlet. Each cmdlet is a mini-script or program. This is similar to shell scripting; batch scripts in Windows or Bash scripts in Linux, where each line of code we enter calls a defined program.

Most scripts in PowerShell are written in the same way—the script can be run as if it were a cmdlet, with parameters to modify the behavior and actions. This means we can use them interactively as well, allowing us to share our efforts with our less technically inclined colleagues and friends. Before we start writing scripts, however, it would be good to set up a way to easily use PowerShell interactively. The provided shell is much improved with PowerShell 7, including highlighting to make it easier to see what we are typing and improved copy and paste. However, I prefer another tool—Windows Terminal.

Windows Terminal – an alternative terminal emulator

If you use Linux or macOS, you don't need to do this part, as you already have multi-tabbed terminals, you lucky people. For Windows users, we had to open multiple applications; in the past, I might have had Windows Console (Command Prompt), Windows PowerShell, PowerShell 7, Azure Cloud Shell, PuTTY, Git Bash, and Python all open at once, running as separate applications. Since 2020, however, there is a much better choice—Windows Terminal. It can run multiple instances of any command-line program in separate tabs, which is enough to convince me on its own, but it also has support for emojis and glyphs, a split-pane function, and an allegedly fun new font called Cascadia Code, plus it's open source. There are lots of details in this blog post if you want to know more: `https://devblogs.microsoft.com/commandline/introducing-windows-terminal/`.

Windows Terminal is hosted on GitHub at `https://github.com/Microsoft/Terminal`, and you can download and install the `.msixbundle` file from there. You can also install it using Winget if you installed that earlier, or if you are on Windows 11. The preferred way, however, is to install it from Microsoft Store. This allows the application to be automatically updated—as it is open source, software updates are frequent and often necessary, as they include bug fixes as well as improvements.

Installing Windows Terminal from Microsoft Store

Installing from the Windows Store is a breeze. Here's how to do it:

1. Type `store` into your search bar in Windows and launch the Microsoft Store app.
2. Type `Windows Terminal` into the search bar in the Store app.
3. Click **Get**, as shown in the following screenshot:

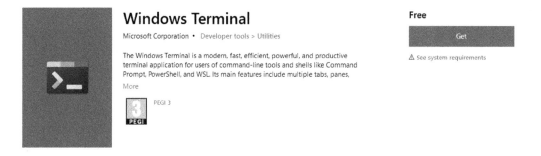

Figure 2.15 – Getting Windows Terminal: not suitable for toddlers

4. After a few minutes, Terminal will be available in your **Start** menu.

And that's it. Windows Terminal will now be updated automatically. Let's start configuring it for our purposes. Because we've already installed PowerShell 7, Terminal will default to that when you open it; if we hadn't, it would default to Windows PowerShell instead. Depending on which other applications you have installed on your client, it may automatically pick them up and make them available. Click the *down* icon in the toolbar to see what is already available and select an application other than the default, as illustrated in the following screenshot:

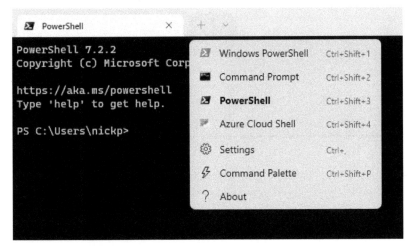

Figure 2.16 – The basic applications available in Windows Terminal

That's great, but it doesn't begin to cover the number of command-line applications you might have. Let's see how we can do that. I've got Python on my machine because I often enjoy a change of perspective. If you want to follow along and you don't have Python installed, you can download it from here: `https://www.python.org/downloads/`.

Python by default installs to `C:\Users\<yourname>\AppData\Local\Programs\Python\<version number>`, as in the following screenshot. You'll need to make a note of the path, and enable viewing hidden files in **File Explorer**:

> nick parlow > AppData > Local > Programs > Python > Python310

Name	Date modified	Type	Size
DLLs	21/04/2022 13:04	File folder	
Doc	21/04/2022 13:04	File folder	
include	21/04/2022 13:03	File folder	
Lib	21/04/2022 13:04	File folder	
libs	21/04/2022 13:04	File folder	
Scripts	21/04/2022 13:04	File folder	
tcl	21/04/2022 13:04	File folder	
Tools	21/04/2022 13:04	File folder	
LICENSE.txt	23/03/2022 22:22	Text Document	32 KB
NEWS.txt	23/03/2022 22:23	Text Document	1,219 KB
python.exe	23/03/2022 22:22	Application	97 KB
python3.dll	23/03/2022 22:22	Application extens...	61 KB
python310.dll	23/03/2022 22:22	Application extens...	4,342 KB
pythonw.exe	23/03/2022 22:22	Application	96 KB
vcruntime140.dll	23/03/2022 22:22	Application extens...	95 KB
vcruntime140_1.dll	23/03/2022 22:22	Application extens...	37 KB

Figure 2.17 – Where Python is

To configure Windows Terminal to access Python, you'll need to set up a new profile. Here's how you can do this:

1. Start Windows Terminal.

2. Click the *down* button on the toolbar, and select **Settings**.

3. Select **Add a new profile** in the left-hand pane, and click on **New empty profile**, as shown in the following screenshot:

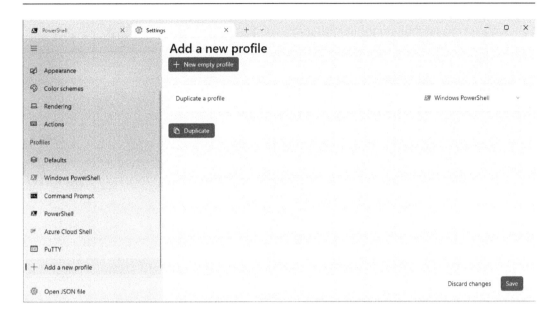

Figure 2.18 – Creating a new profile

4. Fill in the name—in my case, I'm using `Python 3.10`, so I know which version of Python it will launch.

5. Fill in the path to the `python.exe` executable file.

6. Select a starting directory, if you like. I like to put all my rubbish in one place.

7. I like to use icons. You can find Python icons here: `C:\Users\<username>\AppData\Local\Programs\Python\Python310\Lib\test\imghdrdata`.

8. Click **Save**.

You can see an overview of this in the following screenshot:

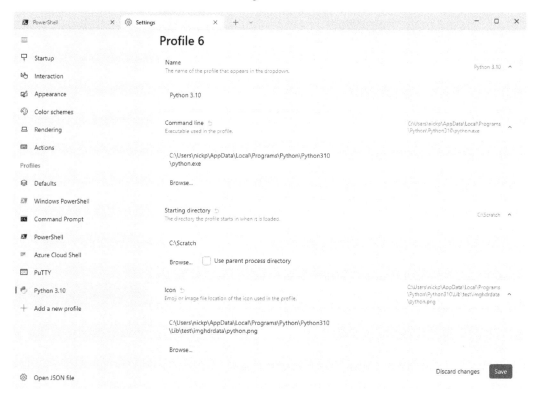

Figure 2.19 – Creating a new profile, completed

And we're done. Now, when you click on the *down* button in the toolbar, you'll see **Python 3.10** as an option. Why have I used Python as an example here? Why didn't I use the PowerShell 7 Preview version? Because Windows Terminal is pretty clever. If you install PowerShell 7 Preview after installing Windows Terminal, just restart Windows Terminal, and voilà! PowerShell 7 Preview will be an option. Cool, eh?

Here, you can see Python running in Windows Terminal:

```
Python 3.10.4 (tags/v3.10.4:9d38120, Mar 23 2022, 23:13:41) [MSC v.1929 64 bit (AMD64)] on win32
Type "help", "copyright", "credits" or "license" for more information.
>>>
```

Figure 2.20 – Running Python in Windows Terminal

There's another thing we must do. We've discussed the importance of being able to start PowerShell as an administrator; we need to do that for Windows Terminal as well. The easiest way to do that is to pin the Terminal app to the taskbar. If you right-click the icon on the taskbar, we can then right-click the **Terminal** icon in the pop-up menu and select **Run as administrator**, as follows:

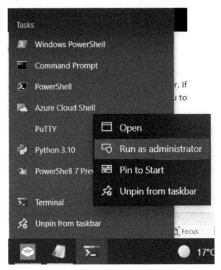

Figure 2.21 – Running Windows Terminal as an administrator

If you open the settings for a profile in Windows Terminal, then you can set just that profile to run as an administrator. There are lots of other things you can do with Windows Terminal. The settings are available through the **user interface (UI)**, or there is a convenient settings file in **JavaScript Object Notation (JSON)** that you can edit directly.

Summary

In this chapter, we have explored cmdlets quite thoroughly. By now, we should understand the naming conventions, the syntax that cmdlets use, how to find out the parameters a cmdlet takes, and what to put in them. We then looked at some ways of discovering new cmdlets and modules, both on our local machine and with the PowerShell Gallery. Finally, we discussed working interactively with PowerShell and looked at an exciting new application for Windows users; Windows Terminal.

In the next chapter, we're going to take a long hard look at the pipeline; how it works, how to string cmdlets together, how to understand what's gone wrong, and what to do about it. We'll also look at another great application for working with PowerShell, and this time everyone can install it, not just Windows users.

Exercises

1. Which of these is the correct cmdlet to obtain the contents of a file in PowerShell: `Get-Content` or `Read-Content`?

2. What happens if you type `"alive alive" |` oh into the shell, and why?

3. How many parameter sets does the `Get-ChildItem` cmdlet have? Which parameter determines which set we will use?

4. If you see the `Get-ChildItem c:\foo *.exe` cmdlet, you can tell that `c:\foo` is an argument being passed to the `-Path` parameter. Which parameter is `*.exe` being passed to?

5. Without actually trying it, will the `Get-ChildItem c:\foo -Filter *.exe, *.txt` cmdlet run? If not, why not?

6. How might you find cmdlets to work with **Amazon Web Services (AWS)**?

7. How might you find cmdlets to work with AliCloud?

8. How could you change the text size in Windows Terminal?

3

The PowerShell Pipeline – How to String Cmdlets Together

Almost all **operating systems (OSs)** have the concept of a **pipeline**, allowing the output of one process to be fed into the input of the next. This concept is credited to Douglas McIlroy in 1973 when he was working on version 3 of Unix at Bell Labs. This initial implementation envisaged the output of every command as a file-like structure, on which the next command could operate.

This chapter will explain how PowerShell adheres to this vision and differs from it. We'll start by exploring the pipeline concept, then look at some basic ways of manipulating the contents of the pipeline before taking a medium-depth dive into how the pipeline works in PowerShell, and how we can troubleshoot it when it doesn't.

By the end of this chapter, we'll understand how information passes from one cmdlet to the next, how to manipulate that information so that we only work with the stuff we need, and how to work out what's going wrong when we get an error message.

In this chapter, we're going to cover the following topics:

- How to bring cmdlets together – the pipeline

- Selecting and sorting objects

- Filtering objects

- Enumerating objects

- Formatting objects

- How the pipeline works – parameter binding

- Troubleshooting the pipeline – pipeline tracing

How to bring cmdlets together – the pipeline

Since Unix and the C programming language in the 1970s, operating systems have abstracted computer input and output into **standard streams**. These are *abstract devices* that belong to the operating system. They allow any program running on that operating system to accept standardized input, often from a keyboard, and provide standardized output, usually to a screen, without needing to know anything about how the input got there, or where the output is going. The three most common are **standard input (stdin)**, **standard output (stdout)**, and **standard error (stderr)**. The stdin stream is almost always from the keyboard and can be captured by the PowerShell Read-Host cmdlet. The stdout stream is the successful output of the cmdlet. The stderr stream contains any error messages produced by the program and is sent to a separate stream so as not to interfere with any successful output.

PowerShell expands on these streams a bit and has six output streams instead of two. Each of these streams can be captured either with an explicit PowerShell cmdlet or by specifying one of the common parameters when running a cmdlet, as shown in the following table:

Stream #	Description	Cmdlet	Common Parameters
1	Success	Write-Output	None – this is the default output
2	Error	Write-Error	-ErrorAction and -ErrorVariable
3	Warning	Write-Warning	-WarningAction and -WarningVariable
4	Verbose	Write-Verbose	-Verbose
5	Debug	Write-Debug	-Debug
6	Information	Write-Information	-InformationAction and -InformationVariable

Table 3.1 – PowerShell streams

Stream 1 is the equivalent of stdout, while stream 2 is the equivalent of stderr. The PowerShell pipeline passes the contents of stream 1, success, from one cmdlet to the next in the pipeline. When we see red error messages on the screen, they are not output in stream 1 – they are output in stream 2. This is because we don't want error messages (or verbose messages or anything other than an output object) being passed into the next cmdlet and causing another error. After all, the second cmdlet has no way of interpreting that information.

The pipeline may consist of one or more PowerShell cmdlets, separated by a pipe character (|). Every PowerShell cmdlet is part of a pipeline, even if it's just one cmdlet. There is an implicit pair of cmdlets, Out-Default | Out-Host, at the end of every pipeline so that the output in stream 1 of the cmdlet gets formatted and written to the screen. Some cmdlets have no stream 1 output, so we see nothing on the screen after running them. For example, in *Chapter 2, Exploring PowerShell Cmdlets and Syntax*, we ran the following cmdlet:

```
Set-Alias -Name processes -Value Get-Process
```

Once the cmdlet finished running, we were returned to the prompt. If we look at the help file for Set-Alias, we will see that it has no output by default, so we see nothing on the screen when it runs successfully. Set-Alias is still a pipeline, though; Out-Default still runs, it just receives no output.

Cmdlets execute from left to right, with the output object of the cmdlet on the left being passed to the next cmdlet in the pipeline on the right. For ease of reading (and typing), the pipe symbol can be used as a line break when working interactively. Try pressing *return* or *Enter* after the pipe symbol:

```
Get-process |
Get-member
```

You should see a continuation prompt (>>) after pressing *return/Enter* after the pipe symbol, as shown here:

```
PS /home/nickp> get-process |
>> get-member

   TypeName: System.Diagnostics.Process

Name                    MemberType    Definition
----                    ----------    ----------
Handles                 AliasProperty Handles = Handlecount
Name                    AliasProperty Name = ProcessName
NPM                     AliasProperty NPM = NonpagedSystemMemorySize64
PM                      AliasProperty PM = PagedMemorySize64
SI                      AliasProperty SI = SessionId
VM                      AliasProperty VM = VirtualMemorySize64
WS                      AliasProperty WS = WorkingSet64
```

Figure 3.1 – Using the pipe symbol as a line break

We keep referring to objects – it would be useful to describe exactly what we mean. This is what we'll do in the next section.

What is an object?

When we run commands in Linux and the Windows console, the commands output a byte stream to stdout; this is interpreted as a text file, held in memory. When we want to manipulate the contents of this output, we must use the same tools that we would use to search and manipulate text; this may be Perl, sed, AWK, or a host of others.

This means that we become adept at text manipulation; I've got about seven volumes of Perl books on my desk, dating back to the mid-nineties. PowerShell cmdlets don't produce a text-like byte stream; instead, they produce objects and collections of objects, which are table structures held in memory, that are produced when we run Get-Process, as shown here:

```
PS /home/nickp> Get-Process
                                                    Property
NPM(K)    PM(M)     WS(M)     CPU(s)      Id   SI ProcessName
------    -----     -----     ------      --   -- -----------
     0     0.00      3.52       0.10      47   46 bash
     0     0.00      0.32       0.09       1    1 init
     0     0.00      0.22       0.00      46   46 init
     0     0.00    172.23      25.38    4514   46 pwsh                    Collection
     0     0.00    115.63      18.65    4678   46 pwsh        Object
     0     0.00      2.65       0.04    4677   46 sudo
```

Figure 3.2 – The Get-Process collection of objects

Each line in the table is an object. Each column is a property of the objects in the table. The whole table is a collection of objects. From *Figure 3.1*, we know that each object is of the System.Diagnostics. Process type and has the list of properties and methods associated with that object type. With the pipeline, we can send this collection to another cmdlet to extract further information, or just call the specific property we are interested in. If we want to know the value of a property that isn't displayed by default, such as how much privileged processor time had been consumed in the lifetime of a particular process, we could type the following:

```
(Get-Process -id 4514).PrivilegedProcessorTime
```

Where did that 4514 come from? It's the Id property of one of the pwsh processes in *Figure 3.2*. From this, I can see that my pwsh process has 11.75 seconds in privileged mode. I know – we probably don't want to know that for a process as trivial as pwsh, but we might be interested in the value for other processes if we were investigating a storage performance issue on a database server. Run the following code:

```
Set-Alias -Name processes -Value Get-Process
(get-process -id (processes).id).privilegedprocessortime
```

Here, we will get the privileged process time for all the processes currently running on our client, using the alias we have set for Get-Process.

Not all cmdlets produce a single type of object. Some cmdlets may produce more than one, and we need to be careful how we process these and pass their output in the pipeline. For instance, consider the Get-ChildItem cmdlet. It gets the contents of a directory or folder. A directory may contain two basic types of items – that is, files and sub-directories. These two types will have different properties – for instance, we can't nest a sub-directory inside a file. A pipeline that has been set up to manipulate file objects may fail if it is also passed directory objects. Let's have a look; type the following:

```
(Get-ChildItem -Path c:\scratch\ | Get-Member).TypeName |
Select-Object -Unique
```

Here, we can see that the C:\scratch directory on my Windows machine contains both directories and files, as shown in the following screenshot:

```
PowerShell                  ×  +  ˅
PS C:\Users\nickp> (Get-ChildItem -Path C:\scratch\ | Get-Member).TypeName | Select-Object -Unique
System.IO.DirectoryInfo
System.IO.FileInfo
PS C:\Users\nickp> |
```

Figure 3.3 – Checking the types of objects in a directory

What are we doing there? This looks a bit complicated. Well, we're taking the output of the Get-ChildItem C:\scratch cmdlet and passing it to Get-Member. We're only interested in the TypeName property, so we put the pipeline in parentheses so that we can easily access just the property we need. Once we've got the collection of all TypeName instances, we pass it in a second pipeline to Select-Object, which we tell to only return unique values by using the -unique parameter. Clever, eh?

We're going to look at basic ways of manipulating these objects in the next few sections. Let's start with selecting and sorting objects.

Selecting and sorting objects

Many of the cmdlets we might run will produce a large amount of output, and, likely, much of it will not be interesting. Therefore, it's useful to be able to select just the bits we need and sort them into a meaningful order. There are two cmdlets for doing this: Select-Object and Sort-Object. We will often see these referred to by their aliases – select and sort.

Using Select-Object

We used `Select-Object` in the *What is an object?* section to select the unique properties of objects in a collection. However, we can use it to do so much more. Look at the help file for `Select-Object` by running the following command:

```
Get-Help Select-Object
```

Here, we can see that there are four parameter sets, all of which work in one of two ways – we can either use the cmdlet to work with one or more properties of a collection, or we can use it to select a subset of objects in a collection. Let's try the first one by typing the following:

```
Get-Process | Select-Object Name, Id
```

Here, we'll see a collection of objects with two properties – Name and Id. Now, let's run that in `Get-Member`, as follows:

```
Get-Process | Select-Object Name, Id | Get-Member
```

Here, we can see that we've taken that collection of `System.Diagnostics.Process` objects and changed them into `Selected.System.Diagnostics.Process` objects – these objects only have two properties – the Name and Id properties we used in the `Select-Object` cmdlet:

```
PS /home/nickp> Get-Process | Select-Object Name, Id | Get-Member

    TypeName: Selected.System.Diagnostics.Process

Name         MemberType   Definition
----         ----------   ----------
Equals       Method       bool Equals(System.Object obj)
GetHashCode  Method       int GetHashCode()
GetType      Method       type GetType()
ToString     Method       string ToString()
Id           NoteProperty int Id=47
Name         NoteProperty string Name=bash
```

Figure 3.4 – The properties of our new objects

We've still got the same number of objects, but now, they only have the properties we're interested in. This has two benefits; first, PowerShell will run much quicker while working on these smaller objects, but also PowerShell will require less memory. The downside is that we no longer have access to the properties we *didn't* select from the original objects in the pipeline.

The second way we can use `Select-Object` is to select a subset of objects from a collection. The parameters for doing that are in the first parameter set; `-first`, `-last`, and `-skip`. Each of these parameters requires an integer as an argument. `-first` 5 will select the first five objects in the pipeline, whereas `-last` 2 will select the last two objects in the pipeline, like this:

```
PS /home/nickp> 1,2,3,4,5,6,7,8 | Select-Object -first 5
1
2
3
4
5
PS /home/nickp> 1,2,3,4,5,6,7,8 | Select-Object -last 2
7
8
```

Figure 3.5 – Selecting a subset of objects

We can use the `-skip` parameter to miss out values at the start or end, like this:

```
1,2,3,4,5,6,7,8 | Select-Object -First 2 -skip 1
```

This will return the integers 2 and 3 which are the first two if we skip the first one.

> **Activity 1**
> How might we return 2, 3, 4, 7, and 8 from that array?

The problem with running `Select-Object` in this way is that unless we can control the order of the objects in the collection, we're just grabbing random objects. This brings us to our next cmdlet, `Sort-Object`.

Ordering objects with Sort-Object

When we run `Get-Process`, the processes are returned in alphabetical order, by process name. This is determined in the PowerShell source code. We can, however, change the order in which the objects are presented (and by implication, re-order them in the pipeline) using the `Sort-Object` cmdlet.

`Sort-Object` can sort a collection of objects on one or more properties. We don't need to run it with any parameters; if we don't specify a property to sort on, it will sort the collection based on the default sort property of the first object in the pipeline, which is defined deep within the PowerShell source code and is not easy to find.

What does this mean? Remember that Get-ChildItem produces two types of output. By default, when you run Get-ChildItem, you get a list of all the first type of object (System. IO.DirectoryInfo, or directories), and then a list of all the second type of object (System. IO.FileInfo, or files), as shown in the first example in the following screenshot:

```
PS C:\Users\nickp> Get-ChildItem -Path C:\scratch\

    Directory: C:\scratch

Mode                 LastWriteTime         Length Name
----                 -------------         ------ ----
d----         19/04/2022     15:26                myPowershell
-a---         21/04/2022     22:33             27 bar.txt
-a---         21/04/2022     21:41              0 New Text Document.txt

PS C:\Users\nickp> Get-ChildItem -Path C:\scratch\ | Sort-Object

    Directory: C:\scratch

Mode                 LastWriteTime         Length Name
----                 -------------         ------ ----
-a---         21/04/2022     22:33             27 bar.txt
d----         19/04/2022     15:26                myPowershell
-a---         21/04/2022     21:41              0 New Text Document.txt
```

Figure 3.6 – The effect of running Select-Object with no parameters

In the second example, Get-ChildItem -Path C:\Scratch\ | Sort-Object, we have a list of all the objects arranged alphabetically and mixed; it ignores the object type.

We can add a property name to sort our collection on that property. For instance, we could run Get-Process and sort on the working set size, like so:

```
Get-Process | Sort-Object -Property ws
```

This is nice. However, it's sorted them in the default order, ascending, so the processes we are most likely to be interested in – those with the highest memory consumption – are at the bottom of the table. We can fix that with another parameter, -Descending:

```
Get-Process | Sort-Object -Property WS -Descending
```

This produces a much more useful output, as shown here:

```
PS /home/nickp> Get-Process | Sort-Object -Property ws -Descending

NPM(K)     PM(M)      WS(M)      CPU(s)       Id  SI ProcessName
------     -----      -----      ------       --  -- -----------
     0      0.00     170.64       25.82     4514  46 pwsh
     0      0.00     151.45       16.70     5141  46 pwsh
     0      0.00     133.93        5.64     5389 ...26 pwsh
     0      0.00     116.98       42.00     4678  46 pwsh
     0      0.00       3.50        0.24       47  46 bash
     0      0.00       2.83        0.06     5327 ...26 bash
     0      0.00       2.64        0.04     4677  46 sudo
     0      0.00       1.97        0.44     5077  46 top
     0      0.00       0.31        0.12        1   1 init
     0      0.00       0.21        0.00       46  46 init
     0      0.00       0.21        0.00     5326 ...26 init
```

Figure 3.7 – Using Sort-Object to sort in descending order

We can even sort on multiple properties at once. For instance, we could try doing the following:

```
Get-Process | Sort-Object -Property SI, WS -Descending
```

This orders our list by **Session ID (SI)**, and then by **Working Set (WS)**.

Let's take a look at the help file. Here, we can see that Sort-Object has three parameter sets that all work in much the same fashion; the only difference is the -top, -bottom, and -stable parameters. The -top and -bottom parameters are fairly self-explanatory, but -stable is less so. When we run Sort-Object, it will output objects of equal value in an order according to its internal logic, not necessarily in the order that they are received. The -stable parameter (as well as -top and -bottom) will preserve the order that Sort-Object received the objects in if the sorted properties are equal.

We can now see how we can combine these two cmdlets, Sort-Object and Select-Object, to produce meaningful collections of interesting information. For instance, we could type the following:

```
Get-Process | Sort-Object CPU -Descending | Select-Object
-First 5
```

This will get us the five most CPU-intensive running processes, as follows:

```
PS /home/nickp> Get-Process | Sort-Object cpu -Descending | Select-Object -First 5

NPM(K)    PM(M)     WS(M)     CPU(s)      Id  SI ProcessName
------    -----     -----     ------      --  -- -----------
     0     0.00    116.98      42.00    4678  46 pwsh
     0     0.00    170.64      25.82    4514  46 pwsh
     0     0.00    155.34      19.21    5141  46 pwsh
     0     0.00    133.93       5.87    5389 ...26 pwsh
     0     0.00      1.97       0.44    5077  46 top
```

Figure 3.8 – Combining Sort-Object and Select-Object

What if we don't want the top five, though? What if we want all the processes that are using *a lot* of CPU? That's where filtering comes in.

Filtering objects

We can filter objects in a more sophisticated way using the Where-Object cmdlet. Where-Object also looks at the properties of the objects in the pipeline, but it can also make decisions about which objects to output and which to discard. Try this:

```
Get-Process | Where-Object -Property CPU -gt -Value 1
```

This will return a list of processes where the CPU property has a value greater than 1. In practice, we very rarely see people include the -Property and -Value names for the parameters, as they are positional. It is far more likely that you will see this written as follows:

```
Get-Process | where CPU -gt 1
```

Wait, though. What's that -gt? The -gt parameter is a **comparison operator**, an important concept in coding.

Understanding comparison operators

Comparison operators are expressed as switch parameters when using the Where-Object cmdlet, resulting in the help file being a long and complex document, with many parameter sets, as only one comparison operator can be used at a time. The basic comparison operators are shown in the following table:

Comparison	Operator	Case-Sensitive Operator
Equality	`-eq`	`-ceq`
Inequality	`-ne`	`-cne`
Greater than	`-gt`	`-cgt`
Less than	`-lt`	`-clt`
Greater than or equal to	`-ge`	`-cge`
Less than or equal to	`-le`	`-cle`
Wildcard equality	`-like`	`-clike`

Table 3.2 – Basic comparison operators

By default, the operators are not case-sensitive, so `-eq top` is functionally the same as `-eq TOP`. There are also several NOT operators to obtain the opposite, such as `-NotLike`. Additionally, we have more advanced comparison operators, such as the following:

- `-match` to get values based on regular expressions.
- `-in` to get objects where the property has a value in a specified array. We'll discuss arrays in *Chapter 4, PowerShell Variables and Data Structures*.
- `-contains` to get objects where the specified value might be in a property that contains an array, rather than a single value.

Let's explore how some of these might work. Try running the following commands to get a list of your running PowerShell processes:

```
Get-Process | Where-Object ProcessName -eq pwsh
Get-Process | Where-Object ProcessName -like pwsh
Get-Process | Where-Object ProcessName -like *pwsh
Get-Process | Where-Object ProcessName -like *wsh
Get-Process | Where-Object ProcessName -contains pwsh
Get-Process | Where-Object ProcessName -in "pwsh", "bash"
```

The last one works because we have given `Where-Object` a two-item array of values, `"pwsh"` and `"bash"`, and asked it to return any objects with a `ProcessName` property value in that array. In practice, the array probably wouldn't be a list of strings like that but something much more complicated, derived by running another cmdlet.

> **Activity 2**
>
> Why doesn't `Get-Process | Where-Object ProcessName -contains *wsh` produce any output?

That's all very interesting, but what happens if we want to find something more complicated, such as a filter on two properties, or find values within a range?

Understanding Where-Object advanced syntax

So far, we've been using `Where-Object` with what is known as the **basic syntax**. For more complicated operations, there is a more advanced option: using the `-FilterScript` parameter. This parameter allows us to pass a short script object to the cmdlet, which then runs on each item in the pipeline.

Filter scripts are **script blocks**, and script blocks must be enclosed in curly brackets. They allow us to combine filters using **Boolean operators** such as `-and`, `-or`, and `-not`. Let's see how one of our previous examples might work using advanced syntax. Earlier in this section, we typed the following:

```
Get-Process | Where-Object ProcessName -eq pwsh
```

This gave us a list of all our running `pwsh` processes when using the basic syntax.

Writing the same command using the advanced syntax would look like this:

```
Get-Process | Where-Object -FilterScript {$PSItem.ProcessName
-eq 'pwsh'}
```

The filter script is the bit enclosed in curly brackets – that is, `$PSItem.ProcessName -eq 'pwsh'`. Let's break this down. `-eq 'pwsh'` is familiar to us, as we used it earlier, but what about `$PSItem.ProcessName`? This is a construction that allows us to access the `ProcessName` property of the object currently being processed. `$PSItem` is a **variable** that represents the current object in the pipeline. In practice, you will very rarely see `$PSItem` outside of textbooks; the variable is almost always written as `$_` (*dollar underscore*); for example, `$_.ProcessName -eq 'pwsh'`. In the basic syntax, we didn't need quotes around `pwsh`, but in the advanced syntax, we do so that the script knows that we are passing it a string value, like so:

```
PS C:\Users\nickp> Get-Process | Where-Object ProcessName -eq pwsh

NPM(K)    PM(M)     WS(M)    CPU(s)      Id  SI ProcessName
------    -----     -----    ------      --  -- -----------
    88   147.73     20.99     51.25     540   1 pwsh
   103    74.84     74.09     42.06    5432   1 pwsh
   110   126.75    125.91     25.86    8088   1 pwsh
   104   112.72    125.61     29.02   19948   1 pwsh
   101   133.21    138.13     14.86   23736   1 pwsh

PS C:\Users\nickp> Get-Process | Where-Object -FilterScript {$PSItem.ProcessName -eq pwsh}
ParserError:
Line |
   1 | … t-Process | Where-Object -FilterScript {$PSItem.ProcessName -eq pwsh}
     |                                                                       ~
     | You must provide a value expression following the '-eq' operator.

PS C:\Users\nickp> Get-Process | Where-Object -FilterScript {$PSItem.ProcessName -eq 'pwsh'}

NPM(K)    PM(M)     WS(M)    CPU(s)      Id  SI ProcessName
------    -----     -----    ------      --  -- -----------
    91   149.47     64.53     52.09     540   1 pwsh
   103    74.84     74.09     42.06    5432   1 pwsh
   110   126.75    125.91     25.86    8088   1 pwsh
   104   112.72    126.05     29.14   19948   1 pwsh
   101   133.21    138.13     14.94   23736   1 pwsh
```

Figure 3.9 – Three ways of filtering with Where-Object, one of which is wrong

Without the quotes, the cmdlet will interpret pwsh as the next cmdlet. If you look closely at the error, you will see that it doesn't get as far as that, though, because -eq is missing a value. It doesn't matter much if you use single or double quotes here, but the best practice is to use single quotes unless you need some of the special powers of double quotes, which we will talk about in *Chapter 4*, *PowerShell Variables and Data Structures*.

Multiple filters in the advanced syntax

Now that we understand the syntax, we can start using it to combine filters to produce more complex results. Try this:

```
Get-Process | Where-Object -FilterScript {$PSItem.ProcessName
-eq 'pwsh' -and $PSItem.CPU -gt 1}
```

This should give you a list of your pwsh processes where the CPU value is greater than 1. Now, if you change the CPU value to something higher, you should see the output change:

```
PS /home/nickp> Get-Process | Where-Object -FilterScript {$PSItem.ProcessName -eq 'pwsh' -and $PS
Item.CPU -gt 1}

NPM(K)    PM(M)      WS(M)     CPU(s)      Id  SI ProcessName
------    -----      -----     ------      --  -- -----------
     0     0.00     125.91      25.82    4514  46 pwsh
     0     0.00      74.09      42.00    4678  46 pwsh
     0     0.00     126.06      29.46    5141  46 pwsh
     0     0.00     138.13      15.18    5389 …26 pwsh

PS /home/nickp> Get-Process | Where-Object -FilterScript {$PSItem.ProcessName -eq 'pwsh' -and $PS
Item.CPU -gt 25}

NPM(K)    PM(M)      WS(M)     CPU(s)      Id  SI ProcessName
------    -----      -----     ------      --  -- -----------
     0     0.00     125.91      25.82    4514  46 pwsh
     0     0.00      74.09      42.00    4678  46 pwsh
     0     0.00     126.06      29.47    5141  46 pwsh
```

Figure 3.10 – Combining filters with Where-Object advanced syntax

Be aware that the script block syntax is unforgiving. Unless we type it carefully and exactly right, we will not get the result we are hoping for. For instance, let's say we type the following:

```
Get-Process | Where-Object -FilterScript {$PSItem.ProcessName
-eq 'pwsh' -and CPU -gt 25}
```

Here, we will get an error saying You must provide a value expression following the '-and' operator. Because we can see the error, we can fix it by replacing CPU with $PSItem.CPU. However, let's say we only want processes named pwsh or bash, and we type this:

```
Get-Process | Where-Object -FilterScript {$PSItem.ProcessName
-eq 'pwsh' -or 'bash'}
```

Here, we *don't* get an error, we just get the wrong result, as shown in the following screenshot. The correct syntax is shown in the second example in the following screenshot:

```
PS /home/nickp> Get-Process | Where-Object -FilterScript {$PSItem.ProcessName -eq 'pwsh' -or 'bas
h'}

NPM(K)     PM(M)     WS(M)    CPU(s)     Id  SI ProcessName
------     -----     -----    ------     --  -- -----------
     0      0.00      1.70      0.24      47  46 bash
     0      0.00      1.70      0.06    5327 …26 bash
     0      0.00      0.18      0.12       1   1 init
     0      0.00      0.09      0.00      46  46 init
     0      0.00      0.09      0.00    5326 …26 init
     0      0.00    125.91     25.82    4514  46 pwsh
     0      0.00     74.09     42.00    4678  46 pwsh
     0      0.00    129.37     30.13    5141  46 pwsh
     0      0.00    138.13     15.32    5389 …26 pwsh
     0      0.00      0.72      0.04    4677  46 sudo
     0      0.00      0.60      0.44    5077  46 top

PS /home/nickp> Get-Process | Where-Object -FilterScript {$PSItem.ProcessName -eq 'pwsh' -or $PSI
tem.ProcessName -eq 'bash'}

NPM(K)     PM(M)     WS(M)    CPU(s)     Id  SI ProcessName
------     -----     -----    ------     --  -- -----------
     0      0.00      1.70      0.24      47  46 bash
     0      0.00      1.70      0.06    5327 …26 bash
     0      0.00    125.91     25.82    4514  46 pwsh
     0      0.00     74.09     42.00    4678  46 pwsh
     0      0.00    129.37     30.16    5141  46 pwsh
     0      0.00    138.13     15.32    5389 …26 pwsh
```

Figure 3.11 – Careful with that syntax, Eugene

We can also use the advanced syntax to access properties of properties. Let's run the following:

```
Get-Process | Get-Member
```

Here, we can see that the ProcessName property is a string, so it has the properties of a string object. This means we can run something like this:

```
Get-Process | Where-Object -FilterScript {$_.ProcessName.Length
-lt 5}
```

Here, we are looking for all the processes running on the machine with a ProcessName that's fewer than 5 characters. We're also using the more common $_ in place of $PSItem. You must get used to this.

Filter optimization

Consider the following two cmdlets:

```
Get-Process | Sort-Object -Property CPU -Descending | Where-
Object CPU -gt 1
Get-Process | Where-Object CPU -gt 1 | Sort-Object -Property
CPU -Descending
```

They produce the same results (at least, they do on my machine). However, on my client, the first one takes 29 milliseconds, while the second one only takes 20 milliseconds. Try it yourself with the Measure-Command cmdlet, like this:

```
Measure-Command {Get-Process | Sort-Object -Property CPU
-Descending | Where-Object CPU -gt 1}
Measure-Command {Get-Process | Where-Object CPU -gt 1 | Sort-
Object -Property CPU -Descending}
```

Now and then, because they're both very short pipelines, you may get a surprising result, but if you run them 10 times in a row, the second cmdlet will be quicker than the first in some way almost every time. This variation is caused by the other things running on your client, competing with PowerShell for resources.

Earlier in this chapter, we talked about reducing the amount of processing and memory PowerShell requires to produce a result. Filter optimization is a great way to do this. We should filter objects as early as possible in the pipeline to reduce the number of objects PowerShell has to work on. There's a basic rule: **filter left**.

We don't just have the Where-Object cmdlet for filtering. Many cmdlets also have filtering parameters that are either explicit, where the parameter name is -Filter, or parameters that will perform common filtering tasks. For instance, the Get-ChildItem cmdlet has -File and -Directory parameters to limit its output to just those object types. Where possible, use the built-in parameters of the cmdlet to filter objects before passing them into the pipeline for further processing.

Activity 3

How can we find a list of cmdlets that have a -Filter parameter?

We've now got a pretty good grasp of how to limit the objects in the pipeline to just the ones we're interested in. Next, we'll look at how we can perform operations on those objects.

Enumerating objects

Often, we will want to perform an operation on the objects that we're working with. Most of the time, there will be a cmdlet to do this, but sometimes, there won't. For instance, say we want to output the filename and path of some items in a folder. There is no convenient property that will produce just the filename and path; there are properties such as `pspath`, which will get us what we want and a bit extra, but nothing that gets exactly what we want. There is, however, a method on the objects that are produced by `Get-ChildItem` that will: `tostring()`. We can execute this method on each item by enumerating them, like so:

```
Get-ChildItem myfiles | Foreach-Object -MemberName tostring
```

This will produce exactly the output I want, as follows:

```
PS /home/nickp> Get-ChildItem myfiles | ForEach-Object -MemberName tostring
/home/nickp/myfiles/AnotherTextFile
/home/nickp/myfiles/ATextFile
/home/nickp/myfiles/AThirdTextFile
```

Figure 3.12 – Basic enumeration

This is a pretty simple example. Like `Where-Object`, `Foreach-Object` has basic and advanced syntax, and the advanced syntax looks very similar to what we saw in the previous section. You must provide a script block to the `-Process` parameter of `ForEach-Object`. To run the last cmdlet with the advanced syntax, we would type the following:

```
Get-ChildItem myfiles | ForEach-Object -Process {$_.tostring()}
```

As shown in the following screenshot, the output is the same. Note that when using a script block, the method name, `tostring`, must be followed by an open and close bracket pair:

```
PS /home/nickp> Get-ChildItem myfiles | ForEach-Object -Process {$PSItem.tostring()}
/home/nickp/myfiles/AnotherTextFile
/home/nickp/myfiles/ATextFile
/home/nickp/myfiles/AThirdTextFile
```

Figure 3.13 – Advanced enumeration

If the method takes arguments, then we would put them in parentheses as a comma-separated list, like so:

```
('Powerhell').Insert(5, 'S')
```

This will correct the spelling by inserting the `'S'` string at position 5 in the original string. We don't see interactive enumeration as much as we used to, since usually, cmdlets are written to perform most of the things we might have wanted to enumerate interactively. However, this is an important concept in scripting, as we will see in *Chapter 5, PowerShell Control Flow – Conditionals and Loops*. There is one useful technique we can use it for, though – repeating a process a set number of times. Try this:

```
1..10 | Foreach-Object {Get-Random}
```

So, in the first part of the pipeline, we are using a range operator (. .) to create an array of 10 integers from 1 to 10. We're not using the `$PSItem` pipeline variable in the second cmdlet, though – we're just instructing it to run once for each item in the pipeline. As you can see, we're not limited to just putting object methods into the script block; we can put cmdlets and scripts in there too.

Parallel enumeration

One of the problems with enumeration is that it can take a very long time if there are a lot of objects, or if the process is complicated. With PowerShell 7, we gained the ability to run `ForEach-Object` processes in parallel. Try running the following code, which will print out the numbers 1 to 10:

```
1..10 | ForEach-Object {
$_
Start-sleep 1}
```

As you press *Enter* after each line, you should see a continuation prompt until you close the curly brackets. Slow, eh? 10 seconds to print out 10 numbers. Now, let's try it with parallel processing:

```
1..10 | ForEach-Object -Parallel {
$_
Start-Sleep 1}
```

Now, you should see the numbers being printed out in groups of five. We can alter the number of parallel processes with the `-ThrottleLimit` parameter.

Now that we've explored some useful cmdlets for manipulating the pipeline and had our first taste of scripting (yes, that's what you did just now), we will have a look at how the pipeline works.

How the pipeline works – parameter binding

The main difference between the output of PowerShell cmdlets and more generic shells is that instead of being file-like, the output is an **object**, with a type, properties, and methods. So, how does an object produced by one cmdlet get passed to another cmdlet?

Cmdlets can only accept input via their parameters. There is no other way, so it follows that the output objects of one cmdlet must be fed to a parameter of the next cmdlet in the pipeline. Consider the following cmdlet pipeline:

```
Get-Process | Sort-Object -Property CPU
```

We can only see one parameter here, `-property`, and it's being given an argument of CPU. So, what's going on? `Sort-Object` is being given two parameters, but we can't see one of them. This is called **pipeline parameter binding**.

PowerShell takes the output of the first cmdlet, `Get-Process`, and must do something with it, so it looks for a parameter on the second cmdlet that can accept the object that PowerShell is holding. There are two ways this can happen; `ByValue` and `ByPropertyName`. Let's look at them in detail.

`ByValue` is the default method, and PowerShell will always try that first, so let's start with that.

Understanding ByValue parameter binding

Let's have a look at the help file for `Sort-Object` by typing the following:

```
Get-Help Sort-Object -Full
```

Have a look through the parameters. You will see that only one parameter can accept objects from the pipeline: `-InputObject`. The help file has this to say about it:

```
-InputObject <System.Management.Automation.PSObject>
        To sort objects, send them down the pipeline to `Sort-
Object`. If you use the InputObject parameter to submit a
collection of items, `Sort-Object` receives one object that
represents the collection. Because one object cannot be sorted,
`Sort-Object` returns the entire collection unchanged.
        Required?                       false
        Position?                       named
        Default value                   None
        Accept pipeline input?          True (ByValue)
        Accept wildcard characters?     false
```

Here, we can see that it only accepts input `ByValue`, and it only accepts `PSObject` type input. `PSObject` is pretty broad; it means anything that is an object in PowerShell. So, we can use it to sort an array of numbers because they are objects of the `System.Int32` type, as shown in the following screenshot. Notice that, as described in the help file, we can't successfully pass an array directly to the `-InputObject` parameter; it must go through the pipeline. If we try to explicitly feed it an array via the parameter, it sees a single array object and returns the array unsorted. We need it to pass through the pipeline one item at a time:

```
PS /home/nickp> 1,3,5,4,2 | sort-object
1
2
3
4
5
PS /home/nickp> sort-object -InputObject 1,3,5,4,2
1
3
5
4
2
```

Figure 3.14 – Correct and incorrect use of the -InputObject parameter

Let's have a look at another. We can see from the help file for Get-ChildItem that it has a parameter, -path, that accepts pipeline input ByValue, and accepts string objects. This means we can do something like this, where we put the myfiles string into the pipeline:

```
'myfiles' | Get-ChildItem
```

Here, we will get a meaningful output – a list of all the items in the myfiles directory. If we had a cmdlet pipeline that outputs paths as strings, we could feed this into Get-ChildItem to get the contents. The important thing to remember when using ByValue is that the type of object you are passing into the pipeline must match the type of object that is specified by the parameter of the next cmdlet that accepts pipeline input.

Get-ChildItem is interesting because the parameter that accepts pipeline input is not the -InputObject parameter – it's -path. What happens if you try to pipe a string to Get-ChildItem, but you also explicitly specify the -path parameter? You will get an error, as shown here:

```
PS /home/nickp> 'myfiles' | Get-ChildItem -Path myfiles
Get-ChildItem: The input object cannot be bound to any parameters for the command either because
the command does not take pipeline input or the input and its properties do not match any of the
parameters that take pipeline input.
```

Figure 3.15 – Pipeline sabotage

The preceding error says that there is no parameter to accept pipeline input, even though we know there is. This is because we bound a value to Get-ChildItem before we started processing the objects in the pipeline, effectively removing that parameter from those available. If we see this error, it's always worth checking that we haven't already used the parameter before we throw our laptops at the wall in frustration.

Let's have a look at the other method of binding pipeline content to a parameter: ByPropertyName.

ByPropertyName parameter binding

PowerShell will always try to bind to a parameter ByValue first. It will only try to shoehorn the pipeline objects using ByPropertyName if ByValue is not available. What happens if your first cmdlet produces objects of the wrong sort for the pipeline-accepting parameter of the next cmdlet? Well, PowerShell will look and see if there is a parameter in the second cmdlet that accepts pipeline input where there is a matching property name – usually, -Id or -Name.

Unsurprisingly, Stop-Process is a cmdlet that stops processes. If we look at the help file, we will see that three parameters accept pipeline input: -InputObject, which accepts objects ByValue, and -Id and -Name, which accept ByPropertyName. Now, let's type the following:

```
Get-Random  |  Stop-Process
```

Here, we will get an error – the same one shown in *Figure 3.15*. We know that Stop-Process has three parameters that take pipeline input, so it's not the first reason. We haven't explicitly bound anything to any parameters either, so it must be because the type of object we have in the pipeline is the wrong sort of object. If we use Get-Member to determine the type of objects Get-Random produces, and then refer to the help file for Stop-Process, we will see that Get-Random produces System.Int32 objects, but Stop-Process requires System.Diagnostics.Process objects. So, if we've not got the right sort of objects in our pipeline, why didn't PowerShell try to do anything ByPropertyName? Well, it did, but none of the properties of the object that were output by Get-Random have a property name that matches the -Id or -Name parameters in Stop-Process. Let's have some fun. Type the following:

```
New-Object -TypeName PSObject -Property @{'Id' = (Get-Random)}
  | Stop-Process -WhatIf
```

What are we doing there? We're using the New-Object cmdlet to create a generic PowerShell object (-TypeName PSObject) with a single property, Id, which we populate by running the Get-Random cmdlet to produce a random number. We will be able to see it in the output if we pipe the cmdlet into Get-Member:

```
PS /home/nickp> New-Object -TypeName PSObject -Property @{'Id' = (Get-Random)} | Get-Member

   TypeName: System.Management.Automation.PSCustomObject

Name        MemberType   Definition
----        ----------   ----------
Equals      Method       bool Equals(System.Object obj)
GetHashCode Method       int GetHashCode()
GetType     Method       type GetType()
ToString    Method       string ToString()
Id          NoteProperty System.Int32 Id=724849817
```

Figure 3.16 – Creating custom objects

Once we've created this new custom object, we can pipe it into `Stop-Process`. The object type is not right, so it can't bind to `-InputObject`, but the object has a property name that matches the `-Id` parameter, so it binds there. Finally, because we don't want to have too much fun, we're using the `-WhatIf` parameter, just in case `Get-Random` provides us with a legitimate process ID. `-WhatIf` is one of the common parameters available in most PowerShell cmdlets, and it tells us what would happen if we ran the cmdlet without actually changing anything.

Parenthetical commands

A few times now, we have run cmdlets in parentheses, as we did previously. Parentheses are a way of overriding the order in which PowerShell runs. The same as in mathematics, parentheses are an instruction to do something *first*. When we use them in PowerShell, the content inside the parentheses must be completed before anything else in that segment of the pipeline is processed. This gives us another way to pass input directly to a parameter.

In the preceding example, we tried to run the following:

```
Get-Random | Stop-Process
```

This didn't work. While the object type (`System.Int32`) was correct for the `-Id` parameter, the `PropertyName` value was incorrect. With parentheses, we can explicitly pass that content to the `-Id` parameter, like so:

```
Stop-Process -Id (Get-Random)
```

First, PowerShell will produce a random number, and then pass it to the `-Id` parameter for us. We will see many more useful examples of parentheses as we go through this book.

Troubleshooting the pipeline – pipeline tracing

We've done a lot of work in this chapter, so now it's time to kick back and have some fun with `Trace-Command`. At least, I think it's fun; other opinions are available. This cmdlet does, however, really let us get into the nuts and bolts of how PowerShell works so that we get to see it in action.

Run the following code:

```
Trace-Command -Name ParameterBinding -Expression {New-Object
-TypeName PSObject -Property @{'Id' = (Get-Random)} | Stop-
Process -WhatIf} -PSHost
```

Here, we're running `Trace-Command` and asking it to record `ParameterBinding` events. We're giving it the cmdlet we ran previously as an expression in a script block, and then with `-PSHost`, we're telling it to output to the screen, rather than its default, which is the debug stream that we saw right at the start of this chapter when we were talking about streams.

We've now got a screen full of yellow writing, which is messy; we're going to need to have a dig around in there. These are the questions we're interested in:

- Where did the custom object bind?

- How did the custom object bind?

Here's my output, tidied up, with comments below each line:

1. `DEBUG: BIND PIPELINE object to parameters: [Stop-Process]`

   In this line, we're starting by binding to the parameters of `Stop-Process`.

2. `DEBUG: PIPELINE object TYPE = [System.Management.Automation.PSCustomObject]`

   This tells us what sort of object we have in the pipeline.

3. `DEBUG: Parameter [InputObject] PIPELINE INPUT ValueFromPipeline NO COERCION`

   This tells us that `-InputObject` only takes the `ByValue objects`.

4. `DEBUG: BIND arg [@{Id=1241688337}] to parameter [InputObject]`

   `arg [1241688337]` is the random number that was generated.

5. `DEBUG: Binding collection parameter InputObject: argument type [PSObject], parameter type [System.Diagnostics.Process[]], collection type Array, element type [System.Diagnostics.Process], no coerceElementType`

   This shows us that the object types don't match.

6. `DEBUG: BIND arg [@{Id=1241688337}] to param [InputObject] SKIPPED`

   Here, we're skipping binding to `-InputObject`.

7. `DEBUG: Parameter [Id] PIPELINE INPUT ValueFromPipelineByPropertyName NO COERCION`

   This line shows that the `-Id` parameter accepts `ByPropertyName` as input.

8. `DEBUG: BIND arg [1241688337] to parameter [Id]`

   `DEBUG: Binding collection parameter Id: argument type [Int32], parameter type [System.Int32[]], collection type Array, element type [System.Int32], no coerceElementType`

   This shows us that the object types match.

9.   DEBUG: BIND arg [System.Int32[]] to param [Id] SUCCESSFUL

Here, we are told we have successfully bound to the -Id parameter.

So, we have the answers to our questions – the object in the pipeline bound to the -Id parameter, ByPropertyName.

That was a whirlwind introduction to Trace-Command. If your pipeline is failing, and you are sure that your object types match, or that you have matching property names, and you haven't bound something explicitly to the only parameter that accepts pipeline input, then this cmdlet is your best hope of understanding what's happening.

Summary

We covered some really interesting and quite technical topics in this chapter. We started by describing what the pipeline does, and then looked at techniques for selecting and sorting objects. We then looked at filtering objects and talked about the importance of using filtering to allow PowerShell to work as efficiently as possible.

From there, we introduced a topic that will be important later, enumeration, and looked at one of the newer features of PowerShell 7, parallel enumeration. In the last part of this chapter, we took a deeper dive into how the pipeline accomplishes its magic and examined the two methods of parameter binding: ByValue and ByPropertyName. Finally, we played with a cmdlet that allows us to get under the hood of how the pipeline is working: Trace-Command.

Most of the time, the pipeline *just works*. However, for cases when it doesn't, this chapter has given us the essential knowledge we need to understand what it is doing and, hopefully, how to fix it. Sometimes, cmdlet authors do not provide a way for their cmdlets to accept pipeline input. This chapter has shown us how to spot that and given us one technique for working around it.

This chapter concludes the introductory part of this book on PowerShell mechanics. In the next chapter, we're going to start doing some coding by looking at variables and data structures. Hold tight.

Exercises

The following are some exercises to help you solidify your knowledge of this chapter:

1.   How can we use PowerShell to display just the day of the week it is today?

2.   We need to get a list of CPU usage and the locations of all our running processes, and we don't want a lot of unnecessary information. How do we do that?

3.   Now that we've got our list, how can we get the path names in reverse alphabetical order?

4.   There's a lot of stuff here. How do we ensure it only lists the processes that have a CPU usage of greater than 5?

5. What is the most efficient way to get a list of read-only files from our home drive?

6. We need to get the size of all the files in our home directory. We just want the name and the size in bytes.

7. We have a file that contains a list of process names, called `processes.txt`. we need to use it to discover information about the processes on our local machine, so we will need to find a cmdlet that can get content from the file.

8. Without *actually running the cmdlet*, what will happen if we run this without `-WhatIf` on a Windows host?

```
'bobscomputer' | Stop-Computer -WhatIf
```

If it's not right, what would the right cmdlet be?

What would happen if we ran it on a Linux host? Tip: think about this. Don't try it. Especially don't try it without `-WhatIf`.

Further reading

As I get older, I find the history of computing more and more fascinating; concepts and devices that were bleeding edge when I was in my twenties are now dusty old relics. However, these old relics go some way to explaining why we are where we are. The Unix Oral History Project has a great section on the concept of pipes: `https://dspinellis.github.io/oral-history-of-unix/frs122/unixhist/finalhis.htm`.

4

PowerShell Variables and Data Structures

It's time to really understand what we mean when we talk about variables. Variables are a common concept in computer science and mathematics, so it's important to have a good grasp of what they are and how they are used in PowerShell.

We'll start by exploring what a variable is, both literally and metaphorically. We will look at how we can use them in PowerShell and contrast the way PowerShell works with other languages. We will explore the concept of primitives, the basic building blocks of data, before moving on to the common data structures that PowerShell uses. Finally, we'll have some fun with splatting, an important and useful technique for simplifying cmdlets.

In this chapter, we're going to cover the following main topics.

- Understanding PowerShell variables
- Exploring object types
- Discovering value types
- Typing explained
- Navigating reference types
- Splatting – using hashtables for fun and profit

Understanding PowerShell variables

A variable is like a box. We can put stuff in it. We can take that stuff out and put something else in it. The box may contain one thing, or it may contain many things. It may contain multiple things of the same type, for instance, 30 pairs of socks, or it can be like my kitchen drawer, and contain all sorts of different things, including string. We can organize the things it contains in different ways or not organize them, like my kitchen drawer. It may contain nothing at all.

A variable is really a label for a region of memory. That's all it is – a name and an address in memory. When you tell PowerShell to use the contents of a variable, you're telling it to go to that area of memory and use what it finds there. Using a label gives us two advantages; firstly, it saves a lot of typing, especially if the variable contains many objects. Secondly, it allows us to assign meaning, something that tells us, and other people reading our code, what the purpose of the variable is, and a clue as to what it likely contains. This is far more important and useful than it may appear right now.

Figure 4.1 – Ceci n'est pas une variable. With apologies to Magritte

PowerShell is intended to be easy to use, so variables can be created dynamically, unlike some languages, such as Java, where we must declare the variable before we can put something in it. What do I mean? Consider this line of code; don't type it, just think about it:

```
$MyVariable = 'some stuff'
```

What am I doing there? I'm dynamically creating a variable with some stuff in it.

If I were to do that in a more Java-like style, I would write this:

```
New-Variable -Name MyVariable
Set-Variable -Name MyVariable -Value 'some stuff'
```

Which creates a variable, gives it a name, and then we put a value in it. In practice, this is very rare. Most people, in most situations, create variables on the fly.

If you read those lines of code closely, you will see that the first example contains $MyVariable, and in the second one, it's MyVariable, without the $ sign. Let's talk about why.

Variables are not their contents

We very rarely want to manipulate a variable. Going back to the box metaphor, unless we are five years old, we're usually more interested in the contents of the box, not the box itself. MyVariable is the name assigned to the variable, the label that we can use to refer to it. $MyVariable refers to the contents of the variable. This is the stuff we are interested in. Let's demonstrate.

```
PS C:\Users\nickp> $MyVariable  = "some stuff"
PS C:\Users\nickp> $MyVariable
some stuff
PS C:\Users\nickp> MyVariable
MyVariable: The term 'MyVariable' is not recognized as a name of a cmdlet, function, script file, or
executable program.Check the spelling of the name, or if a path was included, verify that the path is
 correct and try again.
PS C:\Users\nickp> Get-Variable MyVariable

Name                          Value
----                          -----
myVariable                    some stuff

PS C:\Users\nickp> Get-Variable $MyVariable
Get-Variable: Cannot find a variable with the name 'some stuff'.
PS C:\Users\nickp> Write-Output MyVariable
MyVariable
PS C:\Users\nickp> Write-Output $MyVariable
some stuff
PS C:\Users\nickp> |
```

Figure 4.2 – MyVariable is not $MyVariable

In the first line in *Figure 4.2*, we're dynamically creating a variable called MyVariable and putting some stuff into it:

```
$MyVariable = "some stuff"
```

In the second line, we ask PowerShell for the contents of MyVariable by typing $MyVariable, and we get some stuff back.

In the third line, we've just typed the name of the variable, MyVariable, and PowerShell has not understood what we want.

In the fourth line, we explicitly ask for MyVariable with the Get-Variable cmdlet, and again we get the some stuff string, but we also get some other stuff that isn't part of the string; the Get-Variable cmdlet has returned a PSVariable object, not the contents of the variable, which is the some stuff string. We can confirm what sort of variable it is by using Get-Member. Type the following:

```
Get-Variable MyVariable | Get-Member
```

In the fifth line, PowerShell quite reasonably tells us we don't have a variable called some stuff – we're passing the contents of MyVariable to Get-Variable here, not the name of the variable.

In the sixth line, it may look like we're passing a variable to Write-Output, but we're not. We're passing a string with the value MyVariable, not the contents of MyVariable.

The seventh line passes the contents of MyVariable to Write-Output correctly by referring to $MyVariable.

In practice, if we always preface our variable names with a $ sign, we'll almost always be right. This brings us to names; what is a good variable name, and what is not?

Naming variables

There are two things we should consider when naming a variable. Firstly, names we can use, and secondly, names we *should* use.

Names we can (and can't) use

Variable names can contain any combination of letters, numbers, question marks, and the underscore symbol, _. They are not case sensitive. We can use other characters as well if we enclose the variable name in curly braces { }, but we don't do this. Really – it makes life difficult, and there's almost never any need for it. Examples of good and bad names are listed in the following table:

Possible Variable Name	Impossible Variable Name
Z54	z54!
ComputerName	$ComputerName
Computer_Name	Computer-Name
{Computer Name}	Computer Name
ComputerName?	{Computer Name{ }}

Table 4.1 – Names we can and can't use

Now that we know what sort of names we *can* use, what sort of names *should* we use?

Names we should (and shouldn't) use

One of the purposes of using variables is to assign meaning. We do this by making the names meaningful; a variable name should give some clue as to the variable's contents or purpose. While MyVariable is a perfectly legal and suitable name when we're typing one or two lines of code, when we write a script, it doesn't give us any clue as to what it contains or how we wanted it to be used; it just tells us that it's a variable and that it's *mine*.

My day job often involves debugging code written by other people. I have nightmares caused by scripts with 20 or 30 variables called a, I, x, y, ii, x3, agtd, and so on. I don't know what they mean, and I bet the original author doesn't remember, either. When naming variables, we should understand that our code will be read many more times than it is written, often by us, sometimes years after we wrote it. Let's do ourselves a favor and write meaningful variable names.

We should also use consistent names, such as ComputerName1, ComputerName2, and ComputerName3, not ComputerName1, computer_name2, and ComputerNameThree. The PowerShell best practice guidelines suggest using Pascal case widely, where each word is capitalized, as this is easy to read and works well with screen readers. Other languages, such as Python, suggest variable names should be all lowercase and the words separated with underscores: `computer_name`. Whichever we choose, being consistent will make our lives easier.

We don't use question marks, either. It's scruffy, and it can cause complications.

Finally, we should avoid trying to use the names of automatic or preference variables. Wait, what?

The three common types of PowerShell variable

So far, we've been talking about a particular type of PowerShell variable – **user-created variables**. There are two other types: **automatic variables** and **preference variables**. User-created variables only exist for as long as the session or script that generated them is running; once we close our PowerShell window, those variables are destroyed. This is called **scope**, and we'll cover it in *Chapter 8, Writing Our First Script – Turning Simple Cmdlets into Reusable Code*. Automatic and preference variables exist for every session or script.

Automatic variables

These are used internally by PowerShell. We've already used one: `$PSItem`, or `$_`, which refers to the current object in the pipeline. We can assign a value to it if we like, but PowerShell will clear it when the current running pipeline completes, as in *Figure 4.3*:

```
PS C:\Users\nickp> $PSItem = "some stuff"
PS C:\Users\nickp> $PSItem
PS C:\Users\nickp>
```

Figure 4.3 – Don't use the names of automatic variables

After setting `$PSItem` to `"some stuff"`, the pipeline completes, and the variable is cleared, losing the information we were trying to store. Happily, most automatic variables are protected, as in *Figure 4.4*:

```
PS C:\Users\nickp> $PSVersionTable

Name                           Value
----                           -----
PSVersion                      7.2.4
PSEdition                      Core
GitCommitId                    7.2.4
OS                             Microsoft Windows 10.0.19044
Platform                       Win32NT
PSCompatibleVersions           {1.0, 2.0, 3.0, 4.0…}
PSRemotingProtocolVersion      2.3
SerializationVersion           1.1.0.1
WSManStackVersion              3.0

PS C:\Users\nickp> $PSVersionTable = "some stuff"
WriteError: Cannot overwrite variable PSVersionTable because it is read-only or constant.
PS C:\Users\nickp>
```

Figure 4.4 – You can't overwrite some automatic variables

You can see a list of the automatic variables in the help topic about_Automatic_Variables, or you can see them online at https://docs.microsoft.com/en-us/powershell/module/microsoft.powershell.core/about/about_automatic_variables.

Preference variables

Preference variables store information about how PowerShell works, enabling us to customize how PowerShell behaves. For instance, we could use a preference variable to ensure the -WhatIf parameter is applied by default to all cmdlets we run (that support it). Let's see how that works in *Figure 4.5*:

```
PS /home/nickp> $WhatIfPreference
False
PS /home/nickp> $WhatIfPreference = $true
PS /home/nickp> $WhatIfPreference
True
PS /home/nickp> Get-Process

 NPM(K)    PM(M)     WS(M)    CPU(s)      Id  SI ProcessName
 ------    -----     -----    ------      --  -- -----------
      0     0.00      3.53      0.06     341 340 bash
      0     0.00      0.19      0.14       1   1 init
      0     0.00      0.22      0.00     340 340 init
      0     0.00     89.46      3.24     407 340 pwsh

PS /home/nickp> Stop-Process -id 407
What if: Performing the operation "Stop-Process" on target "pwsh (407)".
PS /home/nickp>
```

Figure 4.5 – Using preference variables

In the first line, we check the value of the WhatIfPreference variable; it's False, the default. That makes sense because we've just started the PowerShell session. In the second line, we assign the value True by setting $whatIfPreference = $true.

Then we check the value again. Sure enough, it's now True. Let's see how things work now. We run Get-Process to get the Id parameter of a suitable process; in this case, I'm going to get the ID of the pwsh process, 407. Now, when we run Stop-Process -Id 407, we would normally expect the pwsh session to end; it doesn't because, by default, now all processes run with the -WhatIf parameter set to True.

Changing preference variables this way only persists while the current session or script is running. If you stop and restart PowerShell, they're all set back to the defaults. If you need to persist a preference, you can change your PowerShell profile, a PowerShell script that can be found by querying the PROFILE variable by typing $PROFILE. You'll learn about editing scripts in *Chapter 8, Writing Our First Script – Turning Simple Cmdlets into Reusable Code*.

There's a full explanation of each of the preference variables in the help topic `About_Preference_Variables`, or you can read more about them online at `https://docs.microsoft.com/en-us/powershell/module/microsoft.powershell.core/about/about_preference_variables`.

Finally, we can see the current values held in all variables by typing `Get-Variable` with no parameters.

Now that we understand a bit about the variable – the box – we can start looking at what we can put in there. Let's have a look at object types.

Exploring object types

In the last section, we talked about types of variables. Now, we're going to talk about **object types** – the things that go in the box. The type of the object in the variable tells the computer what to do with it – what properties it has and what we can do with it. Type the following:

```
$MyVariable = "some stuff"
$MyVariable | Get-Member
```

We should see something like the output in *Figure 4.6*:

```
PS /home/nickp> $MyVariable = "some stuff"
PS /home/nickp> $MyVariable | Get-Member

   TypeName: System.String

Name            MemberType     Definition
----            ----------     ----------
Clone           Method         System.Object Clone(), System.Object ICloneable.Clon…
CompareTo       Method         int CompareTo(System.Object value), int CompareTo(st…
Contains        Method         bool Contains(string value), bool Contains(string va…
CopyTo          Method         void CopyTo(int sourceIndex, char[] destination, int…
EndsWith        Method         bool EndsWith(string value), bool EndsWith(string va…
EnumerateRunes  Method         System.Text.StringRuneEnumerator EnumerateRunes()
Equals          Method         bool Equals(System.Object obj), bool Equals(string v…
```

Figure 4.6 – It's a string

We've put a string in there, and we know this because we're told it – TypeName is `System.String`. At the moment, `MyVariable` contains a string. We can change what the type is by assigning something else to it. Try typing the following without quotation marks:

```
$MyVariable = 4.2
```

Then, use `Get-Member` to check the contents. Now we've got a `System.Double` object type in there, a floating-point number.

We can do even better things. Type the following, and check the contents of the variable with `Get-Member`:

```
$MyVariable = (Get-Process)
$MyVariable | Get-Member
```

Now we have the output of `Get-Process` held in our variable, and the contents have a type of `System.Diagnostics.Process`.

Variables can hold any type of object. Remember, everything in PowerShell is an object. We covered some of the specifics of PowerShell objects in *Chapter 3, The PowerShell Pipeline – How to String Cmdlets Together*, but it is a good idea to review them from a more generic programming perspective.

What is an object? – redux

Picture a bicycle. What color is it? What sort of handlebars does it have? What is the wheel diameter? My bike has ape hanger handlebars, 15" wheels, and is a scuffed red glitter. Your bike may be a more sensible item altogether, with riser handlebars, 20" wheels, and in a serviceable black. My son Tom's bike has pursuit handlebars, 22" wheels, and is white.

That's three objects, there, of the (non-existent) `TypeName Imaginary.Bike`. We can list the objects in *Table 4.2*. All the objects have the same set of **properties**: Name, Handlebar, Wheel (inch), and Color properties. In each instance, they have different values for the properties. Other properties may include a basket, lights, and so on. Some of those properties may be optional, but some are not; a bicycle will always have two wheels of a fixed diameter, and a color.

Name	MyBike	YourBike	TomsBike
Handlebar	Ape hanger	Riser	Pursuit
Wheel (inch)	15	20	22
Color	Red	Black	White

Table 4.2 – Our bikes

We can create those bikes in PowerShell, list out the properties of each, and we can see that they are objects of the `Imaginary.Bike` type by using `Get-Member`:

```
PS /home/nickp> $MyBike

Name    Color Wheel(inch) Handlebar
----    ----- ----------- ---------
MyBike  red            15 Ape Hanger

PS /home/nickp> $YourBike

Name     Color Wheel(inch) Handlebar
----     ----- ----------- ---------
YourBike Black          20 Riser

PS /home/nickp> $TomsBike

Name     Color Wheel(inch) Handlebar
----     ----- ----------- ---------
TomsBike white          22 Pursuit

PS /home/nickp> $TomsBike | Get-Member

   TypeName: Imaginary.Bike
```

Figure 4.7 – Three imaginary bikes

Our bikes also have a common set of things we can do with them. We can pedal them to make them speed up. We can use the brakes to make them slow down. These are **methods**, and we looked at them when we covered Get-Member in *Chapter 1, Introduction to PowerShell 7 – What It Is and How to Get It*. We would expect objects of the same type to have the same methods as each other.

This concept of an object is common to most modern programming languages, and most programming languages handle them in similar ways. The imaginary exercise we have just gone through is as relevant in Python as it is in PowerShell. Here are the same three imaginary bikes in Python:

```
>>> pprint(vars(mybike))
{'color': 'red', 'handlebar': 'Ape Hanger', 'name': 'MyBike', 'wheel_inch': 15}
>>> pprint(vars(yourbike))
{'color': 'black', 'handlebar': 'Riser', 'name': 'YourBike', 'wheel_inch': 20}
>>> pprint(vars(tomsbike))
{'color': 'white', 'handlebar': 'Pursuit', 'name': 'TomsBike', 'wheel_inch': 22}
>>> print (type(tomsbike).__name__)
ImaginaryBike
>>>
```

Figure 4.8 – Three imaginary bikes in another language

The difference in PowerShell is everything is an object. With that in mind, let's explore some common types of objects that we will want to put in variables. Let's start with value types.

Discovering value types

Value types are the building blocks of programming in PowerShell. Other languages have **primitive** types that derive from the base classes of the relevant language; PowerShell does not because (all together now) everything is an object and is derived from the System.Object class in .NET. In general, value types in PowerShell are analogous to (but not exactly the same as) primitives. The memory location that holds a value-type object holds the actual data. There are also reference types, which we'll look at later, that hold a reference to the actual data; the data is held elsewhere, possibly in multiple locations. Value-type data is a fixed size, in bits. Value types have a single value. To illustrate, let's look at some value types. We'll start with the simplest value type, the **Boolean** type.

> **Memory locations – CompSci101 alert!**
>
> Data is stored in two different places in memory, the **stack,** and the **heap**. The stack is for static allocations (things that don't change), and the heap is dynamic. The heap stores global information and is exactly like it sounds; it's just a heap of data with a tree-like structure. It's not of fixed size and allows random access. Access to the data can be quite slow, and the heap becomes fragmented over time.
>
> The stack is an orderly memory space of fixed size. It has a linear structure, where the last bit of data to be put on the stack is the first bit to be removed. Access to information is much quicker than in the heap. However, because space is limited, we occasionally get a stack overflow where we try to put more data into a stack than it can hold – the computer science equivalent of crossing the streams (Ghostbusters reference). Each thread of a running application has its own stack, but they all share the application heap.
>
> When we create a variable, it goes in the stack. The data the variable refers to may be in the stack (for a value-type variable), or it may be in the heap (for a reference-type variable), but the variable is always in the stack.

Booleans

A Boolean-type variable can hold one of two values; true or false. That's it. It's called a System. Boolean or [bool]. [bool] is an accelerator and saves us from having to type a much longer class name; it's an alias for the type System.Boolean. Booleans are easy to assign; we use the automatic variables $True and $False. Try the following:

```
$MyBoolean = $True
$MyBoolean | Get-Member
```

We can see that the type is System.Boolean. Variables with this type are useful in scripting, as we will see in *Chapter 5, PowerShell Control Flow – Conditionals and Loops*. In that chapter, we'll also see a similar but subtly different value type, the [switch] type – that can also only be true or false but has a different set of members.

Integers

Integers are whole numbers, that is, numbers without a decimal point. There are three main integer types, [int32], [int64], and [byte]. [int32] is the default type and is a signed value 32 bits long, meaning it can hold decimal values between -2,147,483,648 and +2,147,483,647. If we create a variable that holds a whole number between those values, then PowerShell will give it the type [int32]:

```
$MyNumber = 42
$MyNumber | Get-Member
```

If we try and assign a number outside that range, then PowerShell will give it the [int64] type, which is 64 bits long and can hold numbers between -9, 223, 372, 036, 854, 775, 808 and +9, 223, 372, 036, 854, 775, 807.

We will sometimes see [int] and [long] in books and on web pages instead of [int32] and [int64] – the terms are interchangeable.

[byte] is a special type of integer; it has no sign and is a whole number between 0 and 255, making it 8 bits long – 1 byte.

Activity one

Why not have a single integer type – [int64]? Why bother complicating things?

Real numbers

In mathematics, real numbers are numbers that exist – they can be whole numbers (42), decimals (3.1), fractions (1/3), or irrational numbers (pi, the square root of two). Imaginary numbers like the square root of -1 are not real numbers, although they are incredibly useful. In PowerShell, whole numbers are expressed using the integer types we've just discussed, and common irrational numbers are served by the [math] type. We mostly use real number types to express floating point numbers.

There are three common variable types for working with real numbers, [single] (or [float]), [double] (or [long]), and [decimal]. The [single] variable type is 32 bits and has seven digits of precision (the numbers to the right of the decimal point). The [double] variable type is 64 bits and has 15 or 16 digits of precision. By default, PowerShell creates variables of the type [double] when you use a decimal number:

```
$MyRealNumber = 42.0
$MyRealNumber | Get-Member
```

The [Decimal] type is 128 bits long and has a sliding scale of precision up to 28 digits. This is used in scientific and financial calculations.

Char

The [char] type describes a single character, a member of the UTF-16 character set that we're currently using. It's a 16-bit value that corresponds to a symbol in the current character map. Try the following:

```
[char]$MyChar = 24
$MyChar
```

On my machine, I see an up-arrow ↑. You may see something different. What you won't see is 24. We did something new there; we preceded the variable with a type accelerator. To understand why, we need to talk about typing.

Typing explained

Now we understand some basic types, we need to cover typing and how languages, particularly PowerShell, manipulate the type of the object in the variable. How does a computer know what type of object it is? Languages can be divided into those that only support **static typing**, where the object type the variable can hold is declared when the variable is created and doesn't change, and those that support **dynamic typing**, where the contents of the variable determine what the type is. In dynamically typed languages, the type of the variable can change. Try the following:

```
$MyVariable = 'some stuff'
$MyVariable | Get-Member
$MyVariable = 42
$MyVariable | Get-Member
```

We can see that the object type of $MyVariable changes depending on what is inside it, making PowerShell a dynamically typed language. In fact, PowerShell is described as **Type-Promiscuous** by Bruce Payette in *PowerShell in Action*, because it will try to make the thing that we put in a variable do whatever we want. So long as the object in the variable has the right sort of property, PowerShell doesn't care what type it is. Let's play around.

Dynamic versus static typing

If we type $x = '4', we get [string]. If we type $x = 4 without the quotes, we get [int32].

Now, let's see what happens if we type the following:

```
$x = '4' + 4
```

Try it, and pipe $x to Get-Member just to confirm the type. PowerShell has tried its best to interpret what you want. It's chosen to treat the second 4 as a string and added the two strings together, giving 44. Amazing, right? Try it the other way around:

```
$x = 4 + '4'
```

Now it's treating the second `'4'` as an integer and returns 8. This does not work in most languages:

```
Python 3.10.4 (tags/v3.10.4:9d38120, Mar 23 2022, 23:13:41) [MSC v.1929 64 bit
Type "help", "copyright", "credits" or "license" for more information.
>>> x = '4' + '4'
>>> x
'44'
>>> x = 4 + 4
>>> x
8
>>> x = '4' + 4
Traceback (most recent call last):
  File "<stdin>", line 1, in <module>
TypeError: can only concatenate str (not "int") to str
>>> x = 4 + '4'
Traceback (most recent call last):
  File "<stdin>", line 1, in <module>
TypeError: unsupported operand type(s) for +: 'int' and 'str'
>>>
```

Figure 4.9 – Python is not promiscuous

In Python, we can add strings together, called **concatenating**, and we can add integers together (called **adding**), and Python will happily dynamically type the variable contents as either a string or an integer. We cannot, however, mix strings and integers together; Python throws an error.

This is mostly a blessing, but sometimes it's a mixed blessing. Because PowerShell works so hard trying to do what we want, it will sometimes do things we don't want. It may be that we always want the contents to be a string, but some data entry error or an ill-defined operation puts an integer in there. This affects what we can do with that variable afterward because it has changed the object type to an integer. In a less-accommodating language, we get an error that tells us exactly what has gone wrong, but PowerShell may give us unexpected results, which take an age to debug if we're lucky or cause a disaster if we're not.

Casting variables

Luckily, we can make PowerShell act more like a statically typed language by defining the contents of the variable when we create it by using an accelerator, `[int32]`:

```
[int32]$MyNewVariable = '42'
$MyNewVariable | Get-Member
```

And it's an `[int32]` type, even though we gave it a string. Note this won't work if we give it something that is less easy to interpret as an integer:

```
[int32]$MyNewVariable = 'Forty Two'
```

This throws an error. Importantly, it will throw an error even if we just type the following:

```
$MyNewVariable = 'Forty Two'
```

Because when we created `MyNewVariable` a few lines previously, we defined it as the `[Int32]` type, and so now that is all it can ever hold. This can also lead to some confusing results.

We might expect this cmdlet to throw an error as we try to put a floating-point number into `MyNewVariable`:

```
$MyNewVariable = 4.2
```

But no. PowerShell just picks the closest integer and uses that instead:

```
PS C:\Users\nickp> $MyNewVariable = 4.2
PS C:\Users\nickp> $MyNewVariable
4
PS C:\Users\nickp> $MyNewVariable | Get-Member

    TypeName: System.Int32
```

Figure 4.10 – PowerShell doing as it's told

We can cast the variable, though, to a new type, like this:

```
[single] $MyNewVariable = 4.2
```

And we now have the correct value in there. Casting is an incredibly useful technique that we'll be using a lot later, especially in *Chapter 7, PowerShell and the Web – HTTP, REST, and JSON*. It allows us to take a collection of strings and turn them into XML and JSON objects that can be used to interact with web-based applications.

There are a couple of common ways of using casting to change the type of a variable's contents. Firstly, we can create a new variable by copying the contents as a defined type. Let's create a variable we know contains an integer:

```
[int32] $MyVariable = 42
```

We can cast that to a new variable as a string:

```
$MyString = [string] $MyVariable
$MyString | Get-Member
```

We can do it the other way around, as well:

```
[string] $MyOtherString = $MyVariable
```

> **Activity two**
>
> What is the difference between $myString and $MyOtherString?
>
> Hint: what types of objects can we subsequently put in each variable?

Secondly, we can do it without creating a new variable; we can just use [string] $MyVariable in our code, and PowerShell will treat the contents as an object of the correct type if it can.

That's as much as we need to do on simple value types, and how PowerShell uses dynamic and static typing. It's time to look at the more complex compound variable types – reference types.

Navigating reference types

Now we understand a bit about typing, and how value types work, we can talk about the other main type of object – **reference types**. We compared value type objects to primitives in other languages in the previous section, *Discovering value types*. Reference-type objects are the equivalent of data structures. Reference-type objects only hold a reference in the stack to more data in the heap; this is important because reference-type objects do not have a defined size. In general, a reference type may hold up to 2 GB of data. To prove it, I turned the Shakespeare play Hamlet into a string, by downloading it as a text file from Project Gutenberg:

```
PS C:\Users\nickp> [string]$shakespeare = (Get-Content C:\Users\nickp\Downloads\hamlet.txt)
PS C:\Users\nickp> $shakespeare.GetType()

IsPublic IsSerial Name                                     BaseType
-------- -------- ----                                     --------
True     True     String                                   System.Object

PS C:\Users\nickp> $shakespeare.Length
196788
```

Figure 4.11 – Stringifying Hamlet

As we can see, there are around 197,000 characters in the whole string.

I did two interesting things there; I used the length property of the string type to see how long my string was, in characters, but I also used the GetType() method to check the object type rather than using the pipeline to pass it to Get-Member. Before we talk more about properties and methods and the other exciting things we can do with strings, I want to start with a simple reference-type object, the array.

Arrays

An array is a data structure of fixed length that contains a collection of objects. They don't have to be the same type of object, and they are not necessarily sorted or ordered. An array can contain zero or more objects. We can tell PowerShell we want to create an array by either casting the variable as an array implicitly using the comma character , or explicitly with [array]. Try the following:

```
$MyArray = 1,2,3
$MyArray.GetType()
```

Did you try it? You do need to. As we go through this section, I'll be calling back to the arrays we create here. It would be awful if you got to the end of the section and had to come back and start again because you didn't create the array the first time around.

To create a single-item array, you can do the following:

```
$number = ,1
[Array]$MyTinyArray = 1
```

The output can be seen in the following screenshot:

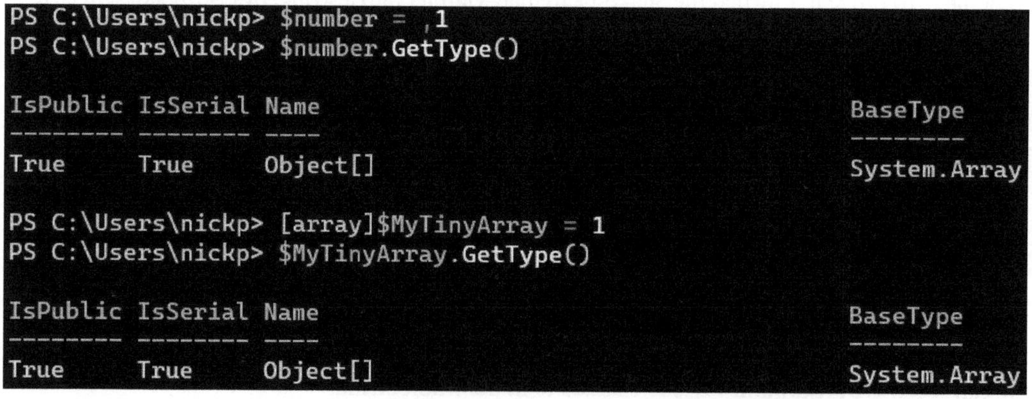

Figure 4.12 – Two single-element arrays

We can see that we create Object[] of BaseType as System.Array each time.

We can also create arrays using the range operator (..). Try the following:

```
$NewArray = 1..10
```

We should get an array containing all the numbers from 1 to 10, inclusive.

Finally, we can use the array operator @():

```
$AnotherArray = @(1..5; "some stuff")
```

Note we have to use a semicolon, not a comma, when separating different types of objects and using expressions. This is useful when we start scripting and using the splatting technique, which we'll cover in the last section of this chapter.

Array basics

Each object in the array is called an element. We can list the elements by calling the whole array ($NewArray), like any other variable:

```
PS C:\Users\nickp> $NewArray = 1..10
PS C:\Users\nickp> $NewArray
1
2
3
4
5
6
7
8
9
10
PS C:\Users\nickp>
```

Figure 4.13 – Listing the elements of an array

We can choose to call a single element in an array by passing its index. This gets the first element:

```
$NewArray[0]
```

This will get the second-to-last element:

```
$NewArray[-2]
```

We can call multiple elements:

```
$NewArray[0,2,5,7]
```

And we can call a range of elements:

```
$NewArray[6..9]
```

We can change the values of elements of an array by assigning them directly:

```
$NewArray[5] = 5
```

We can add elements to an array by using the += operator:

```
$NewArray += 11
```

But it's tricky to delete an element from an array; instead, create a new array that only holds the elements you want.

By default, an array can hold objects of multiple types:

```
$ScruffyArray = 1, 'socks', (Get-Process)
```

We can constrain the type of the objects in an array so that it can only hold objects of one type:

```
[Int32[]]$IntArray = 1..5
```

Now try the following:

```
$IntArray += 'socks'
```

Oops. We get an error:

```
PS C:\Users\nickp> [Int32[]]$IntArray = 1..5
PS C:\Users\nickp> $IntArray += 'socks'
MetadataError: Cannot convert value "socks" to type "System.Int32". Error: "Input
 string was not in a correct format."
PS C:\Users\nickp> $IntArray.GetType()

IsPublic IsSerial Name                                            BaseType
-------- -------- ----                                            --------
True     True     Int32[]                                         System.Array

PS C:\Users\nickp> $IntArray[2].GetType()

IsPublic IsSerial Name                                            BaseType
-------- -------- ----                                            --------
True     True     Int32                                           System.ValueType
```

Figure 4.14 – You can't leave that in there

If we have a look, we can see that the type of the IntArray object is [int32[]] with a base type of System.Array, and the type of the elements is [Int32]. We saw this syntax in *Chapter 2, Exploring PowerShell Cmdlets and Syntax*, when we were looking at the Get-Help cmdlet. An empty pair of square brackets denotes a parameter that can take multiple values; in other words, an array:

```
SYNTAX
    Get-Command [[-Name] <System.String[]>] [[-ArgumentList] <System.Object[]>]
    [-All] [-CommandType {Alias | Function | Filter | Cmdlet | ExternalScript |
    Application | Script | Workflow | Configuration | All}]
    [-FullyQualifiedModule
    <Microsoft.PowerShell.Commands.ModuleSpecification[]>] [-ListImported]
```

Figure 4.15 – System.String accepts an array

Finally, we can add arrays together:

```
$BigArray  = $NewArray + $IntArray
```

That's the basics covered. Let's look at the properties and methods we can use with arrays.

Properties and methods of arrays

It is difficult to use `Get-Member` to see the properties and methods available on an array. PowerShell does not pass the array into the pipeline; it passes each element in the array in order. Try it by typing the following:

```
$NewArray | Get-Member
```

All we get back are the properties and methods for the `[Int32]` type.

To see the properties and methods of the array type, you'll need to either go to the help topic about_ Arrays or look online here: https://docs.microsoft.com/en-us/powershell/ module/microsoft.powershell.core/about/about_arrays.

Let's have a brief look at some of the more important ones.

Count, Length, and Rank

These are common properties of arrays. `Count` is an alias for `Length`. They both tell us how many elements are in the array. $NewArray.Count and $NewArray.Length are the same. This is back to the muscle memory thing of old admins, again. You'll see both in the PowerShell literature.

`Rank` is interesting if you're working with datasets. All the arrays we have been working with are **one-dimensional** and have a rank of 1. The objects in the array exist on an imaginary line – even $ScruffyArray, which contains the output of Get-Process. Most arrays you are likely to work with in PowerShell are one-dimensional. In data science, however, we quite often need to use multidimensional arrays; they're complicated, and I haven't seen a good PowerShell module for manipulating them. If you are really interested, have a look at the about_Arrays help topic. Just know it's possible if you need to do a little bit with multidimensional arrays.

Clear, ForEach, and Where

These are common methods of arrays. Where the element of an array supports the `Clear` method, you can use it on the array to clear all the elements. If the element doesn't support it, though, you'll get an error.

```
PS C:\Users\nickp> $a = @(0..3)
PS C:\Users\nickp> $a.ForEach({$_ * $_})
0
1
4
9
PS C:\Users\nickp> $a.Clear()
PS C:\Users\nickp> $a
PS C:\Users\nickp>
```

Figure 4.16 – Some methods are more useful than others

The ForEach method allows us to iterate through each element in an array and perform an operation on it. Type the following in to get the squares of the numbers in the array:

```
@(0..3).ForEach({$_ * $_})
```

Personally, I find this type of code golf willfully complicated and it goes against PowerShell's best practices. It's fine if we're doing a couple of lines, but I wouldn't put it in a script. We'll cover how to do this in a more readable way in *Chapter 5, PowerShell Control Flow – Conditionals and Loops*.

The Where method is similar, although more useful in one-liners. To get the elements of $NewArray greater than 5, we could type the following:

```
$NewArray.where({$_ -gt 5})
```

It's functionally the same as this:

```
$NewArray | Where-Object {$_ -gt 5}
```

And arguably less readable. We covered Where-Object in *Chapter 3, The PowerShell Pipeline – How to String Cmdlets Together*. Remember, PowerShell will output each member of an array into the pipeline in turn. So, why have these as methods at all? If we are working with very large arrays, then using the method on the array rather than using the pipeline is faster. The following cmdlet takes about 300 ms to complete on my laptop:

```
Measure-Command {@(0..100000).ForEach({$_ * $_})}
```

The following cmdlet takes about 400 ms:

```
Measure-Command {@(0..100000) | ForEach-Object{$_ * $_}}
```

So, it depends on where we want to save time. If the fastest possible code is our aim, then use the method on the array. If we want our code to be quickly understood when we return to it, then use the pipeline.

Array performance

One place where it is worth saving time, however, is in our manipulation of arrays. While it looks like we can change arrays by adding elements, this is not actually the case. Arrays are a fixed size. Every time we add an element, we create a new array. Let's say we see something like this:

```
$SlowArray = @()
1..10000 | Foreach-Object { $Slowarray += $_ }
```

We're actually creating and discarding 10,000 arrays. A lot of the documentation will tell us that the alternative is to use a .NET type instead of arrays – [System.Collections.ArrayList], like this:

```
$ArrayList = [System.Collections.ArrayList]@()
1..10000 | ForEach-Object { $Null = $ArrayList.Add($_) }
```

Here we have the same sort of programming style, where we create the array variable and then add to it, but we have to call a non-PowerShell type and then use the Add() method. It works, but it's quite complicated, especially when we're just starting out.

Another alternative is to be clever about how we create our array and construct it like this:

```
$AutoArray = (1..10000 | ForEach-Object {$_})
```

This produces the same array as the other two with the speed of the ArrayList object type, but with the simplicity of using all PowerShell code. I ran these three cmdlets inside Measure-Command, so you can see the difference:

```
PS C:\Users\nickp> $SlowArray = @()
PS C:\Users\nickp> (Measure-Command{1..10000 | ForEach-Object {$SlowArray += $_}}).Tot
alSeconds
2.3771013
PS C:\Users\nickp> $ArrayList = [System.Collections.ArrayList]@()
PS C:\Users\nickp> (Measure-Command{1..10000 | ForEach-Object {$Null=$ArrayList.Add($_
)}}).TotalSeconds
0.0564523
PS C:\Users\nickp> (Measure-Command{$AutoArray = (1..10000 | ForEach-Object {$_})}).To
talSeconds
0.0481883
```

Figure 4.17 – Three ways of creating the same array

I first came across this observation on Tobias Weltner's excellent blog, https://PowerShell. one. I thoroughly recommend reading his articles.

Copying arrays

Now we have a pretty good idea of what an array is, we can look at one of the key differences between value types and reference types: how copying variables works. Try this:

```
$a = 42
$b = $a
$a = 'socks'
```

Without typing any more – what is in $b? If you said 42, you would be right. Of course it is. The value of $a is held in the stack, so when we create $b, we copy the value 42 to the top of the stack and call it $b (if you got an error saying 'socks' isn't of type [Int32], close your PowerShell session and start a new one).

Copying arrays doesn't work like that. Try the following:

```
$Array1 = 1,2,3
$Array2 = $Array1
$Array1[2] = 5
$Array2
```

Argh! What happened there? Array2 contains the updated value! That's because all we did when we copied Array1 to Array2 was copy the reference to the data in the heap, the process storage area. When we then changed the element, we didn't create a new array; we just changed the data in the old location. The references remain the same, so all copies of Array1 will also reference the new data.

How do we get around this? Easy. At least, easyish. Have a go by doing the following:

```
$Array1 = 1,2,3
$Array2 = $Array1 | ForEach-Object {$_}
```

And, voilà, we can now make changes to Array1 without it affecting Array2:

```
$Array1[2] = 5
$Array2
```

We made PowerShell put each element in Array1 into the pipeline and pipe it into Array2, creating a separate array of data. It's a bit slow and clunky, but it works, and it's simple.

That's enough about arrays for now. We'll be doing lots more with them throughout the book. Let's look at the second reference type we're going to cover: strings.

Strings

A string is a sequenced collection of [char] type objects – it's text. As we saw at the start of this section on reference types, strings are a reference type, and they are immutable – read-only. If you want to change a string, you need to create a new string and destroy the old one.

Strings have two properties, Chars and Length. Chars returns the [char] object at the given index:

```
$String = "PowerShell"
$String.Chars(0)
```

Chars is a parameterized property – we must give it a value, known as an **overload**. It takes a single [int32]; anything else will throw an error. We can pass it a variable that contains a single [int32], however. The Length property returns the length of the string object in characters:

```
$String.Length
```

See the following screenshot for how this all looks:

```
PS C:\Users\nickp> $String = "PowerShell"
PS C:\Users\nickp> $string.Chars(0)
P
PS C:\Users\nickp> $char = 2
PS C:\Users\nickp> $string.Chars($char)
W
PS C:\Users\nickp> $string.Length
10
```

Figure 4.18 – Properties of strings

Strings have a lot of methods. Where most of the methods on value types involve changing the object type, there are a lot of methods on strings to change the formatting. Have a look at this:

```
$String | Get-Member -MemberType Method | Measure-Object
```

And we'll see there are 52 methods available on strings. We'll not cover them all here, but let's try a few of the common ones. Remember, each time we use these methods, we're manipulating the output of the string, not the contents of the string.

To get the string all in uppercase:

```
$String.ToUpper()
```

To get it all in lowercase:

```
$String.ToLower()
```

To output the string as an array of single characters:

```
$String.ToCharArray()
```

To replace a character in a string:

```
$String.Replace('o','X')
```

After all that, type and see that the actual content of the variable is unchanged:

```
$String
```

`Replace()`, along with `Join()` and `Split()`, are also available as PowerShell string operators:

```
$List = 'one,two,three,four'
$List.Split(',')
```

This can also be written as the following:

```
$List -Split ','
```

This is shown in the following screenshot:

```
PS C:\Users\nickp> $List = 'one,two,three,four'
PS C:\Users\nickp> $List.split(',')
one
two
three
four
PS C:\Users\nickp> $List -Split ','
one
two
three
four
```

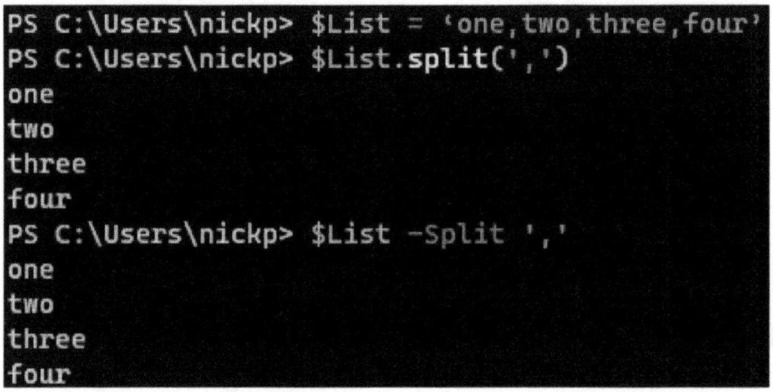

Figure 4.19 – Two ways to split

Quite often we find we have a date, but it's in text format and ends up as a string. The `ToDateTime` method allows us to capture that string as a `[DateTime]` type, but we need to supply the culture we want as part of the method. We can do it like this:

```
$Culture = Get-Culture
[String]$DateString = '1/5/2024'
$ImportantDate = $DateString.ToDateTime($Culture)
```

We can see in the following screenshot that `$ImportantDate` is a `[DateTime]` object:

```
PS C:\Users\nickp> $Culture = Get-Culture
PS C:\Users\nickp> [string]$DateString = '1/5/2024'
PS C:\Users\nickp> $ImportantDate = $DateString.ToDateTime($Culture)
PS C:\Users\nickp> $ImportantDate

01 May 2024 00:00:00

PS C:\Users\nickp> $DateString.GetType()

IsPublic IsSerial Name                                          BaseType
-------- -------- ----                                          --------
True     True     String                                        System.Object

PS C:\Users\nickp> $ImportantDate.GetType()

IsPublic IsSerial Name                                          BaseType
-------- -------- ----                                          --------
True     True     DateTime                                      System.ValueType
```

Figure 4.20 – Converting a string to a DateTime object

Even easier, though, if we have the chance, is to use the [DateTime] value type accelerator and cast the variable as the right type of object:

```
[DateTime]$Anniversary = '1/5/2024'
```

Single and double quote marks

In PowerShell, single and double quote marks behave differently. They can both be used to define a string, but they have different purposes. Try this:

```
$MyName = 'Nick'
Write-Output 'My Name is $MyName'
Write-Output "My Name is $MyName"
```

We can see in the following screenshot that the output is very different:

```
PS C:\Users\nickp> $MyName = 'Nick'
PS C:\Users\nickp> Write-Output 'My Name is $MyName'
My Name is $MyName
PS C:\Users\nickp> Write-Output "My Name is $MyName"
My Name is Nick
```

Figure 4.21 – Single and double quotes

Double quotes tell PowerShell to expand the variables it finds before processing. The shell alerts us to what it is going to do by coloring the variable green when we use double quotes.

To print the contents of a variable when it's going to be immediately followed by another character, enclose the variable name in curly braces:

```
"${MyName}: Engineer"
```

To print the variable, and not the contents of the variable, use the backtick character `` ` ``:

```
Write-Output "The value of `$MyName is $MyName"
```

We'll be doing plenty with strings as we go through the book, but now we should look at another important reference type, the hashtable.

Hashtables

A hashtable is a PowerShell implementation of a type of data structure called a dictionary. They consist of a list of **key-value** pairs. We use hashtables to look up values for a given key or check which key holds a given value; they are basically lookup tables. Let's create a hashtable and play around with it:

```
$Hash = @{}
```

We're using @{} to create a hashtable there. We shouldn't confuse it with @(), which will create an array. Now we've got our hashtable, we should put something in it. We can do this when we create the hashtable, like this:

```
$MyBike = @{HandleBar = "ApeHanger"; Color = "Red"; Wheel = 15}
```

Note that we use a semicolon to separate the pairs, not a comma as we do in arrays:

```
PS C:\Users\nickp> $Hash = @{}
PS C:\Users\nickp> $Hash.GetType()

IsPublic IsSerial Name                                     BaseType
-------- -------- ----                                     --------
True     True     Hashtable                                System.Object

PS C:\Users\nickp> $MyBike = @{HandleBar = "ApeHanger"; Color = "Red"; Wheel = 15}
PS C:\Users\nickp> $MyBike.Add("Bell", $True)
```

Figure 4.22 – Creating and populating hashtables

We can add key-value pairs to the hashtable using the add method as follows:

```
$MyBike.Add('Bell', $True)
```

The add method requires two parameters separated by a comma; the first is the key and must be in quotes, and the second is the value. If this is a string, it must also be in quotes:

```
$MyBike.Add('Condition','Poor')
```

Note that, unlike an array, PowerShell treats a hashtable as a single object:

```
$MyBike | Measure-Object
```

Compare this with the following:

```
$NewList = @(1,2,3,4)
$NewList | Measure-Object
```

However, we can use the Count property to return the number of key-value pairs:

```
$MyBike.Count
```

Now that we have our hashtable, what can we do with it? The obvious use is to look up values:

```
$MyBike.condition
```

And it returns the value poor. We can also use the key like we would use an index in an array:

```
$MyBike['Wheel']
```

We can use this method to add key-value pairs as well:

```
$MyBike['Gears'] = 'Fixed'
```

The big advantage of using the square brackets is it allows us to pass an array of keys and get the values back:

```
$MyBike['HandleBar', 'Condition', 'Gears']
```

Or, we can use a variable to hold the array:

```
$BikeDetails = 'HandleBar', 'Condition', 'Gears'
$MyBike[$BikeDetails]
```

We can list out all the key-value pairs in the hashtable one at a time with the GetEnumerator() method:

```
$MyBike.GetEnumerator()
```

Hold on. Can't we do that just by typing $MyBike? No. If we try to do that, we get the whole hashtable as a single object. It will look like key-value pairs, but it won't behave like a set of separate ones. Try the following:

```
$MyBike | ForEach-Object {[Array]$BikeProperties += $_}
$BikeProperties.Count
$MyBike.GetEnumerator() | ForEach-Object {[Array]$NewBikeProperties +=
$_}
$NewBikeProperties.Count
```

We can see there that only one object passed through the pipeline in the first line.

We can remove key-value pairs as well with the `remove` method:

```
$MyBike.Remove('Gears')
```

We can test for the presence of a key:

```
$MyBike.ContainsKey('HandleBar')
```

And we can test for the presence of a value:

```
$MyBike.ContainsValue('poor')
```

Ordered hashtables

By default, hashtables are not ordered, and this doesn't really matter because we're only ever looking for the values they contain in the key-value pairs. Sometimes, however, we want our hashtable to be arranged in a particular way. We can use the `[ordered]` keyword to do this. Note this doesn't go before the variable; it goes on the right-hand side:

```
$OrderedHash = [ordered]@{a=10;b=20;c=30}
```

And you can see the difference in the following screenshot:

```
PS C:\Users\nickp> $ScruffyHash = @{a=10;b=20;c=30}
PS C:\Users\nickp> $ScruffyHash.GetEnumerator()

Name                           Value
----                           -----
c                              30
a                              10
b                              20

PS C:\Users\nickp> $OrderedHash = [ordered]@{a=10;b=20;c=30}
PS C:\Users\nickp> $OrderedHash

Name                           Value
----                           -----
a                              10
b                              20
c                              30

PS C:\Users\nickp> $OrderedHash.GetType()

IsPublic IsSerial Name                                     BaseType
-------- -------- ----                                     --------
True     True     OrderedDictionary                        System.Object
```

Figure 4.23 – Ordered hashtable

Notice that it's now a different type – OrderedDictionary. We can still get values by passing the key, but because it is ordered, we can also now just pass the index of the key pair:

```
$OrderedHash.c
$OrderedHash[1]
```

Finally, you may have noticed that we're back to bikes again. That's because there's another cool thing we can do with hashtables – we can turn them into objects:

```
$MyImaginaryBike = [PSCustomObject] $MyBike
```

As you can see from the following screenshot, we now have a PSCustomObject called $MyImaginaryBike with a set of properties matching the original hashtable key-value pairs:

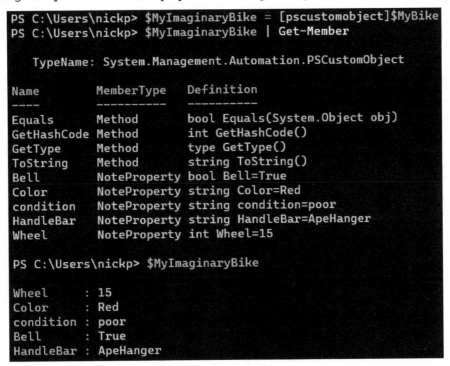

Figure 4.24 – Turning a hashtable into an object

Cool, eh? We'll be using hashtables a lot in the rest of the book because they're such a useful type.

There are other reference types as well that cover other types of data structures, such as queues and stacks, but we don't tend to use them as much, certainly not in everyday PowerShell. Before we finish this chapter, we'll cover one final use for hashtables: splatting.

Splatting – a cool use for hashtables

Some PowerShell cmdlets take a lot of parameters, and it can be confusing to feed them all into the cmdlet one at a time, all on the same line. Hashtables to the rescue. Try the following:

```
$Colors = @{
ForegroundColor = 'red'
BackgroundColor = 'white'
}
Write-Host 'all the pretty colors' @Colors
```

Notice that we don't use $Colors; we use @Colors. Also, notice it doesn't matter which way round we use it:

```
Write-Host @Colors 'OK, just red and white, then'
```

This will work as well, because we've explicitly named the parameters in the hashtable:

```
PS /home/nickp> $Colors = @{
>> ForegroundColor = 'red'
>> BackgroundColor = 'white'
>> }
PS /home/nickp> Write-Host 'all the pretty colors' @Colors
all the pretty colors
PS /home/nickp> Write-Host @Colors 'OK, just red and white, then'
OK, just red and white, then
PS /home/nickp>
```

Figure 4.25 – A basic example of splatting

We could use an array, but that will only work for positional parameters; the first value in the array will be the first positional parameter, the second value will be the second, and so on. Because most cmdlets don't have more than one or two positional parameters, this is nothing like as useful as a hashtable.

We'll be using splatting a lot as we go on, but for this chapter, that's it. Time to summarize what we've covered.

Summary

This has been a long chapter, but we've learned a lot. We started by looking at variables and how they are used in PowerShell. After that, we took another look at objects from a computer science perspective and learned about their properties and methods. This gave us a grounding to start exploring object types, and we looked at some of the value types, which are equivalent to the computer science concept of primitives. From there, we saw how value types can be grouped together into data structures or reference types. Finally, for a bit of fun, we looked at how splatting can save us time and effort.

In the next chapter, we are going to be looking at flow control in PowerShell, conditional statements such as `if` and `else`, and loops using `ForEach` and `While`. We'll also be installing more software because that's the fun stuff, right?

Exercises

1. What's wrong with the variable `My Variable`?

2. Without trying the code, what `TypeName` will this cmdlet return?

    ```
    New-Variable -Name MyVariable -Value "somestuff"
    Get-Variable MyVariable | Get-Member
    ```

3. How can we change the view of the errors PowerShell shows us?

4. What automatic variable can we use to clear the contents of an array or hashtable?

5. How might we compare two integers?

6. What is the object type of `MyVariable` here?

    ```
    $MyVariable = ,1
    ```

7. How would we get each character in a string into an array?

8. What's going to go wrong here, and why?

    ```
    Write-Output 'My Name is $MyName'
    ```

9. How can we create an object of type `OrderedDictionary`?

Further reading

There is a lot of reading for this chapter because we've only really brushed the surface of the subject. We really should read the help topics associated with what we've been doing in this chapter, and some of the official PowerShell language documentation:

- about_Variables: https://docs.microsoft.com/en-us/powershell/module/microsoft.powershell.core/about/about_variables

- about_Automatic_Variables: https://docs.microsoft.com/en-us/powershell/module/microsoft.powershell.core/about/about_automatic_variables

- about_Preference_Variables: https://docs.microsoft.com/en-us/powershell/module/microsoft.powershell.core/about/about_preference_variables

- about_Objects: https://docs.microsoft.com/en-us/powershell/module/microsoft.powershell.core/about/about_objects

- PowerShell types: https://docs.microsoft.com/en-us/powershell/scripting/lang-spec/chapter-04

- PowerShell Variables: https://docs.microsoft.com/en-us/powershell/scripting/lang-spec/chapter-05

- about_Booleans: https://docs.microsoft.com/en-us/powershell/module/microsoft.powershell.core/about/about_booleans

- about_Arrays: https://docs.microsoft.com/en-us/powershell/module/microsoft.powershell.core/about/about_arrays

- PowerShell Arrays: https://docs.microsoft.com/en-us/powershell/scripting/lang-spec/chapter-09

- about_HashTables: https://docs.microsoft.com/en-us/powershell/module/microsoft.powershell.core/about/about_hash_tables

- PowerShell hashtables: https://docs.microsoft.com/en-us/powershell/scripting/lang-spec/chapter-10

- about_Splatting: https://docs.microsoft.com/en-us/powershell/module/microsoft.powershell.core/about/about_splatting

PowerShell Control Flow – Conditionals and Loops

So far, everything we have done has been one thing after another, to paraphrase Arnold Toynbee. That's fine, but it doesn't reflect how we want things to happen in the real world. Most of the time, we want our code to do different things depending on the circumstances, and sometimes we want it to do something a number of times. This is where control flow is necessary. In this chapter, we are going to look at how to make PowerShell do different things in a script, depending on what it finds – these are called **conditionals**. Then we are going to look at how to make PowerShell repeat a process, both for a predetermined number of times and for an indefinite number. Because an indefinite number may be effectively infinite, we are going to look at how to break out of and continue looping behavior.

Doing this effectively requires writing multiple lines of code, so first, we are going to talk about **Integrated Development Environments** (**IDEs**) and then install the one that is recommended for PowerShell 7, Visual Studio Code.

In this chapter, we are going to cover the following main topics:

- An introduction to IDEs and VS Code

- Conditional control – `if`, `else`, `elseif`, and `switch`

- Loops – `foreach`, `do while`, `do until`, `while`, and `for`

- Breaking and continuing

- Let's play a game

An introduction to IDEs and VS Code

The console is great for running a line or two of code or for quickly checking whether an idea will work, but it cannot save our code, and we can't edit it. We need an editor. The simplest editor is whichever text editor we have installed on our machine, for instance, Notepad on Windows or Vi on Linux. These will do the bare minimum in that we can write our code, save it, and come back and edit it. They won't do any more than that, though, and there are much better options available.

An IDE will highlight commands and keywords and do some syntax checking, and the good ones will also come with a built-in console to allow us to test our code by running short sections of it, sometimes just a line or the whole thing at once. They also usually have some sort of debugging facility, allowing us to stop our code at certain points and check the contents of variables. Most languages come with some form of IDE, for instance, Python has **IDLE**, the **Integrated Development and Learning Environment**, but I don't know many people who use it for their work, and Windows PowerShell has the **Integrated Scripting Environment**, or **ISE**, which is excellent, but has not been made available for PowerShell 7. Instead, the recommended IDE for PowerShell 7 is **Visual Studio Code** (**VS Code**), an open source JavaScript-based environment from Microsoft.

VS Code is highly extensible (translation – lots of people have written add-ons for it) and can be used with a wide range of languages. All we need to do is download our choice of language modules. There are also add-ons that check syntax, allow us to use code snippets, connect us to code repositories, such as Git, integrate testing, and generally do anything we could do with a far more expensive IDE, such as Eclipse. Rather than talk about it, let's get it installed.

Installing VS Code

VS Code can be installed on Windows, Linux, macOS, and Raspberry Pi – that's right, there's a Raspbian install. It's pretty simple. Go to the VS Code download page at `https://code.visualstudio.com/download`, and click on the relevant package for the machine and operating system we are working on; so for a Raspberry Pi, we would select the `.deb` ARM download. Once it's downloaded, change to the folder or directory where we've saved the package.

Linux

VS Code is a graphical tool, so we need to use a desktop environment with Linux. For Ubuntu and other Debian-based versions, we just need to run the following commands:

```
sudo apt update
sudo apt install ./<filename>.deb
```

For Raspbian, it's easier still:

```
sudo apt update
sudo apt install code
```

These commands will do it.

Things are a little more complicated for Red Hat distros. The easiest way is probably with snapd, in which case the following will work:

```
sudo snap install code -classic
```

There are more detailed instructions on installing VS Code for Linux at `https://code.visualstudio.com/docs/setup/linux`.

macOS

To install VS Code on macOS, download the relevant Mac installer `.zip` file and extract the contents. Drag the `Visual Studio Code.app` to the `Applications` folder, which will make VS Code available in **Launchpad**.

Windows

In Windows, we have a choice of user or system installations. If we follow the user install option, the application gets installed by default in `C:\Users\<username>\AppData\Local\Programs\Microsoft VS Code` and is only available for the user who installed it. If we use the system installer, then it gets installed in `C:\Program Files\Microsoft VS Code` and requires administrator privileges to install. Automatic updates are easier if we install the user installation package, so let's go ahead and download that one:

1.   Once it's downloaded, browse to the `Download` location and double-click the `.exe` file.

2.   Accept the **End-User License Agreement (EULA)** and click **Next**.

3.   Change the installation location if you want, and click **Next**.

4.   Decide whether you want a *Start* menu folder, and click **Next**.

5. On the **Select Additional Tasks** dialog, decide whether you want a desktop icon and file and directory context menu options, enabling you to open files and folders directly in VS Code. I'd recommend you accept the defaults of adding VS Code to your PATH environment variable and registering code as an editor for supported file types. Click **Next**:

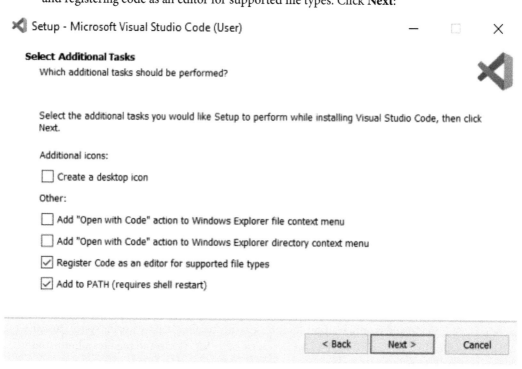

Figure 5.1 – Select Additional Tasks for the VS Code installation

6. Review the installation options and click **Install**.

7. Click **Finish** and admire your new VS Code installation.

A really quick way for Windows

If we've got the PowerShellGet module installed, then we can run the following:

```
Install-Script Install-VSCode -Scope CurrentUser ; Install-VSCode.PS1
```

Press Y to agree Yes, and that's it. This method is great for when we know what we're doing with VS Code, but if this is our first time with it, let's do things manually so we can see exactly what's going on.

Configuring VS Code for PowerShell

Now we've got VS Code installed, we need to tell it to recognize the PowerShell language. On installation VS Code has no idea about PowerShell. We need to install an extension. Open VS Code, if it isn't already open, by typing Code in the search bar and selecting the application in the results. In the main window, click on the *Extensions* icon on the far-left edge of the window – it looks like a pile of boxes:

Figure 5.2 – Finding the PowerShell extension for VS Code

Type powershell in the extensions search bar. We want the PowerShell extension by Microsoft; it's the first result, as shown in the following screenshot. Click on it, and then click the blue **Install** button in the main pane:

Figure 5.3 – Installing the PowerShell extension for VS Code

Let's get started. Press *Ctrl + N* to open a new file. We'll be asked to select a language. We don't have to do this, but doing so means we have assistance ready from the start; we can type without specifying a language, but the syntax checking and highlighting won't be available until we save our file as a PowerShell script by using the .ps1 file extension. Go ahead and click to select **PowerShell** from the dropdown. We can change the language at any time by clicking on the language name in the bottom-right corner; if we haven't selected a language then it says **Plain Text**.

The first thing we should see after selecting PowerShell is that the PowerShell integrated terminal has started at the bottom of the screen. We can run PowerShell cmdlets in there, and when we run our code from the top window, the results will appear in the terminal. Try this – in the top window, type write-outp.

You should see VS Code give you a helpful autocomplete option like this:

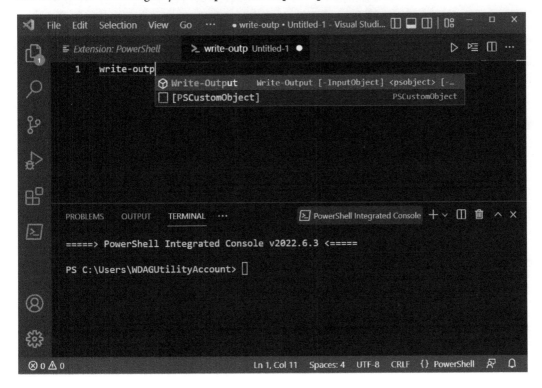

Figure 5.4 – Autocomplete in VS Code

Not only does it autocomplete for you, but it also gives hints about how the cmdlet is used; if you hover over the suggestion, you will see a > to the right of it. Click on that to read more about the cmdlet. Complete the cmdlet with some suitable text string, and press *Ctrl + S* to save it – give it a suitable filename ending in .ps1; I've used HelloWorld.ps1. Now click the play icon (arrow) at the top right of the window to run the code. It should look something like this:

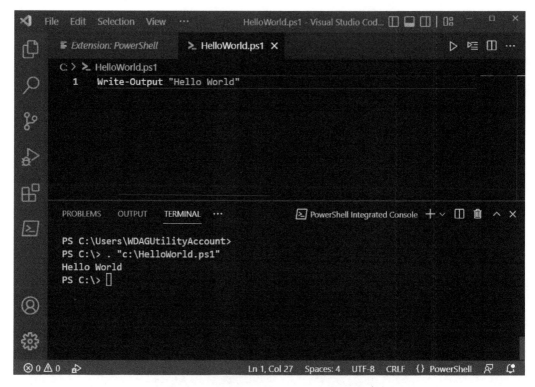

Figure 5.5 – Running PowerShell in VS Code

If you get an output that looks like the preceding screenshot, congratulations. You've run your first script!

Top tip for switching terminal environments

If you're running on Windows, you've probably got at least two different versions of PowerShell installed – PowerShell 7 and Windows PowerShell. How do you swap between them? Click on the curly braces ({}) next to the word **PowerShell** in the bottom right of the screen. Open **PowerShell Session Menu,** and you'll be given the option to switch between the different versions of PowerShell you have installed and registered in your PATH environment variable. You can use the $PSVersionTable variable to check which version you're running.

VS Code is incredibly powerful and has hundreds of features and extensions, meaning we can spend a good chunk of our day using it, but this has a few drawbacks to be aware of:

- Because it is open source and frequently updated, blog articles and tutorials on the internet (or, heaven forfend, a book on PowerShell programming) can become rapidly out of date. We need to carefully research how to use a feature or understand why something doesn't work and be wary of any source more than a year or two old.

- Because it is open source and extensible, there can be quite a steep learning curve. As we go through the book, we'll cover quite a few of the common use cases and features, but we'll barely scratch the surface of the things we can do with this software. The official Microsoft documentation is up to date, if not particularly user-friendly. We should supplement our reading with trustworthy articles and useful websites, such as Stack Overflow and Spiceworks.

- Because it is open source and extensible, anyone can write extensions for it. This means that sometimes extensions will be brilliant, and sometimes they will be less useful. It can also be the case that an extension that was marvelous two years ago has now fallen into disrepair because the author wrote it as a fun project and is now concentrating on other things.

These drawbacks aside, VS Code is incredibly useful. When we come across something that makes us wince in frustration, we should pause, be kind, and work around it. Better still, fix it; that is part of the joy of open source software.

Now we have VS Code installed and ready to use, let's move on to the actual topic of the chapter; PowerShell control flow. We are going to start with conditionals.

Conditional control – if, else, elseif, and switch

Conditional control flow is based on a simple statement. If this thing is true, then do that thing. The first part is a Boolean expression. The second part is an action based on the resolution of the Boolean. A Boolean expression will resolve to one of two values: true or false. We discussed Boolean operators in *Chapter 3, The PowerShell Pipeline – How to String Cmdlets Together*, in the *Understanding Where-Object advanced syntax* section. Consider the following two statements:

```
1 -eq 1
1 -eq 2
```

The first one resolves to the Boolean-type object true. The second one resolves to false. Try it if you don't believe me. It's not often that we need to check whether 1 is the same as 2, but we frequently need to compare variables:

```
PS C:\temp\poshbook> 1 -eq 1
True
PS C:\temp\poshbook> 1 -eq 2
False
PS C:\temp\poshbook> (1 -eq 1).GetType()

IsPublic IsSerial Name                                     BaseType
-------- -------- ----                                     --------
True     True     Boolean                                  System.ValueType
```

Figure 5.6 – Just checking

That covers the first part of our logic; next, we need to be able to perform an action based on the result of our test. Let's get VS Code ready for some fun. Let's close VS Code for now.

Go to your PowerShell prompt (not the one in VS Code) and type the following to create a working directory, move to it, and start VS Code inside it:

```
New-Item -Path C:\Temp\Poshbook -ItemType Directory
Set-Location -Path C:\Temp\Poshbook
Code .
```

The period after Code is important. Don't miss it, or you will be working in the wrong location. VS Code will start and ask whether you want to trust the authors of the files in this folder. We probably do, as we are going to be the authors. We're going to need a new file to work in, so press *Ctrl + N* to create a new file and select **PowerShell** as the language. Press *Ctrl + S* to save it as Conditionals. ps1. We have our blank canvas. Let's go to work.

The if statement

The first conditional we'll look at is the simplest – the if statement. We can use this to perform an action based on whether an expression is true or false. Type this in the script pane:

```
$x = 5
if ($X -gt 4) {
    Write-Output '$x is bigger than 4'
}
```

The brackets contain an expression that needs to be evaluated. The curly braces contain a scriptblock that will run if the expression resolves to true. Now, highlight your lines and press *F8*. Your code will run, and you should see the output in the terminal window:

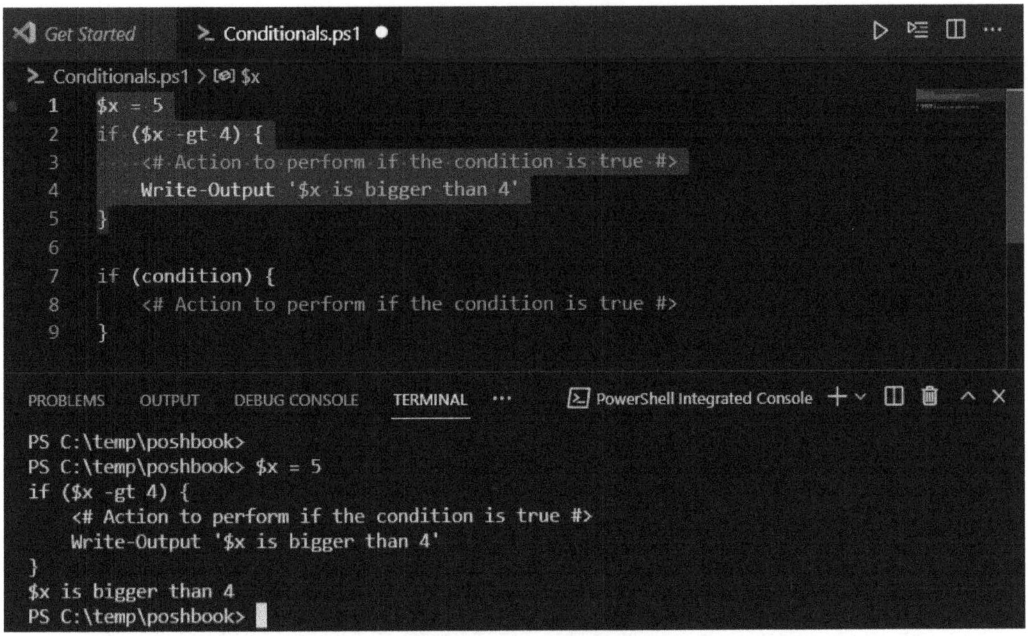

Figure 5.7 – The if statement

Be careful to use single quotes; review *Chapter 4, PowerShell Variables and Data Structures*, to understand why. If you use double quotes in the action, then you will see the output 5 is bigger than 4, because you've expanded the $x variable.

> **Top tip**
>
> After you type if, pause for a second to let VS Code catch up. It will offer you a choice of cmdlets and keywords. Click on if in the list, and it will construct the statement for you, as shown in lines 7 to 9 in *Figure 5.7*. All you need to do is fill in the condition and the action.

Look at the green text on lines 3 and 8. Those are comments. We use them to make our code more readable and to clarify what we are doing. A single-line comment is started with #; everything after the # will be ignored by PowerShell. A multi-line comment starts with <# and ends with #>. These comments were autogenerated by VS Code; we can leave them in or delete them. It makes no difference to how the code runs.

We can test whether a statement is false as well. Type this below line 9:

```
if (!($x -lt 4)) {
    Write-Output ' $x is bigger than 4'
}
```

We're using ! as a -not operator there. We could write line 11 as follows:

```
for (-not($x -lt 4)) {
```

But you won't see the -not operator written out like that very often – most people use !. If you highlight that code and press *F8* then you get the output $x is bigger than 4, again:

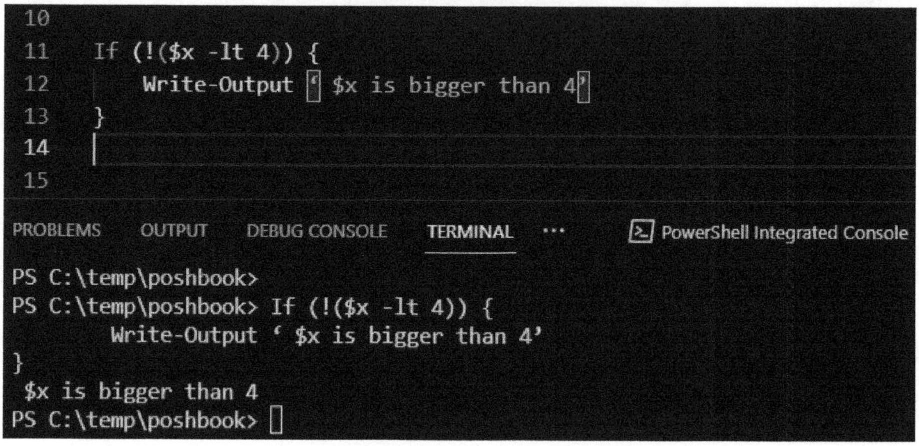

Figure 5.8 – Reversing a condition with the -not operator

If $x is smaller than 4, we will get no output, and the script will move on to the next line after the if statement – we don't need to do anything else. What happens if we want the script to do one thing if a statement is true and something else if a statement is false?

The else statement

We can use the else statement to specify a second action if the test condition for the if statement isn't true. Type this starting on line 15 – use the autocomplete for the else statement and notice we are using -lt in the condition, not -gt:

```
if ($x -lt 4) {
    Write-Output '$x is smaller than 4'
}

else {
    <# Action when all if and elseif conditions are false #>
    Write-Output '$x is not smaller than 4'
}
```

Now select lines 15-22 and hit *F8*:

```
15    if ($x -lt 4) {
16        Write-Output ' $x is smaller than 4'
17    }
18
19    else {
20        <# Action when all if and elseif conditions are false #>
21        Write-Output '$x is not smaller than 4'
22    }
23
```

PROBLEMS   OUTPUT   DEBUG CONSOLE   **TERMINAL**   ...   PowerShell Integrated Console

```
PS C:\temp\poshbook>
PS C:\temp\poshbook> if ($x -lt 4) {
    Write-Output ' $x is smaller than 4'
}

else {
    <# Action when all if and elseif conditions are false #>
    Write-Output '$x is not smaller than 4'
}
$x is not smaller than 4
PS C:\temp\poshbook>
```

Figure 5.9 – Using the else statement

Notice the remark on line 20 from autocompleting the else statement: Action when all if and elseif conditions are false. The else statement is a catch-all if no conditions are true. But how do we test for multiple conditions? We could write multiple if statements, one after another, but each statement would execute regardless of the statement before. We could nest if statements inside each other, but that would be a lot of work.

The elseif statement

We can use elseif to specify multiple conditions to test for multiple conditions within a single if statement. Type this on line 24. Use autocomplete to help get everything right:

```
if ($x -lt 5) {
    Write-Output '$x is less than 5'
}
elseif ($x -gt 5) {
    Write-Output '$x is bigger than 5'
}
else {
```

```
        Write-Output '$x is 5'
    }
```

Highlight the code you've just entered and hit *F8*. You should see the output as follows:

```
>_ Conditionals.ps1 > ...
23
24     if ($x -lt 5) {
25         <# Action to perform if the condition is true #>
26         Write-Output '$x is less than 5'
27     }
28     elseif ($x -gt 5) {
29         <# Action when this condition is true #>
30         Write-Output '$x is bigger than 5'
31     }
32     else {
33         <# Action when all if and elseif conditions are false #>
34         Write-Output '$x is 5'
35     }


PROBLEMS    OUTPUT    DEBUG CONSOLE    TERMINAL    ···         >_ PowerShell Integrated Console

$x is 5
PS C:\temp\poshbook>
```

Figure 5.10 – Using the elseif statement

You can have as many elseif statements as you need, but once one is true, the parent if statement will exit. Try this:

```
if ($x -lt 5) {
    Write-Output '$x is less than 5'
}
elseif ($x -lt 6) {
    Write-Output '$x is less than 6'
}
else {
    Write-Output '$x is 5'
}
```

We get the output $x is less than 6. The else statement never gets to run.

The ternary operator

PowerShell 7 has a new operator that allows us to construct simple if/else statement pairs in a single line. On line 15 of our code, we have the following example:

```
if ($x -lt 4) {
    Write-Output ' $x is smaller than 4'
}
else {
    <# Action when all if and elseif conditions are false #>
    Write-Output '$x is not smaller than 4'
}
```

We can rewrite this with the ternary operator like so:

```
($x -lt 4) ? '$x is smaller than 4' : '$x is not smaller than 4'
```

This is great and will save a lot of typing, but it's also less readable. The question mark character (?) can also be used as an alias for the Where-Object cmdlet, but it's not being used that way here. Remember that our code will be read many more times than it is written.

What happens if multiple statements are true? Let's look at a way we can handle that.

The switch statement

We could test for multiple conditions with multiple if statements, but that might get complicated, so there is a special statement to test for multiple true conditions – switch. The switch statement tests each condition and executes the associated scriptblock for that condition. Every condition that is true will execute. Let's see how it works. On a new line, type the following:

```
$Array   = 1,2,3,4,5

switch ($Array) {
    1 {Write-Output '$Array contains 1'}
    3 {Write-Output '$Array contains 3'}
    6 {Write-Output '$Array contains 6'}
}
```

If you select the code and press *F8* you should see the following output:

```
50    $Array = 1,2,3,4,5
51
52    Switch ($Array) {
53        1 {Write-Output '$Array contains 1'}
54        3 {Write-Output '$Array contains 3'}
55        6 {Write-Output '$Array contains 6'}
56    }
57

PROBLEMS    OUTPUT    DEBUG CONSOLE    TERMINAL    ...        PowerShell Integrated Console

PS C:\temp\poshbook>
PS C:\temp\poshbook> $Array = 1,2,3,4,5

Switch ($Array) {
    1 {Write-Output '$Array contains 1'}
    3 {Write-Output '$Array contains 3'}
    6 {Write-Output '$Array contains 6'}
}
$Array contains 1
$Array contains 3
PS C:\temp\poshbook>
```

Figure 5.11 – Using the switch statement

There are lots of things we can do with the `switch` statement. Consider the following example:

```
$String = "Powershell 7"
Switch -Wildcard -CaseSensitive ($String) {
    7 { Write-Output 'contains 7' }
    "Pow*" { Write-Output 'contains Pow'}
    'pow*' { Write-Output 'contains pow'}
    '*she*' { Write-Output 'contains she'}
    {$String.Length -gt 7} { Write-Output "long string"}
    Default {Write-Output "No powershell here"}
}
```

Here, we are running through a string. We've used the `-Wildcard` and `-CaseSensitive` parameters to check for matching portions of the string and make sure that the cases match as well. We're evaluating a property of the string, not just the content, and finally, we are setting a default output:

```
73
74    $String = "Powershell 7"
75    Switch -Wildcard -CaseSensitive ($String) {
76        7 { Write-Output 'contains 7' }
77        "Pow*" { Write-Output 'contains Pow'}
78        'pow*' {Write-Output 'contains pow'}
79        '*she*' { Write-Output 'contains she'}
80        {$String.Length -gt 7} { Write-Output "long string"}
81        Default {Write-Output "No powershell here"}
82    }
```

```
PROBLEMS  2    OUTPUT    DEBUG CONSOLE    TERMINAL    ···    ⟩_ PowerShell Integrated Console

PS C:\temp\poshbook>
PS C:\temp\poshbook> $String = "Powershell 7"
Switch -Wildcard -CaseSensitive ($String) {
    7 { Write-Output 'contains 7' }
    "Pow*" { Write-Output 'contains Pow'}
    'pow*' {Write-Output 'contains pow'}
    '*she*' { Write-Output 'contains she'}
    {$String.Length -gt 7} { Write-Output "long string"}
    Default {Write-Output "No powershell here"}
}
contains Pow
contains she
long string
PS C:\temp\poshbook> █
```

Figure 5.12 – Switch options

Let's have a look at the lines of code in the screenshot:

- In line 75, we're setting parameters for the switch statement – notice they have to come before the expression to be evaluated that is enclosed in brackets.

- In line 76, we're asking whether the string contains the integer 7. In lines 77 and 78, we're demonstrating the use of the -CaseSensitive parameter.

- In line 80, we're evaluating a property of the string, its length. Notice that this has to go in a scriptblock, so it needs curly braces, not brackets.

- Finally, on line 81, we are setting a default output – this will only be produced if no other conditions in the switch statement get matched.

Activity 1

Why doesn't the output produce the line contains 7?

We can also use a `-Regex` parameter to evaluate against a regular expression. This can't be used with the `-Wildcard` or `-Exact` parameter. The `-Exact` parameter is the opposite of `-Wildcard` and is the default.

Loops – foreach, do while, do until, while, for

Automation theory tells us that machines are better than people at performing repetitive tasks; they will perform the task any number of times in exactly the same way each time. When we are writing code, we call this iteration or looping. We're going to look at four examples of looping in PowerShell that are relatively common. We'll start with the `foreach` loop, before looking at `do while` and its counterpart, `do until`. We'll then look at the more generalized `while` statement and finish with a look at the `for` statement and see how it differs from `foreach`. Let's get started by creating a new file, setting it as a PowerShell file, and saving it as `loops.ps1`.

The foreach loop statement

This is the most common loop statement. We've seen `foreach` before, when we looked at the `Foreach-Object` cmdlet in *Chapter 3, The PowerShell Pipeline – How to String Cmdlets Together*. They're similar in function, but not the same, and have very different syntax. `foreach` loops have the following syntax:

```
foreach ( $element in <expression> ) {<scriptblock>}
```

If `foreach` is at the start of a statement, then PowerShell will treat it as the `foreach` loop statement, not an alias for `ForEach-Object`. We can see this happening in the following screenshot:

Figure 5.13 – The foreach statement and foreach as an alias for ForEach-Object

In line 1, `foreach` is at the start of the line, or statement, and in line 2 it comes after a pipeline character. `PSScriptAnalyzer`, part of the PowerShell extension for VS Code, has recognized `foreach` as an alias of `ForEach-Object` in line 2 and given it a wavy yellow underline to denote poor practice, but not in line 1. If we hover the mouse over `foreach` in line 2, we can see that it is moaning because we have used an alias, and it's right. What else is going on in that image?

In line 1, we've got a `foreach` statement – it consists of the `foreach` keyword, a grouped expression in brackets, and a scriptblock in curly braces. The grouped expression takes the format (`$element in [expression]`) and produces a collection of objects. Once the collection is complete, the scriptblock operates on each object in turn. In this case, we are collecting all the objects in the current directory that end in `.ps1`. We then perform an operation on them – we get their length (`$f.length`) and add it to the `$l` variable using the compound operator, `+=`. It doesn't matter what variable we use to denote the elements in the collection so long as it isn't an automatic variable or a variable we are using elsewhere.

In the second line, we are using the `ForEach-Object` cmdlet to do exactly the same thing. What's the difference?

When we use the `foreach` keyword to create a loop, the expression is run to produce an array, which is held in memory. Each element is then run into the scriptblock one at a time. If your expression creates a very large array then you may experience memory issues.

When we use the `ForEach-Object` cmdlet as part of a pipeline, each element in the array created by `Get-ChildItem *.ps1` passes through the entire pipeline one at a time; this means it uses a lot less memory, as the whole array doesn't exist in memory, just single elements. The downside is it may well take longer to process.

Let's try a `foreach` loop for ourselves. Type the following:

```
$l = 0 ; foreach ($f in Get-ChildItem *.ps1) {$l += $f.length} ; $l
```

That's not quite the same as the line in *Figure 5.13*. We're using a semicolon (`;`) as a statement separator; this allows us to put multiple statements on one line instead of splitting it over multiple lines. This is easier to type but not easier to read. Let's go through the command;

- Our first statement is `$l = 0 ;`. This creates the `$l` variable and sets it to 0. This means each time we run the whole line, it will reset `$l` to 0.

- The second statement is `Foreach ($i in Get-ChildItem *.ps1) {$l += $i.length} ;`. This is where we create our array and loop through each element of it.

- Our final statement is just `$l` – this returns the value of `$l` at the end of the loop.

We can see how this looks in the following screenshot:

```
>_ foreachloop.ps1 > [e] $length
   1    $l = 0 ; foreach ($f in Get-ChildItem *.ps1) {$l += $f.length } ; $l

PROBLEMS  1     OUTPUT     DEBUG CONSOLE     TERMINAL     JUPYTER

PS C:\temp\poshbook>
PS C:\temp\poshbook> $l = 0 ; foreach ($f in Get-ChildItem *.ps1) {$l += $f.length } ; $l

2032
PS C:\temp\poshbook>
```

Figure 5.14 – The foreach loop and statement separator

We'll be using foreach loops quite a lot, as they are the most common type of loop. Let's move on to the next types, do while and do until.

The do while and do until loop statements

The do while and do until loops share the same syntax, which puts the scriptblock first:

```
do {<scriptblock>} until/while (<condition> is true)
```

Because the condition is last, they will always execute the scriptblock at least once.

Try this. Type the following:

```
$number = 0
do { $number ++
Write-Output "The number is $number"
} while ($number -ne 5)
```

Let's take a closer look at what we've just done:

- In the first line, we're creating a $number variable and setting it to 0.

- In the second line, we are starting a do while loop with the do keyword, opening a scriptblock with a curly brace, {, and incrementing by 1 the $number variable using the ++ increment operator.

- In the third line, we're performing another operation, writing output to the screen.

- In the final line, we are closing the scriptblock with a curly brace, }, then using the while keyword to supply the condition, in brackets. In this case, it is while $number is not equal to 5.

What is your last line of output? For me, it is The number is 5. This is because the scriptblock is run before the condition is evaluated. Try this:

```
$number = 0
Do {Write-Host "The number is not Zero"}
While ($number -ne 0)
```

As we can see in the following screenshot, the scriptblock has been executed even though the condition is false.

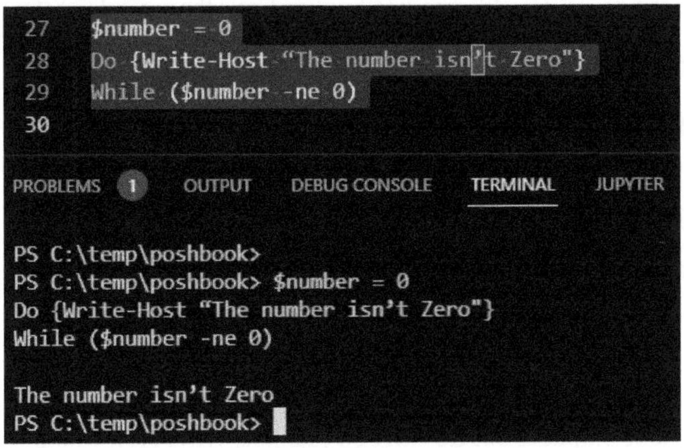

Figure 5.15 – The computer is lying to you

The do until loop works the same way, but until the condition is true:

```
$number = 0
do { $number ++
Write-Host "The number is $number"
} until ($number -eq 5)
```

Let's see how those loops look next to each other:

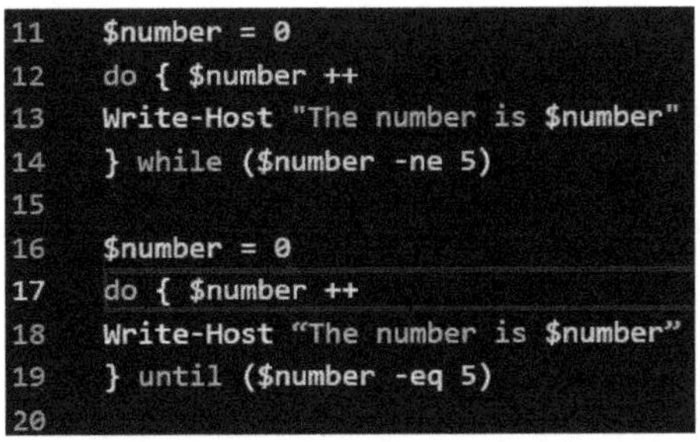

Figure 5.16 – do while and do until

Generally, we use do until loops when the test condition is expected to be positive and do while loops when the test condition is expected to be negative. It is not while or until that determines true or false, but the condition associated with it. You can just as easily have "not equals" (negative) with until and "equals" (positive) with while. Remember, though, that the scriptblock will execute the first time the condition is not met. What can we do about that?

The while loop

The while loop turns the do while loop back to front and puts the condition before the scriptblock:

```
while (<condition> is true) {<scriptblock>}
```

This means if the condition is not true, then the scriptblock never executes. There is no until statement.

Try it. Type this:

```
$number = 0
while ( $number -ne 5) { $number ++
Write-Host "The number is $number"}
```

> **Activity 2**
> This produces the same output as our do while example. Why? How would you prove that the scriptblock doesn't execute when the condition is true?

Let's look at our final loop next, the for loop.

The for loop

Despite its name, the for loop is more like a while loop than a foreach loop. It's a counting loop that depends on a condition being true, like while, but it is much more flexible. The syntax is more complicated as well:

```
for (<Iterator> ; <condition> ; <iteration>) { <scriptblock> }
```

The iterator is the variable we're going to iterate, similar to the $number variable we used previously when we looked at the while loop. The condition is the same as the while loop condition, and the iteration is the action we perform on the iterator each time we go round the loop. Try this:

```
for ($i = 0 ; $i -lt 5 ; $i ++) {Write-Host $i}
```

That's not hugely exciting; it just looks like a complicated way to do exactly the same as the `while` loop previously. However, the `for` loop allows us to index the element of the loop and move around based on that index. Try this:

```
$fruits = @('banana', 'apple', 'pear', 'plum')
for ($i = 1 ; $i -lt ($fruits.length) ; $i ++) {
    Write-Host $fruits[$i] "is after"  $fruits[$i-1]
}
```

You should see the output shown in the following screenshot:

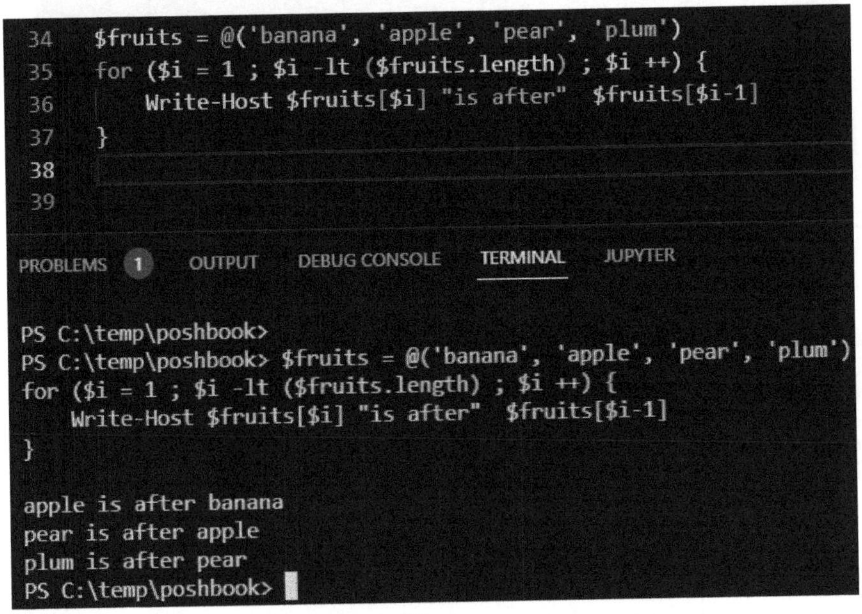

Figure 5.17 – Ordering fruit around with a for loop

Here's another thing we can do with a `for` loop that makes it special. We can change the contents of our array. Try this:

```
$fruits = @('banana', 'apple', 'pear', 'plum')
foreach ($fruit in $fruits) {$fruit = "tasty $fruit"}
Write-Host $fruits
```

Well, that didn't work. We might have hoped that by changing `$fruit` it would affect the original array, but it doesn't, because the `foreach` loop operates on copies of the elements in the array. We can use the `for` loop to do it though:

```
$fruits = @('banana', 'apple', 'pear', 'plum')
for ($i = 0 ; $i -lt ($fruits.length) ; $i ++) {
```

```
    $fruits[$i] = "tasty $($fruits[$i])"
}
Write-Host $fruits
```

And we should see the output as follows:

```
44    $fruits = @('banana', 'apple', 'pear', 'plum')
45    foreach ($fruit in $fruits) {$fruit = "tasty $fruit"}
46    Write-Host $fruits
47
48    $fruits = @('banana', 'apple', 'pear', 'plum')
49    for ($i = 0 ; $i -lt ($fruits.length) ; $i ++) {
50        $fruits[$i] = "tasty $($fruits[$i])"
51    }
52    Write-Host $fruits

PROBLEMS  1    OUTPUT    DEBUG CONSOLE    TERMINAL    JUPYTER

PS C:\temp\poshbook>
PS C:\temp\poshbook> $fruits = @('banana', 'apple', 'pear', 'plum')
for ($i = 0 ; $i -lt ($fruits.length) ; $i ++) {
    $fruits[$i] = "tasty $($fruits[$i])"
}
Write-Host $fruits
tasty banana tasty apple tasty pear tasty plum
PS C:\temp\poshbook>
```

Figure 5.18 – Using a for loop to make fruit tasty

We're doing something new in line 50, there. We're using $ (), the sub-expression symbol, to make sure PowerShell correctly interprets what we mean. While we can expand simple variables inside double quotes, more complex expressions need a little more. Without wrapping $fruits[$i] in a pair of brackets preceded by a dollar sign, PowerShell won't correctly unpack it.

We're nearly done with loops. We've looked at the foreach loop, which performs an operation for each element in an array. We've looked at do while and while, which repeat an operation while a condition is true. Then we looked at do until, which performs an operation until a condition becomes true. Finally, we looked at the more complicated for loop, which repeats an operation a predetermined number of times. What we need next is a way of controlling our loops. What happens if the condition in a while loop never becomes false? Let's look at loop control with break and continue.

Breaking and continuing

The break and continue statements are related and allow us to control how our loops behave. We can also use them in switch statements. It's important not to use them outside of loops or switch statements as they can lead to unpredictable behavior. A break statement can be used to stop a loop iterating altogether, while continue can be used to stop an iteration and move on to the next one. Let's look at break first.

The break statement

Let's play with the trusty while loop. Type this:

```
$number = 0
while ( $number -ne 5) { $number ++
if ($number -eq 3) {
    break
    }
    Write-Host "The number is $number"
}
```

Hopefully, you'll see that the last number printed is 2. The conditional if statement says to stop looping if $number is 3. The break statement only acts on the loop it is nested inside.

The continue statement

The continue statement stops the current iteration of the loop, not the whole loop, and moves on to the next iteration. Try this:

```
$number = 0
while ( $number -ne 5) { $number ++
if ($number -eq 3) {
    continue
    }
    Write-Host "The number is $number"
}
```

This time, the loop prints out the numbers 1 to 5, but omits 3. It breaks out of the current iteration before it reaches the Write-Host statement, and starts the next one. You should see the result in the following screenshot:

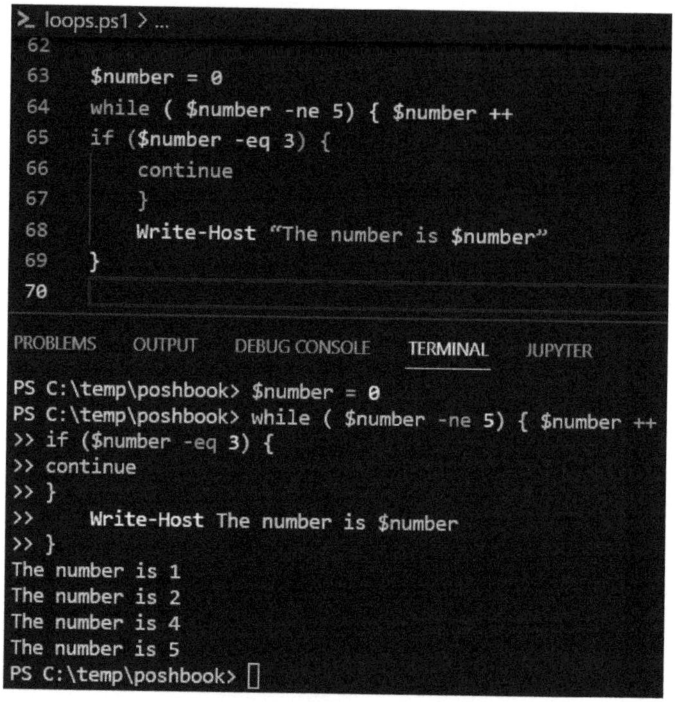

Figure 5.19 – Using continue

We can also use `break` and `continue` in `switch` statements, like this:

```
$String = "Powershell 7", "python"
switch -Wildcard -CaseSensitive ($String) {
    {$_} {Write-output "processing $_ :"}
    '*7' { Write-Output 'contains 7'}
    "Pow*" { Write-Output 'contains Pow'}
    'pow*' {Write-Output 'contains pow'}
    '*she*' { Write-Output 'contains she'; continue}
    {$String.Length -gt 7} { Write-Output "long string"}
    {$String.Length -lt 7} {Write-Output "No powershell here"}
}
```

This is similar to the `switch` block we used earlier in the chapter, in the *The switch statement* section. The difference is we are now passing an array of strings, not a single one. The `continue` statement in line 7 means that the `long string` and `No powershell here` outputs are never executed; instead, the `switch` statement moves on to the next element in the array, `python`. Now replace `continue` with `break`. We can see that the entire `switch` statement stops – `python` is never processed.

That's enough for now on loops. We'll be using them a lot in the rest of the book. Let's have some fun now, instead.

Let's play a game

We're all familiar with number-guessing games. Let's use what we've learned in this chapter to write a game in PowerShell. This is a common challenge set in many programming tutorials, so we're not going to be any different. In the UK, it is sometimes called the Brucie Game because of its similarity to the popular UK TV gameshow Bruce Forsyth's Play Your Cards Right. The Brucie bonus here is that we get to learn something.

The program generates a random integer between 1 and 100. We then need to get user input in the form of another integer. We compare the guess with the hidden number and decide whether it's right. If it is, we go to the end of the program. If it isn't, then we need to decide whether it is too high or too low and output an appropriate message before going back and asking for another guess. We can represent this as a flow chart, which will be helpful when it comes to writing our code:

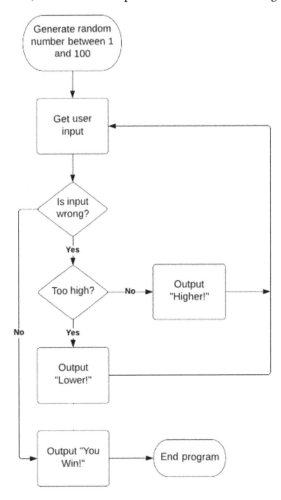

Figure 5.20 – Flow chart for the Brucie game

The first thing we need to do is open a new file; mine is called `Brucie.ps1`. Let's go to work.

The first box calls for a random integer between 1 and 100. That's easy:

```
[int]$Hidden = Get-Random -Minimum 1 -Maximum 101
```

Now we need to tell the player what to do, and get an input from them:

```
Write-Host "Let's play the Brucie Game! Guess the hidden number
between 1 and 100. give me a number below"
$guess = [int] (Read-Host)
```

Now we have our two numbers in variables called `$Hidden` and `$guess`. We need to compare them. The best way to do this is to use an `if-else` statement. If the number is wrong, we do one thing, else we print `You Win!`:

```
[int]$Hidden = Get-Random -Minimum 1 -Maximum 101
Write-Host "Let's play the Brucie Game! Guess the hidden number
between 1 and 100. give me a number below"
$guess = [int] (Read-Host)
if ($guess -ne $hidden) {
    <# Action to perform if the condition is true #>
} else {Write-Host "You Win"}
```

What action do we need to perform? We need to see whether it is higher or lower. We'll need another `if-else` there:

```
if ($guess -ne $hidden) {
    <# Action to perform if the condition is true #>
    if ($guess -lt $hidden) {
        Write-Host "Higher!"
    } else { Write-Host "Lower!"}
} else {Write-Host "You Win!"}
```

And that is that. Wait, no it isn't. We need to give them multiple guesses. We need a loop. We could use all sorts of loops here, but probably the easiest is a `while` loop. Have a think about how you might do it before moving on and seeing how I did it.

Don't peek. Think.

OK. Here's my solution:

```
[int]$Hidden = Get-Random -Minimum 1 -Maximum 101
Write-Host "Let's play the Brucie Game! Guess the hidden number
between 1 and 100.
give me a number below"
$guess = 0
```

```
while ($guess -ne $hidden) {
    $guess = [int] (Read-Host)
    if ($guess -lt $hidden) {
        Write-Host "Higher!"
    } elseif ( $guess -gt $hidden) { Write-Host "Lower!"}
}
Write-Host "You Win"
```

Here's the whole thing working:

```
Brucie.ps1 > ...
1    [int]$Hidden = Get-Random -Minimum 1 -Maximum 101
2    Write-Host "Let's play the Brucie Game! Guess the hidden number between 1 and 100.
3    give me a number below"
4    $guess = 0
5    while ($guess -ne $hidden) {
6        $guess = [int] (Read-Host)
7        If ($guess -lt $hidden) {
8            Write-Host "Higher!"
9        } elseif ( $guess -gt $hidden) {
10           Write-Host "Lower!"
11       }
12   }
13   Write-Host "You Win"
14
```

PROBLEMS **3**   OUTPUT   DEBUG CONSOLE   **TERMINAL**   JUPYTER

```
PS C:\temp\poshbook> . "c:\temp\poshbook\Brucie.ps1"
Let's play the Brucie Game! Guess the hidden number between 1 and 100.
give me a number below
50
Higher!
75
Lower!
67
Lower!
60
Lower!
55
Lower!
53
Lower!
52
You Win
PS C:\temp\poshbook>
```

Figure 5.21 – The Brucie game

On line 4, I've initialized $guess as 0 so that the loop has something to work with.

On line 5, I've changed my first `if` statement to a `while` statement. I've also closed the loop with a curly brace and made `Write-Host "You Win"` the final statement of the program.

On line 6, I've brought my input-gathering statement inside the loop. Try leaving it outside. That gets old quickly because we're never changing the value of `$guess` from 0.

The only other change I made was on line 9, where I replaced `else` with an `elseif` statement, otherwise the loop prints `Lower!` even when we're right.

And that's it. Make sure you save a working copy of the game so we can work with it later. We've covered a lot of ground in this chapter; let's summarize.

Summary

We started the chapter by looking at IDEs and installing the recommended environment for PowerShell 7, VS Code. VS Code is a large and ever-changing application. We need to spend time familiarizing ourselves with it and keep regularly updated as the features and capabilities change frequently. We have seen that it is easy to use and very powerful.

We then looked at the two main ways of controlling flow within a program: conditionals and loops. We spent a lot of time on the `if`, `else`, and `elseif` conditional statements and then looked at the related `switch` statement.

After that, we looked at loops. We started with a loop that will iterate through all the elements in an array – the `foreach` loop – and explored how it differs from the `ForEach-Object` cmdlet. We looked at `do while` and `do until`, which will repeat a loop while a condition is true or false, and then we looked at the `while` loop, which swaps the position of the condition and the scriptblock. The last loop we looked at in this section was a counting loop – `for`.

Finally, we finished this chapter by writing a short number-guessing game in PowerShell, the Brucie game. I hope you enjoyed doing this, as this sort of exercise will really cement how to write code in PowerShell.

In the next chapter, we're going to be looking at how PowerShell can be used to interact with files. We're going to be reading content, writing content, and generally playing around.

Exercises

1. What output will `$x = 4 ; IF ($x -gt 4) {Write-Host '$x is larger than 4'}` produce?

2. Write a statement that will produce an output for the line `$x = 4 ; IF ($x -gt 4) {Write-Host '$x is larger than 4'}` when $x is not larger than 4.

3. Write a statement that will produce output from `$x = 4 ; IF ($x -gt 4) {Write-Host '$x is larger than 4'}` when $x is exactly 4.

4. Write a statement that will produce an output for the line `$x = 4 ; IF ($x -gt 4)` `{Write-Host '$x is larger than 4'}` when $x is not larger than 4, as in question 2, but this time use the `ternary` operator.

5. What is going wrong here?

    ```
    $processes = Get-process | foreach ($process in $processes)
    {$process.name}
    ```

6. Rewrite `$number = 0 ; Do {$number ++ ; Write-Host "Number is` `$number"} While ($number -eq 5)` so that it works, but without using a do until loop.

7. Make this statement work: `For ($i = 0 ; $i -lt 5 ) {Write-Host $i}`.

8. We should only use `break` and `continue` statements in loops and one other place. Where?

9. How would you make it so the Brucie game limits the number of guesses a user could make?

Further reading

This was a big chapter, so there is plenty of further reading here:

- Developing PowerShell with VS Code: `https://docs.microsoft.com/en-us/` `powershell/scripting/dev-cross-plat/vscode/using-vscode`

- About `if`: `https://docs.microsoft.com/en-us/powershell/module/` `microsoft.powershell.core/about/about_if`

- About `switch`: `https://docs.microsoft.com/en-us/powershell/module/` `microsoft.powershell.core/about/about_switch`

- About `foreach`: `https://docs.microsoft.com/en-us/powershell/module/` `microsoft.powershell.core/about/about_foreach`

- About `do`: `https://docs.microsoft.com/en-us/powershell/module/` `microsoft.powershell.core/about/about_do`

- About `while`: `https://docs.microsoft.com/en-us/powershell/module/` `microsoft.powershell.core/about/about_while`

- About `for`: `https://docs.microsoft.com/en-us/powershell/module/` `microsoft.powershell.core/about/about_for`

- About `break`: `https://docs.microsoft.com/en-us/powershell/module/` `microsoft.powershell.core/about/about_break`

- About `continue`: `https://docs.microsoft.com/en-us/powershell/module/` `microsoft.powershell.core/about/about_continue`

PowerShell and Files – Reading, Writing, and Manipulating Data

So far, our PowerShell journey has been on the screen. Wouldn't it be neat to be able to write the output of our cmdlets to a file somewhere so that we could save it for later or send it to other people? That's what we're going to do in this chapter. First, we're going to look at formatting output for the screen so that we can just focus on the things we're interested in or present output in a more useful manner. Next, we're going to look at writing the output to a text file using Out-File. I do this multiple times a day and it's an incredibly useful technique, but it is very limited, so we're also going to look at creating **Comma-Separated Value (CSV)** files for consumption by another program, such as Microsoft Excel, and HTML files so that we can display our output as a web page.

Once we're comfortable with the output, we're going to dive into a short section that will help us understand how PowerShell interacts with filesystems, before looking at how we can use PowerShell to read and manipulate data in common file types, such as text and CSV files. Finally, we'll wrap the chapter up with a short walkthrough of a fun project and leave you with a challenge.

In this chapter, we are going to cover the following topics:

- Understanding formatting
- Writing to a text file
- Using ConvertTo- and Export- cmdlets
- Handling files
- Working with file
- Let's have some fun!

Understanding formatting

Let's think about our old friend, `Get-Process`. We know that when we run it, it displays a list of the running processes on our machine. For each process, it displays some of the properties. We know from running `Get-Process | Get-Member` that there are many more that it doesn't display unless we ask for them explicitly. This is the case for pretty much every PowerShell cmdlet; the output we see is rarely the complete output of every property the objects in the pipeline possess. How does that happen? Welcome to the **default format**.

PowerShell decides on the format for displaying output based on the `TypeName` of the object in the pipeline. If the `TypeName` has an associated **default formatting view**, then PowerShell will use it. If there isn't a default formatting view, for instance, if it is a `PSCustomObject`, then the shell will determine whether there is a **default property set** and, if so, display that. If there are fewer than five default properties, they will be displayed in a table; if there are more than five, then they will be displayed as a list. Finally, if the object has neither a default formatting view nor a default property set, then all the properties will be displayed.

We can see part of the default formatting view for `Get-Process` in the following screenshot:

```
 process.format.ps1xml
  4        <View>
  5          <Name>process</Name>
  6          <ViewSelectedBy>
  7            <TypeName>System.Diagnostics.Process</TypeName>
  8          </ViewSelectedBy>
  9          <TableControl>
 10            <TableHeaders>
 11              <TableColumnHeader>
 12                <Label>NPM(K)</Label>
 13                <Width>7</Width>
 14                <Alignment>Right</Alignment>
 15              </TableColumnHeader>
 16              <TableColumnHeader>
 17                <Label>PM(M)</Label>
```

Figure 6.1 – Part of the default formatting view for System.Diagnostics.Process objects

It is possible to redefine the properties that are displayed by default, but I've never found it necessary to do so, so it's beyond the scope of this book. If it's something you think you might like to do, then have a look at the help files for the `FormatData` cmdlets by running the following:

```
Get-Help *FormatData
```

We don't need to do anything as drastic as updating `FormatData` to change the way our output is formatted, though. In the rest of this section, we're going to look at three common ways of changing the way our data is displayed using `Format` cmdlets. First, let's look at my favorite, `Format-List`.

Format-List

Most cmdlets we use will display output as a table with the object name and a few well-chosen properties. `Format-List` allows us to display the object properties and values as a list. Note that `Format-List` displays the properties in the default property set, not the ones in the default format view if a view exists. Have a look at the following screenshot to see what we mean:

```
PS /home/nickp> Get-Process

 NPM(K)      PM(M)      WS(M)     CPU(s)      Id  SI ProcessName
 ------      -----      -----     ------      --  -- -----------
      0       0.00       3.52       0.08       8   7 bash
      0       0.00       0.32       0.10       1   1 init
      0       0.00       0.22       0.00       7   7 init
      0       0.00      94.12       2.71      73   7 pwsh

PS /home/nickp> Get-Process | Format-List

Id      : 8
Handles : 4
CPU     : 0.08
SI      : 7
Name    : bash

Id      : 1
Handles :
CPU     : 0.1
SI      : 1
Name    : init
```

Figure 6.2 – The default format and the list format

We can see that running `Get-Process` on its own produces some very different information from what we get when we pipe it into `Format-List`. In fact, `Format-List` doesn't look very good at all, there – so why do I use it so much? Try getting the information for a single process and using `Format-List` with the wildcard operator, (`*`), as follows:

```
Get-Process pwsh | Format-List *
```

There! Lots of information. We can also just select certain properties to display by passing a comma-separated list to the `-Property` parameter of `Format-List`, as follows:

```
Get-Process pwsh | Format-List -Property Name, Id, CPU, Responding
```

`Format-List` has the `fl` alias, so an awful lot of the stuff I ask people for when I'm troubleshooting their servers has `| fl *` somewhere near the end.

Format-Table

If we want a subset of data for a number of objects, then the table format is convenient. If we want different data to the default format view, then we can use `Format-Table`. Try this:

```
Get-Process | Format-Table -Property Name, Id, CPU, Responding
```

This will get us a subset of properties for each process in a convenient table format.

Quite often, when we run `Format-Table`, we don't actually see all the data we've asked for; instead, the output is truncated with an ellipsis (...). Happily, there are two other parameters of `Format-Table` that can help us out. Firstly, we can use the `-AutoSize` parameter to remove white space between columns and set each column to the width of its largest entry. However, if that still doesn't get everything, then we can use the `-Wrap` parameter to display each entry across multiple lines. Try this to see the difference:

```
Get-Process | Format-Table -Property Name, Id, CPU, Path, Modules
Get-Process | Format-Table -Property Name, Id, CPU, Path, Modules
-Wrap
```

That's quite handy. Let's look at our last format cmdlet, `Format-Wide`.

Format-Wide

The `Format-Wide` cmdlet allows us to show data in a wide list format, which makes it easier to read on a screen. It resembles the standard Linux list output (`ls`), but without the coloring rules that make the list command so useful. It will only display a single property of each object and defaults to a `Name` property unless we specify something else using the `-Property` parameter. It has two parameters that allow us to control the display – `-Column`, which specifies a set number of columns, and `-AutoSize`, which tries to fit in as many as possible without truncating the data. Try this:

```
Get-ChildItem | Format-Wide
Get-ChildItem | Format-Wide -Column 5
Get-ChildItem | Format-Wide -AutoSize
```

Personally, I don't find I use the `Format-Wide` cmdlet anything as much as I should. It's useful for concisely seeing a list of objects and saves scrolling up and down looking for an item.

Formatting gotchas

In *Chapter 3, The PowerShell Pipeline – How to String Cmdlets Together*, we discussed a very important rule: **Filter Left**. Well, here we have another important rule: **Format Right**. Although the `Format-` cmdlets produce readable text on the screen, that's because the formatting data objects they produce are processed by the shell. We really can't use the output from a `Format-` cmdlet anywhere else in the pipeline, except to feed it into one of the specialized `Out-` cmdlets, such as the `Out-Default` | `Out-Host` pair that is implicit on the end of every PowerShell pipeline.

There is, however, a very useful Out- cmdlet that we haven't looked at yet, and we'll cover it in the next section.

Writing a text file

We started this chapter by promising to cover writing PowerShell output to a file. Let's do that. We have learned that we can feed the output of the Format- cmdlets into an Out- cmdlet and there is a specific cmdlet for writing data to a file; Out-File.

Out-File will write the output from any cmdlet to a text file. We can format the output first using a Format- cmdlet if we want to, but we don't have to; if we don't, we get the default output of the cmdlet. Let's try it:

```
Get-Process | Out-File -FilePath C:\temp\poshbook\procsRaw.txt
Get-Process | Format-Table -Property Name, Id, CPU, Path, Modules |
Out-File -FilePath C:\temp\poshbook\procsNoWrap.txt
Get-Process | Format-Table -Property Name, Id, CPU, Path, Modules
-Wrap | Out-File -FilePath C:\temp\poshbook\procsWrap.txt
```

As we can see, the content of the text files looks exactly the same as the screen outputs; all we've done is redirect the output to a file instead of the screen.

There are a few parameters we can use with Out-File:

- -FilePath specifies the path and name of the file we want to create. By default, Out-File will overwrite any pre-existing file with the same name, unless that file is read-only.

- -Append will add the output to an existing file, again, if it is not set to read-only.

- -NoClobber will check whether a file already exists and prevent it from being overwritten. We'll see an error message saying that the file already exists.

- -Force will allow us to ignore the read-only attribute on existing files.

- -Encoding can change the default encoding of the file from ASCII to a range of other formats; a popular one is UTF-8.

Out-File also has a couple of aliases that we might see quite often. The greater-than symbol (>) is an alias for Out-File -FilePath, and we just need to type a path and file name after it. A double greater-than symbol (>>) is an alias for Out-File -Append -FilePath and again, just needs a path and filename. We can't use any other parameters with these aliases. For example, Get-Process > C:\temp\processes.txt will take the output of Get-Process and save it to C:\temp.txt – if we then run Get-Date >> C:\temp\processes.txt, it will append the output of Get-Date to the same file.

Out-File only produces a file. It doesn't put any object in the pipeline, so must be the last cmdlet in a pipeline.

The first important thing to remember is that what gets written to the file is *exactly* what we would see on the screen.

The other important thing to remember is that a file we create with `Out-File` is a text file. We can call it a CSV file if we want, but it won't be. The data won't be converted; no commas will be inserted. Let's demonstrate:

```
Get-Process | Format-Table -Property Name, Id, CPU, Path, Modules
-Wrap | Out-File C:\temp\poshbook\procsWrap.csv
```

As expected, the contents of the CSV file created in the last line look horrible. Here's what it looks like if I try to open it in MS Excel, my usual app for manipulating CSV files:

[32;1mName	Id	CPU Path	Modules][0m	
[32;1m----	--	--- ----	-------][0m	
Acrobat 2944 1466.40625 C:\Program Files\Adobe\Acrobat DC\Acrobat\Acrobat.exe			{System.Diagnostics.ProcessMo	
System.Di				
		agnostics.ProcessModule		
System.Diagnosti				
		cs.ProcessModule		
System.Diagno				
		stics.ProcessModule		
		(KERNELBASE.dll)â€¦}		
Acrobat 15600 13.90625 C:\Program Files\Adobe\Acrobat DC\Acrobat\Acrobat.exe			{System.Diagnostics.ProcessMo	
System.Di				
		agnostics.ProcessModule		
System.Diagnosti				
		cs.ProcessModule		

Figure 6.3 – This is not a CSV file

We'll have a look at how we can produce different types of files in the next section, using the `ConvertTo-` and `Export-` cmdlets.

Using ConvertTo- and Export- cmdlets

If we want our PowerShell objects in a format other than text, we're going to need to process them somehow. There are two groups of cmdlets that let us do that. The `ConvertTo-` cmdlets convert the objects in our pipeline into data of a particular type, such as CSV or HTML data. The `Export-` cmdlets combine the equivalent `ConvertTo-` cmdlet with an `Out-File` function to produce a file of the relevant type. In this chapter, we're going to cover three common file types; CSV, XML, and HTML.

CSV

Let's look at the `ConvertTo-CSV` cmdlet first. With this cmdlet, we can take the output of another cmdlet and turn it into a CSV datastream. Try this:

```
Get-Process | ConvertTo-Csv
```

You'll see something like the following screenshot:

```
PS C:\Users\nickp> Get-Process | ConvertTo-Csv
"Name","SI","Handles","VM","WS","PM","NPM","Path","CommandLine","Parent","Company","CPU","FileVersion","ProductVersion",
"Description","Product","__NounName","SafeHandle","Handle","BasePriority","ExitCode","HasExited","StartTime","ExitTime",
"Id","MachineName","MaxWorkingSet","MinWorkingSet","Modules","NonpagedSystemMemorySize64","NonpagedSystemMemorySize","Pa
gedMemorySize64","PagedMemorySize","PagedSystemMemorySize64","PagedSystemMemorySize","PeakPagedMemorySize64","PeakPagedM
emorySize","PeakWorkingSet64","PeakWorkingSet","PeakVirtualMemorySize64","PeakVirtualMemorySize","PriorityBoostEnabled",
"PriorityClass","PrivateMemorySize64","PrivateMemorySize","ProcessName","ProcessorAffinity","SessionId","StartInfo","Thr
eads","HandleCount","VirtualMemorySize64","VirtualMemorySize","EnableRaisingEvents","StandardInput","StandardOutput","St
andardError","WorkingSet64","WorkingSet","SynchronizingObject","MainModule","PrivilegedProcessorTime","TotalProcessorTim
e","UserProcessorTime","MainWindowHandle","MainWindowTitle","Responding","Site","Container"
"Acrobat","1","167","116379648","1826816","2646016","11752","C:\Program Files\Adobe\Acrobat DC\Acrobat\x86\Acrobat\Acrob
at.exe","""C:\Program Files\Adobe\Acrobat DC\Acrobat\x86\Acrobat\Acrobat.exe"" --type=compute-only-renderer --ipc-rdr-ch
annel=ko.ddd28f44.ac45e400.2 --ipc-co-channel=ko.8a670d33.95e7ea97.1 --proc=5 --helperprocpid=21816 --channeltype=2 /n /
prefetch:2 /CR","System.Diagnostics.Process (Acrobat)","Adobe Systems Incorporated","30.4375","22.2.20191.0","22.2.2019
1.0","Adobe Acrobat DC ","Adobe Acrobat DC","Process","Microsoft.Win32.SafeHandles.SafeProcessHandle","3140","8","False
","30/08/2022 11:39:35","","1413120","204800","System.Diagnostics.ProcessModuleCollection","11752","11752","26
46016","2646016","91168","91168","3911680","3911680","9986048","9986048","119001088","119001088","True","Normal","264601
6","2646016","Acrobat","255","1","","System.Diagnostics.ProcessThreadCollection","167","116379648","116379648","False",,,,
"1826816","1826816",,"System.Diagnostics.ProcessModule (Acrobat.exe)","00:00:14.0937500","00:00:30.4375000","00:00:16.34
```

Figure 6.4 – Nasty

Ugh. Horrible, right? However, we can then pipe that into `Out-File` as follows:

```
Get-Process w* | ConvertTo-Csv | Out-File C:\temp\poshbook\
ProcessesConvertTo.csv
```

It will produce a real CSV file of all the processes starting with w that we can open in an application that reads CSV, such as MS Excel or Google Sheets. Not only that but it also ignores the default format information and just dumps everything.

Even better, there is a cmdlet that will do the whole thing in one operation – `Export-Csv`:

```
Get-Process | Export-Csv C:\temp\poshbook\ProcessesExport.csv
```

Let's take a closer look.

ConvertTo-Csv

This cmdlet has a few parameters we will be interested in:

- `-NoTypeInformation`: A lot of the scripts we might see on the internet will include this parameter, but we don't need it anymore. Prior to PowerShell 6.0, by default, the `ConvertTo-Csv` cmdlet included an introductory line that detailed the object type that had been converted, so any scripts that were written for earlier versions of PowerShell almost always included this parameter to remove that line. Since PowerShell 6.0, the default is to *not* include type information. Including the parameter won't cause a problem, but we don't need it in PowerShell 7.x.

- `-IncludeTypeInformation`: Use this if you *do* want to know the type of the object in the first line of the CSV stream.

- `-Delimiter`: We usually want our CSV file to use a comma as the field delimiter character, but sometimes we might need to produce a **Tab-Separated Values** (**TSV**) file using the tab delimiter, `` `t ``, or perhaps use a colon or semicolon. We can use this parameter to specify a different delimiter character – for example, in the following:

```
Get-Process | ConvertTo-Csv -delimiter ';'| Out-File C:\temp\
poshbook\ProcessesConvertTo.csv
```

- This is handy when we are converting `DateTime` objects, which in some **UI cultures**, include a comma in the value for `"DateTime"`; `"Monday, August 6, 2022 17:55"`.

- `-UseQuotes`: This parameter controls how the cmdlet applies double-quote characters. By default, every value is double-quoted, turning it into a string, but sometimes we might want to keep the values as integers or floating point numbers. We can use this parameter to control the quoting behavior.

- `-QuoteFields`: If we need even finer control over quoting behavior, we can specify the fields in which we want the values to be double-quoted. The first line of the CSV file is the field names and it may take a bit of experimentation to get this right.

Once we've converted our objects into a CSV datastream, we can either pipe it to `Out-File` or consume it in some other way; for instance, we might want to create a number of CSV objects and then aggregate and manipulate them before outputting a single file.

Export-Csv

The `Export-Csv` cmdlet combines `ConvertTo-Csv` with `Out-File` in a single cmdlet. It has the same interesting parameters that we've already discussed for those cmdlets. Here are the matching `Out-File` parameters:

- `-Path (instead of -FilePath)`

- `-Force`

- `-NoClobber`

- `-Encoding`

- `-Append`

Here are the parameters from `ConvertTo-Csv`:

- `-Delimiter`

- `-NoTypeInformation`

- `-IncludeTypeInformation`

- `-QuoteFields`
- `-UseQuotes`

The parameters for `Export-Csv` work the same as the equivalent parameters in `ConvertTo-Csv` and `Out-File`. There are no aliases for `Export-Csv`.

XML

eXtensible Markup Language (**XML**) is a specialized language intended to be both machine- and human-readable. It's handy for transferring data structures across networks and between systems. *Figure 6.1* at the start of this chapter is an example of XML. We'll be seeing more of it as we go through the book, but for now, all we need to know is that there are two cmdlets associated with writing objects as XML data – `ConvertTo-Xml` and `Export-Clixml`.

ConvertTo-Xml

This cmdlet only has a handful of parameters:

- `-As`: This parameter allows us to specify the output format; whether it's a single string, an array of strings, or an `XmlDocument` object.
- `-Depth`: We can use this to limit the number of levels and sublevels the document can contain. By default, this isn't specified.
- `-NoTypeInformation`: This stops the object type information from being written.

Export-Clixml

Common Language Infrastructure XML (**Clixml**) can be used to store objects in a file and then recreate those objects from the file. The `Export-Clixml` cmdlet is pretty simple. It has one of the `ConvertTo-Xml` parameters, `-Depth`, and then the following `Out-File` parameters:

- `-Path` (instead of `-FilePath`)
- `-Force`
- `-NoClobber`
- `-Encoding`

Let's create an XML file we can use later:

```
Get-Date |Export-Clixml -Path C:\temp\poshbook\date.xml
```

Try opening that in an editor such as notepad or VS Code. You should see something like the following:

```
1   <Objs Version="1.1.0.1" xmlns="http://schemas.microsoft.com/powershell/2004/04">
2     <Obj RefId="0">
3       <DT>2022-08-09T15:57:54.1378531+01:00</DT>
4       <MS>
5         <Obj N="DisplayHint" RefId="1">
6           <TN RefId="0">
7             <T>Microsoft.PowerShell.Commands.DisplayHintType</T>
8             <T>System.Enum</T>
9             <T>System.ValueType</T>
10            <T>System.Object</T>
11          </TN>
12          <ToString>DateTime</ToString>
13          <I32>2</I32>
14        </Obj>
15      </MS>
16    </Obj>
17  </Objs>
```

Figure 6.5 – A date represented in XML

The important bit is line 3. That's the actual data; the rest is formatting information and information about the type of object. Keep this file and we'll use it later in the chapter.

HTML

It is really useful to be able to convert our PowerShell output into HTML, as we can display it in a web browser. This is a popular technique for writing reports in system administration. We can use it to produce dashboards and other online reports. There are better techniques for creating data that can be consumed by web APIs and we'll be looking at those in the next chapter. There is only one cmdlet for creating HTML code; `ConvertTo-Html`. If we want to write it to a file, we'll need to use `Out-File`. Try this:

```
Get-Date | ConvertTo-Html | Out-File -FilePath C:\temp\poshbook\date.
html
```

If you then open `Date.html` in your web browser, you should see something like this:

DisplayHint	DateTime	Date	Day	DayOfWeek	DayOfYear	Hour	Kind
DateTime	09 August 2022 16:45:01	09/08/2022 00:00:00	9	Tuesday	221	16	Local

Figure 6.6 – A date as HTML

That's not particularly inspiring. Let's take a closer look at the cmdlet to see whether we can make it more interesting

ConvertTo-Html

The `ConvertTo-Html` cmdlet has quite a few interesting parameters that we can use to format our output:

- `-As`: This parameter allows us to format the output as a table or as a list. By default, we get a table.

- `-Body`: This allows us to add text after the opening `<body>` tag. This is the main part of any web page. We're not going to explain how HTML works here – if you would like a refresher on HTML, then `https://www.w3schools.com/` is an excellent and free online resource.

- `-Head`: This allows us to write text in the `<head>` section.

- `-Title`: This allows us to give the page a title. Unlike `-Body` and `-Head`, it only takes a single string.

- `-PreContent`: This allows us to write text before the table we create.

- `-PostContent`: This allows us to add text after the table.

- `-Meta`: This allows us to add metatags to the head.

- `-Fragment`: This omits the `<head>` and `<body >` tags and just writes the HTML to produce the table. This is handy if we are going to concatenate a bunch of fragments into one single web page.

- `-CssUri`: This allows us to specify a CSS file to provide additional formatting, such as different fonts, background colors, and so on. I encourage you to have a look at `http://www.csszengarden.com/` to see some of the amazing things we can do with CSS.

Let's have a play. Open a new file in VS Code, select CSS as the language, and type the following exactly as written:

```
Table {
    color: blue ;
    text-align: center;
    background-color: bisque;
}

Body {
    background-color: cadetblue;
    font-family: 'Trebuchet MS';
    color: yellow;
}
```

Save it as `style.css` in your working directory, `C:\temp\poshbook`.

Create a new PowerShell file in the same directory and try this:

```
$params = @{
    As = 'List'
    Title = 'My Date Page'
    Body = 'Here is my Date'
    CssUri = 'Style.css'
}
Get-Date | ConvertTo-Html @params | Out-File C:\temp\poshbook\
FancyDate.Html
C:\temp\poshbook\FancyDate.html
```

If you select and run your code, you should see the following output:

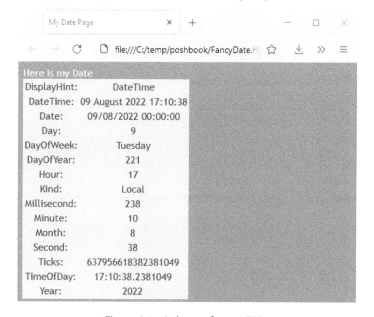

Figure 6.7 – A date as fancy HTML

There is a great article on how to write HTML documents in PowerShell here: https://leanpub.com/creatinghtmlreportsinwindowspowershell/read.

That's a good start on how to create files. Next, let's briefly divert to PSProviders, PSDrives, and the New-Item cmdlet.

Handling files

Before we can work with files, we need to be able to find them, and understand how PowerShell works with hierarchical data structures such as filesystems.

A brief note about PSProviders and PSDrives

PowerShell connects to data structures through software called **providers**. These allow PowerShell to present a data structure as a filesystem (including the filesystem). On Windows, this allows us to search for and manipulate objects in the Registry and the Certificate Store as if they were files. Arguably, it is less useful on Linux. Let's have a look. Run this:

```
Get-PSProvider
```

You should see a list of providers and associated drives. We can connect to the associated drive with the Set-Location cmdlet:

```
Set-Location Env:
```

Note we have to use the name of the drive, not the name of the provider, and we need to follow it with a colon.

Once in the data structure, we can use Get-ChildItem to search for objects, as in the following screenshot, which lists out the environment variables as if they were filesystem objects:

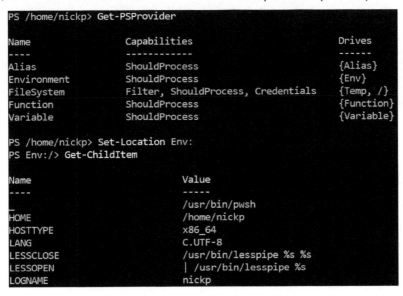

Figure 6.8 – The environment provider

Providers are dynamic; that is, they don't need to know what is in the store before connecting to it and so they are popular as a way of providing access to data structures. While there are only a few included in PowerShell by default, you will find that some modules will add new providers, especially in Windows. For instance, if we install the ActiveDirectory module, then we will have access to an AD: drive containing the Active Directory data.

Note that just installing the provider is not enough. We also need to have a drive object before we can browse it. The drive is the thing we work with; the provider is the software that lets us access it. Most modules will create the required drive as well as install the provider. We can create our own drives quite easily. In my home directory on my Ubuntu machine, I have a directory called `MyFiles`. I can make this a drive by running the following:

```
New-PsDrive -Name MyFiles -Root /home/nickp -PSProvider FileSystem
```

Then, I can browse the `MyFiles:` drive, like so:

```
PS Env:/> New-PSDrive -Name MyFiles -Root /home/nickp -PSProvider FileSystem

Name            Used (GB)     Free (GB) Provider     Root                                  Current
                                                                                           Locatio
                                                                                                 n

----            ---------     --------- --------     ----                                  -------
MyFiles            106.85      369.04 FileSystem     /home/nickp

PS Env:/> Get-ChildItem MyFiles:

    Directory: /home/nickp

UnixMode   User          Group          LastWriteTime         Size Name
--------   ----          -----          -------------         ---- ----
drwxr-xr-x nickp         nickp          04/28/2022 13:02       512 myfiles
-rw-r--r-- nickp         nickp          06/23/2022 15:09        10 newstuff
-rw-r--r-- nickp         nickp          03/25/2022 00:15      3690 packages-microsof
                                                                  t-prod.deb
-r--r--r-- nickp         nickp          04/29/2022 14:11        15 processes.txt
-rw-r--r-- nickp         nickp          06/23/2022 15:15         0 System.Collection
                                                                  s.Hashtable
```

Figure 6.9 – Creating a new drive

Item- cmdlets

We use the `-Item` and `-Childitem` cmdlets to move around the filesystem and find items. We're not going to cover them in detail here, as they are self-explanatory. Read the associated help files to understand their simple syntax:

- `Get-ChildItem` lists the items found in a location:

    ```
    Get-ChildItem -Path C:\Windows
    ```

- `Copy-Item` lets us make a copy of an item in a different location:

    ```
    Copy-Item -Path 'C:\Temp\File.txt'  -Destination 'C:\New'
    ```

- `Move-Item` lets us move an item to a different location:

    ```
    Move-Item -Path 'C:\Temp\File.txt'  -Destination 'C:\New'
    ```

- Rename-Item lets us change the name of an item:

    ```
    Rename-Item -Path 'C:\New\File.txt' -NewName 'NewFile.txt'
    ```

- Remove-Item lets us delete an item:

    ```
    Remove-Item -Path 'C:\New\NewFile.txt'
    ```

- Get-Item lists the item and its value; it doesn't get the contents. Most of the time, we want to use Get-ChildItem instead when we're working in the filesystem, but if we wanted to know the value of an environment variable, then we would use this cmdlet. Try this. Type the following:

    ```
    Get-Item -Path C:\temp\poshbook
    ```

    Then, try this and see the difference:

    ```
    Get-ChildItem -Path C:\temp\poshbook
    ```

    Get-Item has returned the properties of the C:\temp\poshbook folder, whereas Get-ChildItem has returned the folder and its contents.

- Set-Item: Again, this is not hugely useful in the filesystem. However, if we wanted to change the value of an environment variable or an alias, then we would use this cmdlet.

- New-Item: We can use this to create files and folders, as well as create new aliases and variables:

    ```
    New-Item -Path C:\New\File.txt
    ```

- Invoke-Item: Performs the default action on an item. For instance, if it's an executable file, it will run it. If it is a TXT file, it will open the file in the default text editor:

    ```
    Invoke-Item -Path C:\temp\poshbook\FancyDate.html
    ```

There are also two cmdlets for moving around in and between drives; Get-Location and Set-Location. Many of these cmdlets have aliases associated with them that echo the equivalent bash and Windows commands – for instance, Get-ChildItem can be called by using ls or dir. Note, however, that the parameters are still those for PowerShell, not for the bash or Windows command. For example, Dir /p will not produce a paginated directory listing – it will produce an error.

Now that we know how to find our files and move them around, let's look at what is inside them.

Working with files

Using PowerShell to read the contents of files and manipulate that data is a common task. We're going to look at three cmdlets in this section. First, let's explore the generic Get-Content cmdlet.

Get-Content

The Get-Content cmdlet can get any type of data in a file and store it as an array of strings or bytes (as a bytestream). By default, each line in the file will be interpreted as a single string. We will only get meaningful content if the file can be interpreted as an array of strings; otherwise, we must fetch it as a bytestream. This is useful if we are getting the contents of an executable file, for example. It's got a few parameters. Here are the more interesting ones:

- -Path specifies the item we want. This accepts an array of string values so that we can concatenate multiple files into a single array.

- -TotalCount is the total number of lines to read from the file. The default is -1, which will read to the last line, but we can check just the first few lines of a file to make sure that it is as we expect it to be without loading the whole thing.

- -ReadCount is the number of lines that can be sent through the pipeline at a time.

- -AsByteStream allows us to get the content as bytes rather than as strings.

- -Credential allows us to supply alternative credentials to open the file.

- -Delimiter allows us to specify the character that is used to separate strings. By default, it is the newline character (`n), but we can use anything we like.

- -Encoding can be used to specify that the contents are encoded in a different format to the default; **UTF-8 with no Byte Order Mark (utf8NoBOM)**.

- -Raw will return the entire contents as a single string.

- -Tail is like -TotalCount, but works backward and gets lines from the end. We can't use it with -TotalCount.

Get-Content is similar in function to the cat command in Linux and, unsurprisingly, cat is an alias for it.

Get-content is one of the most common ways of bringing data into PowerShell so that we can work with it, but it's not very flexible. For instance, if we try to get a CSV file, then it will interpret the file as text, rather than a specially formatted file. Let's have a look at how we can import information in a structured way.

Import- cmdlets

Like the Export- cmdlets, the Import- cmdlets perform two operations at once. They combine Get-Content with a specialist parser that will interpret the information and format it correctly for the original file type, allowing us to manipulate something that looks like the original objects. Let's look at Import-Csv first.

Import-Csv

The `Import-Csv` cmdlet only has a few parameters:

- `-Delimiter`: Just in case the file is using something other than a comma to separate values
- `-Path`: To identify the file to be imported
- `-Header`: To specify manual column name information if your CSV file doesn't have it
- `-Encoding`: If your file has come from a system that didn't output it as `utf8NoBOM`.

The cmdlet expects the file to contain string objects and outputs `PSCustomObjects` with note properties that match the column headers in the original file. Let's have a play:

```
Get-Process | Export-Csv processes.csv
$procs = Import-Csv processes.csv
$procs.name
```

This will output the name values of each object in the array. The next command will show us that we haven't recreated process objects, we've created new `PSCustomObjects`:

```
$procs | Get-Member
```

The following command will retrieve the second element in the array. Because there is no default view or default properties list, all properties will be displayed:

```
$procs[1]
```

You should see something like this:

```
PS /home/nickp> Get-Process | Export-Csv processes.csv
PS /home/nickp> $procs = Import-Csv processes.csv
PS /home/nickp> $procs.name
bash
init
init
pwsh
PS /home/nickp> $procs | Get-Member

    TypeName: System.Management.Automation.PSCustomObject
```

Figure 6.10 – Importing a CSV file

Importing CSVs into PowerShell is great if you have, for instance, a list of users and you need to pipe them through a loop to get their home drive size, or you want to create a lookup table.

Import-Clixml

If you have an XML file that was generated by PowerShell, then you can use the `Import-Clixml` cmdlet to recreate something that looks much more like the original objects. There aren't many parameters to this cmdlet. Here are the most interesting ones:

- `-Path` specifies the file to be imported.

- `-Skip` allows us to skip a specified number of objects in the file.

- `-First` gets only a specified number of objects from the start of the file. Clixml files can be huge, so this is handy if we want to check what's inside.

- `-IncludeTotalCount` tells us how many objects are in the file. Interestingly, it has an accuracy property that tells us how reliable the estimate is.

Let's have a play with it. Try this:

```
Get-Date | Export-Clixml -Path date.xml
Notepad date.xml
$date = (Import-Clixml -Path date.xml)
$date | Get-Member
$date
```

We can see that what we get back is a date object. Let's try another one:

```
Get-Process | Export-Clixml processes.xml
$XmlProcs =Import-Clixml processes.xml
```

If we then call `$XmlProcs`, we can see that the output displays exactly as we'd expect for the `Get-Process` cmdlet:

```
PS /home/nickp> $XmlProcs

 NPM(K)    PM(M)      WS(M)     CPU(s)      Id  SI ProcessName
 ------    -----      -----     ------      --  -- -----------
      0     0.00       3.52       0.07    5500 ...99 bash
      0     0.00       0.32       0.10       1   1 init
      0     0.00       0.22       0.00    5499 ...99 init
      0     0.00     339.20      71.34    5565 ...99 pwsh
```

Figure 6.11 – Recreating objects with Import-Clixml

However, they're not quite the objects we exported. Let's run the following:

```
$XmlProcs | Get-Member
```

We can see that they are Deserialized.System.Diagnostics.Process objects. This tells us that they have been turned into a data object and then retrieved from a file, and they are not live objects.

One of the most common uses for this is to store credentials securely. Try this:

```
$cred = Get-Credential
```

We're asked to enter a username and password.

We can pipe the credential variable into an XML file:

```
$cred | Export-Clixml Credential.xml
```

That file can now be stored on a disk somewhere. It is encrypted by the Export-Clixml cmdlet.

We can then import it back using Import-Clixml:

```
$newcred = Import-Clixml Credential.xml
```

We get a credential object. You can see in the following screenshot what the XML file looks like. The password is the encrypted hex string:

```
PS /home/nickp> $cred = Get-Credential

PowerShell credential request
Enter your credentials.
User: nickp
Password for user nickp: *********

PS /home/nickp> $cred | Export-Clixml -Path Credential.xml
PS /home/nickp> Get-Content ./Credential.xml
<Objs Version="1.1.0.1" xmlns="http://schemas.microsoft.com/powershell/2004/04">
  <Obj RefId="0">
    <TN RefId="0">
      <T>System.Management.Automation.PSCredential</T>
      <T>System.Object</T>
    </TN>
    <ToString>System.Management.Automation.PSCredential</ToString>
    <Props>
      <S N="UserName">nickp</S>
      <SS N="Password">530063006f006f0070000310032003300e00</SS>
    </Props>
  </Obj>
</Objs>
PS /home/nickp> $newcred = Import-Clixml ./Credential.xml
PS /home/nickp> $newcred

UserName                    Password
--------                    --------
nickp      System.Security.SecureString
```

Figure 6.12 – Storing encrypted credentials

Note that the encryption uses our login credentials for the machine we were using when we encrypted the file. No other user can decrypt that easily and we can't then decrypt those credentials on another machine.

We can't use just import any XML file with `Import-Clixml`. If we try it with something that hasn't been correctly formatted for the cmdlet, we'll get an error, like this:

```
PS C:\Users\nickp> Import-Clixml .\DISM.psm1-help.xml
Import-Clixml: Element 'Objs' with namespace name 'http://schemas.
microsoft.com/powershell/2004/04' was not found. Line 2, position
2.
PS C:\Users\nickp>
```

Figure 6.13 – We can't import just anything

In this case, the schema of the XML file is incorrect for the `Import-Clixml` cmdlet; there are important lines missing, as we can see from the error message. Don't try running this code – you may well not have the DISM file referenced in the cmdlet.

That's about it for this chapter. Before we summarize, though, let's play around and consolidate some learning from this chapter and earlier chapters.

Let's have some fun – measuring the most frequent words in a text file

One of my favorite programming books is *Exercises in Programming Style* by Cristina Videira Lopes. It is inspired by the 1947 book by Raymond Queneau, *Exercices de Style*, in which the author tells the same story in 99 different styles. Lopes's book contains 41 Python programs that accomplish the same task with different programming styles. This book is truly mind-expanding and really changed the way I saw writing code; it is as much an art as any other form of creative writing. The book itself is not cheap, but all the programs are available on GitHub: `https://github.com/crista/exercises-in-programming-style`. I'd encourage you to have a quick look, even if you don't know any Python.

The problem each program solves is to determine the frequency of the words in a text file and sort them in descending order; this is an example of a **term frequency** problem, and it is a fairly common exercise given to computer science students. Let's have a go at it:

1. First, create a new folder in VS Code, and then create a new PowerShell file in your new folder called `wordcountBasic.ps1`

   The file I'm going to use is an English translation of Franz Kafka's classic, *The Trial*, but any large text file will do. I downloaded it from here: `https://www.gutenberg.org/ebooks/7849.txt.utf-8`

   Go ahead and download it and save it in your new folder as `thetrial.txt`.

2. Now that we have our data, the next thing to do is to putt the contents of the file into a variable. That's easy. We'll need to get it as a single huge string, rather than an array of strings:

    ```
    $TheTrial   =   Get-Content -Path .\thetrial.txt -Raw$TheTrial =
    get-content -path .\thetrial.txt -Raw
    ```

3. Now, we can use one of the methods available for string objects to split the text into an array of single-word strings:

    ```
    $TrialWords = $TheTrial.Split(" ")
    ```

    Notice that there's a space inside the pair of double quotes.

4. Let's see how many words we've got:

    ```
    $TrialWords.Length
    ```

    I get 79,978 words. This code may take a while to run.

5. Now… the next bit is tricky. We need to count how many times each word appears in the text. This is where the power of the shell really shines. Doing the next bit in Python would require a few lines of string manipulation, but PowerShell comes with a built-in cmdlet, Group-Object:

    ```
    $GroupedWords = $TrialWords | Group-Object
    ```

6. The trouble with that line is it will group the objects alphabetically, which is not what we want. We want them grouped by frequency, so we need a Sort-Object cmdlet in the pipeline as well:

    ```
    $GroupedWords = $TrialWords | Group-Object | Sort-Object Count
    ```

7. We also don't want to see all the words; we just want the most frequent words. Let's get the most frequent 10. We can use a formula of [-1..-10] to get them from the array. We're using [-1..-10] because by default, the sort order is ascending and we want it descending. We could run $GroupedWords[-1..-10].

8. And that's it! Here's my whole program and the output:

```
wordcountBasic.ps1 > ...
1    $TheTrial  =  Get-Content -Path .\thetrial.txt -Raw
2    $TrialWords = $TheTrial.Split(" ")
3    $GroupedWords = $TrialWords | Group-Object | Sort-Object Count
4    $GroupedWords[-1..-10]
```

PROBLEMS   OUTPUT   DEBUG CONSOLE   **TERMINAL**   JUPYTER

```
PS C:\temp\poshbook>
PS C:\temp\poshbook> . "c:\temp\poshbook\wordcountBasic.ps1"

Count Name                         Group
----- ----                         -----
 4081 The                          {The, The, the, the…}
 2566 to                           {to, to, to, to…}
 1642 he                           {he, he, he, he…}
 1640 and                          {and, and, and, and…}
 1502 of                           {of, of, of, of…}
 1201 a                            {a, a, a, a…}
 1130 in                           {in, in, in, in…}
  993 was                          {was, was, was, was…}
  920 That                         {That, that, that, that…}
  857 his                          {his, his, his, his…}
```

Figure 6.14 – The ten most frequent words in any English book (written by a man)

We've achieved something here, although it's probably not what we wanted to achieve. It looks to me like the list of the 10 most frequent words in any book in English, written by a man. What can we do about that?

The computer science discipline of **Natural Language Processing** involves the concept of **stop words**. These are common words in a language that shouldn't be counted when analyzing the text. There are plenty of lists of stop words available on the internet for free. What we need to do is build a loop that compares each word in the array to a list of stop words and only adds them to a new array if they are *not* in the list.

> **Activity**
>
> Rewrite the program using a loop to compare each word in the `$TrialWords` array to the words in a list of stop words. Use the stop words file at `https://raw.githubusercontent.com/stopwords-iso/stopwords-en/master/stopwords-en.txt`.
>
> Hint 1:
>
> You won't want to use a PowerShell array for this – why? It's probably best to use an array list. Construct it like this:
>
> `$Words = [System.Collections.ArrayList]@()`
>
> Hint 2:
>
> You will need to split the array on more characters than just a space because of words that have full stops and other punctuation immediately after them. For some characters, you'll need to use an escape character – the backtick (`) – for them to be interpreted properly. I found replacing the second line in the preceding code with this line to be effective:
>
> `$TestWords = $TheTrial.Split(" ", "`t", "`n", ",","`"",".",`
> [System.StringSplitOptions]::RemoveEmptyEntries)`
>
> `RemoveEmptyEntries` prevents null strings from being counted.
>
> `t is the tab character.
>
> `n is the newline character.
>
> ` " allows us to use a double quote mark as a delimiter.
>
> Hint 3:
>
> Is `That` the same word as `that`? You will want to make sure that all the characters in your words are in the same case.

Have fun! I've written one way to do it at the end.

Summary

This is quite a long chapter and it is really only an introduction. We will cover more ways of ingesting data with PowerShell as we go through the book. We've come a long way, though.

We started out by looking at how we can format output for the screen using three common formatting cmdlets: `Format-List`, `Format-Table`, and `Format-Wide`. We then looked at how we could output that formatted data to a text file with `Out-File`. We took some time to understand the limitations of this approach before we explored two families of cmdlets: `ConvertTo-` and `Export-`.

We took quite a deep look at the cmdlets for handling CSV files, `ConvertTo-Csv` and `Export-Csv`, and understood how the `ExportTo-Csv` cmdlet combines the `ConvertTo-Csv` and `Out-File` cmdlets. We then looked at `ConvertTo-Xml` and `Export-Clixml`. Finally, we looked at `ConvertTo-Html` and experimented with how we can use it to produce interestingly formatted documents by referencing a CSS file.

We then briefly discussed `PSProviders` and `PSdrives` and understood that these are more useful in a Windows environment, but are still relevant for Linux and macOS.

We looked at `Get-Content`, the most common way of bringing data into PowerShell, and learned that it produces either an array of strings or bytes – to import data in a more structured way, we would need to use something else: the `Import-` cmdlets. We looked at `Import-Csv` and `Import-Clixml` and saw how they can be used to construct PowerShell objects from structured data.

Finally, we did some programming and looked at how we can analyze text files using PowerShell.

In the next chapter, we will be looking at how we can use PowerShell to interact with systems on the internet and the common file formats we will need.

Exercises

1. How would you produce a wide list of the names of all the files in your temp directory, with three columns?

2. What will happen if we run this code?

    ```
    Get-Process | Format-Wide -column 5 | Where-Object id -gt 100
    ```

3. Using PowerShell, write an `"I love PowerShell"` string to a new file in the directory you are working in.

4. Add a "`Sooo much`" string to the file from *question 3*.

5. Write a statement to create a file containing all the items in your working directory to a CSV file, but separated with semicolons rather than commas.

6. How many functions are defined in your PowerShell session?

7. How would you import the text file from *question 4* using a space as a string separator?

8. How would you import the file you created in *question 5* and what sort of objects would you get?

9. What does the following error tell us?

    ```
    Import-Clixml: Element 'Objs' with namespace name 'http://
    schemas.microsoft.com/powershell/2004/04' was not found.
    ```

Further reading

We really should read all the help files for the cmdlets we've used in this chapter. We know how to find them, so we're not going to list them here.

*   To learn about HTML and CSS, go to the W3Schools website: `https://www.w3schools.com/`

*   To learn more about Serialization, have a look here: `https://docs.microsoft.com/en-us/dotnet/standard/serialization/introducing-xml-serialization`

7
PowerShell and the Web – HTTP, REST, and JSON

Up until now, we've worked in a very small space – our client machine. It's nice, but the world doesn't work like that. Pretty much every device we use is connected to other machines and also, usually, the internet. Devices need to be able to interact with services provided over the web to download data, interact with cloud applications, and play games. In this, chapter we're going to look at ways we can use PowerShell to work with objects in the world outside our box.

We'll start out with a brief chat about web services and then look at the basic PowerShell tool for interacting with them; `Invoke-WebRequest`. We'll go on to look at **Application Programming Interfaces** (**APIs**). We'll talk about the dominant type of API in use today – **Representational State Transfer** (**REST**). Once we've got a good grip on that and the tool we can use to work with it, `Invoke-RestMethod`, we'll look at some of the ways of exchanging information with web services using **JavaScript Object Notation** (**JSON**), and the tools we use to convert JSON data into PowerShell objects, and vice versa. Finally, we'll tackle a short exercise.

This chapter will give us the basic techniques we'll need for some of the work we'll do in later chapters of the book and build on some of the work we did in the last chapter. We'll see that those techniques apply to data on the web as well.

In this chapter we are going to cover the following main topics:

- Working with HTTP
- Getting to grips with APIs
- Working with REST
- Working with JSON

Working with HTTP

The world we live in has a dominant philosophy, a set of concepts and practices that has largely defined information technology for the last 30 years; the client/server paradigm. There are alternatives; centralized computing with dumb terminals, such as mainframe computing, thin client computing with applications such as Citrix, or peer-to-peer computing such as we might see in BitTorrent or blockchain applications. Tim Berners-Lee envisaged the World Wide Web as a peer-to-peer network, but it hasn't really stayed that way. The client/server model is prevalent. In general, the device on our desk or in our hands is the client, and it is connected to a remote server to receive or manipulate information. It differs from a dumb terminal in that some of the processing is carried out on the client, and some of it on the server.

In this chapter, we're going to look at how information is exchanged between clients and servers on the internet using the foundational protocol of the World Wide Web; **Hypertext Transfer Protocol (HTTP)**. This is the protocol we use to browse websites.

The basic cmdlet for working with HTTP in PowerShell is `Invoke-WebRequest`, so let's have a look at how we can use the `Invoke-WebRequest` cmdlet to work with data on the web.

The `Invoke-WebRequest` cmdlet is an incredibly versatile tool that allows us to create an HTTP request and submit it to a web service. Because the range of requests we might make is huge, the cmdlet is pretty complicated, with over thirty parameters. Let's start with the simple stuff. Let's get a list of hyperlinks to relevant news topics. In a web browser, go to this address: `https://neuters.de`. This is a text-based website that aggregates the most recent Reuters news articles. It's nice and simple.

Now, open PowerShell and type the following:

```
$News = Invoke-WebRequest https://neuters.de
```

This will send a GET request to the address and store the response in the $News variable.

Now let's see what we've got by calling the contents of $News. Type this:

```
$News
```

You should see something that looks like the following figure:

```
PS C:\Users\nickp> $News = Invoke-WebRequest https://neuters.de
PS C:\Users\nickp> $News


StatusCode        : 200
StatusDescription : OK
Content           : <!DOCTYPE html><html lang="en"><head><title>Neuters - Reuters Proxy</title><link rel="stylesheet"
                    href="/main.css?v=0"><meta name="viewport" content="width=device-width, initial-scale=1"></head><body>…
RawContent        : HTTP/1.1 200 OK
                    Server: nginx
                    Date: Thu, 20 Oct 2022 09:57:31 GMT
                    Connection: keep-alive
                    Keep-Alive: timeout=5
                    Vary: Accept-Encoding
                    Content-Type: text/html; charset=utf-8
                    Content-Length: 1760…
Headers           : {[Server, System.String[]], [Date, System.String[]], [Connection, System.String[]], [Keep-Alive,
                    System.String[]]…}
Images            : {}
InputFields       : {}
Links             : {@{outerHTML=<a
                    href="/business/energy/americas-new-nuclear-power-industry-has-russian-problem-2022-10-20/">America's new
                    nuclear power industry has a Russian problem</a>; tagName=A;
                    href=/business/energy/americas-new-nuclear-power-industry-has-russian-problem-2022-10-20/},
                    @{outerHTML=<a href="/world/europe/ukraine-curbs-power-usage-after-russian-attacks-destroy-some-energy-pla
                    nts-2022-10-19/">Ukrainian forces push toward Kherson, Kyiv orders electricity curbs</a>; tagName=A; href=
                    /world/europe/ukraine-curbs-power-usage-after-russian-attacks-destroy-some-energy-plants-2022-10-19/},
```

Figure 7.1 – Invoke-WebRequest gets the HTTP response

That's great, but it's not pretty. If we look a little closer at our output, we can see that one of the sections is called Links. We can use that to just get the hyperlinks from the page by calling it like this:

```
$News.Links
```

Unfortunately, they are all relative links, but we should turn them into absolute links by adding the root location, which we can do quite easily. If we pipe the output of $News.Links to Get-Member, we can see that it has a property called href, which just contains the link, as follows:

```
Name        MemberType   Definition
----        ----------   ----------
Equals      Method       bool Equals(System.Object obj)
GetHashCode Method       int GetHashCode()
GetType     Method       type GetType()
ToString    Method       string ToString()
href        NoteProperty string href=/world/us/bidens-strategic-silence-trump-may-be-tested-days-ahead-2023-04-02/
```

Figure 7.2 – href property

We can concatenate that with the root domain. Type the following code:

```
$News.Links | Foreach {"https://neuters.de" + $_.href}
```

And you should see a list of absolute links, like in the following figure:

```
PS C:\Users\nickp> $News.Links | Foreach {"https://neuters.de" + $_.href}
https://neuters.de/world/europe/russian-commander-admits-situation-is-tense-his-forces-ukraine-2022-10-19/
https://neuters.de/world/uk/uk-pm-truss-tries-reassert-authority-rebellion-grows-2022-10-19/
https://neuters.de/markets/europe/global-markets-view-usa-2022-10-19/
https://neuters.de/world/middle-east/iranian-climber-elnaz-rekabi-cheered-by-fans-return-iran-2022-10-19/
https://neuters.de/business/energy/exclusive-us-says-russia-oil-price-cap-will-not-be-aimed-opec-2022-10-19/
https://neuters.de/business/autos-transportation/investor-group-unions-push-hyundai-address-child-labor-us-suppliers-202
2-10-19/
https://neuters.de/markets/us/us-awards-28-billion-ev-battery-grid-projects-2022-10-19/
https://neuters.de/world/uk/uk-consumer-price-inflation-101-september-ons-2022-10-19/
https://neuters.de/
https://neuters.de/search
https://neuters.de/about
```

Figure 7.3 – Scraping the neuters.de site for links

If you got something like that, congratulations, you have just **scraped** your first website with PowerShell. Scraping is the process of automating the retrieval of data from a website.

`Invoke-WebRequest` has only one mandatory parameter; `-Uri`. It is positional, so any string following the cmdlet will be treated as an input for this parameter. The `-Uri` parameter accepts the URL of the source.

> **URI versus URL**
>
> We are probably all familiar with the acronym **URL**, which is short for **Uniform Resource Locator**. We may be less familiar with **URI**, which is short for **Uniform Resource Identifier**. URI is an umbrella term that consists of two different ways to identify a resource; it may be either a name (**Uniform Resource Name (URN)**) or a location (URL). A URL always provides the location of the resource. URLs are a subset of URIs, consist of a scheme and a path, and may include other elements. The schemes we are probably most familiar with are `http:` and `https:`, so an absolute URL would be `https://neuters.de`, containing both the scheme (`https:`) and the address (`neuters.de`) separated by a double slash (`//`).
>
> What about URNs, though? A URN consists of the scheme (`urn:`), one or more **namespace identifiers** (**NIDs**), and a **namespace-specific string** (**NSS**). An example would be `urn:ietf:rfc:1149`, which identifies my favorite protocol definition.
>
> The twist is that the `-Uri` parameter only supports the `http:` and `https:` schemes, so can only accept URLs. However, according to the World Wide Web Consortium, the international standards authority for the web, URI is a more precise and technically correct term than URL.

Let's take a closer look at some of the parameters that we can use with `Invoke-WebRequest`:

- `-Method` will accept any of the standard HTTP methods: GET, PUT, POST, DELETE, and a few others. If we omit it, then the default method is GET. If we need to use a custom method, then we can use the `-CustomMethod` parameter. We can't use both `-Method` and `-CustomMethod` in the same cmdlet. This parameter allows us to send information to a web address.

- `-OutFile` specifies a path and name to write the output to a file. Note this only writes the response HTML to the file, not things such as the response code. This parameter prevents the output from being placed in the pipeline. If we want the output to be available to the pipeline and to be written to a file, then we need to use the `-PassThru` parameter as well.

- `-Headers` can be used to submit specific header information as part of the web request. The information must take the form of a hashtable or dictionary.

- `-Body` can submit specific body content, such as a query. We can't use `-Body` and `-Form` in the same cmdlet.

- `-Form`. The `-Form` parameter is used to submit information to an HTML form at the target address. We can find lots of information on the web about how to use the `-Form` parameter to quickly and easily log in to websites using Windows PowerShell. Unfortunately, most of them don't work with PowerShell 7 because the HTML is parsed differently. We'll discover why shortly.

- `-Proxy` allows us to specify an alternative proxy server to the one set on our client. It is normally used with either the `-ProxyUseDefaultCredentials` parameter, which passes the current user credentials to the proxy, or with the `-ProxyCredentials` parameter, which allows us to specify alternative credentials.

- `-NoProxy` lets us bypass the client proxy altogether. We can't use it in the same cmdlet as `-Proxy`.

- `-SessionVariable` can be used when connecting to a stateful web service; we can use the `-SessionVariable` the first time we run `Invoke-WebRequest`, and then use the `-WebSession` parameter with the same value for each subsequent connection to ensure we persist the session state. This is useful if we need to log in to a web service before using it. Note that we supply a string to `-SessionVariable`, but then supply the string as a variable to `-Websession`, like so:

```
Invoke-WebRequest -Uri https://reddit.com -SessionVariable sv
Invoke-WebRequest -Uri https://reddit.com/settings -WebSession
$sv
```

- `-SkipCertificateCheck` will ignore SSL/TLS certificate problems. For obvious reasons, we shouldn't use this parameter unless we are sure that the site we are connecting to is secure, and any certificate problems we see are not a sign of a problem. Sometimes, a certificate problem is fairly innocuous and may be down to a harried admin who hasn't renewed their certificate, and sometimes it's malicious.

- `-SkipHttpErrorCheck`: By default, if `Invoke-WebRequest` gets a HTTP error code as a response, it will report it as an error, in red, rather than as an output. If we want to capture the error response and process it, then we can use this parameter. For an example, see the following figure:

```
PS C:\Users\nickp> Invoke-WebRequest https://google.com -Method OPTIONS
Invoke-WebRequest:


 Error 405 (Method Not Allowed)!!1

    *{margin:0;padding:0}html,code{font:15px/22px arial,sans-serif}html{background:#fff;color:#2
auto 0;max-width:390px;min-height:180px;padding:30px 0 15px}* > body{background:url(//www.google
00% 5px no-repeat;padding-right:205px}p{margin:11px 0 22px;overflow:hidden}ins{color:#777;text-d
media screen and (max-width:772px){body{background:none;margin-top:0;max-width:none;padding-righ
.google.com/images/branding/googlelogo/1x/googlelogo_color_150x54dp.png) no-repeat;margin-left:-
-resolution:192dpi){#logo{background:url(//www.google.com/images/branding/googlelogo/2x/googlelo
t 0% 0%/100% 100%;-moz-border-image:url(//www.google.com/images/branding/googlelogo/2x/googlelog
 only screen and (-webkit-min-device-pixel-ratio:2){#logo{background:url(//www.google.com/images
ogo_color_150x54dp.png) no-repeat;-webkit-background-size:100% 100%}}#logo{display:inline-block;


 405. That's an error.
  The request method OPTIONS is inappropriate for the URL /.  That's all we know.
PS C:\Users\nickp> Invoke-WebRequest https://google.com -Method OPTIONS -SkipHttpErrorCheck

StatusCode       : 405
StatusDescription : MethodNotAllowed
Content          : <!DOCTYPE html>
                   <html lang=en>
```

Figure 7.4 – Using -SkipHttpErrorCheck

In the figure here, the first cmdlet, in the red box, doesn't use the -SkipHttpErrorCheck parameter, so PowerShell treats the response as an error. In the second cmdlet, in the green box, we've used the parameter and we can see the actual HTTP response that the server sent.

There are another thirty parameters we can use with Invoke-WebRequest but these are the most commonly used ones. Let's take a look at why the -Form parameter isn't as useful in PowerShell 7.

Why don't we see Forms information in PowerShell 7?

As we mentioned, the -Form parameter doesn't work as well in PowerShell 7 as it does in Windows PowerShell. If we examine the objects returned by Invoke-WebRequest with Get-Member, we can't see the Forms property in PowerShell 7 but we can in Windows PowerShell. It's worth taking a closer look and understanding why. The Invoke-WebRequest cmdlet produces different types of objects in PowerShell 7 and Windows PowerShell. We can see in the following figure the difference in output. In the upper blue frame, we can see that Windows PowerShell produces objects with a TypeName of HtmlWebResponseObject, and we can see the properties of this type include Forms:

```
PS C:\Users\nickp> $reddit = Invoke-WebRequest -Uri 'https://www.reddit.com/login'
PS C:\Users\nickp> $reddit | gm


   TypeName: Microsoft.PowerShell.Commands.HtmlWebResponseObject

Name            MemberType Definition
----            ---------- ----------
Dispose         Method     void Dispose(), void IDisposable.Dispose()
Equals          Method     bool Equals(System.Object obj)
GetHashCode     Method     int GetHashCode()
GetType         Method     type GetType()
ToString        Method     string ToString()
AllElements     Property   Microsoft.PowerShell.Commands.WebCmdletElementCollection AllElements {get;}
BaseResponse    Property   System.Net.WebResponse BaseResponse {get;set;}
Content         Property   string Content {get;}
Forms           Property   Microsoft.PowerShell.Commands.FormObjectCollection Forms {get;}
Headers         Property   System.Collections.Generic.Dictionary[string,string] Headers {get;}
Images          Property   Microsoft.PowerShell.Commands.WebCmdletElementCollection Images {get;}
InputFields     Property   Microsoft.PowerShell.Commands.WebCmdletElementCollection InputFields {get;}
Links           Property   Microsoft.PowerShell.Commands.WebCmdletElementCollection Links {get;}
```

Figure 7.5 – Invoke-WebRequest in Windows PowerShell

In PowerShell 7, next, we can see that we get a `BasicHtmlWebResponseObject`, which doesn't have a `Forms` property:

```
PS C:\Users\nickp> $reddit = Invoke-WebRequest -Uri 'https://www.reddit.com/login'
PS C:\Users\nickp> $reddit | gm


   TypeName: Microsoft.PowerShell.Commands.BasicHtmlWebResponseObject

Name                 MemberType Definition
----                 ---------- ----------
Equals               Method     bool Equals(System.Object obj)
GetHashCode          Method     int GetHashCode()
GetType              Method     type GetType()
ToString             Method     string ToString()
BaseResponse         Property   System.Net.Http.HttpResponseMessage BaseResponse {get;set;}
Content              Property   string Content {get;}
Encoding             Property   System.Text.Encoding Encoding {get;}
Headers              Property   System.Collections.Generic.Dictionary[string,System.Collections.G
Images               Property   Microsoft.PowerShell.Commands.WebCmdletElementCollection Images {
InputFields          Property   Microsoft.PowerShell.Commands.WebCmdletElementCollection InputFie
Links                Property   Microsoft.PowerShell.Commands.WebCmdletElementCollection Links {g
RawContent           Property   string RawContent {get;set;}
RawContentLength     Property   long RawContentLength {get;}
RawContentStream     Property   System.IO.MemoryStream RawContentStream {get;}
RelationLink         Property   System.Collections.Generic.Dictionary[string,string] RelationLink
StatusCode           Property   int StatusCode {get;}
StatusDescription    Property   string StatusDescription {get;}

PS C:\Users\nickp> |
```

Figure 7.6 – Invoke-WebRequest in PowerShell 7

This is because PowerShell 7 uses basic parsing by default.

In Windows PowerShell, we can use the information held in the Forms property of the web page to create a variable with properties that match the fields on the form, and then submit the variable as part of our cmdlet, using the -Form parameter. Because the objects returned by Invoke-WebRequest don't have a property called Forms, many of the instructions found on the internet for using the cmdlet this way won't work in PowerShell 7.

That doesn't mean we can't use Invoke-WebRequest to fill in forms, however. We just need to understand what the form fields are beforehand; we will struggle to work it out with PowerShell 7 alone. We also need to be aware that many of the examples we see on the internet are written for the Windows PowerShell version of the Invoke-WebRequest cmdlet.

Authentication

Many websites use some form of authentication, so authentication is a big part of Invoke-WebRequest. The first thing to do is to set the type of authentication in use. We can use the -UseDefaultCredentials parameter to try and authenticate with the current environment login, but if we're using an external address, rather than something inside our organization, then we will probably need to supply site-specific information. The -Authentication parameter accepts the following:

- None: This is the default. If the -Authentication parameter is not filled, then Invoke-WebRequest will not use any authentication.

- Basic: This will send a Base64-encoded set of credentials. Hopefully, we're connecting to an HTTPS URL, because Base64 encoding is not the same as encryption. This is not a very secure way of sending credentials. We will also need to use the -Credential parameter to supply the username and password.

- Bearer: This will require a Bearer token to be supplied as a secure string using the -Token parameter. A token is basically a long string that can be used to identify the sender of the request. Bearer authentication is an HTTP authentication scheme that was developed as part of OAuth 2.0 – the Open Authorization standard. Not all bearer authentication is OAuth, however. Because we are passing a token assigned by the remote server, it should only be used over HTTPS so that it is encrypted.

- Oauth: This is an open standard for access delegation. It's used by many big internet companies such as Amazon, Google, and Microsoft to provide authorization and authentication. Usually, it takes a bearer token, as mentioned previously.

Let's have a look at how this works. On my client, I've installed PowerShell Universal, a module from the good people at Ironman Software (https://blog.ironmansoftware.com/). This lets me run a lightweight server on my client and create endpoints.

> **Don't try to do this on your client**
>
> It takes quite a lot of configuration that we're not going to cover in this book and requires a subscription to use the authentication functions. I'm including it here so that we can see how the process works.

I've created an endpoint at `http://localhost:5000/me` that requires an authentication token to access. I've created the token on the server, and stored it as a secure string as follows:

```
$apptoken = ConvertTo-SecureString -String <mytoken> -AsPlainText
```

The token isn't really `<mytoken>`; it's a very much longer random string. Now I can access the endpoint by providing the token using the `$apptoken` variable:

```
Invoke-WebRequest -Uri http://localhost:5000/me -Authentication Bearer
-Token $apptoken
```

As we can see in the following figure, without supplying authentication, I get a `401` error; I'm unauthorized. When I supply authentication in the second cmdlet, I get the content of the page, `Hello World`:

```
PS C:\Users\nickp> Invoke-WebRequest -Uri http://localhost:5000/me
Invoke-WebRequest: Response status code does not indicate success: 401 (Unauthorized).
PS C:\Users\nickp> Invoke-WebRequest -Uri http://localhost:5000/me -Authentication Bearer -Token $apptoken

StatusCode        : 200
StatusDescription : OK
Content           : Hello World
RawContent        : HTTP/1.1 200 OK
                    Date: Tue, 25 Oct 2022 16:23:14 GMT
                    Server: Kestrel
                    Cache-Control: no-cache
                    Transfer-Encoding: chunked
                    Content-Type: application/json

                    Hello World
```

Figure 7.7 – Providing authentication using the -Authentication and -Token parameters

Quite often, however, we will need to provide authentication via the `-Headers` parameter. This is a little more involved than using `-Authentication`. We need to provide the token as part of the web request but point it to the correct header. In the case of my local test endpoint, I can do it like this:

```
Invoke-WebRequest -Uri http://localhost:5000/me -Headers @
{Authorization = "Bearer $admtoken"}
```

Note that if we supply the token in the header, we must *not* encode it using the `ConvertTo-SecureString` cmdlet. I've saved the unencoded token as `$admtoken`, (not `$apptoken`) as we can see here:

```
PS C:\Users\nickp> Invoke-WebRequest -Uri http://localhost:5000/me -Headers @{ Authorization = "Bearer $apptoken"}
Invoke-WebRequest: Response status code does not indicate success: 401 (Unauthorized).
PS C:\Users\nickp> Invoke-WebRequest -Uri http://localhost:5000/me -Headers @{ Authorization = "Bearer $admtoken"}

StatusCode       : 200
StatusDescription : OK
Content          : Hello World
RawContent       : HTTP/1.1 200 OK
                   Date: Tue, 25 Oct 2022 16:36:15 GMT
                   Server: Kestrel
                   Cache-Control: no-cache
                   Transfer-Encoding: chunked
                   Content-Type: application/json
```

Figure 7.8 – Passing authentication data using the -Headers parameter

In the first line, I'm trying to pass the encoded token, stored in the $apptoken variable. In the second line, I'm passing the unencoded token store in the $admtoken variable.

Note that the SecureString object type provides a *measure of security*, according to Microsoft. It's not truly secure. Read more here: https://learn.microsoft.com/en-us/dotnet/api/system.security.securestring.

Now we've covered making basic requests, let's take a look at how we can interact with websites more programmatically.

Getting to grips with APIs

Most modern systems communicate between client and server using an API. This is a list of agreed requests and responses between the two components. This sounds complicated, but it is quite simple. If we put the https://random.dog/woof.json URL into a browser, we get back the URL of a random dog, from a database of dog images. We also get the size of the file, in bytes.

Our browser is the client, and it sends an HTTP GET request to an API endpoint (/woof.json) on the server at the https://random.dog URL. In response to this request, the server sends a message containing a URL back to us, in the first frame in the following figure. We can look at the headers in the second frame below and see that the content type is **JSON**. We can then display the URL in a browser to see a picture of an adorable dog, below. Note that I'm using Firefox, here, which allows us to see the headers as well as the content. Other browsers will only show the JSON content.

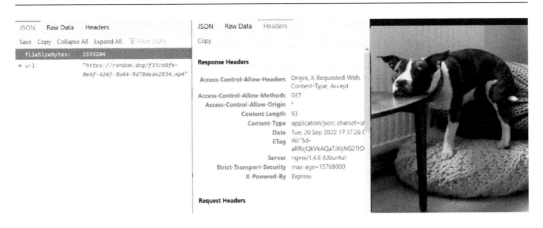

Figure 7.9 – Dog via API

The server isn't sending a web page for the browser to display; it's just sending data that contains a URL, and every time we request the page, it sends a different URL. We'll take a good look at this data in the later section of this chapter entitled *Working with JSON*, so don't worry about it too much now.

There are four common types of APIs in general use:

- **Remote Procedure Call (RPC)** APIs
- SOAP APIs
- REST APIs
- WebSocket APIs

They fall into two categories – **stateful**, where the connection between client and server is maintained over a number of requests, and **stateless**, where each request from a client is treated as a unique event and doesn't persist any information over to the next request. Let's take a closer look.

RPC APIs

RPC APIs call a function in software on a server – they tell a server to do something using a specific piece of code, and the server will return an output that may or may not contain data. They may not do this over HTTP; there is a separate protocol called, appropriately enough, RPC, which is often used over local networks. We are not going to concern ourselves with RPC APIs in this chapter, but they are undergoing a bit of a resurgence on the internet, particularly for blockchain applications. RPC APIs were historically stateful, but more modern implementations of this model are usually not.

SOAP APIs

SOAP APIs use the **Simple Object Access Protocol** to exchange messages using XML. We see these APIs most usually when working with Windows servers running Microsoft **Internet Information Server** (**IIS**) rather than Linux servers, which usually run Apache or NGINX software. As we have seen in *Chapter 6, PowerShell and Files – Reading, Writing, and Manipulating Data*, XML is not the easiest language to work with and Windows is a less common operating system than Linux for web servers, so SOAP APIs are not the most popular. SOAP is most commonly stateless.

REST APIs

REST is a style of software architecture for client-server, machine-to-machine communication. A REST API conforms to this style. They are flexible and lightweight, most often based on the HTTP protocol. REST APIs are stateless and can receive output in many forms, including HTML and XML. JSON is the most common form of output, however. REST APIs are generally the simplest APIs to work with and certainly the most common on the internet.

WebSocket APIs

WebSocket APIs use JSON to move data between clients and servers. Like REST APIs, they are based on HTTP, but unlike REST APIs, WebSocket APIs also use their own protocol, called the WebSocket protocol, an extension of HTTP, which allows for a wider range of operations. They are stateful and bi-directional; the server may initiate communication with a connected client. This makes them extremely powerful, but also harder to use.

Let's take a closer look at how we can work with the most common API type – the REST API.

Working with REST

The most common API we will work with is the REST API. We most frequently encounter REST APIs when we use **web applications**. A web application is usually a tiered client/server application. A typical application would consist of three tiers or layers:

- **A presentation layer** – the web browser or app on the client device
- **An application layer** – the web server
- **A storage layer** – usually a database running on the web server or a separate server

We use REST APIs to communicate between the presentation layer (the browser) and the application layer (the web server); how the application layer communicates with the storage layer (the database) is up to the application developer, but it will often be Python or PHP.

REST APIs are usually implemented using HTTP, which means they use a familiar set of HTTP commands such as GET, PUT, and POST. Because of the way web applications are usually designed, REST APIs are frequently associated with database operations; **Create, Read, Update, and Delete (CRUD)**. The following table summarizes how the commands map to operations.

Database operation	REST API request	Example
Create	POST	Create a new user
Read	GET	Get a picture of a dog
Update	PUT	Change an address
Delete	DELETE	Delete a chatroom post

Table 7.1 – How REST relates to CRUD

The websites we've looked at so far utilize APIs, and we've worked with them using Invoke-WebRequest. Let's take a look at a different cmdlet we can use.

Invoke-RestMethod

The Invoke-RestMethod cmdlet can be used to query a REST API endpoint, such as http://random.dog/woof.json. How does Invoke-RestMethod differ from Invoke-WebRequest? Let's look at the random.dog/woof.json API endpoint with both to compare the output:

```
PS C:\Users\nickp> Invoke-WebRequest -Uri https://random.dog/woof.json

StatusCode        : 200
StatusDescription : OK
Content           : {"fileSizeBytes":196058,"url":"https://random.dog/71c33af4-4d09-4836-b996-816f95c10667.webm"}
RawContent        : HTTP/1.1 200 OK
                    Server: nginx/1.4.6
                    Server: (Ubuntu)
                    Date: Mon, 21 Nov 2022 17:31:25 GMT
                    Connection: keep-alive
                    X-Powered-By: Express
                    Access-Control-Allow-Origin: *
                    Access-Control-Allow-Headers…
Headers           : {[Server, System.String[]], [Date, System.String[]], [Connection, System.String[]], [X-Powered-By,
                    System.String[]]…}
Images            : {}
InputFields       : {}
Links             : {}
RawContentLength  : 93
RelationLink      : {}


PS C:\Users\nickp> Invoke-RestMethod -Uri https://random.dog/woof.json

fileSizeBytes url
------------- ---
        81506 https://random.dog/e5bb2521-5775-4e01-a6df-82e1291d39a4.jpg
```

Figure 7.10 – Comparing Invoke-WebRequest and Invoke-RestMethod

In the first example, in the red box, I've used `Invoke-WebRequest`. In the second example, in the green box, I've used `Invoke-RestMethod`. Both cmdlets parse the response correctly, but they are doing different things. `Invoke-WebRequest` is displaying the HTTP response from the endpoint, including the headers and content. `Invoke-RestMethod` is only looking at the content and is displaying it as a custom object with a set of properties corresponding to names in the dictionary included in the content. Wait, what? Where did the dictionary come from? Remember, `Invoke-RestMethod` works with REST API endpoints. A REST API provides output in JSON, or less frequently in XML. JSON and XML outputs usually consist of a collection of name-value pairs; a dictionary. If we use `Invoke-RestMethod` to interrogate an HTML page that doesn't output in JSON or XML, then we get a single object, consisting of the raw HTML from the page. We will cover JSON in more detail in the next section of this chapter, *Working with JSON*. Let's take a closer look at the output we get when we access an API endpoint.

If we pipe `Invoke-RestMethod` to `Get-Member`, we can see that we have a `System.Management.Automation.PSCustomObject` with two properties; `fileSizeBytes` and `url`:

```
Invoke-RestMethod -Uri https://random.dog/woof.json | Get-Member
```

The parameters for `Invoke-RestMethod` are quite similar to `Invoke-WebRequest`. We can summarize them in *Table 7.2*. As we can see, `Invoke-WebRequest` has the `-HttpVersion` parameter, which was introduced in PowerShell 7.3, while `Invoke-RestMethod` does not, and `Invoke-RestMethod` has parameters that deal with relative links (`-FollowRelLink` and `-MaximumFollowRelLink`) and `-StatusCodeVariable`, which can assign the HTTP response status code to a separate variable. This is useful when combined with the `-SkipHttpErrorCheck` parameter:

```
Invoke-WebRequest
      [<CommonParameters>]

      -CustomMethod
      [-AllowUnencryptedAuthentication]
            [-Authentication
<WebAuthenticationType>]
      [-Body <Object>]
      [-Certificate <X509Certificate>]
          [-CertificateThumbprint
<String>]
      [-ContentType <String>]
      [-Credential <PSCredential>]
      [-DisableKeepAlive]

      [-Form <IDictionary>]
      [-Headers <IDictionary>]
      [-HttpVersion <Version>]
      [-InFile <String>]


      [-MaximumRedirection <Int32>]
      [-MaximumRetryCount <Int32>]
      [-Method <WebRequestMethod>]

      -NoProxy
      [-OutFile <String>]
      [-PassThru]
    [-PreserveAuthorizationOnRedirect]
      [-Proxy <Uri>]
    [-ProxyCredential <PSCredential>]
      [-ProxyUseDefaultCredentials]


      [-Resume]
      [-RetryIntervalSec <Int32>]
      [-SessionVariable <String>]
      [-SkipCertificateCheck]
      [-SkipHeaderValidation]
      [-SkipHttpErrorCheck]
      [-SslProtocol <WebSslProtocol>]


      [-TimeoutSec <Int32>]
      [-Token <SecureString>]
```

```
Invoke-RestMethod
      [<CommonParameters>]

      -CustomMethod
      [-AllowUnencryptedAuthentication]
            [-Authentication
<WebAuthenticationType>]
      [-Body <Object>]
      [-Certificate <X509Certificate>]
          [-CertificateThumbprint
<String>]
      [-ContentType <String>]
      [-Credential <PSCredential>]
      [-DisableKeepAlive]
      [-FollowRelLink]
      [-Form <IDictionary>]
      [-Headers <IDictionary>]


      [-InFile <String>]
      [-MaximumFollowRelLink <Int32>]
      [-MaximumRedirection <Int32>]
      [-MaximumRetryCount <Int32>]
      [-Method <WebRequestMethod>]

      -NoProxy
      [-OutFile <String>]
      [-PassThru]
    [-PreserveAuthorizationOnRedirect]
      [-Proxy <Uri>]
    [-ProxyCredential <PSCredential>]
      [-ProxyUseDefaultCredentials]
          [-ResponseHeadersVariable
<String>]
      [-Resume]
      [-RetryIntervalSec <Int32>]
      [-SessionVariable <String>]
      [-SkipCertificateCheck]
      [-SkipHeaderValidation]
      [-SkipHttpErrorCheck]
      [-SslProtocol <WebSslProtocol>]
      [-StatusCodeVariable <String>]
      [-TimeoutSec <Int32>]
```

`[-TransferEncoding <String>]`
`[-Uri] <Uri>`
`[-UseBasicParsing]`
`[-UseDefaultCredentials]`
`[-UserAgent <String>]`
`[-WebSession <WebRequestSession>]`
	`[-Token <SecureString>]`
	`[-TransferEncoding <String>]`
	`[-Uri] <Uri>`
	`[-UseBasicParsing]`
	`[-UseDefaultCredentials]`
	`[-UserAgent <String>]`
	`[-WebSession <WebRequestSession>]`

Table 7.2 – The parameters of Invoke-WebRequest and Invoke-RestMethod, compared

There are some minor differences in a couple of the parameters, for example, the `Invoke-RestMethod` `-Uri` parameter can also accept `file:` and `ftp:` schemes, as well as `http:` and `https:`.

To really get to grips with `Invoke-RestMethod` though, we need to understand the content that we are retrieving when we use it. To do that, let's take a closer look at the most common data format, JSON.

Working with JSON

What is JSON? First of all, it's *not* a language; it's a data format. While it has JavaScript in the name, it is used by many modern languages to generate, parse, and exchange data. It is also intended to be human-readable; we just have to know how to read it. JSON stores data in a dictionary-like format of key-value pairs. The first term is the key, and the second term is the value. The key is a string, and the value may be another string, a Boolean, a number, an array, or a JSON object. A JSON object consists of one or more key-value pairs, so because the value can be another object, JSON objects can be nested. Let's type the cmdlet:

```
PS C:\Users\nickp> (Invoke-WebRequest random.dog/woof.json).content
```

Then, we get something like the following JSON response.

```
{"fileSizeBytes":176601,"url":"https://random.dog/6b41dccd-90ca-4ce8-
a0e2-800e9ab92aa7.jpg"}
```

This consists of two key-value pairs:

```
"fileSizeBytes":176601
"url":"https://random.dog/6b41dccd-90ca-4ce8-a0e2-800e9ab92aa7.jpg"
```

In the first pair, `fileSizeBytes` is the key, and the value is `176601`, which is fairly obviously the file size, in bytes. The second pair has a key of `url`, and the value is the URL that follows. The key and the value are separated by a colon (`:`).

Both pairs are enclosed in a single set of braces (`{ }`). The braces tell us that this is a single object consisting of the enclosed pairs. The pairs in an object are separated by a comma (`,`). There is no comma after the last pair in an object. If we wanted to include an array, we would enclose it in square brackets. Let's write one that describes a well-known television character. Open VS Code, create a new file, and save it as something appropriate, such as `C:\temp\poshbook\ch7\enterprise.json`. Then, type the following:

```
{
"Name": "Enterprise",
"Designation": "NCC-1701",
"Captain": {
    "FirstName": "James",
    "Initial": "T",
    "LastName": "Kirk"
    },
"BridgeCrew": ["Uhura", "Spock", "Sulu", "Chekhov", "Riley"],
"PhotonTorpedoes": 240000000,
"JediName": null,
"IsAwesome": true
}
```

The following figure shows how it should look in VS Code. It's a valid JSON file and demonstrates the valid JSON data types and syntax.

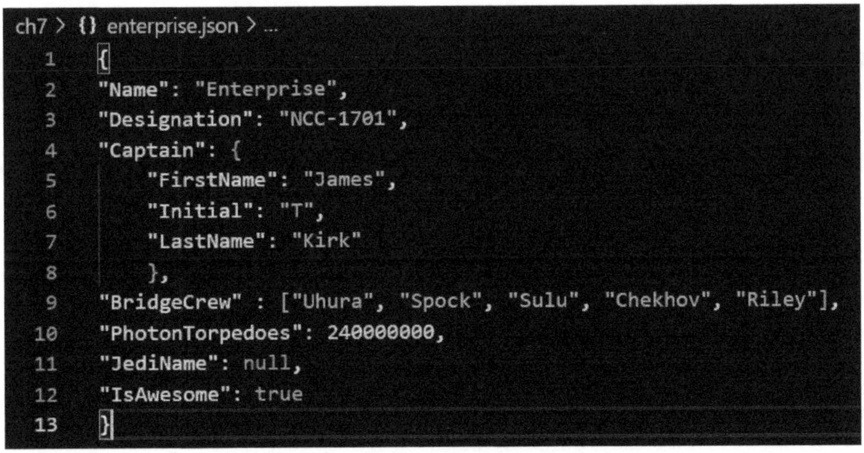

Figure 7.11 – To boldly demonstrate JSON

`Name` and `Designation` contain string values, `Captain` contains another JSON object, and `BridgeCrew` contains an array of strings (but it could be an array of other valid data types, or even of more JSON objects). Obviously, it has no `JediName`, and it is definitely awesome.

As we can see, VS Code can parse JSON and help us ensure our syntax is correct through color coding.

There are a few other points to remember. First of all, whitespace between elements is ignored; `"Initial": "T"` is as valid as `"Initial": "T"`. Do everyone a favor by being consistent with how you use whitespace, though. Secondly, there is no particular number format. `240000000` is not an integer or a floating-point value; it's just a number. Finally, there is no provision for comments within JSON; this should encourage us to write clear and descriptive code.

Now we have a reasonable understanding of what JSON is, how can we use it in PowerShell? PowerShell doesn't work with JSON the way it does with XML, so we need to be able to convert our JSON data into a custom PowerShell object and convert PowerShell objects into JSON. There are a pair of cmdlets that can do this for us, `ConvertFrom-Json` and `ConvertTo-Json`. Let's look at `ConvertFrom-Json` first.

ConvertFrom-Json

`ConvertFrom-Json` will parse JSON content from a location and turn it into a custom PSObject. Let's see how it works.

Open a PowerShell console and try getting the content using the following:

```
$starship = Get-Content 'C:\temp\poshbook\ch7\enterprise.json'
```

As we can see from the following figure, we can import the content fine, but if we use `Get-Member`, we can see we have imported that content as a string:

```
PS C:\Users\nickp> $starship = Get-Content 'C:\temp\poshbook\ch7\enterprise.json'
PS C:\Users\nickp> $starship | Get-Member

   TypeName: System.String
```

Figure 7.12 – Importing JSON with Get-Content alone

Turning the data held in the JSON file into a string is going to make it difficult to use and manipulate. Now, let's try using `ConvertFrom-Json`:

```
$starship = (Get-Content 'C:\temp\poshbook\ch7\enterprise.json' |
ConvertFrom-Json)
```

This time, we've imported it as a custom PSObject, which is much more useful. Doing it this way creates an object with properties corresponding to the key-value pairs contained in the JSON, which we can then access the same way as we can with the properties of any other PowerShell object, as in the following figure:

```
PS C:\Users\nickp> $starship = (Get-Content 'C:\temp\poshbook\ch7\enterprise.json' | ConvertFrom-Json)
PS C:\Users\nickp> $starship | Get-Member


   TypeName: System.Management.Automation.PSCustomObject

Name            MemberType   Definition
----            ----------   ----------
Equals          Method       bool Equals(System.Object obj)
GetHashCode     Method       int GetHashCode()
GetType         Method       type GetType()
ToString        Method       string ToString()
BridgeCrew      NoteProperty Object[] BridgeCrew=System.Object[]
Captain         NoteProperty System.Management.Automation.PSCustomObject Captain=@{FirstName=James; Initial=T;
Designation     NoteProperty string Designation=NCC-1701
IsAwesome       NoteProperty bool IsAwesome=True
JediName        NoteProperty object JediName=null
Name            NoteProperty string Name=Enterprise
PhotonTorpedoes NoteProperty long PhotonTorpedoes=240000000

PS C:\Users\nickp> $starship.Captain

FirstName Initial LastName
--------- ------- --------
James     T       Kirk
```

Figure 7.13 – Importing JSON with ConvertFrom-Json

Let's take a closer look at the ConvertFrom-Json cmdlet.

ConvertFrom-Json is a simple cmdlet that hides a lot of complicated work. As we've seen, we can use it to convert a JSON string into a custom PSObject. We can also use it to create an ordered hashtable from a JSON string; this is necessary because JSON allows duplicate key names, where only the case of the string may be different. Because PowerShell is case-insensitive, only the last key-value pair would be converted; instead, ConvertFrom-Json throws an error. The other reason is that JSON allows keys that are empty strings; this would lead to a PSObject with a property name that is an empty string, which isn't allowed. See the following figure for examples of these errors:

```
PS C:\Users\nickp> '{ "key": "lower case", "Key": "Capitalised" }' | ConvertFrom-Json
ConvertFrom-Json: Cannot convert the JSON string because it contains keys with different casing.
Please use the –AsHashTable switch instead. The key that was attempted to be added to the existin
g key 'key' was 'Key'.
PS C:\Users\nickp> '{ "": "empty string key"}' | ConvertFrom-Json
ConvertFrom-Json: The provided JSON includes a property whose name is an empty string, this is on
ly supported using the –AsHashTable switch.
```

Figure 7.14 – Reasons to use the -AsHashtable parameter

Let's look at the parameters:

- -AsHashtable will convert the JSON string into an ordered hashtable, which preserves the ordering of the JSON keys. We looked at ordered hashtables in *Chapter 4, PowerShell Variables and Data Structures*. While not as useful as a PSObject, ordered hashtables are easier to work with than strings, and in some circumstances are faster to process than a PSObject.

- -Depth allows us to set the maximum depth of nesting that we will process; as we saw at the start of this section, JSON key-value pairs can contain JSON objects, which in turn can contain further JSON objects. The default value of -Depth is 1024.

- -InputObject only accepts strings; either the string itself, a variable that contains a string, or an expression that generates a string, as we saw in the enterprise.json example previously. We can't pass a file to it directly; we need to get the file content first using Get-Content. Obviously, it accepts pipeline input.

- -NoEnumerate will read an array of strings as a single string, resulting in a single output object. Consider the example in the following figure:

```
PS C:\Users\nickp> '["fish", "cat", "dog"]' |
>> ConvertFrom-Json |
>> ForEach-Object {Write-Output "Pet: $_"}
Pet: fish
Pet: cat
Pet: dog
PS C:\Users\nickp> '["fish", "cat", "dog"]' |
>> ConvertFrom-Json -NoEnumerate |
>> ForEach-Object {Write-Output "Pet: $_"}
Pet: fish cat dog
```

Figure 7.15 – Using the -NoEnumerate parameter

In the first cmdlet, we get three separate objects. When we include the -NoEnumerate parameter, we get a single object, fish cat dog.

Now we've seen how to convert JSON into a format that PowerShell can easily work with, let's look at how we can convert PowerShell objects into JSON.

ConvertTo-Json

ConvertTo-Json will take any PowerShell object and convert it into a JSON-formatted string. It does this by converting the properties of the object into key-value pairs, where the property name is the key, and discarding any methods the object has. Let's see it working. If you didn't create the $starship variable as a PSObject previously, do so now:

```
$starship = (Get-Content 'C:\temp\poshbook\ch7\enterprise.json' |
ConvertFrom-Json)
```

Now, let's say we've been in a battle, and need to update our photon torpedo count. We can type the following:

```
$starship.PhotonTorpedoes = 1900000000
```

This will update it on the PSObject, and then we use ConvertTo-Json to produce a JSON-formatted object to replace the original that we imported:

```
$starship | ConvertTo-Json | Out-File "C:\temp\poshbook\ch7\
klingonattack.json"
```

If we open that in VS Code, we can see that it is a correctly formatted JSON file with the updated torpedo count:

```
ch7 > {} klingonattack.json > ...
  1   {
  2       "Name": "Enterprise",
  3       "Designation": "NCC-1701",
  4       "Captain": {
  5         "FirstName": "James",
  6         "Initial": "T",
  7         "LastName": "Kirk"
  8       },
  9       "BridgeCrew": [
 10         "Uhura",
 11         "Spock",
 12         "Sulu",
 13         "Chekhov",
 14         "Riley"
 15       ],
 16       "PhotonTorpedoes": 1900000000,
 17       "JediName": null,
 18       "IsAwesome": true
 19   }
```

Figure 7.16 – After a Klingon attack

We can see in line 16 that the torpedo count has changed. VS Code still sees this as valid JSON with no errors. We can see the formatting has changed from the original file; each element of the `BridgeCrew` array is on its own line because of the formatting rules that `ConvertTo-Json` uses, but other than that it's the same as the original `enterprise.json` file. We could then feed this JSON string to an API to update the information on a server.

Like `ConvertFrom-Json`, `ConvertTo-Json` is a deceptively simple cmdlet that hides a lot of work behind a short list of parameters. Let's take a look at them:

- `-AsArray` will convert a PSObject into a JSON array unconditionally. Consider the following examples in the following figure.

```
PS C:\Users\nickp> "string1", "string2" | ConvertTo-Json
[
  "string1",
  "string2"
]
PS C:\Users\nickp> "string1" | ConvertTo-Json
"string1"
PS C:\Users\nickp> "string1" | ConvertTo-Json -AsArray
[
  "string1"
]
```

Figure 7.17 – The -AsArray parameter

- In the first line, I'm converting two strings into JSON. `ConvertTo-Json` automatically treats them as an array and puts them in square brackets because they are two separate objects. In the second line, I'm only feeding a single string into the pipeline, and `ConvertTo-Json` treats it as a single string. But what if I want it to be formatted as a single-member array? Then, I use the `-AsArray` parameter, and I get my square brackets.

- `-Compress` removes whitespace and indented formatting from the JSON output. The output will be on a single line.

- `-Depth` specifies how many levels of nested objects can be included in the JSON output. We can have between zero and one hundred levels of nesting, but the default is a miserly two levels, which can catch people out. We get a warning if our output has more than this level. Consider the JSON in the following figure:

```
ch7 > {} nesting.json > ...
  1   {
  2       "Name": "Enterprise",
  3       "Designation": "NCC-1701",
  4       "Captain": {
  5         "FirstName": "James",
  6         "MiddleName": {
  7             "Initial": "T",
  8             "StandsFor": "Tiberius",
  9             "really?": {
 10                 "response": "yes, really"
 11             }
 12       },
```

Figure 7.18 – nesting.json

If we ingest it into a variable, then convert it back into JSON, and then we get the warning in the following figure. Notice that the third level of nesting, on the line beginning with `"really?"`, is not converted into a JSON object, but into a string representing a hashtable:

```
PS C:\Users\nickp> $nesting | ConvertTo-Json
WARNING: Resulting JSON is truncated as serialization has exceeded the set depth of 2.
{
  "Name": "Enterprise",
  "Designation": "NCC-1701",
  "Captain": {
    "FirstName": "James",
    "Initial": {
      "StandsFor": "Tiberius",
      "really?": "@{value=yes really}"
    },
```

Figure 7.19 – We need to increase -Depth

- -EnumsAsStrings will convert all the values of the **enum** type in the input object into their equivalent strings. What does that mean? An enum type enumerates a value as one of a set of predefined constants. An example is the DayOfWeek property of a DateTime object. When we type (Get-Date).DayOfWeek, it returns a string, Saturday, but the value is actually held as an integer between 1 and 7. Have a look at the example in the following figure:

```
PS C:\Users\nickp> (Get-Date).DayOfWeek
Saturday
PS C:\Users\nickp> (Get-Date).DayOfWeek | ConvertTo-Json
6
PS C:\Users\nickp> (Get-Date).DayOfWeek | ConvertTo-Json -EnumsAsStrings
"Saturday"
```

Figure 7.20 - Using the -EnumAsStrings parameter

- -EscapeHandling controls how certain characters are escaped, such as the newline character (`n). There are three possible settings – Default, where only control characters are escaped, EscapeNonAscii, where all non-ASCII and control characters are escaped, and EscapeHtml, where special HTML characters such as <, >, ?, &, ', and " are escaped.

- -InputObject accepts any type of PowerShell object explicitly or via the pipeline, as an expression, or as a variable.

Most of these parameters are formatting controls intended to make it easier to work with APIs, which may have different expectations of the input we give them. There is one more command that helps us get our data into a format that can be consumed by an API; Test-Json.

Test-Json

The Test-Json cmdlet will test the validity of a string as a JSON object. This is extremely useful when writing scripts to work with APIs to make sure our data can be consumed correctly. It is especially useful when we consider that not everything we produce with ConvertTo-Json is necessarily good JSON. Consider the examples in the following figure:

```
PS C:\Users\nickp> $date = Get-Date
PS C:\Users\nickp> "{'date': $date}" | Test-Json
Test-Json: Cannot parse the JSON.
False
PS C:\Users\nickp> "{'date': $date}" | ConvertTo-Json
"{'date': 01/14/2023 17:37:25}"
PS C:\Users\nickp> "{'date': $date}" | ConvertTo-Json | Test-Json
Test-Json: Cannot parse the JSON.
False
PS C:\Users\nickp> "{'date': 01/14/2023 17:22:21}" | Test-Json
Test-Json: Cannot parse the JSON.
False
PS C:\Users\nickp> "{'date': '01/14/2023 17:22:21'}" | Test-Json
True
```

Figure 7.21 – Getting things wrong with ConvertTo-Json

In the first line, we create a variable called $date and put the current date in it. This is an object of the DateTime type. Unsurprisingly, when we try the cmdlet in line 2, Test-Json is unhappy. In line 3, we convert the expression into JSON using ConvertTo-Json, and then test it again in line 4. Horror! Although it has been converted successfully, it's still not compliant JSON. In line 5, we can try testing just the string output from line 3, and we can see what the problem is. While ConvertTo-Json has taken the value from the $date variable, it hasn't formatted it correctly as a string. When we correct the formatting in line 6, we can see that Test-Json is now happy. The clever way to do it, of course, is like this:

```
PS C:\Users\nickp> $date = Get-Date
PS C:\Users\nickp> "{'date': $($date.date)}" | ConvertTo-Json
"{'date': 05/30/2023 00:00:00}"
PS C:\Users\nickp> "{'date': $($date.date)}" | ConvertTo-Json | Test-Json
True
PS C:\Users\nickp> 
```

Figure 7.22 – The right way to do it

There are a couple of parameters with Test-Json that allow us to define custom JSON schemas if we need to produce specialized or custom JSON for particular systems, but we don't need to go into them here. One interesting quirk of the cmdlet is that the -InputObject parameter found on almost all cmdlets is called -Json here, but functionally it is the same; it takes a string, either explicitly or via the pipeline.

Let's have some fun – who is on the International Space Station?

Since I was small, I have been fascinated by space. One of my earliest memories is sitting up with my mam and dad to watch an Apollo moon landing on a creaky old black and white television. It wasn't Apollo 11. I'm not quite that old. As an exercise, let's see whether we can find out who is on the ISS, and present that data on a web page. We'll need to refer to some of the stuff we learned about in the last chapter to accomplish this; *Chapter 6, PowerShell and Files – Reading, Writing, and Manipulating Data*, as well as what we've learned in this chapter. We're not going to walk through it – try and accomplish this on your own. There are lots of ways to do this, and I've put my solution in the answers. Here are some hints though.

> **Activity**
> We can break this down into two tasks:
> Task 1 – use an API to find out who is on the ISS, right now
> Task 2 – display this data in an HTML file

There is an API with the data we require at http://api.open-notify.org/astros.json

You could use `Invoke-WebRequest`, but it's probably easier to use `Invoke-RestMethod`

You will probably want to use `ConvertTo-Html` to produce the web page. You may need to study the help file for this cmdlet to understand some of the formatting options.

Here's my finished attempt:

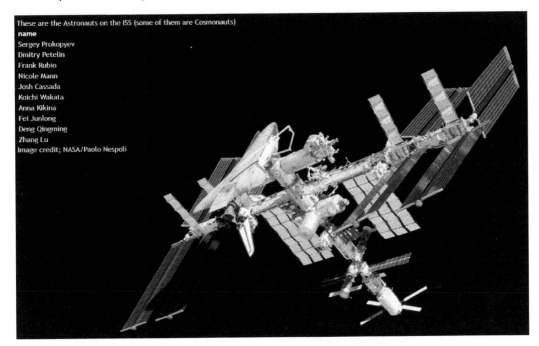

These are the Astronauts on the ISS (some of them are Cosmonauts)
name
Sergey Prokopyev
Dmitry Petelin
Frank Rubio
Nicole Mann
Josh Cassada
Koichi Wakata
Anna Kikina
Fei Junlong
Deng Qingming
Zhang Lu
Image credit; NASA/Paolo Nespoli

Figure 7.23 – Just beautiful

This should stretch us a little bit, but we've got all the knowledge we need to get this done and have some fun along the way.

Summary

We've come on a bit of a journey in this chapter and started to interact with the world outside our local machines. The techniques we covered will be used throughout the book, so we will get plenty of opportunity to become properly familiar with them.

We started out by looking at how we can work with HTML data over HTTP using the `Invoke-WebRequest` cmdlet. We saw that this is a complex cmdlet with many options, and we covered the parameters frequently used with it. We focused on authentication, as this will be a key technique required for retrieving and posting data. We also saw that it is difficult to manipulate the data we ingest using this cmdlet, as it is text-based.

We then talked about an easier way to ingest data from servers over a network, using an API. We discussed the common types of API, in particular the most common, REST APIs.

We then looked at the PowerShell cmdlet for working with REST – `Invoke-RestMethod`. We saw how similar this cmdlet is to `Invoke-WebRequest`, but that instead of producing a page of HTML, it outputs data in a structured format.

We went on to explore the most common format for this data, JSON. We looked at the three cmdlets in PowerShell for working with JSON data; `ConvertFrom-Json`, `ConvertTo-Json`, and `Test-Json`.

Finally, we used our new knowledge to produce an HTML web page displaying the names of the astronauts currently on board the ISS.

This chapter marks the end of the coding fundamentals section of this book; we've covered data structures, flow control, file manipulation, and connecting to the internet. In the next chapter, we are going to start looking at turning our lines of scruffy code into scripts and tools that we can share with other people. It'll be fun.

Exercises

1. How would we send a delete request to the following URL: `https://httpbin.org/delete`?

2. What parameters would we need to use `Invoke-WebRequest` with a stateful endpoint?

3. We try to connect to a website and see the following error:

    ```
    Invoke-WebRequest: The remote certificate is invalid because of
    errors in the certificate chain: NotTimeValid
    ```

    How can we continue to the site with `Invoke-WebRequest`?

4. Which type of API is stateful? What does this mean?

5. We sign up to a web service and get an authentication token. We encode the token using `ConvertTo-SecureString`, store it in a variable called `$token`, and then use the variable to create a web request like this:

    ```
    Invoke-WebRequest -Uri 'https://webservice.com/endpoint'
    -Headers @{Authorization = "Bearer $token"}
    ```

    We get an authentication error. Have we done something wrong, or is the token bad?

6. Get the latitude and longitude of the ISS right now. You can use `http://api.open-notify.org/iss-now.json`.

7. How many universities in the UK have the letter 'x' in their name? Use the API at `http://universities.hipolabs.com/search?country=United+Kingdom` to find out.

8. How can we use `Test-Json` to validate our generated JSON against a custom schema?

Further reading

- More on APIs here:

  https://www.packtpub.com/product/understanding-apis-and-restful-apis-crash-course-video/9781800564121

  https://www.digitalfluency.guide/apis/introduction-to-apis

- Lots more on REST here:

  https://restfulapi.net/

- A good JSON tutorial, but with some JavaScript:

  https://www.w3schools.com/js/js_json_intro.asp

- How to use JSON schemas:

  https://json-schema.org/understanding-json-schema

Part 2:
Scripting and Toolmaking

This part walks you through turning a set of cmdlets into a script, introduces functional programming, shows you how to turn scripts into modules, and how to share those modules with colleagues and others using GitHub and GitLab. It also includes a chapter on PowerShell security, so that you don't inadvertently distribute code that is less secure than it could be.

This part has the following chapters:

- *Chapter 8, Writing Our First Script – Turning Simple Cmdlets into Reusable Code*
- *Chapter 9, Don't Repeat Yourself – Functions and Scriptblocks*
- *Chapter 10, Error Handling – Oh No! It's Gone Wrong!*
- *Chapter 11, Creating Our First Module*
- *Chapter 12, Securing PowerShell*

8

Writing Our First Script – Turning Simple Cmdlets into Reusable Code

Starting in this chapter, we're going to look at how we can put the basic concepts we've learned together into scripts and tools that we can reuse, adapt, and distribute for others. In the coming chapters, we're going to look at creating functions and script blocks, error handling and debugging, creating modules that allow us to distribute our code as tools, and finally, securing PowerShell. In this chapter, though, we're going to start with the basics: turning a handful of cmdlets into a script.

We'll start by discussing scripts in general and why we might want to write one. After that, we'll take a quick look at where we can find PowerShell scripts online, and then we'll cover how we can run scripts.

Once we understand how to use other people's scripts, we'll dive into writing our own. First, we'll learn how to identify changing values in a working cmdlet pipeline, then we'll learn how to turn those into parameters so we can pass the values into the cmdlets when we run the script, rather than having to edit the script each time. We'll cover how to make parameters mandatory, how to take values from the pipeline, and how to create switch parameters, before moving on to cover how to help ourselves and others use our scripts.

In the second part of this chapter, we'll cover how to add comments and comment blocks to our script that explain what we're trying to do in each part and help us and others edit and adapt the script. Next, we'll look at how we can write help information that can be accessed from outside the script using the Get-Help cmdlet. After that, we'll move on to a script construct that can help us understand what is going on when the script is producing unexpected output – the Write-Verbose cmdlet. Finally, we'll cover how to add help messages for mandatory parameters, which will prompt users with information about how to use the parameter.

In this chapter, we are going to cover the following main topics:

- Introduction to scripting
- Writing a script
- Identifying changing values
- Working with parameters
- Providing help for our script

Introduction to scripting

A script is a sequence of instructions written in a human-readable form for a computer to carry out. They are usually written in a scripting language such as PowerShell, Python, or JavaScript. We covered the differences between scripting languages and programming languages back in *Chapter 1, Introduction to PowerShell 7 – What It Is and How to Get It*; the key thing to remember is that scripting languages are interpreted and so need a program (such as PowerShell) to be running on the client to run the script, whereas programming languages are compiled; they will run directly in the operating system.

Scripting, to me, is an art form. It's probably the truest cybernetic art form; what we write in a script has to make sense to both human beings and machines. In *Chapter 6, PowerShell and Files – Reading, Writing, and Manipulating Data*, we talked about *Exercises in Programming Style* by Cristina Videira Lopes, where a term frequency task was solved in dozens of different ways. This is equally true of scripts in PowerShell. There is no one way to write a script, and what seems lovely to one person may be really ugly to another; I have a deep loathing of code golf, where a script is written with as few lines and characters as possible, but that is a personal preference – other people love it. Simplicity, and clean and functional code – these things are beautiful, and it requires a creative and inventive mind to write it. In this chapter, we're going to cover how I approach writing scripts.

Why do we want to write scripts?

Fundamentally, because we are lazy. A script allows us to capture a series of steps that may be complicated or time-consuming, and repeat them easily without work. Secondly, because we are fallible and easily distracted. The longer and more complicated a task is, the more likely we are to make a mistake. Writing a script means the task will be completed in the same way every time. If we can get it right once and capture that process, then we almost never need to get it right again. We can go and make our mistakes somewhere else. Finally, because we don't want to do the thing at all; if we write a script, we can give it to somebody else to do.

Script writing is an example of toolmaking, where we create something to make our task easier to accomplish. Some script writing might be proper automation, but generally, automation includes the concept of a feedback loop, where the tool responds to an external stimulus without user intervention. A central heating boiler is a tool; it makes heating your house much easier than building a fire in each room. A thermostat is automation; when the temperature is too low, it turns the boiler on, and when it is too high, it turns the boiler off. If we've set it correctly, then we should never be too warm or too cold.

There is some theory around toolmaking and automation that is worth considering, as it can help us decide whether we want to write a script or not. Let's quickly cover the three basic principles of automation:

- **Compensatory principle**: This is based on the concept that machines are better at some tasks than people, and people are better at some tasks than machines. Automation and tools based on this principle divide work based on the strengths and weaknesses of people and machines.

- **Complementarity principle**: Constantly using tools to accomplish difficult tasks can de-skill the human operator; we forget how to do things. Then, when we really need to take over, when things are going wrong, we can't fix the problem. We use this principle where the human operator must retain the skills that the automation is replacing. Aircraft autopilots are a good example of this; the operator doesn't use them all the time or may only use part of them so that they retain the skills they need when the autopilot can't land the plane because of weather or a mechanical failure.

- **Left-over principle**: This is the principle we most commonly associate with scripting. It's the idea that we automate everything we can, and then manually do what is left over.

Of course, it's a little bit more complicated than that. Sometimes, tasks are too hard to automate, or we do them so rarely it's not worth bothering. We'll not save any time or effort by writing a script. A rule of thumb is to script anything that will take less time to script than you will spend doing it manually over three years. So, if you have a task that you do every weekday that takes 5 minutes, and it will take you 4 hours to script, then that works out at 62 hours over 3 years. By spending 4 hours scripting it, you'll save over a week of work for yourself, over 3 years. Let's start by understanding where we can get scripts that other people have written.

Getting scripts

We discussed different places to get PowerShell modules and cmdlets in *Chapter 2, Exploring PowerShell Cmdlets and Syntax*. We can use those same places to find PowerShell scripts as well. Let's just recap them:

- **PowerShell repositories**: Whether it's the official PowerShell repository at `https://www.powershellgallery.com/`, the Microsoft Learn repository at `https://learn.microsoft.com/en-us/samples/browse/`, or an internal one, repositories are great places to find scripts. Generally speaking, scripts in the PowerShell Gallery have undergone some minimal validation and will have information about the author, the version, and the license for use.

- **GitHub**: This is also a good source for PowerShell scripts, but they're generally not validated and may not be complete or functional.

- **Online elsewhere**: There are very good scripts elsewhere online. For example, the Practical 365 site (`https://practical365.com`) has some extremely useful scripts for working with Microsoft 365. However, the quality of online scripts may be variable.

Whenever we get a script from an author we don't know or trust, we should be careful to understand what the script does and how it does it before running it in an environment we care about. We should do this even when we do trust the author, of course. It is worth starting a sandbox or virtual machine to test the script first.

Running scripts

There are two things we need to be aware of before we can run a script. The first is that PowerShell scripts always have an extension of `.ps1`. Files with this extension are not registered as executables, so double-clicking them in Windows Explorer will open them in Notepad or another editor; it won't run the script. Files with this extension also require a relative or absolute path to run from the PowerShell terminal, so with either `PS C:\myscripts> .\MySuperScript.ps1` (relative path) or `PS C:\> C:\myscripts\MySuperScript.ps1` (absolute path) without the `.\`, the script won't run.

Secondly, PowerShell has an execution policy for running scripts, but only on Windows computers. By default, on a Windows client, the execution policy is `Restricted`, which means that scripts cannot run. Happily, we can change this for the current user by running the following cmdlet:

```
Set-ExecutionPolicy -ExecutionPolicy RemoteSigned -Scope CurrentUser
```

This will allow the current user to run scripts that have been written on the local machine, or scripts downloaded from the internet that include a code signature. We'll be covering execution policy and code signing in detail in *Chapter 12, Securing PowerShell*, but for now, run this cmdlet so that we can get on with writing a script.

If we are using a Linux or Mac client, we don't need to do this. The policy is effectively `Unrestricted` for those computers because of differences in the way security is implemented in the Linux and macOS operating systems.

That's enough introduction; let's get on with what we're here for: writing a script.

Writing a script

How do we go about writing a script? Pretty much every script I write from scratch starts with writing down the steps and cmdlets I need to complete a task. Once I can complete the task with only the information in the list, and all the cmdlets work, I know I am ready. Let's start our script with a working command. As an example, consider the following cmdlet:

```
Invoke-RestMethod -Uri 'https://api.weatherapi.com/v1/current.
json?q=London&aqi=no' -Method GET -Headers @{"key" = "fp3eofkf3-0ef-
```

```
2kdwpoepwoe03eper30r"}| ConvertTo-Html | Out-File "c:\temp\poshbook\
ch8\WeatherData.html"
```

This cmdlet gets some weather data for my location from the API service from the Weather API, using a personal key, and writes it to an HTML file for display. Obviously, I've not put my real personal key in the preceding cmdlet, so it will fail with an API key error if we run that exact code. Let's consider how we might turn this cmdlet into a script. To continue, we'll need to get our own personal key.

Getting a Personal Key for the Weather API Service

To work through this chapter, we'll need our own personal key for the Weather API service:

1. Go to `https://www.weatherapi.com` and click the **Sign Up** button.

2. Enter an email address (twice) and a new password (twice), accept the terms and conditions, complete the CAPTCHA, and we will be sent a verification email.

3. Clicking the link in the verification email will open a web page to tell us that we are verified, and will invite us to log in.

4. Do this by clicking the login link and entering our email address and the password we have just created. At the top of the next page is our personal API key. This is the key we will use to run this cmdlet.

5. Copy it and save it in a text file somewhere safe. You can always find it again by logging in to the service.

Now we've got a key, let's open VS Code and create a new file. Call it `weatherdata.ps1`. Type the following, using the key we've just generated from the Weather API instead of `<our new key here>`:

```
Invoke-RestMethod -Uri 'https://api.weatherapi.com/v1/current.
json?q=London&aqi=no' -Method GET -Headers @{"key" = "<our new key
here>"}| ConvertTo-Html | Out-File "c:\temp\poshbook\ch8\WeatherData.
html"
```

Let's think about tidying this cmdlet up so that it is more readable. The cmdlet does two things; it gets information from the API, and it outputs that information to a file, so let's split those up:

```
$response = Invoke-RestMethod -Uri 'https://api.weatherapi.com/v1/
current.json?q=London&aqi=no' -Method GET -Headers @{"key" = "<our new
key here>"}
$response | Convertto-Html | Out-File "c:\temp\poshbook\ch8\
WeatherData.html"
```

So now, we are storing the response in a variable and then outputting it in the second line.

How else might we make this more readable? That first cmdlet is very long. We could break out the headers and the URI to make it more readable, as we can see in the following figure:

```
ch8 > ⋋_ weatherdata.ps1 > ...
  1    $headers = @{"key" = "<New key here>"}
  2
  3    $uri = "https://api.weatherapi.com/v1/current.json?q=London&aqi=no"
  4
  5    $response = Invoke-RestMethod -Uri $uri -Method GET -Headers $headers
  6
  7    $response | Convertto-Html | Out-File "c:\temp\poshbook\ch8\WeatherData.html"
  8    |
```

Figure 8.1 – Readable code

If we save `weatherdata.ps1`, we can now run it from the PowerShell console by switching to the directory we save it in and running the following at the prompt:

.\weatherdata.ps1

While the code is readable, it's not very flexible. It does one thing, and if we want it to do something slightly different (for instance, produce the data for a different city) or if we want to share it with someone else, we need to make some changes. Let's look at where we might start with that.

Identifying changing values

Let's think about things we might want to change in this code. We want it to get weather information from the web and write it to a HTML document. This means it's unlikely that we want to change the `Invoke-RestMethod`, `Convertto-Html`, and `Out-File` cmdlets. Think about what values might change before we move on.

Ready? Good.

These are some things that we might want to be able to change the values of when we run the script:

- We might want to change the city.

- We might want to change where we save the HTML output.

- We might want to change the API key.

- We might not want to hardcode the API key in the script at all.

We can pass values for these things when we call the script by making them parameters within the script. The next section will be all about parameterizing our script.

Working with parameters

Parameters are values for script variables that can be passed when we run the script, rather than being hardcoded into the script. As we've just seen in the previous section, we run the script in much the same way as we run any other cmdlet, and, as with cmdlets, we can pass parameter values to our script. Let's look at how we do that.

The first thing we need is the `CmdletBinding` attribute. Attributes are a way of telling PowerShell how we want it to process the elements of our script. We've used them before in *Chapter 4, PowerShell Variables and Data Structures*, when we learned how to cast variables. The `CmdletBinding` attribute tells PowerShell that we want it to treat the script as a cmdlet. Some of the big advantages this has are that our script will be able to access common parameters such as `-Verbose`, as well as positional binding. Let's add it. At the top of our script, create a new line and add this:

```
[CmdletBinding()]
```

Next, we need to create a `Param()` block to hold the variables we want to use as parameters. On a line directly under the `CmdletBinding` attribute, type this:

```
Param()
```

The `Param()` block must precede all the code that we're going to write. We will add our parameters inside the brackets, so it's best to press *Enter* a couple of times inside the brackets so that we have some space to add them:

```
[CmdletBinding()]
Param(

)
```

Now, we're ready to start creating parameters.

Creating useful parameters

The most useful parameters are values that change. Let's start with the city we're getting weather data for. The city is embedded in the `$uri` variable, which is a string. We can easily create a new variable to just hold the city name and pass it to the `$uri` variable. Try this:

```
[CmdletBinding()]
Param(
$City = "London"
)
```

And change the `$uri` variable to look like this:

```
$uri = "https://api.weatherapi.com/v1/current.json?q=$($City)&aqi=no"
```

Remember we need to use double quotes here (") so that the $City variable will be expanded. We can check our code against the following figure:

```
ch8 > 𝟤 weatherdata.ps1 > ...
   1    [CmdletBinding()]
   2    Param(
   3    $City = "London"
   4
   5    )
   6
   7    $headers = @{"key" = "<New key here>"}
   8
   9    $uri = "https://api.weatherapi.com/v1/current.json?q=$($City)&aqi=no"
  10
```

Figure 8.2 – Adding the CmdletBinding attribute and a param() block

This will write the value of $city into the $uri value when we run it.

> **Test, Test, Test**
>
> This is really important; if we make two changes and the script stops working, we will have to work out which change broke the script. Test after every change. Make sure it all still works before moving on to another change.

Let's test it. From the console, make sure we're in the directory where we've saved the script, and type the following:

```
.\WeatherData.ps1 -City Paris
```

Now, check the WeatherData.html file. It should look like this:

location

@{name=Paris; region=Ile-de-France; country=France; lat=48.87; lon=2.33; tz_id=Europe/Paris; localtime_epoch=1678214253; localtime=2023-03-07 19:37}

@{last_updated_epoch=167 wind_mph=13.6; wind_kph precip_in=0; humidity=53; gust_kph=22}

Figure 8.3 – Welcome to beautiful Paris

If this has worked for you, congratulations! You have parameterized your first script. Let's look at what we've done.

By putting the $City variable into the Param() block, we've made it accessible from outside the script so that we can pass values to it when we run the script. By assigning a value to the variable, writing $City = "London", we've set a default value so that if we don't pass a value via a parameter, the script will still run.

We can put as many variables as we like in the Param() block, but we must separate each one with a comma (,). Let's do another one; try the following activity.

Activity 1

How might we pass the location where we want to save the output? And how might we make that as easy as possible?

Hint: if we pass just a filename, it will save the output in the same location as the script is running from. Would we want that every time?

Let's look at what we could do with the key. Keys are a long string of random characters, so it's not going to be practical to type that into a parameter. How might we get around this?

We could save the key to a file, and then use Get-Content to extract the string from the file and use it that way. In *Chapter 7, PowerShell and the Web – HTTP, REST, and JSON* we saw there are two ways of passing a key to Invoke-RestMethod. We can either pass it to the -Key parameter or include it in the -Headers parameter, as we are doing in this script. The important difference is that in one scenario the key must be encoded, and in the other, it must be plain text. Can you remember which is which? Look back to the last chapter to find out.

If you remembered, well done. If you worked it out from how our script currently works, even better. We're already passing an unencoded string in the header, so we don't need to encode our key before saving it.

Open a new text document using your preferred text editor and save it as key.txt in the same folder as the script – in my case, c:\temp\poshbook\ch8. Copy and paste your WeatherApi key into it and save it.

Now all we need to do is add a parameter that points to the file, and a line that gets the content from the file. Then, we can add that to the $headers variable. It might look something like this:

```
[CmdletBinding()]
Param(
$City = "London",
$KeyFile = "key.txt"
)
$key = Get-Content $KeyFile
$headers = @{"key" = "$key"}
```

We've identified our changing values and created our parameters.

Activity 2

Knowing what we know from previous chapters, how might we rewrite our script so that we can accept multiple values for the -City parameter?

Hint 1: Look at a help file for a cmdlet that accepts multiple strings in a parameter to see how we could write an attribute for the -City parameter. Get-Random accepts multiple objects for -InputObject.

Hint 2: We're going to want a way of processing each string in turn. Remember, multiple strings passed into a parameter are an array.

Hint 3: We're going to want to send each city to a different output.

Let's look at how we might improve them using attributes.

Specifying type

We can limit the possibility of errors by specifying the type of the parameter in the same way as we specify the type of a variable, by typing the attribute before the variable. In your script, replace the $City = "London" line with this:

```
[String] $City = "London"
```

Now, whatever we pass in the -City parameter will be cast to a string.

Making parameters mandatory

We might want our script to require an explicit value for the -City parameter each time we run it. We could do that by changing the -City parameter like this:

```
[CmdletBinding()]
Param(
[Parameter(Mandatory = $true)]
$City = "London"
)
```

We've added the line [Parameter(Mandatory = $true)] before the $City parameter. Note that there is no comma (,) after the attribute. Now we've done that, the script ignores the default value for the parameter ("London"), and it prompts for a city:

```
PS C:\temp\poshbook\ch8> .\WeatherData.ps1

cmdlet weatherdata.ps1 at command pipeline position 1
Supply values for the following parameters:
City: paris
PS C:\temp\poshbook\ch8>
```

Figure 8.4 – Mandatory parameters

In the figure, we can see that because we didn't include a value for the -City parameter, we get prompted. One of the most useful things we can do with a script is to make it accept parameter values from the pipeline. Let's have a look at how we can do that.

Taking values from the pipeline

We covered how parameters can take values from the pipeline in *Chapter 3, The PowerShell Pipeline – How to String Cmdlets Together*. In this section, we're going to see how easy it is to make our script accept pipeline values. Remember, there are two ways that a parameter can take values from the pipeline: ByValue and ByName. For our script, it would be best if we let the -City parameter accept pipeline input by value, so let's do this:

```
[CmdletBinding()]
Param(
[Parameter(ValueFromPipeline)]
$City = "London",
```

All we've done is add the line [Parameter(ValueFromPipeline)] to the Param() block. We can see the difference it makes in the following figure:

```
PS C:\temp\poshbook\ch8> "cwmbran" | .\WeatherData.ps1
weatherdata.ps1: The input object cannot be bound to any parameters for the command either because
 the command does not take pipeline input or the input and its properties do not match any of the
parameters that take pipeline input.
PS C:\temp\poshbook\ch8> "cwmbran" | .\WeatherData.ps1
PS C:\temp\poshbook\ch8>
```

Figure 8.5 – Accepting values from the pipeline

In the first example, we can see that we've created a string, "cwmbran", and tried to pass it through the pipeline to the script. The script doesn't accept values from the pipeline, and we get an error message in red telling us just that. If we then alter the -City parameter to accept values from the pipeline, we can see the script completing without error in the second example.

Let's see what happens if we try feeding two values into the script through the pipeline, as in this example:

```
"Manila","Cardiff" | .\weatherdata.ps1
```

We will only get an output for the last item. To make this work properly, we need to include the part of the script we want to repeat for each item in a process { } block, like this:

```
34    [CmdletBinding()]
35    Param(
36    [Parameter(ValueFromPipeline)]
37    [string[]]$City = "London",
38    $OutputFile = "WeatherData.html",
39    $OutputPath = "C:\temp\poshbook\ch8",
40    $KeyFile = "key.txt",
41    [switch] $Joke
42    )
43
44    process {
45        foreach ($item in $City) {
46
47            Write-Verbose "Processing $item"
48
49            $Output = "$($OutputPath)\$($item)_$($OutputFile)"
50
51            $key = Get-Content $KeyFile
52
53            $headers = @{"key" = "$key"}
54
55            $uri = "https://api.weatherapi.com/v1/current.json?q=$($item)&aqi=no"
56
57            $response = Invoke-RestMethod -Uri $uri -Method GET -Headers $headers
58
59            $response | Convertto-Html | Out-File $Output
60        }
61    }
62
```

Figure 8.6 – Making pipeline input work properly

I'm opening a process { } block on line 44, and then closing it on line 61. I can now feed multiple cities into the pipeline and get an HTML file for each of them, like this:

```
"Bristol", "Brighton" | .\weatherdata.ps1
```

Note that doesn't mean we can get rid of the foreach loop from *Activity 2* entirely, though. If we pass multiple cities explicitly using the -City parameter, we will still need to process them individually with a loop.

There are lots of other things we can do with parameters, which are detailed in the article here: https://learn.microsoft.com/en-us/powershell/scripting/lang-spec/chapter-12.

Many of them can be used to validate the parameter input: making sure that it is the correct type, or even selecting input from a list of accepted values.

Switch parameters

There's one last feature of parameters we should talk about before moving on: switch parameters. Many of the cmdlets we've been using have parameters that act as switches; they don't take a value, they just have to be present to change the behavior of the cmdlet. For example, using the -Full parameter in Get-Help changes the amount of help information that is returned. We can do that in our script too. Try this – after the param() block, add the following lines:

```
If ($Joke.IsPresent) {
Write-Output "Why did the chicken cross the road?"
}
```

Then on the last line of the param() block, add the following line before the closing parenthesis. Remember, you will also need to add a comma after the previous parameter:

[switch] $Joke

The following figure shows how it looks in my script and shows the output when we use our new -Joke parameter:

```
34    [CmdletBinding()]
35    Param(
36    [Parameter(ValueFromPipeline)]
37    [string[]]$City = "London",
38    $OutputFile = "WeatherData.html",
39    $OutputPath = "C:\temp\poshbook\ch8",
40    $KeyFile = "key.txt",
41    [switch] $Joke
42    )
43
44    process {
45        If ($Joke.IsPresent) {Write-Output "Why did the chicken cross the road?"}
46
47        foreach ($item in $City) {
48
49            Write-Verbose "Processing $item"
50
```

PROBLEMS   OUTPUT   DEBUG CONSOLE   TERMINAL   PORTS   PowerShell Extension

```
PS C:\temp\poshbook\ch8> .\weatherdata.ps1 -Joke
Why did the chicken cross the road?
PS C:\temp\poshbook\ch8>
```

Figure 8.7 – Only joking

In line 40, I've added a comma after the parameter, so PowerShell knows there's another parameter coming. I've added the new -Joke switch parameter in line 41, and then on lines 44-46, I've added an If statement to tell PowerShell what to do if the switch is present. Finally, I've used the switch in the terminal at the bottom when I called the script, and the script told me the best joke in the world. Simple, huh?

Note that when we're looking at other people's scripts on the internet, we may well see a different construction for switch parameters. Instead of using If ($Joke.IsPresent), we will often see If ($Joke -eq $true). While this will work, it's a much older way of doing things and could be confusing. Using the .IsPresent method of the parameter is the way Microsoft recommends.

We'll be using parameters a lot as we go through the rest of the book, but for now, let's look at the other main topic of this chapter, providing help in our scripts.

Providing help for our script

Writing scripts is great fun, and we learn new things every time we write one. We include the new techniques or shortcuts, finish the script, put it to work, and then forget about it. The next time we look at it might be months or even years later, by which time we might well have forgotten how it works or why we wrote it the way we did. The answer to this is to write comprehensive help for the script, explaining how our script works and how to use it. This is even more important for scripts that we make available for other people to use.

In this section, we're going to cover four ways of providing help. First, we're going to briefly look at how we can comment our code to help ourselves and others. After that, we'll look at creating comment-based help for use with the Get-Help cmdlet. Then, we're going to look at the Write-Verbose cmdlet, and how we can use it to understand what the script is doing. Finally, we'll look at how we can provide help for mandatory parameters.

Let's start with commenting our code.

Comments

We briefly mentioned comments in *Chapter 5, PowerShell Control Flow – Conditionals and Loops*. We saw that a single line may be turned into a comment by adding a hash at the start (#), and we could create multiline comments by enclosing a body of text like this: <# ... #>. However, we didn't really talk about why comments are useful. PowerShell is a scripting language – a particularly friendly one, in my opinion. Most of the time, it is reasonably obvious to someone who knows the language what a line of code will do, but a line of explanation means that we don't need to parse each line to know what was intended. And, of course, what we write doesn't always do what we intend. A comment that records what we want the line to do makes our lives a lot easier when we're digging through four or five hundred lines of code. When the script is being adapted by somebody else, comments are invaluable. Have a look at the example below:

```
# concatenate the strings to produce an output filename
$Output = "$($OutputPath)\$($item)_$($OutputFile)"
```

The comment line tells us exactly what the slightly unreadable code is hopefully going to achieve.

Comment blocks

Comments are intended to be read in an editor of some sort. To make them easier to read, we will want to split a long comment across multiple lines. We could use the backtick character (`` ` ``) to escape manual line breaks, but that doesn't really make it easier to read, particularly for some editors and some fonts. It's better to use the blockquote construct, <#...#>. Have a look at the following figure:

```
foreach ($item in $City) {
    <# This block of code  is repeated for each city ($item) in the $city array.
    it creates a new filename for each city, then constructs a uri ($uri) and uses
    Invoke-RestMethod to fetch the data from that uri. finally it converts the
    response to HTML and writes it to the new filename #>

    $Output = "$($OutputPath)\$($item)_$($OutputFile)"

    $key = Get-Content $KeyFile

    $headers = @{"key" = "$key"}

    $uri = "https://api.weatherapi.com/v1/current.json?q=$($item)&aqi=no"

    $response = Invoke-RestMethod -Uri $uri -Method GET -Headers $headers

    $response | Convertto-Html | Out-File $Output
}
```

Figure 8.8 – Comment blocks

The comment block is in green and explains the intention of the following lines. Let's have a look at some dos and don'ts for writing good comments:

- Comment on a separate line; adding a comment on the same line makes the line either too long or causes it to wrap in the editor.

- Comment before the line you're explaining; prepare the reader for what's coming next in the script, not what's been.

- Don't comment on the obvious; generally speaking, too many comments are better than too few but don't waste your time explaining things that don't need it. Better to comment what a block of simple lines does than each individual line.

Let's look at how we can provide help for our script with the Get-Help cmdlet.

Comment-based help

The Get-Help cmdlet reads XML help files included with the main PowerShell program, and for modules and functions that have them. However, it can also read correctly formatted comments embedded in a script. This is called **comment-based help**. We can write comment-based help by adding special help comment keywords at the start of our script.

There are a number of rules to remember about writing comment-based help:

- It must be either at the start or the end of a script. For a couple of reasons, including the best practices for comments we covered previously, we should put it at the start.

- Comment-based help must be contiguous. We can't split it up into different comment blocks.

- Each section of the help must start with a legitimate keyword. The keyword is not case-sensitive, but it must be preceded by a dot (.).

- There must be two blank lines after the comment-based help.

Luckily, VS Code makes writing comment-based help a breeze. Let's see it working.

In our script, create a new line at the start of the script, and type comm. As we can see in the following figure, VS Code will offer us the comment-help function helper if we have the PowerShell extension installed.

```
ch8 > ≥ weatherdata.ps1
  1    comm
  2    [Cmd □ comment-help                                    Function Help
  3    Para □ block-comment                                   Comment Block
  4    [str □ [SuppressMessageAttribut…    Function: Suppress PSScript…
  5    $Out □ [SuppressMessageAttribut…    Parameter: Suppress PSScrip…
  6    $Out □ [SuppressMessageAttribute]    Suppress PSScriptAnalyzer …
  7    $KeyFile = "key.txt"
  8    )
  9
```

Figure 8.9 – The comment-help function in VS Code

Go ahead and select it. VS Code will create a comment-based help template for us with the most commonly used keywords, correctly formatted, and even add the two blank lines after the block for us.

Let's have a look at the common sections:

- .SYNOPSIS: This section should be one line that summarizes what the script does.

- .DESCRIPTION: This is where we put the full description, including how it works, what it should be used for, different ways to use it, and so on.

- .NOTES: This is where we should put warnings about incompatibilities, prerequisites for running the script (for instance, that we need to have a weatherapi key saved to a text file), and any other useful information that doesn't fit in the description.

- .LINK: This will provide a link for Get-Help -Online to consume. Personally, I never use it and delete it from the help section.

- .EXAMPLE: We can put examples of usage here to explain how to use the parameters. Separate each example with a new .EXAMPLE keyword on a new line.

I'll admit, the first time I did this, it was a real thrill seeing my script help looking like the real thing. It doesn't get old:

```
PS C:\temp\poshbook\ch8> get-help .\weatherdata.ps1

NAME
    C:\temp\poshbook\ch8\weatherdata.ps1

SYNOPSIS
    A short one-line action-based description, e.g. 'Tests if a function
    is valid'

SYNTAX
    C:\temp\poshbook\ch8\weatherdata.ps1 [[-City] <String[]>]
    [[-OutputFile] <Object>] [[-OutputPath] <Object>] [[-KeyFile]
    <Object>] [<CommonParameters>]
```

Figure 8.10 – Retrieving comment-based help for a script

This works just like anything else with Get-Help. To see the notes, type Get-Help .\weatherdata. ps1 -Detailed. To get everything, use the -Full parameter.

Activity 3

Write a short comment-based help for the script. Test it by calling Get-Help .\weatherdata. ps1 from the console.

That's it for comment-based help. It's incredibly useful, whether we read it in the editor or using the Get-Help cmdlet. I recommend we use it as often as we can. Let's look at something else now, that isn't strictly help, but is definitely helpful: the Write-Verbose cmdlet.

Write-Verbose

Back in *Chapter 3, The PowerShell Pipeline – How to String Cmdlets Together*, we talked briefly about the standard streams: output streams that exist in most programming languages and classify and direct output. The verbose stream is one of them and is intended for messages that help users understand what a cmdlet is doing. It's particularly useful for troubleshooting long-running cmdlets that don't appear to be doing anything. Every PowerShell cmdlet has a -Verbose switch parameter that allows us to see what the cmdlet is doing and whether it's got stuck, although not all of them produce a verbose stream output. We can see this in action already in our script because the Invoke-RestMethod cmdlet has a particularly useful verbose output. Try this:

```
.\weatherdata.ps1 -Verbose
```

You should see something like the following figure:

```
PS C:\temp\poshbook\ch8> .\weatherdata.ps1 -Verbose
VERBOSE: HTTP/1.1 GET with 0-byte payload
VERBOSE: received -byte response of content type application/json
VERBOSE: Content encoding: utf-8
PS C:\temp\poshbook\ch8>
```

Figure 8.11 – Verbose output from inside our script

We're able to access this verbose output because we have used the CmdletBinding() attribute at the start of the script, which gives us access to advanced functions. Without it, we can call the -Verbose parameter without an error, but it won't produce any output.

We can do even more than this, though; we can write our own verbose stream messages with the Write-Verbose cmdlet. Why is this useful? Because when we are processing many items in a loop in our script, it can tell us which item in the loop is failing. Let's say we ask our script to produce the data for three cities as follows:

```
.\weatherdata.ps1 -City "London", "Paris", "Llareggub"
```

Then, we'll get an error saying that when Invoke-RestMethod ran, a matching location couldn't be found, but the line of code that threw the error is as follows:

```
Invoke-RestMethod -Uri $uri -Method GET -Headers $headers
```

So it could be any of the cities that doesn't exist.

We can fix this by changing the start of the foreach loop:

```
foreach ($item in $City) {

    Write-Verbose "Processing $item"
    $Output = "$($OutputPath)\$($item)_$($OutputFile)"
```

We've added the line `Write-Verbose "Processing $Item"` at the start of the loop, which means that if we use the `-Verbose` parameter now, the script tells us which city it's processing, and we can see which of our cities is fictitious, as in the following figure:

```
PS C:\temp\poshbook\ch8> .\weatherdata.ps1 -City "London", "Paris", "Llareggub"
Invoke-RestMethod: C:\temp\poshbook\ch8\weatherdata.ps1:40
Line |
  40 |  … $response = Invoke-RestMethod -Uri $uri -Method GET -Headers $headers …
     |                                                           ~~~~~~~~~~~~~~~~~~~~~~~~~~~~~~~~~~~~~~~~~~~~~~~~~~~~~~~~~~~~~~
     | {"error":{"code":1006,"message":"No matching location found."}}
PS C:\temp\poshbook\ch8>
PS C:\temp\poshbook\ch8>
PS C:\temp\poshbook\ch8> .\weatherdata.ps1 -City "London", "Paris", "Llareggub" -Verbose
VERBOSE: Processing London
VERBOSE: HTTP/1.1 GET with 0-byte payload
VERBOSE: received -byte response of content type application/json
VERBOSE: Content encoding: utf-8
VERBOSE: Processing Paris
VERBOSE: HTTP/1.1 GET with 0-byte payload
VERBOSE: received -byte response of content type application/json
VERBOSE: Content encoding: utf-8
VERBOSE: Processing Llareggub
VERBOSE: HTTP/1.1 GET with 0-byte payload
VERBOSE: received -byte response of content type application/json
Invoke-RestMethod: C:\temp\poshbook\ch8\weatherdata.ps1:40
Line |
  40 |  … $response = Invoke-RestMethod -Uri $uri -Method GET -Headers $headers …
     |                                                           ~~~~~~~~~~~~~~~~~~~~~~~~~~~~~~~~~~~~~~~~~~~~~~~~~~~~~~~~~~~~~~
     | {"error":{"code":1006,"message":"No matching location found."}}
PS C:\temp\poshbook\ch8>
```

Figure 8.12 – Using Write-Verbose to illuminate the Bible-black

When we run the script in the first line, all we see is the error, but when we run it with the `-Verbose` parameter, it tells us which city it was processing when it encountered the error. Let's look at the final type of help we'll cover in this chapter: parameter help messages.

Parameter help messages

As well as controlling how parameters work in a script, we can also write helpful comments to guide people in using parameters in our scripts. These comments only apply to mandatory comments and are available if the mandatory parameter isn't provided. Let's try it. Edit the `$City` parameter like this:

```
Param(
[Parameter(Mandatory, HelpMessage="Enter one or more city names
separated by commas")]
[string[]]$City = "London",
```

Now, when we run it without supplying a value for the $City parameter, we get a message suggesting we type an interrobang (! ?) for help:

```
PS C:\temp\poshbook\ch8> .\weatherdata.ps1

cmdlet weatherdata.ps1 at command pipeline position 1
Supply values for the following parameters:
(Type !? for Help.)
City[0]: !?
Enter one or more city names separated by commas
City[0]: london
City[1]:
PS C:\temp\poshbook\ch8> |
```

Figure 8.13 – Accessing the HelpMessage parameter

Once we type the interrobang, the message we wrote in the script is presented. It's as easy as that; just remember that we can only use parameter help messages with mandatory parameters.

That about wraps it up for this chapter. Let's review what we've learned.

Summary

In this chapter, we've moved on from learning the building blocks of PowerShell syntax, and now we're beginning to put things together. The techniques we've learned may not be familiar to us, but with time and practice, they will become familiar and easy. As we go through the rest of the book, we will have plenty of opportunities to use them.

We started by talking about what scripts are and why we might want to write scripts at all. We looked briefly at where we can find other people's scripts, and what we need to do to run them on our machines.

We've done a lot of practical work in this chapter. Firstly, we looked at how we might make it easier for people to read what we're doing by breaking long pipelines up and substituting variables for hardcoded values in cmdlets, particularly values that might change.

We moved on to look at how we could pass those values into the script from outside using parameters, and we looked at various ways we could define and manipulate those parameters by making them mandatory or taking values from the pipeline.

We then looked at how we could make our scripts more easily understood by providing comments, before creating full-blown comment-based help for them, so that we can use the Get-Help cmdlet.

After that, we looked at using the Write-Verbose cmdlet to provide verbose output. This helps us understand what our script is doing when it doesn't seem to be working as we hoped.

Finally, we looked at providing help messages for mandatory parameters to make it easier for people to run our scripts.

In the next chapter, we're going to look at how we can make our code simpler and easier to write using script blocks, lambdas, and functions.

Further reading

- Output streams: `https://learn.microsoft.com/en-us/powershell/module/microsoft.powershell.core/about/about_output_streams`

- Some automation theory: `https://poshidiot.wordpress.com/2018/06/12/how-do-i-know-what-to-automate/`

- *The Practice of Cloud System Administration*, Limoncelli, T., Hogan, C., and Chalup, S. (2017) Boston: Addison-Wesley, *Chapter 12*.

- *Time Management for System Administrators*, Sebastopol: Limoncelli, T. (2008), O'Reilly Media, Inc., *Chapter 13*.

- *Why the Fitts list has persisted throughout the history of function allocation*: de Winter, J. C. F., and Dodou, D. (2014), Journal of Cognition, Technology & Work

- Learn more about attributes and parameters: `https://learn.microsoft.com/en-us/powershell/scripting/lang-spec/chapter-12`

Exercises

1. On attempting to run a script we've written, another user on our machine gets an error message that says `running scripts is disabled on this system`. What do we have to do to allow them to run the script?

2. We have a young relative who loves *Dungeons and Dragons*, but they've lost their 20-sided die. We write a short PowerShell script for them, `Get-Die.ps1`, as follows:

   ```
   Get-Random -Minimum 1 -Maximum 20
   ```

   This will produce a random number between 1 and 20 every time it is run. Which value in this line of code is most likely to change if they lose another die with a different number of sides?

3. In the `Get-Die.ps1` script from the previous question, how would we parameterize the changing value?

4. What type of parameter should it be, and how would we specify it?

5. They like the script, and now they've lost their four-sided die. They've discovered that they can put any number they like into the parameter. While this was quite cool at first, now they want the script to only let them roll the dice that are used in the game. How could we do that? We

need to know that *Dungeons and Dragons* uses 4-, 6-, 8-, 10-, 12-, and 20-sided dice, and we'll also need to read the link about parameters given in the text.

6. Our relative explains that sometimes they need to roll more than one die of the same type at a time and asks whether there is a way to do this. Well, of course there is… let's write it for them.

7. They've noticed that sometimes they forget to put the number of dice in, and they get a total of 0. How could we stop that from happening?

8. We're not always going to be around, and sometimes they aren't sure what to put in the parameters. How could we make it easier for them?

9. They are really trying our patience. Every now and then, they need to roll something they call a d100. This is a 10-sided die, with numbers going up in tens: 0, 10, 20, 30, and so on, plus a roll of a normal 10-sided die, which added together gives them a number between 1 and 100. Promising ourselves we'll never babysit for them again, how do we do that?

9

Don't Repeat Yourself – Functions and Scriptblocks

In this chapter, we're going to look at one of the basic principles of software development and learn how to apply it to save ourselves effort and make our code easier to maintain: **Don't Repeat Yourself**, also known as the **DRY** principle. In *The Pragmatic Programmer*, by Andy Hunt and Dave Thomas, the principle is stated as *"Every piece of knowledge must have a single, unambiguous, authoritative representation within a system."* Some programmers will take this principle to its logical conclusion and have no repeating code anywhere. We're writing scripts, and so we will apply the principle just as much as is convenient. We will talk about the concept of functions within code. By the end of the chapter, we will have seen how to write functions in our scripts to replace repeating code and learned how doing this makes our scripts easier to adapt and repair. We will also learn about another type of expression that is related to functions: **scriptblocks**. Along the way, we will also inevitably have to discuss the concept of **scope**.

In this chapter, we are going to cover the following topics:

- Why do we care about repeating code?
- How to turn repeating code into a function
- The concept of scope
- Exploring scriptblocks
- Let's do something useful

Why do we care about repeating code?

The obvious reason is that it is boring to figure out how to do something in PowerShell and then keep repeating the same lines over and over. For example, back in *Chapter 4, PowerShell Variables and Data Structures*, we discussed objects by referring to TypeName Imaginary.Bike. The Imaginary. Bike object had three properties: handlebar, wheel, and color. Let's say we want to write a short script that validates that an imaginary bike has all its properties. It might look something like this:

```
$mybike = @{handlebar = "ApeHanger"; color = "Red"; wheel = 15}

if (!($mybike.handlebar)) {
    write-output "this bike has no handlebars"
}
if (!($mybike.wheel)) {
    write-output "this bike has no wheels"
}
if (!($mybike.color)) {
    write-output "this bike has no handlebars"
}
if (!($mybike.gears)) {
    write-output "this bike has no gears"
}
```

In the first line, I'm just defining my imaginary bike. The validation script starts after that. I've thrown in a non-existent property, gears, just to make sure that the code works. We can see that the script has a lot of if statements that do almost exactly the same thing as each other: they check whether an attribute is present and output a message if it is missing. We're not too bothered about the repetition because we're only checking four properties. But what if we needed to check 40 or 400? This is where the DRY principle comes in. We could write a script to do the same thing like this:

```
$properties = @('handlebar', 'wheel', 'color', 'gears')
foreach ($property in $properties) {
    if (!($mybike.($property))) {
        write-output "this bike has no $property"
    }
}
```

Each property we add from now on just needs a single word added to the $properties array, rather than three new lines of code. Great, huh?

We're not just saving ourselves the effort of typing stuff out twice here, though. We're also saving ourselves the effort of finding our typing mistakes in possibly hundreds of lines of code. If that foreach loop works for one property, it will work for all of them, unless we mistyped the property name when we added it to the `$properties` array. We know exactly where to look if something isn't working, and so does anyone who needs to troubleshoot our script after us.

The DRY principle doesn't just refer to excessive code duplication; it can be applied far more widely in software. To quote *The Pragmatic Programmer* again, "*Many people took it [DRY] to refer to code only: they thought that DRY means "don't copy-and-paste lines of source." [...] DRY is about the duplication of knowledge, of intent. It's about expressing the same thing in two different places, possibly in two totally different ways.*"

Imagine if we had written not just one script but a whole bunch of scripts that worked with imaginary bikes. Perhaps we run an imaginary bike shop and want a stock control application. We might find we need to refer to imaginary bike properties frequently in those scripts. It may be that we would end up with lists of properties in lots of places. It's not hard to imagine that those lists might differ. Some might be incomplete. Some might be out of date. If we were to apply DRY to this, then there would be just one list of properties for all the scripts, a single source of truth when it comes to the properties that an imaginary bike might have, and whenever a script needed to refer to the list of properties, this is where they would find them.

To summarize, then, we care about repeating code for three reasons:

- We don't want to write more code than is necessary.

- We want it to be easier to find mistakes.

- We want a single source of truth for our code.

Do we want to reduce code duplication all the time, in every case? Probably not. Going back to the section on automation in *Chapter 8, Writing Our First Script – Turning Simple Cmdlets into Reusable Code*, sometimes the effort required to reduce duplication to the minimum just isn't worth it. Perhaps we're only going to use a piece of code twice; in this case, copying and pasting it is perfectly fine, rather than working out how to do it just once. There are also two other software development principles worth knowing about: **Avoid Hasty Abstraction** (**AHA**) and **You Aren't Gonna Need It** (**YAGNI**). AHA warns us to "*prefer duplication over the wrong abstraction*" and comes from Sandi Metz, the author of *Practical Object-Oriented Design in Ruby*. She encourages us to be flexible in our coding and only create abstractions (such as the second validation script previously) if they are genuinely necessary, and only once we understand exactly how the abstraction needs to work. The YAGNI principle comes from the practice of **Extreme Programming** (**XP**) and states that we should not add functionality until it's needed. As an example, if our imaginary bike had only a single property, then writing the script in the first example, with a single `if` statement, is preferable to writing the script in the second example with an abstraction that isn't going to be used (*You Aren't Gonna Need It*). We should do the simplest thing that could possibly work. One of the main takeaways from this is that software developers love an acronym.

Now we know why we should reduce code duplication, let's look at one of the main ways to do it in PowerShell: by using functions.

How to turn repeating code into a function

A function is a **named** section of code, a piece of code within a script or program that is given a label, and may be used by referring to the label. This is a very common programming paradigm and appears in most imperative programming languages. Some languages, such as PowerShell and Python, call these pieces of code functions. Some call them subroutines, subprograms, methods, or procedures. The paradigm is called procedural programming and lies between the scripting that most people practice with PowerShell and full object-oriented programming in languages such as C++ and Java. Functional programming is a different paradigm, with a declarative style.

> **Imperative, Declarative, Procedural, and Functional**
>
> I'm throwing around a lot of new words here, so it's worth quickly explaining what they mean.
>
> **Imperative** languages are *recipe* languages such as Python and PowerShell. Each step in the script or program tells the computer to do something, and often, how to do that thing. This is usually the first style of programming that people learn; often, it is the only style they learn.
>
> **Declarative** languages tell the computer what the end result should look like, and leave it up to the computer how to get there. We are all familiar with a declarative language: HTML. An HTML document may tell a computer that a string is a `<Heading>`, but it is up to the browser that is interpreting the HTML to decide what a `<Heading>` looks like.
>
> **Procedural** programming is the style of programming we're going to be examining in this chapter: writing procedures, which are called functions in PowerShell, and calling them from within our script. The overall programming style is still imperative.
>
> **Functional** programming is a declarative style of programming, where we create functions on objects and then call the functions. Pure functional programming is often described as declarative programming. Functional programming in PowerShell is not impossible, but it is pretty advanced, so we're not going to cover it in this book. If you are really interested in having a look at it, then visit Chris Kuech's GitHub page at `https://github.com/chriskuech/functional` and have a play with his **functional** module for PowerShell.

Let's have a look at a function. In the PowerShell console, try this:

```
function get-square($a) {$a * $a}
```

Now, type `get-square`, followed by a number, like this:

```
get-square 23
```

As if by magic, the square of our number is returned. While the console is open, we can use `get-square` as often as we like.

What have we done there? Well, we've taken some code, `{$a * $a}`, and given it a label (or name), `get-square`, by using the `function` keyword. We've also told it to expect a variable, `$a`, by placing the variable in brackets directly after the name. Whenever we use the name of the function, the code runs on the object we're passing – in this case, the integer 23.

It's pretty rare we would define and use a function in the console like that. Instead, I usually incorporate functions into my scripts. Let's do that now. Open a new PowerShell file in VS Code so we can carry on playing. Let's do something a little more adventurous. Let's create a function that gets the square root of a number by approximation. Type this:

```
function Get-RoughRoot {
    param (
        $number
    )
    $start = 1
    while (($start * $start) -le $number)  {
        $result = $start
        $start += 1
        }
    return $result
}
Get-RoughRoot 785692
```

All this code does is start at 1, and keep multiplying numbers by themselves until it gets to a number that is larger than the number we originally pass to the function – in this case, 785692. It's pretty rough and ready. If we run this code, we find that the approximate square root of 785,692 is 886, pretty close to the actual square root of 886.392 but not exact. It demonstrates one of the strengths of machines: fast repetition. It's gone through that while loop 887 times.

Notice the param() block that we've opened on the second line. It's the same as the param() blocks we've been using already. In fact, we can turn this function into an **advanced function** by including the cmdletbinding() attribute, and then we could use all the common parameters with Get-RoughRoot. We can do all the same things with the param() block in a function as we can do with the param() block in a script.

> **Activity 1**
>
> If we type 65378 | Get-RoughRoot at the end of our script and run it, what's going to happen? Why is that, and how could we make that line work?

Once we've created our function within a script, we can call it as many times as we like, just by referring to the name of the function and providing values for the parameters. Yes, there is a really easy way to get an accurate square root with PowerShell, and it's much shorter, but where's the fun in that?

What makes a function?

To create functions, we need the following:

- The keyword, `function`, at the start.

- A descriptive and meaningful name. It's best to follow the PowerShell naming conventions and use an approved verb in a verb-noun pair, especially if the function is going to be shared with others.

- A set of PowerShell cmdlets in braces, `{ }`.

We can include a set of parameters, either within a `param()` block after we've opened the braces, or we can include them in brackets appended to the name. It's preferable to use the `param()` block, especially if we've got multiple parameters or if we want to add statements to the parameters – for instance, to control how they accept pipeline input, or what types they accept.

When we're including functions in scripts, it is important to remember that the script is read by the computer from top to bottom, rather than ingested whole before executing. It is important, therefore, that we have defined our functions before we call them in the script. It's usual to define all the functions in a script at the top, after the parameters.

Each function consists of four statement blocks: `begin`, `process`, `end`, and `clean`. We don't need to include these statements for our function to work, but we need to be aware of how PowerShell will read our code if we don't include them.

The `begin` statement block is for statements that set up the function and will only run once when the function is called before the function does anything with its input. Similarly, the `end` block will only run once when the function is called. The `process` block will run for each object in the pipeline that is fed to the function, which is why we need to include it when accepting multiple objects from the pipeline, because if no statement blocks are specified, then PowerShell assigns all statements to the `end` block.

The `clean` statement block was introduced in PowerShell 7.3. It is similar to the `end` statement block, but it will always run, even if the function terminates due to an error or if the function is deliberately halted by pressing *Ctrl* + *C*, whereas the `end` block will not. The other difference is that the `end` block can output objects to the pipeline, and `clean` cannot.

Let's see how this looks in actual code. In the following figure, we've added `begin`, `end`, `process`, and `clean` statement blocks to our `Get-RoughRoot` function:

```
ch9 > ≥ basicfunction.ps1 > ...
     1 reference
 7   function Get-RoughRoot {
 8       param (
 9           [Parameter(ValueFromPipeline)]
10           $number
11       )
12       begin {
13       write-output "for the begin statement, the number is $number"
14       }
15       process {
16           $start = 1
17           while (($start * $start) -le $number)  {
18               $result = $start
19               $start += 1
20               }
21       write-output "The rough root of $number is $result"
22           }
23
24       end {
25           write-output "for the end statement, the number is $number"
26       }
27
28       clean {
29           write-output "no output from the clean block"
30       }
31
32   }
33
34   785692, 3492858  | Get-RoughRoot
```

PROBLEMS ❶   OUTPUT   DEBUG CONSOLE   **TERMINAL**

```
for the begin statement, the number is
The rough root of 785692 is 886
The rough root of 3492858 is 1868
for the end statement, the number is 3492858
PS C:\temp\poshbook>
```

Figure 9.1 – Begin, process, end, and clean statement blocks

The begin statement on line 12 contains a Write-Output cmdlet to display the value that is currently held in the -number parameter. We can see from the output at the bottom that there is no value held in this parameter when the begin block runs. The process block on line 15 then runs and feeds the current value of -number to the pipeline, and repeats for as many values of -number as there are in the pipeline. The end block on line 24 then runs once, and can only see the final value passed by the -number parameter. Finally, the clean block executes on line 28. We can see that it produces no output at all, although it does complete successfully. If you don't believe me, try it – write a line of code that can't run, such as write-rubbish "here is some rubbish". There will be a whole load of red text as PowerShell fails to execute it.

There is also an important keyword to be aware of: `return`. The `return` keyword ends the current iteration of the block that is running. Let's see what happens when we use it. Here is the code for the `Get-RoughRoot` function, with an `if` statement in the `process` block that returns the pop string if the original number is less than 10:

```
function Get-RoughRoot {
    param (
        [Parameter(ValueFromPipeline)]
        $number
    )
    begin {
    write-output "for the begin statement, the number is $number"
    }
    process {
        $start = 1
        while (($start * $start) -le $number)   {
            $result = $start
            $start += 1
                }
        if ($number -lt 10) {
            return "pop"
        }
        write-output "The rough root of $number is $result"
        }

    end {
        write-output "for the end statement, the number is $number"
    }
}
```

Let's now pass a number less than 10 in our pipeline, like this:

```
785692, 4, 3492858   | Get-RoughRoot
```

We will get the output in the following figure:

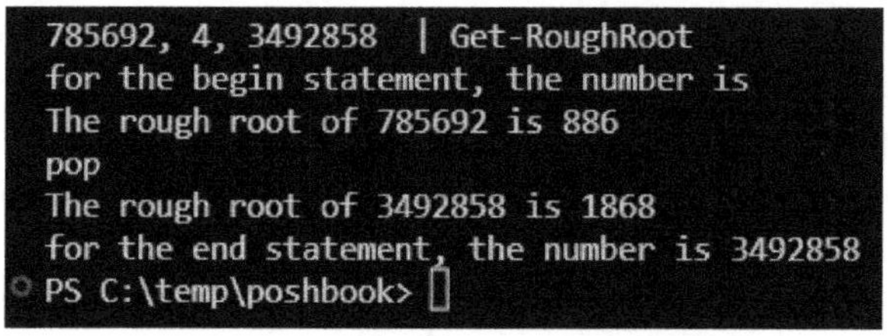

Figure 9.2 – Using the return keyword

We can see that the rough roots of the two large numbers are returned, but the process block has terminated early when fed a number less than 10.

The `return` keyword has returned the value it has been assigned (`pop`), but that is purely optional – we don't need to assign a value to `return`. It's worth noting that this is slightly confusing for those of us who are familiar with other languages. For example, in Python, the `return` statement is used to supply the result of the function. In both Python and PowerShell, `return` statements work in very similar ways but the intention behind them is different; PowerShell will return the output of the function without the `return` keyword, whereas Python will not. For both Python and PowerShell, `return` will stop the function at the point it is used.

Basic and advanced functions

Most of the functions I write within scripts are basic functions, but we can make a function behave like a cmdlet by using the `CmdletBinding` attribute. This gives us access to a range of behaviors that we see in cmdlets, such as the `-whatif` and `-confirm` parameters. It also gives us access to advanced methods such as `WriteCommandDetail` and `WriteError`.

Function parameters

As we've mentioned, parameters for functions work the same way as parameters in scripts, but it's worth recapping them here.

Types of parameters

There are four types of parameters we can use with functions (and scripts!):

- Named parameters
- Switch parameters
- Positional parameters
- Dynamic parameters.

Let's take a closer look.

Named parameters

Named parameters are the parameters we've been working with, where we supply a variable that is used as the parameter's name, like this:

```
Param(
$number
)
```

The name of that parameter, whether it is in a function or a script, is -number. We can use the $number variable anywhere within our function, and it will have the value supplied in the parameter. As we saw in *Chapter 8*, *Writing Our First Script – Turning Simple Cmdlets into Reusable Code*, we can set a default value for a parameter like this:

```
$number = 100
```

We can also specify the type of the parameter by supplying a type value in square brackets before the variable: [int] $number.

Switch parameters

Switch parameters don't require a value, they are simply on or off. If we supply the parameter to the function, then they are on; if they're not supplied, then they are off. We specify the type of the parameter as [switch], like this: [switch] $heads. We can test for the presence of the switch in our function with an if statement, like this:

```
Function get-flip {
    param([switch]$heads)
    if ($heads.ispresent) {"Heads!"}
    else {"Tails!"}
}
```

We don't need the .ispresent property, we could just type if ($heads), but I think that's less clear. We could also use the if ($heads -eq $true) construction, which we may see in older articles on the web, but that is not Microsoft's preferred method.

Positional parameters

These parameters make use of the $Args automatic variable instead of using a param() block. This parameter exists for every basic function and allows us to create unnamed parameters, like this:

```
Function get-product {
$product = $Args[0] * $Args[1]
Write-output "The product of $($Args[0]) and $($Args[1]) is $product"
}
```

This means we can supply parameters like this:

```
Get-product 2 4
```

We can see the result in the following figure:

```
PS C:\Users\nickp> Function get-product {
>> $product = $Args[0] * $Args[1]
>> Write-output "The product of $($Args[0]) and $($Args[1]) is $product"
>> }
PS C:\Users\nickp> get-product 2 4
The product of 2 and 4 is 8
PS C:\Users\nickp>
```

Figure 9.3 – Using positional parameters

We can see the function has correctly assigned the values we supplied. The $Args parameter is an array.

Note that if we use a param() block, then that will override this functionality; it won't work, as we will need to specify positional parameters. By default, parameters are positional, in the order that the parameters are written down, so this will work:

```
Function get-product {
Param($a,$b)
$product = $a * $b
$product
}
Get-product 2 4
```

The value 2 will be assigned to $a, and the value 4 will be assigned to $b. If it is important that a parameter be at a specific position, however, we should use the position attribute, discussed in the next section.

The $Args automatic variable can also be used to splat parameters into a function – review *Chapter 4, PowerShell Variables and Data Structures*, for more about splatting. Let's see how that works in the following figure:

```
PS C:\Users\nickp> function Get-Fifteen20 {Get-Random @Args; $Args}
PS C:\Users\nickp> Get-Fifteen20 -minimum 15 -maximum 20
19
-minimum
15
-maximum
20
PS C:\Users\nickp>
```

Figure 9.4 – Splatting the $Args variable

In the first line, we are creating a simple function called Get-Fifteen20. It runs Get-Random. We tell it to accept arguments from the command line into an array called @Args (note the array symbol, @). After that, we tell it to output the value of the $Args automatic variable. From the output, we can see we first get a random number between 15 and 20 (19), then we get the contents of the $Args variable. We can see it is an array of four objects: -minimum, 15, -maximum, and 20. These are supplied in sequence to the Get-Random cmdlet in the function, giving us an effective PowerShell statement of Get-Random -minimum 15 -maximum 20, which works just fine.

> **Activity 2**
>
> Why doesn't Get-Fifteen20 15 20 work?

Dynamic parameters

Dynamic parameters are only available if a specified condition is true. They are not defined in the param() block, but in a separate DynamicParam{} block – note this uses braces, not brackets. Dynamic parameters are quite an advanced topic and should only be used if absolutely necessary, so we're not going to spend much time on them here. A good example of how they work can be found in the Get-ChildItem cmdlet. Get-ChildItem can be used with any PSProvider – we covered PSProviders in *Chapter 6, PowerShell and Files – Reading, Writing, and Manipulating Data*. Depending on which PSProvider we are using, different parameters of Get-ChildItem are available. For instance, if we are in the FileSystem provider, we have access to parameters such as -File and -Hidden. If we are using the Certificate provider, then we can't use those parameters but we have parameters such as -DnsName and -SslServerAuthentication instead.

Now we've covered the types of parameters, let's take a look at some of the attributes we can apply to our parameters.

Parameter attributes

Attributes are optional arguments that we can use to control how parameters behave – whether they are mandatory or accept pipeline input, for example. To use attributes, we must start each parameter with the Parameter() attribute, which looks like this:

```
Param(
[Parameter(Argument = Value)]
$ParameterName
)
```

The Parameter() attribute takes multiple arguments, but we must separate them with a comma (,). Let's go through the more common parameters.

CmdletBinding

The CmdletBinding attribute makes the function behave like a cmdlet. If we use this attribute within a function, we get access to the common parameters such as -whatif and -confirm. This removes access to the $Args automatic variable for that function.

Mandatory

As we saw in *Chapter 8, Writing Our First Script – Turning Simple Cmdlets into Reusable Code*, we can use the Mandatory argument to ensure a value is provided for a parameter, and the HelpMessage argument to provide help for that mandatory parameter:

```
Param(
[Parameter(Mandatory, HelpMessage="Type one or more integers,
separated by commas." )]
[int[]]
$number
)
```

This means that at least one integer must be supplied with the -number parameter, and a help message can be accessed.

Position

The Position argument allows a parameter to be passed without explicitly naming it and can specify at which position it must be supplied:

```
Param(
[Parameter(Mandatory, Position=0 )]
[int[]]
$number
)
```

The preceding code tells us that the first value passed without a preceding parameter name will be applied to the -number parameter. Two things to note are that named parameters are not counted, and that numbering starts at 0, so the second position is Position=1. Note that if we're using a param() block, the $Args functionality we've just covered won't work, and we'll not be able to splat parameters into a cmdlet within our function.

If we don't use a Position argument, then all the parameters will be assigned positions in the order they are declared in the param() block, but we shouldn't rely on this working exactly as we expect. If we want a parameter to be positional, then we should declare it.

ParameterSetName

We can use the ParameterSetName argument to define parameters that are only present for particular parameter sets. If ParameterSetName is not supplied, a parameter belongs to all parameter sets. I adhere to the philosophy that a function should do one thing, and so I've never really found the need for parameter sets. Some people, however, like to write Swiss Army knife functions that do lots of things, and so parameter sets are useful for them.

ValueFromPipeline

We've used this already in this chapter – it's necessary to allow a function parameter to accept an object from the pipeline. The parameter accepts the whole object.

ValueFromPipelineByPropertyName

If we only want the parameter to accept a property of an object (for instance, a name), then we can use this argument. If the object in the pipeline has a name property, `$object.name`, then that will be used for this parameter. The object property must match the parameter name; otherwise, it won't get passed. For instance, if we pass a string through the pipeline to a function with a `-length` parameter that accepts pipeline values by property name, then the parameter will be populated with the length of the string, not the actual string. If the parameter is called `-stringlength`, then it will be empty because the string doesn't have a `stringlength` property.

ValueFromRemainingArguments

We can use this parameter to hold an indeterminate number of arguments that might be passed to a function, as an array. We can then access those arguments by using the index of their position in the array. This is useful in advanced functions, where we don't have access to the `$Args` automatic variable, and we want to capture an unknown number of arguments.

HelpMessage

As we've seen already, this attribute can be used to provide a helpful message for mandatory parameters.

Alias

I'm including this here for the sake of completeness, but I think I've made my views on aliases quite plain. They can occasionally be useful, but they also lead to confusion and make code less readable. It is possible, however, to use the `Alias` attribute to provide an alias for a parameter.

SupportsWildcards

We can use this parameter if we want a parameter to accept wildcards. Note that this doesn't mean the function supports wildcards – we still need to write code in our function that can handle wildcard input.

Argument completion attributes

There are two argument completion attributes that allow a user to complete the values of a parameter using the *Tab* key. These are similar to the `ValidateSet` attribute. We're not going to cover them in this book, but it's useful to know that it is something we can do if we want to.

Validation attributes

There are currently 14 attributes that we can use to validate parameters and the values supplied for them. We can validate that a value is null, that a value follows a specific pattern such as a credit card number or IP address, and that a value is of a certain length or falls in a certain range. We discovered the `ValidateSet` attribute in *Chapter 8, Writing Our First Script – Turning Simple Cmdlets into Reusable Code*. It works like this:

```
Param(
[Parameter (Mandatory)]
[ValidateSet("Pontypool", "Newport", "Swansea","Llanelli", "Cardiff")]
[string]$team
)
```

This will only accept the string if it appears in the array listed in `ValidateSet`. Note that validation attributes sit outside the `Parameter()` attribute.

While there are plenty more aspects of parameters we could cover, that's enough for now. Let's look at a specialized type of function: filters.

Filters

A filter is a specialized function that automatically runs on all objects in the pipeline. A filter is similar to a function with just a `process{ }` statement block. We can use them like this:

```
PS C:\Users\nickp> filter square {$_ * $_}
PS C:\Users\nickp> 36 | square
1296
PS C:\Users\nickp>
```

Figure 9.5 – Using a filter

Instead of using the `function` keyword, we've used `filter`. We've called our filter `square` and defined it as multiplying the pipeline object by itself. Now we can feed a value to the filter via the pipeline, and get an output. Notice that we can't use it like a function; `square 36` won't work as there's nothing in the pipeline for the filter to work on.

Before we can really get on with using functions, though, we need to talk about an important concept: scope.

The concept of scope

PowerShell uses the concept of scope to protect variables, functions, PSDrives, and aliases from inadvertent change by limiting how they may be accessed and modified. Let's demonstrate:

1. Create a variable and set its value:

    ```
    $ScopeTest = 10
    ```

2. Create a function:

    ```
    Function Set-ScopeTest {$ScopeTest = 15; Write-Output "the value
    of ScopeTest is $ScopeTest"}
    ```

3. Test the value of $ScopeTest by calling the variable:

    ```
    $ScopeTest
    ```

4. Run our function:

    ```
    Set-ScopeTest
    ```

5. We can see from the output that the value of $ScopeTest inside the function is 15. Let's check whether the value has changed permanently:

    ```
    $ScopeTest
    ```

    No, it hasn't. That's because the function is operating on its local scope; it can read the value of the variable, and it can change it while it's running, but it can't change it permanently because the variable exists outside the function. This is known as the scope of the function.

PowerShell has the following types of scopes:

-   **Global**: This is the scope created when a PowerShell session is started. It includes all the automatic variables and functions, plus any that we define at the prompt, such as the $scopeTest variable we just used. Anything that is defined in the global scope is available everywhere inside the current session.

-   **Local**: This is the scope where we are currently working. When we are using the command prompt, our local scope is the global scope. Inside the Set-ScopeTest function, there is a different scope to the global scope. When we changed the $SetScope variable inside our function, it only changed in the local scope of the function, not the global scope. The local scope is relative to other scopes, not a predefined scope, so it may refer to the global scope, a script scope, or a child of the global or script scopes. We can create many nested local scopes. When we run a script or a function, we are creating a new local scope.

- **Script**: This is the scope that is created when we run a script. Only the statements in the script run in the script scope, and those statements see the script scope as the local scope. Each script that is running has its own script scope; they don't share objects.

Parent and child scopes

There is a hierarchy of scopes. A scope that is contained in another scope is called a child scope, and the containing scope is called the parent scope. The global scope is always the root scope, the parent of all scopes, and other scopes are child scopes of the global scope. So, when we ran `Set-ScopeTest` previously, we created a local scope for the function that is a child of the global scope. The local scope can read the variables of the parent scope, but by default, does not change them in the parent scope; it can only change them in its local scope. Let's add a few lines to our `Set-ScopeTest` function to illustrate this:

```
PS C:\Users\nickp> Function Set-ScopeTest {
>>      Write-Output "the value of ScopeTest is $ScopeTest"
>>      $ScopeTest = 15
>>      Write-Output "the value of ScopeTest is $ScopeTest"
>>      Write-Output "Global Variable:"
>>      Get-Variable -Scope global | Where-Object {$_.name -like "Scope*"}
>>      Write-Output "`n"
>>      Write-Output "Local Variable:"
>>      Get-Variable -Scope local | Where-Object {$_.name -like "Scope*"}
>> }
PS C:\Users\nickp> Set-ScopeTest
the value of ScopeTest is 10
the value of ScopeTest is 15
Global Variable:

Name                          Value
----                          -----
ScopeTest                     10


Local Variable:
ScopeTest                         15
```

Figure 9.6 – Illustrating parent and child scopes

The first line we've added gets the value of the $ScopeTest variable that the function inherits from its parent scope (in this case, 10) and writes it to the screen. We then change the value of $ScopeTest within the function, as before, and output the new value. Next, we've got a couple of lines using Get-Variable that retrieve the value of the $ScopeTest variable in the global and local scopes. We can see that even within the function, the global value of $ScopeTest remains 10 – it is only the local instance of $ScopeTest that is changed by the function. What happens if we want to modify the value of a variable in the parent scope with our function, though? Let's take a look at how we can do that.

Scope modifiers

Scopes are used for a reason – to protect ourselves from inadvertent changes – and we should only step outside the automatic scopes with caution, but sometimes we need to do it. PowerShell includes a number of scope modifiers that allow us to change the default scope. They include the following:

- `Global`: This specifies objects in the global scope.

- `Local`: This specifies an object in the current scope.

- `Script`: This specifies an object in the parent script scope, or in the global scope if there is no parent script; we'd use this with functions embedded in scripts.

- `Private`: When this is used while creating variables, this prevents child scopes from using the object.

- `<Variable-namespace>` These refer to PSDrive namespaces, such as `env:` and `variable:`.

There are also a couple of others that we won't cover here: `workflow:`, which is deprecated, and `using:`, which is used with cmdlets such as `Invoke-Command` and `Start-Job`. Scripts operate by default in the `script:` scope. Functions operate in the `local:` scope by default, even when they are defined in a script.

We use the scope modifier between the $ symbol and the variable name, like this:

```
$global:ScopeTest = 10
```

This will create a variable in the global scope called `ScopeTest` and set its value to `10` (remember, the variable name doesn't have a $ symbol – we use the $ symbol to refer to the contents of the variable).

Similarly, we can define the scope of a function like this:

```
Function Global:Set-ScopeTest {$ScopeTest = 15}
```

Note that setting the scope of the function to global doesn't change where the function acts, it changes where it is available. So, a function with a global scope doesn't automatically act on global variables, as we can see here:

```
PS C:\Users\nickp> $ScopeTest
10
PS C:\Users\nickp> Function Global:Set-ScopeTest {$ScopeTest = 15}
PS C:\Users\nickp> Set-ScopeTest
PS C:\Users\nickp> $scopeTest
10
PS C:\Users\nickp> Function Set-ScopeTest {$Global:ScopeTest = 15}
PS C:\Users\nickp> Set-ScopeTest
PS C:\Users\nickp> $scopeTest
15
```

Figure 9.7 – Global functions and global variables

We can see the original value of $ScopeTest is 10. We then define a global function called Set-ScopeTest that sets the value to 15. Calling the function doesn't change the global value of $ScopeTest. To do that, we need to tell the function to work on the global variable, not the local version running inside the function. We do that in the second command, with the following code: $Global:ScopeTest = 15.

As we work through the rest of the book, we'll see the concept of scope, and no doubt be occasionally frustrated by it. Remember that it is there to protect us and provide a set of handy guardrails to prevent us from experiencing hilarious consequences. We should only step outside the default scope after some thought and consideration. We can often avoid this through passing variables as parameters, or explicitly writing output from inside our function and storing it as a variable.

Now we understand functions, let's look at their very close relatives: scriptblocks.

Exploring scriptblocks

A scriptblock is a collection of statements inside braces ({ }) that can be used as a single unit. We've already used them numerous times: in Where-Object cmdlets, if and else statements, foreach loops, and earlier in this chapter, when we were writing functions. In this section, we are going to look at some of the properties of scriptblocks and how we can use them in our code.

Consider everything we've just done on functions. A function consists of the function keyword, a name, and a scriptblock: a set of statements inside braces. We don't need the keyword to use the scriptblock – the keyword supplies a label that we use to call the scriptblock when we need it.

Scriptblocks return the output of all the statements they contain; this may be a single object or an array of objects. We can use the return keyword, and it works the same as it does for a function: it will exit the scriptblock at that point.

We can create parameters for scriptblocks using a param() block, and it will accept all the parameter types and attributes that we use with a function. What we can't do is pass parameters outside the braces, as we can with functions, because there is no name value to attach them to.

How to run a scriptblock

There are many ways to call scriptblocks – lots of cmdlets and statements such as foreach accept them. Sometimes, however, we want to just run the scriptblock. Invoke-Command is one way to do it, like this:

```
$a = 10
Invoke-Command -ScriptBlock {$a * $a}
```

This gives us the output 100. Let's look at some of the other ways we might do it.

Unlike functions, scriptblocks may be stored in variables, like this:

```
$square = {$a * $a}
```

Now, we can use the $square variable in the following ways:

- We can pass it as a parameter to Invoke-Command, either with the -ScriptBlock parameter name or not:

  ```
  Invoke-Command $square
  ```

- Using Get-Member, we can see that $square has a TypeName of System.Management. Automation.ScriptBlock. This type has a method called invoke(), which we can use like this:

  ```
  $square.invoke()
  ```

- Let's say we've put a parameter in our scriptblock, like this:

  ```
  $square = {param($a) $a * $a}
  ```

  Then, we can pass the parameter in the brackets:

  ```
  $square.invoke(20)
  ```

  What we can't do is just call the variable to run the scriptblock:

```
PS C:\Users\nickp> $square
param($a) $a * $a
PS C:\Users\nickp> |
```

Figure 9.8 – How not to run a scriptblock

As you can see, if we call the variable, we get the contents of the scriptblock, not the output. Instead, we use the call operator (&) like this:

```
&$square 20
```

We can leave a space between & and $square as well, & $square, and we will often see it written like that.

- There is one other way: dot sourcing. Instead of the call operator, we can use a period (.) like this:

  ```
  . $square
  ```

We need to be very careful when we call scriptblocks like this. Using Invoke-Command, invoke() and the call operator all run the scriptblock in a child scope, as we would expect. Dot sourcing will run it in the parent scope, as we can see in the following figure:

```
PS C:\Users\nickp> $SbScope = "Global scope!"
PS C:\Users\nickp> $ChangeSbScope = {$SbScope = "Local Scope!"; $SbScope}
PS C:\Users\nickp> $SbScope
Global scope!
PS C:\Users\nickp> &$ChangeSbScope
Local Scope!
PS C:\Users\nickp> $SbScope
Global scope!
PS C:\Users\nickp> . $ChangeSbScope
Local Scope!
PS C:\Users\nickp> $SbScope
Local Scope!
```

Figure 9.9 – The call operator and dot sourcing

In the first line, we've defined a variable, $SbScope, as the Global scope! string. We then define a variable, $ChangeSbScope, as a scriptblock that sets $SbScope to Local scope! and returns it. When we call $ChangeSbScope with the call operator, it runs in the local scope and leaves the global value of $SbScope unchanged: Global scope!. However, when we dot source $ChangeSbScope, we can see that it changes the value of $SbScope in the global scope. Be careful. Don't dot source unless you're absolutely sure that's what you have to do.

Lambdas

Most programming languages have the concept of a **lambda** – an anonymous function, a function without a name. In PowerShell, we have the scriptblock, which is a broader concept that includes lambdas. So in Python, we might have a lambda statement such as the following, which adds a value to itself:

```
Add = lambda a: a + a
Add(20)
```

And we get the output 40. In PowerShell, the equivalent lambda, using a scriptblock, would be as follows:

```
$add = {param($a) $a + $a}
&$add(20)
```

And again, we get 40. Lambdas in Python are limited to expressions and can't include statements, whereas in PowerShell, we are not so restricted.

When do we want to use scriptblocks instead of functions? Generally, we use scriptblocks for short, simple blocks of code that may only occur a couple of times in a script. I often use them in the console as well. If I'm writing a script that is going to be used by other people, then anything more than a line or two of code would go in a function to improve readability and make sure other people know exactly what I was trying to do.

The final case for scriptblocks is for people who come to PowerShell knowing another language, such as Python. Using scriptblocks as a substitute for lambdas allows them to continue writing code in a style they are used to.

That's enough to learn about functions and scriptblocks. Let's look at a practical application.

Let's do something useful

When I am writing PowerShell scripts for customers, I like to make sure that the script records information about what it is doing and any changes it has made in a log file so that I can quickly pinpoint what is going on. I don't write the functionality each time I write a script, however; I just include some saved PowerShell snippets in the script that give me a log file function. Let's think about how we might do that now.

First, we need to think about where we create the log file. I use `C:\temp`, as that directory is usually where we put things that we don't want to keep forever, and it usually has fairly relaxed permissions. We might want to think about a different directory on Linux or macOS, such as `/var/log/`.

We also want to create a file that is as easy to read as possible; I write to a text file but I use the suffix `.log` so that I know what sort of text file it is. The file we create needs to be date-stamped so that we know which file relates to which instance the script was run. This means we need to create it outside the function, at the script level; otherwise, we'll create a new file every time the function is called.

Each file entry needs to be time-stamped so we know in what order the events in the log occurred, and it also needs to record a string that we can pass from outside the function.

It looks like we need two parameters: `$LogFile` and `$LogString`. Let's start writing this:

1. Create a new PowerShell file in VS Code; I'm calling mine `Write-Log.ps1`.

2. First, let's create `$LogFilename`:

    ```
    $LogFile = "c:\temp\MyLogFile" + $(Get-Date -UFormat "%Y-%m-
    %d_%H-%M-%S") + ".log"
    ```

    Don't worry too much about the `-UFormat` parameter of `Get-Date`; it's to produce an easily readable text string that will work with Windows file-naming rules.

3. Now, we need a descriptive name, such as `Write-Log`:

    ```
    Function Write-Log {
    }
    ```

4. We also need a `param()` block for our `$LogString` parameter:

    ```
    Function Write-Log {
    Param(
    $logString
    ```

```
    )
    }
```

5. Now, let's get onto the functionality. We need a variable that holds a string for the current date and time. Here's another way to do it:

```
$stamp = (Get-Date).ToString("yyyy/m/dd HH:mm:ss")
```

6. Now, we need to create a log message by concatenating the $stamp variable and the $LogString variable that we get from the parameter:

```
$LogMessage = "$stamp $Logstring"
```

7. Finally, we need to write it to the log file:

```
Add-Content $Logfile -Value $LogMessage
```

8. And that's it. Let's add a line in the script after the function to check that it works:

```
Write-Log "is this thing on?"
```

And let's run it to see.

Figure 9.10 – Yes it is

Here's my complete code:

```
$LogFile = "c:\temp\MyLogFile" + $(Get-Date -UFormat "%Y-%m-%d_%H-%M-
%S") + ".log"
Function Write-Log {
    Param (
        [string]$LogString
    )
    $stamp = (Get-Date).ToString("yyyy/m/dd HH:mm:ss")
    $LogMessage = "$stamp $Logstring"
    Add-Content $Logfile -Value $LogMessage
```

```
    }

    Write-Log "Is this thing on?"
```

The function I use for work does a number of other things as well, and we'll be looking at some of them in the next chapter – *Chapter 10, Error Handling – Oh No! It's Gone Wrong!*.

Activity 3

This function writes a file to a location on the client. If we regularly run scripts that make use of it, we're going to end up with a lot of files cluttering things up. How might we go about writing a function that clears up old log files when we run the script?

Summary

We've done some interesting stuff in this chapter. We considered some fundamental principles of software engineering, particularly DRY, and saw how we might apply them within PowerShell scripts. We looked in detail at how functions are constructed and how they work. We briefly discussed the difference between basic and advanced functions.

We then discussed the four types of parameters we can use with functions: named, switch, positional, and dynamic parameters. We also learned about the $Args automatic variable and saw how we can use that to splat parameters into cmdlets in our basic function.

Next, we looked at the many types of attributes we can apply to our parameters to control how the script behaves. We concentrated on the more common attributes but acknowledged the existence of completion attributes and validation attributes.

Finally, we looked at a special type of function – the filter – and saw how we could use it to process pipeline objects.

We then spent some time looking at the concept of scope and saw how this is used to protect our environment and keep scripts and functions working in constrained areas of memory. We learned about parent and child scopes and the concept of scope hierarchy. Finally, we looked at how we could force functions and scripts to work outside their default scopes.

We then moved on to scriptblocks and saw how they are related to functions. We talked about different ways of calling them, including dot sourcing – a method we should use with caution. We then learned how scriptblocks relate to a common programming concept: the anonymous function or lambda.

We covered a fair bit of theory, so we finished the chapter looking at how we could construct a function to do something useful that we can apply in many scripts – writing to a log file. I hope you found this useful; I know I use it a lot.

In the next chapter, we're going to be looking at how to handle errors, both in our script and ones we encounter when our script meets the outside world.

Further reading

- For information on the software engineering concepts we covered at the start of the chapter: *The Pragmatic Programmer*, 20th Anniversary Edition, David Thomas and Andrew Hunt, 2019, Addison Wesley. There's lots of other really useful stuff in there as well.

- There are lots of help *About* files included in PowerShell on the topics we've covered in this chapter. It's worth knowing and reading these ones:

  - About Functions: `https://learn.microsoft.com/en-us/powershell/module/microsoft.powershell.core/about/about_functions?view=powershell-7.3`

  - About Advanced Functions: `https://learn.microsoft.com/en-us/powershell/module/microsoft.powershell.core/about/about_functions_advanced?view=powershell-7.3`

  - About Advanced Function Methods: `https://learn.microsoft.com/en-us/powershell/module/microsoft.powershell.core/about/about_functions_advanced_methods?view=powershell-7.3`

  - About Advanced Function Parameters: `https://learn.microsoft.com/en-us/powershell/module/microsoft.powershell.core/about/about_functions_advanced_parameters?view=powershell-7.3`

  - About Advanced Function Argument Completion: `https://learn.microsoft.com/en-us/powershell/module/microsoft.powershell.core/about/about_functions_argument_completion?view=powershell-7.3`

  - About CmdletBinding: `https://learn.microsoft.com/en-us/powershell/module/microsoft.powershell.core/about/about_functions_cmdletbindingattribute?view=powershell-7.3`

  - About Function Output: `https://learn.microsoft.com/en-us/powershell/module/microsoft.powershell.core/about/about_functions_outputtypeattribute?view=powershell-7.3`

  - About ScriptBlocks: `https://learn.microsoft.com/en-us/powershell/module/microsoft.powershell.core/about/about_script_blocks?view=powershell-7.3`

Exercises

1. What does AHA stand for?

2. Why should we be very careful when using dot sourcing?

3. We've created a variable called `$ScriptBlock` and populated it with a scriptblock. Let's say we call it like this:

    ```
    $ScriptBlock
    ```

    We don't get the output we expect. Why not?

4. What parameter argument might we use to check that our input is a valid IP address?

5. We've created a filter, `get-square`, and we're trying to use it like this:

    ```
    Get-square 365
    ```

    Why isn't there any output?

6. What are we doing here?

    ```
    $private:number
    ```

7. What's the main difference between a function and a scriptblock?

8. What are we doing wrong here?

    ```
    Function get-square($a)  {$a*$a}
    15 | get-square
    ```

9. We've spent a lot of time in this chapter getting an inaccurate square root. How would we write a function to get an accurate square root?

    ```
    Function get-root($a) {
    <what goes here?>
    }
    ```

10

Error Handling – Oh No! It's Gone Wrong!

There are, broadly, two types of problems that we encounter when using PowerShell: problems that our code encounters and problems with our code. The first type may be as simple as a `FileNotFound` message in response to `Get-ChildItem`. The second type can be much harder to understand, as it may involve problems related to scope, which we saw in *Chapter 9, Don't Repeat Yourself – Functions and Scriptblocks*, or an unexpected divide by zero error. We'll deal with problems that our code encounters in the first half of this chapter, and then move on to problems we may find in our code in the second half.

We'll start by defining what an error is and look at the two types of errors our code will encounter: terminating and non-terminating errors. We will explore how PowerShell deals with both types, how we can change that behavior, and why we might want to. We will then move on to how we can catch errors so that we can understand them and code around them.

In the second half of the chapter, we will look at how we can identify the causes of errors in our code through the process of debugging and look at some of the options available in VS Code to make the process easier.

These are the main topics we will cover in this chapter:

- What is an error?
- Understanding error actions
- Catching errors
- Exploring debugging
- Debugging with VS Code

What is an error?

As we've seen repeatedly, PowerShell, as with most languages, has its own terminology and definitions for common words. **Error** is no exception (except… sometimes it is, as we'll see. That is an extremely funny joke. You'll laugh later, I promise.). An error in PowerShell is, broadly, anything that might produce red text in the console. Let's look at an example. In the console, type the following:

```
Get-ChildItem -Name nosuchfile
```

We will see a red message saying `Get-ChildItem: cannot find path because it does not exist`.

PowerShell is an extremely friendly and helpful language. It will always try to recover from an error and continue with what it was asked to do. In the preceding instance, it was asked to do one thing, couldn't do it, and delivered a helpful error message written in plain language describing why it was unable to do the thing we asked for.

There is a lot of work going on in the background here. The previous error we see is not just a text string; it is part of a complex error object that was generated when PowerShell couldn't find the file. There is a lot more information available to understand what happened and help us get it working.

The amount of information we see is determined by an automatic variable called `$ErrorView`. By default, in PowerShell 7, this variable is set to `ConciseView`, and PowerShell displays a short friendly message. When we're researching on the internet, we'll see that PowerShell can display a lot more information by setting the `$ErrorView` variable to the `NormalView` value, as we can see in the following screenshot:

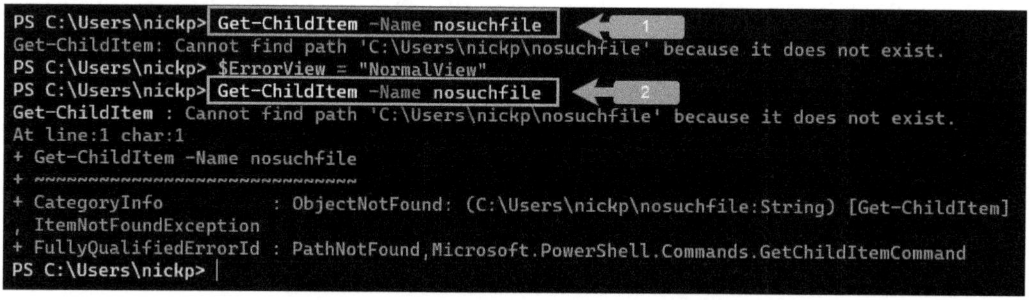

Figure 10.1 – Changing the $ErrorView variable

In the first example, *box 1*, `$ErrorView` was set to the default, `ConciseView`, and we only saw a friendly message. In the second example, *box 2*, we've changed the value of `$errorView` to `NormalView`, and we get additional information telling us where the error occurred (`line:1` and `char:1`) and what category of error it was (`ObjectNotFound`). `ConciseView` was introduced in PowerShell 7; Windows PowerShell continues to use `NormalView` as the default.

For the rest of this chapter, let's set our $ErrorView variable to NormalView by typing the following:

```
$ErrorView = "NormalView"
```

NormalView still isn't the whole story, though. To see the entire error object that was generated, type this:

```
Get-Error
```

And we should see something like this:

```
PS C:\Users\nickp> Get-Error

Exception                    :
    Type                     : System.Management.Automation.ItemNotFoundException
    ErrorRecord              :
        Exception                :
            Type     : System.Management.Automation.ParentContainsErrorRecordException
            Message : Cannot find path 'C:\Users\nickp\nosuchfile' because it does not
exist.
            HResult  : -2146233087
        TargetObject             : C:\Users\nickp\nosuchfile
        CategoryInfo             : ObjectNotFound: (C:\Users\nickp\nosuchfile:String) [],
ParentContainsErrorRecordException
        FullyQualifiedErrorId : PathNotFound
    ItemName                 : C:\Users\nickp\nosuchfile
    SessionStateCategory : Drive
    TargetSite               :
        Name         : GetChildNames
        DeclaringType : System.Management.Automation.SessionStateInternal,
System.Management.Automation, Version=7.3.4.500, Culture=neutral,
PublicKeyToken=31bf3856ad364e35
        MemberType   : Method
        Module       : System.Management.Automation.dll
    Message                  : Cannot find path 'C:\Users\nickp\nosuchfile' because it does
not exist.
```

Figure 10.2 – The error object

Get-Error is a PowerShell 7 cmdlet that allows us to access errors stored in the $Error variable; we won't find this cmdlet in Windows PowerShell. Each error we encounter in a session is written to this variable. It consists of an array of error objects, up to a maximum set by the $MaximumErrorCount automatic variable. By default, this is 256 in PowerShell 7 – hopefully, that'll be enough. We can use Get-Error with the -Newest parameter followed by an integer to get a specified number of errors, starting with the most recent. We can also access individual array members using the standard syntax, like this:

```
$Error[0]
```

This will get the most recent error – this is how we have to do it in Windows PowerShell.

Not every error we encounter will have a friendly message associated with it. Sometimes we will just see the error code, which is highlighted in the box indicated in the previous screenshot. This code is usually either 10 decimal digits, as in the screenshot, starting with -2, or it may be hexadecimal, in which case it will start with 0x, followed by 8 characters. This frequently happens with networking errors.

The code is quite cryptic, but luckily there is a tool we can use to decipher it, called err.exe. It is available as a free download on the Microsoft website; just do a search for err.exe. Once it is downloaded, we don't need to install it; we can just run it as it is from the PowerShell console or from Command Prompt, like this:

```
PS C:\Users\nickp\Downloads> .\err_6.4.5.exe 0x80010002
# for hex 0x80010002 / decimal -2147418110
  RPC_E_CALL_CANCELED                                           winerror.h
# Call was canceled by the message filter.
# as an HRESULT: Severity: FAILURE (1), FACILITY_DEBUGGER (0x1), Code 0x2
# for hex 0x2 / decimal 2
  STATUS_WAIT_2                                                 ntstatus.h
# as an HRESULT: Severity: FAILURE (1), FACILITY_RPC (0x1), Code 0x2
  ERROR_FILE_NOT_FOUND                                          winerror.h
# The system cannot find the file specified.
# 3 matches found for "0x80010002"
PS C:\Users\nickp\Downloads> |
```

Figure 10.3 – Running err.exe

As we can see, the output is only slightly less cryptic, and can be highly context-specific; in this case, if I received the code 0x80010002, as seen in *Figure 10.3*, while I was trying to open a file over a network, I would interpret that as ERROR_FILE_NOT_FOUND.

Now we have a better understanding of what an error is, let's look at the two types of errors we will encounter with PowerShell: terminating and non-terminating.

Terminating and non-terminating exceptions and errors

Programming languages have the concept of an **exception**: an anomalous condition requiring special handling. In general, when a piece of code encounters an exception, it stops what it is doing and switches to executing its exception handler: a function or subroutine that records what has gone wrong. For most languages, an error is an exception, and an exception results in an error.

PowerShell is unusual in that an error isn't always an exception (although an exception is always an error). PowerShell will attempt to recover from errors; it will try to continue what it was doing rather than stop dead. It recognizes two types of error: terminating and non-terminating. Terminating errors are the same as exceptions. PowerShell will output the error and stop what it was doing. Non-terminating errors mean PowerShell will record the error and then carry on if possible (unless we tell it otherwise).

PowerShell exceptions versus .NET exceptions

So, this can be confusing, and much of the information available on this is more so (at least, it confuses me). For instance, Don Jones, in *Learn Windows PowerShell in a Month of Lunches*, explains it as I have here: non-terminating errors are not exceptions. However, Bruce Payette, in *Windows PowerShell in Action*, says that every PowerShell error is an exception, both terminating and non-terminating. Both authors (and their books) are brilliant. I'd hate to say one is right and the other wrong; luckily, I don't have to. A careful reading of pages 532, 543, and 546 of *Windows PowerShell in Action* suggests the following.

Every time PowerShell records an error, there is an underlying .NET exception. Remember, though, that PowerShell sits on top of .NET, and for a .NET exception to be an exception for PowerShell, then it would have to stop PowerShell and start an exception handler function. Non-terminating errors do not stop PowerShell, and the exception handling functions aren't run, so they're not exceptions for PowerShell, even though they are exceptions for .NET. Clear as mud.

Let's illustrate. In the previous section, we looked at the error we received when we tried to get information about a non-existent file, by running Get-ChildItem -Name nosuchfile. Let's try it again, as part of a pipeline. In my ch10 directory, I have two files: foo.txt and bar.txt. Let's see what happens when I run the following:

```
"foo.txt", "nosuchfile", "bar.txt" | Get-ChildItem
```

We can see the results in the following screenshot:

```
PS C:\temp\poshbook\ch10> "foo.txt", "nosuchfile", "bar.txt" | Get-ChildItem

    Directory: C:\temp\poshbook\ch10

Mode                 LastWriteTime         Length Name
----                 -------------         ------ ----
-a---          30/05/2023     17:40              0 foo.txt
Get-ChildItem : Cannot find path 'C:\temp\poshbook\ch10\nosuchfile' because it does not exist
.
At line:1 char:38
+ "foo.txt", "nosuchfile", "bar.txt" | Get-ChildItem
+                                      ~~~~~~~~~~~~~~
+ CategoryInfo          : ObjectNotFound: (C:\temp\poshbook\ch10\nosuchfile:String) [Get-Chil
dItem], ItemNotFoundException
+ FullyQualifiedErrorId : PathNotFound,Microsoft.PowerShell.Commands.GetChildItemCommand
-a---          30/05/2023     17:52              0 bar.txt

PS C:\temp\poshbook\ch10>
```

Figure 10.4 – A non-terminating error

As we can see, PowerShell gets the details for the first item, foo.txt, reports an error for the second item, nosuchfile, and then continues to get information for the third item, bar.txt. This is an example of a non-terminating error.

So, what is a terminating error? This is an error that stops PowerShell altogether – an error that will stop a script or pipeline from running. A good example is a misspelled cmdlet, such as this:

```
PS C:\temp\poshbook\ch10> "foo.txt", "nosuchfile", "bar.txt" | Get-ChildItems
Get-ChildItems : The term 'Get-ChildItems' is not recognized as a name of a cmdlet, function,
script file, or executable program.
Check the spelling of the name, or if a path was included, verify that the path is correct and
 try again.
At line:1 char:38
+ "foo.txt", "nosuchfile", "bar.txt" | Get-ChildItems
+                                      ~~~~~~~~~~~~~~~~
+ CategoryInfo          : ObjectNotFound: (Get-ChildItems:String) [], CommandNotFoundException

+ FullyQualifiedErrorId : CommandNotFoundException
PS C:\temp\poshbook\ch10> |
```

Figure 10.5 – A terminating error

Here, I've used a non-existent cmdlet, Get-ChildItems (remember – PowerShell cmdlets are always singular, never plural), and PowerShell has stopped dead in its tracks on the first attempt to run the cmdlet. If this were a non-terminating error, I would expect to see the error appear three times, once for each filename in the pipeline. Instead, we see it once because the pipeline has terminated altogether.

It's great that PowerShell distinguishes between terminating and non-terminating errors; it's extremely useful in the console environment, but when we're running scripts, we're unlikely to always be around to see the error flash up on the screen and then disappear. When we're writing scripts, we are going to want to turn our non-terminating errors into terminating ones and turn all our errors into exceptions. This is so that we can set an exception handler that will do things such as log errors to a file. Before we look at how we can handle terminating errors, let's look at how we can turn all our errors into exceptions.

Understanding error actions

There are two easy ways to change the way that PowerShell processes errors: the $ErrorAction Preference variable and the -ErrorAction parameter. Let's look at the variable first.

The $ErrorActionPreference variable

The $ErrorActionPreference automatic variable can be used to alter how PowerShell processes errors. By default, it is set to Continue, which means it displays any error and carries on. These are the more important valid settings for the variable:

- Break: This causes PowerShell to enter debug mode when an error occurs. More on debug mode in the second half of this chapter.

- Continue (default): This displays the error message and continues processing.

- Inquire: This displays the error message and asks for permission to continue or stop.

- SilentlyContinue: The error message is not displayed but is added to the $Error variable. PowerShell continues processing.

- Stop: This displays the error message and stops processing. This generates an Action PreferenceStopException exception.

Note that the help document for preference variables (about_Preference_Variables) states that the variable is only effective for non-terminating errors; this is not the case. Changing the variable affects both terminating and non-terminating errors, although after a terminating error, Continue and SilentlyContinue will not force the cmdlet or script to continue; it's still a terminating error.

The $ErrorActionPreference variable is scoped, as we would expect. So, while the value for the session may be Continue, we can set it differently inside our scripts. What we must not do, though, is write $ErrorActionPreference = 'SilentlyContinue' at the top of the script, no matter how tempting it is, or how many times we see people do it on the internet. This suppresses all errors in our script and makes it incredibly difficult to troubleshoot when things go wrong, as well as making Don Jones (the Don of PowerShell) sad. Instead, if there is a cmdlet in our script that we know is going to create a lot of non-terminating errors – for instance, a function that tests for active machines using Test-NetConnection – we can use the -ErrorAction common parameter.

The -ErrorAction parameter

The -ErrorAction parameter is part of the common parameters available to all cmdlets and advanced functions. Note this will only change the actions for non-terminating errors. In the following screenshot, I have set $ErrorActionPreference to Inquire, by typing $ErrorActionPreference = Inquire, and I'm then using the -ErrorAction parameter to try to change the behavior:

```
PS C:\temp\poshbook\ch10> Get-ChildItem -Name nosuchfile -ErrorAction 'SilentlyContinue'
PS C:\temp\poshbook\ch10> Get-ChildItems -Name nosuchfile -ErrorAction 'SilentlyContinue'

Action to take for this exception:
The term 'Get-ChildItems' is not recognized as a name of a cmdlet, function, script file,
or executable program.
Check the spelling of the name, or if a path was included, verify that the path is correct
and try again.
[C] Continue  [I] Silently Continue  [B] Break  [S] Suspend  [?] Help (default is "C"):
```

Figure 10.6 – The -ErrorAction parameter

In the first cmdlet, we're generating a non-terminating error, and the error action is Silently Continue. As we can see, there is no output; the default value of Continue would display the error in red. In the second cmdlet, we're generating a terminating error by getting the cmdlet name wrong, and the -ErrorAction parameter is ignored; we get a prompt for action.

The -ErrorAction parameter has the same values as the $ErrorPreference variable. Let's look at the Ignore value. This suppresses the error message, as with SilentlyContinue. Unlike SilentlyContinue, the error is not written to the $Error variable; it is completely ignored.

> **Activity 1**
>
> What is going to happen if we run the following cmdlets?
>
> `$ErrorActionPreference = "SilentlyContinue"`
>
> `"foo.txt", "nosuchfile", "bar.txt" | Get-ChildItem -ErrorAction "Stop"`

Now we know how to make all our errors terminating errors, let's look at why we might want to do that.

Catching errors

As we've discovered, errors contain lots of useful information we can use to make our code run smoothly. While Get-Error and the $Error variable are useful for real-time troubleshooting, we need to have another way to deal with errors when we are writing scripts.

Try/Catch/Finally

The best way to handle terminating errors in PowerShell is with a Try/Catch/Finally statement. This statement allows us to set up alternate courses of action, depending on whether or not an error occurred. The statement consists of a mandatory Try block, which contains code that might generate an error, and then either a Catch block, a Finally block, or both. The Catch block will run if the code in the Try block generates a terminating error; this is our exception handler. The code in the Finally block will run regardless of whether an error is generated or not; this block is used for any code that may be required to clean up after the code in the Try block. We don't see many instances of the Finally block – I never use it. We can write multiple Catch blocks to handle different errors.

Let's try an example. In a new file in VS Code, type this:

```
function Get-Files {
    PROCESS {
        try {
                $filename = $_
                Get-ChildItem -Path "$_" -ErrorAction "Stop"
        }
        catch {
            write-output "error! file not found: $filename"
        }
    }
}
'foo.txt', 'nosuchfile', 'bar.txt' | Get-Files
```

So, here, we're creating a function called Get-Files. We're starting with a PROCESS block so that we can feed it input from the pipeline. We open a Try block on the third line and include the operating code for the function. Next, we create a variable called $filename and store the current contents of the pipeline in it; we might need that for the Catch block.

> **Activity 2**
>
> Why can't we just use the pipeline variable for the Catch block? Why do we need to store the current pipeline variable in a different variable?

Then, we write the cmdlet that actually does the processing: Get-ChildItem. We add -ErrorAction "Stop" to ensure that all errors are terminating errors; remember that the Catch block will only execute for an exception.

Next, we write the Catch block itself. We use this block to contain code we want to execute if a terminating error is caught; in this case, we just want an onscreen error message and the current string, which we wrote to $filename.

Finally, on the last line, we put our three strings in the pipeline and feed them to our function.

This is how it all looks when we run it:

```
ch10 > trycatch.ps1 > ...
     1 reference
  1  function Get-Files {
  2      PROCESS {
  3          try {
  4              $filename = $_
  5              Get-ChildItem -Path "$_" -ErrorAction "Stop"
  6          }
  7          catch {
  8              write-output "error! file not found: $filename"
  9          }
 10      }
 11  }
 12  'foo.txt', 'nosuchfile', 'bar.txt' | Get-Files
 13
```

```
PROBLEMS   OUTPUT   DEBUG CONSOLE   TERMINAL                    Po

PS C:\temp\poshbook\ch10>
PS C:\temp\poshbook\ch10> . 'C:\temp\poshbook\ch10\trycatch.ps1'


    Directory: C:\temp\poshbook\ch10

Mode                 LastWriteTime         Length Name
----                 -------------         ------ ----
-a---          30/05/2023    17:40              0 foo.txt
error! file not found: nosuchfile
-a---          30/05/2023    17:52              0 bar.txt

PS C:\temp\poshbook\ch10>
```

Figure 10.7 – Using Try/Catch

As we can see in the preceding terminal, `foo.txt` and `bar.txt` are processed, but because `nosuchfile` can't be found, the Catch block action is triggered – in this case, writing an error string to the screen with the filename.

Writing multiple Catch blocks is relatively easy, but we need to know what sort of errors we can expect; specifically, we need to know the full .NET name, including the namespace. We can see from *Figure 10.4* that the .NET exception name when we can't find a file is `ItemNotFoundException`, but we also need the namespace; in this case, it's `System.Management.Automation`. If we don't know what the namespace for an error is, then this one is always worth a try before hunting around on the internet.

We put the error type in square brackets between Catch and the opening brace ({), as in the following screenshot:

```
ch10 > 〉 trycatch.ps1 > ...
        1 reference
    1   function Get-Files {
    2       PROCESS {
    3           try {
    4               $filename = $_
    5               Get-ChildItem -Path "$_" -ErrorAction "Stop"
    6           }
    7           catch [System.Management.Automation.ItemNotFoundException] {
    8               write-output "error! file not found: $filename"
    9           }
   10           catch {"an unspecified error. boo."}
   11       }
   12   }
```

Figure 10.8 – Multiple catch blocks

Our first Catch block starts on *line 7* and will only trigger if an error of the `System.Management.Automation.ItemNotFoundException` type is thrown. All other errors will trigger the second Catch block. Try it; change the cmdlet to `Get-ChildItems` to trigger a `CommandNotFound` error. We should see an unspecified error. boo. written three times.

So, what can we do with Try/Catch? Well, instead of writing to the screen, we can combine it with the logging function we wrote in the last chapter and use the Catch block to write the error message to the log file.

We may see on the internet references to the Trap statement. This goes back all the way to PowerShell v1. It's really fiddly to use and has issues with scope, and the advice is that we should use the newer Try/Catch statement instead. As with the Finally block, I never use the Trap statement.

This almost wraps it up for errors that we might experience running our script; just one last scenario to consider. What about things that aren't errors, but stop our script from running?

Consider this code:

```
Get-ChildItem -path *.csv
```

What happens if there are no .csv files in the directory? PowerShell won't display an error; it won't display anything at all. We might see this as an error for our script, though. Let's look at how we can turn this into a terminating error.

Creating errors

A Throw statement is used to create a terminating error in a script so that the script stops at that point and an exception can be recorded – for instance, written to a log. Let's look at an example. Try this in VS Code:

```
try {
    $files = (Get-ChildItem -Path *.csv)
    if (!($files)) {
        Throw "There are no CSV files here!"
    }
    else {
        #do something with the files
    }
}
catch {
    Write-Output $_.tostring()
}
```

This is a pair of Try/Catch blocks. In the Try block, we're creating a variable, $files, that contains the results of Get-ChildItem -Path *.csv: all the .csv files in the current directory.

Next, we're running an `if` statement with a condition of `! ($files)` – that is, if `$files` is `$null`, then carry out the `Throw` statement, which throws a `There are no CSV files here!` message. This message is wrapped into an error object that is passed to the `Catch` block. We can then display just the message by using `Write-Output $_.tostring()`, just as with a real error. Let's see how it looks:

```
ch10 > ≥ throw.ps1 > ...
1    try {
2        $files = (Get-ChildItem -Path *.csv)
3        if (!($files)) {
4            Throw "There are no CSV files here!"
5        }
6        else {
7            #do something with the files
8        }
9    }
10   catch {
11       Write-Output $_.tostring()
12   }
13
```

```
PROBLEMS    OUTPUT    DEBUG CONSOLE    TERMINAL

PS C:\temp\poshbook\ch10>
PS C:\temp\poshbook\ch10> . 'C:\temp\poshbook\ch10\throw.ps1'
There are no CSV files here!
PS C:\temp\poshbook\ch10>
```

Figure 10.9 – Throwing our own error

As we can see in the red box, the `Throw` statement has produced an error that we can handle in exactly the same way as any other terminating error. How we can write a non-terminating error is something for the next section of this chapter: debugging.

That's enough about how we handle errors. In the next section, we'll take a look at debugging our code.

Exploring debugging

My code has bugs in it. Your code has bugs in it. We're not bad coders; all code has bugs – we just haven't found them all yet. According to Coverity (a code-quality scanning company), quality-controlled professionally written software has around 1 defect (or bug) per 1,000 lines of code. Some of these bugs are never found because the particular set of rare circumstances where the code doesn't behave as expected (an edge case, in the jargon) hasn't occurred.

Bugs largely consist of two types:

- Syntax errors, where we've misspelled a cmdlet or parameter name or missed out a closing bracket or quotation mark. Syntax errors are basically typing errors – just sometimes we've typed the wrong thing thinking it's the right thing. We've seen already how using VS Code can help us enormously with this, by color coding, syntax checking, code hints, and tab autocomplete.

- Logic errors, where our understanding of how PowerShell works is insufficient. For instance, the problems we might run into with scope would fall into this category. Arguably, many of the errors we have already encountered might do as well; a check to see whether a file exists before trying to use it would prevent an unexpected error from being thrown at all, as we've just seen when we discussed the `Throw` statement.

In this section, we are going to have a whistlestop tour through the various features of PowerShell 7 that can help us find and understand the bugs in our code. Before we get into the fun stuff, though, we should remind ourselves of the cardinal rules of troubleshooting:

- **Read the error message**: For example, if the error message is `FileNotFound`, don't start troubleshooting the network connection until we've gone and confirmed with our own eyes that the file is actually where we think it is.

- **Read the help file**: Have we got the names of the parameters correct? Does the cmdlet do what we think it does?

- **Understand how expectation and reality differ**: We need to read the script that we are troubleshooting and understand exactly what we expect it to do and what it is actually doing. An example – I have recently been working with a customer who was having trouble putting his servers into a quiescent state so that he could perform maintenance on them. He believed the script he was using would do that for him, but when we examined it, it did something slightly different. There was nothing wrong with the script; it was his expectation that needed adjusting.

That said, let's look at how we can provide some script instrumentation.

Script instrumentation

Script instrumentation refers to pieces of code embedded within our scripts to give us information about what a script is doing and how well it is doing it. It can mean the progress bars we see when loading modules, messages to say how many times a loop has completed, how many objects were found, or simply how long a portion of the script took to run. In this section, we're going to look at how we can use some of the `write-*` cmdlets to provide us with troubleshooting information. In *Chapter 8, Writing Our First Script – Turning Simple Cmdlets into Reusable Code*, we looked in some detail at the `Write-Verbose` cmdlet, and in *Chapter 3, The PowerShell Pipeline – How to String Cmdlets Together*, we looked at standard streams and the `Write-*` cmdlets associated with each stream. Let's remind ourselves of them here:

Stream #	Description	Cmdlet	Common Parameters
1	Success	`Write-Output`	None – this is the default output
2	Error	`Write-Error`	`-ErrorAction` and `-ErrorVariable`
3	Warning	`Write-Warning`	`-WarningAction` and `-WarningPreference`
4	Verbose	`Write-Verbose`	`-Verbose`
5	Debug	`Write-Debug`	`-Debug`
6	Information	`Write-Information`	`-InformationAction` and `-InformationVariable`

Table 10.1 – PowerShell streams

These streams are intended for different communities; `Write-Output`, `Write-Warning`, `Write-Error`, and `Write-Verbose` are intended for the end user of a script. `Write-Information` is for script operators, and `Write-Debug` is for developers; that's us.

We've used `Write-Output` and `Write-Verbose` previously; we'll not cover them again here. They provide different levels of information for the person running the script. `Write-Error`, however, is new. We can use the `Write-Error` cmdlet to produce a non-terminating error, much the same as we can use `Throw` to generate a terminating error. In the `Write-Error.ps1` script shown next, I've set `$ErrorActionPreference` to the default and replaced the `Throw` message we were using previously with a `Write-Error` cmdlet:

```
ch10 >  write-error.ps1 > ...
    1    try {
    2        $files = (Get-ChildItem -Path *.csv)
    3        if (!($files)) {
    4            Write-Error "There are no CSV files here"
    5        }
    6        else {
    7            #do something with the files
    8        }
    9        Write-Output "the script continues"
   10    }
   11    catch {
   12        Write-Output $_.tostring()
   13    }
   14
```

PROBLEMS   OUTPUT   DEBUG CONSOLE   TERMINAL

```
○ PS C:\temp\poshbook\ch10>
  PS C:\temp\poshbook\ch10> . 'C:\temp\poshbook\ch10\write-error.ps1'
● Write-Error: There are no CSV files here
  the script continues
● PS C:\temp\poshbook\ch10> $error[0]

  Write-Error: There are no CSV files here
○ PS C:\temp\poshbook\ch10> []
```

Figure 10.10 – The Write-Error cmdlet

On *line 4*, I've replaced the Throw statement with Write-Error "There are no CSV files here" and added a Write-Output cmdlet on *line 9*, inside the try statement that opens on *line 1*.

When we run it, we can see that the Write-Error cmdlet outputs a message in red to the console. We can see that it is a non-terminating error because the Write-Output cmdlet on *line 9* also runs and produces a the script continues string in the console. As we can see from the console window in the screenshot, the error is also written to the $Error variable. We control its display with the same $ErrorActionPreference variable we saw earlier in the chapter.

So, when do we use Write-Error, and when do we use Throw? Write-Error is when we want to tell the user that something is wrong but let the script continue with what it is doing. Throw is for when we want the script to stop what it's doing and process the error.

Write-Warning is a cmdlet that I almost never use. It writes text to the warning stream, which is output as yellow text. That's it. It produces yellow text. We can use the $WarningActionPreference variable and the -WarningAction parameter to force the script to stop or silently continue when something is written to the warning stream, but it seems to me this is needless redundancy; better to use Write-Error and write the output to the $Error variable as well. Other opinions are available.

Write-Information is generally used to provide details of what our script has done; it is useful when we're working with log aggregators that target the information stream, for instance, but I generally don't bother with it.

Write-Debug is the cmdlet we're interested in here. This writes to the debug stream and can be accessed by making sure our script is an advanced script, using the CmdletBinding attribute we saw in *Chapter 8, Writing Our First Script – Turning Simple Cmdlets into Reusable Code*. If we've used that attribute, then we have access to the -Debug parameter.

When should we use Write-Verbose and when should we use Write-Debug? The Write-Verbose output is for the user, and we use it to tell the user what the script is doing – for example, a message such as loading files when we have a loop to process and ingest files from a directory. We use Write-Debug inside the loop to enumerate the files that we are loading. Consider the following short script:

```
ch10 >  debugVsVerbose.ps1 > ...
1
2    [CmdletBinding()]
3    param (
4        $Path = "C:\temp\poshbook\ch10"
5    )
6    $files = (Get-ChildItem -Path $path)
7    Write-Verbose "Getting Files..."
8    foreach ($file in $files) {
9        Write-Debug "Current `$file is $file"
10   }
```

```
PROBLEMS    OUTPUT    DEBUG CONSOLE    TERMINAL                    PowerShell Extens

 PS C:\temp\poshbook\ch10> . C:\temp\poshbook\ch10\debugVsVerbose.ps1
 PS C:\temp\poshbook\ch10> . C:\temp\poshbook\ch10\debugVsVerbose.ps1 -Verbose
VERBOSE: Getting Files...
 PS C:\temp\poshbook\ch10> . C:\temp\poshbook\ch10\debugVsVerbose.ps1 -Debug
DEBUG: Current $file is C:\temp\poshbook\ch10\foo
DEBUG: Current $file is C:\temp\poshbook\ch10\bar.txt
DEBUG: Current $file is C:\temp\poshbook\ch10\debugVsVerbose.ps1
DEBUG: Current $file is C:\temp\poshbook\ch10\foo.txt
DEBUG: Current $file is C:\temp\poshbook\ch10\throw.ps1
DEBUG: Current $file is C:\temp\poshbook\ch10\trycatch.ps1
DEBUG: Current $file is C:\temp\poshbook\ch10\write-error.ps1
```

Figure 10.11 – Write-Verbose versus Write-Debug

This contains a Write-Verbose message on *line 7*, outside the foreach loop, and a Write-Debug message inside the loop on *line 9*. The Write-Verbose message targets script users and tells them that the script is doing something, even if they think it isn't. The Write-Debug message is targeted at us and tells us exactly what the script is doing and which file it is processing. Write-Debug and Write-Host actions are controlled by the $DebugPreference and $VerbosePreference variables, respectively. These variables are both set to SilentlyContinue by default and are overridden by their respective -Debug and -Verbose switch parameters, as we can see in the console output in the preceding screenshot.

This is all very well, but this only tells us how to deal with errors we anticipate. What happens when we don't know what's going wrong? We turn to the debugging cmdlets.

Debugging cmdlets

Debugging is hugely complex, and as we dig into it, we quickly come to realize we need a pretty good grasp of computer science to understand it thoroughly. That doesn't mean that a working knowledge of the more common cmdlets isn't incredibly useful. In this section, we're going to look at how to use breakpoints in the console when running scripts. A breakpoint will pause a script from running and start the built-in PowerShell debugger. The cmdlets that set and manipulate them all use the PSBreakpoint noun. These are the PSBreakpoint cmdlets that we should be aware of:

- Set-PSBreakpoint enables a breakpoint at a particular line of a script, variable, or command
- Get-PSBreakpoint lists the breakpoints that are set in a session
- Remove-PSBreakpoint removes the specified breakpoint
- Disable-PSBreakpoint stops a breakpoint from triggering but doesn't remove it
- Enable-PSBreakpoint enables a disabled breakpoint

Let's use the previous debugVsVerbose.ps1 script. If you haven't already, create a new file, save it as debugVsVerbose.ps1, and add this content. You'll need to change the $path variable to a location where you've got some files:

```
[CmdletBinding()]
param (
    $Path = "C:\temp\poshbook\ch10"
)
$files = (Get-ChildItem -Path $path)
Write-Verbose "Getting Files..."
foreach ($file in $files) {
    Write-Debug "Current `$file is $file"
}
```

Now, in the console, *not* in VS Code, navigate to the directory where you saved it, and type the following:

```
Set-PSBreakpoint -Script .\debugVsVerbose.ps1 -Variable file -Mode
read
```

This tells PowerShell that when the debugVsVerbose.ps1 script is run, start the debugger when the value of the $file variable is read. Remember – the variable name doesn't include the preceding dollar sign ($).

Now, run the script to enter debug mode when the variable is read:

```
.\debugVsVerbose.ps1
```

Once we are in debug mode, we can check the values of variables, run cmdlets, interrogate the call stack, display the script, and do lots of other things. Try it; get the current value of $file by typing the following:

```
$file
```

You should see the name of the first file in your location. It should all look something like this:

```
PS C:\temp\poshbook\ch10> Set-PSBreakpoint -Script .\debugVsVerbose.ps1 -Variable file -Mode read

   ID Script               Line Command         Variable        Action
   -- ------               ---- -------         --------        ------
    2 debugVsVerbose.ps1        .               file

PS C:\temp\poshbook\ch10> .\debugVsVerbose.ps1
Hit Variable breakpoint on 'C:\temp\poshbook\ch10\debugVsVerbose.ps1:$file' (Read access)
Hit Variable breakpoint on 'C:\temp\poshbook\ch10\debugVsVerbose.ps1:$file' (Read access)

At C:\temp\poshbook\ch10\debugVsVerbose.ps1:9 char:5
+     Write-Debug "Current '$file is $file"
+     ~~~~~~~~~~~~~~~~~~~~~~~~~~~~~~~~~~~~~~
[DBG]: PS C:\temp\poshbook\ch10>> $file

    Directory: C:\temp\poshbook\ch10

Mode                 LastWriteTime         Length Name
----                 -------------         ------ ----
d----        30/05/2023     17:40                 foo

[DBG]: PS C:\temp\poshbook\ch10>> h

 s, stepInto        Single step (step into functions, scripts, etc.)
 v, stepOver        Step to next statement (step over functions, scripts, etc.)
 o, stepOut         Step out of the current function, script, etc.
```

Figure 10.12 – Using the console debugger

We can see here that in the first command, I set the breakpoint to trigger when $file is read. The next command is to run the script. The console tells us that we've hit a variable breakpoint in yellow and tells us where in the script that breakpoint is. The prompt then switches to the debug mode prompt [DBG]. I type $file, and the contents of the variable are displayed.

The last command I type is h, which is a debugger command, not part of the debugging process. Try this.

Type h to get the help contents. This will show us a list of the commands we can use inside the debugger:

Command	Effect
s, stepInto	Single step (step into functions, scripts, and so on).
v, stepOver	Step to the next statement (step over functions, scripts, etc.). This will run a function or script block as a single step.
o, stepOut	Step out of the current function, script, and so on.
c, continue	Continue the operation.
q, quit	Stop the operation and exit the debugger.
d, detach	Continue the operation and detach the debugger.
k, Get-PSCallStack	Display the call stack.
l, list	List the source code for the current script.
	Use list to start from the current line, list <m> to start from line <m>, and list <m> <n> to list <n> lines starting from line <m>.
Enter	Repeat the last command if it was stepInto, stepOver, or list.
?, h	Displays the help message.

Table 10.2 – PowerShell debugger commands

There are a number of commands that help us navigate through our script and need a little more explanation, as follows:

- StepOver will take us to the next statement; if that statement is a function, the debugger will just run the function. It won't work through it line by line.
- StepInto will take us to the next line of code after the breakpoint and run it. It will step into functions and run them line by line, rather than just running the function.
- StepOut will complete a function if we are in it and take us to the next statement after the function.
- Continue will run the script, either to the end or to the next breakpoint.

- `Get-PSCallStack` will show us where we are in terms of scripts and functions. For instance, if we press the *K* key in our preceding debugger, it will show us that we are in the `debugVsVerbose.ps1` script, at *line 9*. If we were in a function in a script, it would show us the function name and our location within it, followed by the script name and location.

- `List` will show us the script, from whichever line we choose.

- Finally, `quit` will exit the debugger.

In my experience, it's not very often we'll need to debug at the command line. Generally, debugging is easier in an editor such as VS Code. Let's have a look at how we can do that.

Debugging with VS Code

VS Code is probably the best tool for debugging PowerShell. It has all the debugging features most people will need, such as remote debugging capabilities for connecting to other machines; far too many to cover here. This section is going to cover the basics and show how we can use VS Code to perform the basic debugging procedures we've just covered in the command line.

In a new VS Code session, press *Ctrl + Shift + P* to open the Command Palette and type exam; you should see a link for the PowerShell extension examples folder, as shown here:

Figure 10.13 – The PowerShell extension examples folder shortcut

In the File Explorer in the left-hand pane, double-click the `DebugTest.ps1` file to open it.

This is quite a short tutorial script that is provided with the PowerShell VS Code extension. It consists of two functions, Do-Work and Write-Item. Neither function does very much; Do-Work writes two lines of text, using two different cmdlets, Write-Output and Write-Host, and also calls the Write-Item function. Write-Item is a counting function that will count up to the value of the $Count variable, outputting a string each time, with a short delay between each iteration. Do-Work is called by the final line of the script, *line 28*.

Now, let's set a breakpoint. Either select *line 15* by clicking on it and pressing *F9* or hover the mouse to the left of the line number and click. The dull red dot seen in the following screenshot will become bright red:

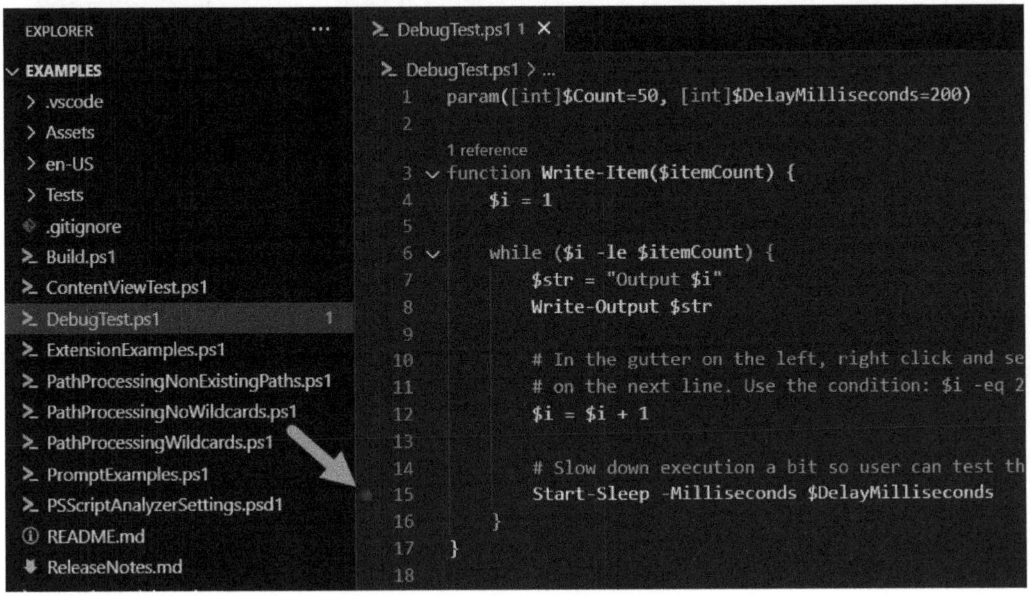

Figure 10.14 – Setting a breakpoint

Now we have a breakpoint set, we can start the debugger. The easiest way to do this is to press *Ctrl + Shift + D*, or we can select **Run** from the **View** menu:

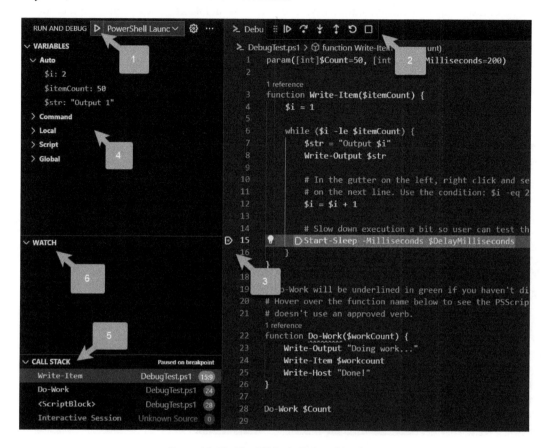

Figure 10.15 – The VS Code Debug interface

The **Debug** view is quite complex, and we'll need to run the file to the breakpoint to see what it does. In the top-left corner, press the green arrow next to **RUN AND DEBUG** (number *1* in *Figure 10.15*). The script will run to the breakpoint on *line 15* and stop. Let's explore the interface. Firstly, we have the run controls (*2*). From left to right, these are *continue, step over, step in, step out, restart*, and *stop*, and are analogous to the controls in the console debugger in the last section. If we hover the mouse over them, we can see the associated keyboard shortcuts; for instance, we can also continue by pressing *F5*. These commands are also available from the **Run** menu in the top toolbar. We can see the breakpoint we've stopped at highlighted in the script (*3*).

The panel on the left contains some really interesting tools in three windows, **VARIABLES**, **WATCH**, and **CALL STACK**. The top window contains the values of all the variables (*4*). There are five subsections here. **Auto** contains the variables around the current breakpoint and their current value; in our case, we are in the Write-Item function, and the variables are $i, $str, and $itemCount. If we hover the mouse over them, we can see the type of the variable. Ironically, **Auto** doesn't show automatic variables. **Command** shows the variables associated with the current command – in this case, Write-Item. If we click the arrow to the left of the word **Command**, we can see automatic variables such as $args and $MyInvocation. If we expand $PSBoundParameters, we can see the parameter associated with Write-Item: [itemCount].

Local, **Script**, and **Global** show the values of all parameters that exist in each of those scopes, and we can see, for instance, that the $i variable exists in the local scope, but not in the script or global scopes.

Let's move on to the **CALL STACK** section (5). Call stacks run from bottom to top, or **last-in, first-out** (**LIFO**), so we can see that we start in the interactive session, and call the script, called <ScriptBlock>, here. This runs to *line 28* and calls the Do-Work function, which runs to *line 24* and calls the Write-Item function, which runs to the breakpoint on *line 15*. This allows us to trace the flow of execution through the script. If we click on the items in the call stack, we can see that the variable values in the top pane change to show their values in the relevant scope. For instance, if we select Do-Work instead of Write-Item, we can see that $PSBoundParameter now contains [workCount].

Finally, we have the **WATCH** section (6), in the middle pane. Here, we can add a variable or an expression that we always want to know the value of. Let's try it. Hover the mouse over the **WATCH** pane and click the + button that appears. In the resulting textbox, type $i*2 and press *Enter*. We should see the expression evaluated to 4. If we now press the **Continue** button or *F5*, the script will run through until it hits the breakpoint again, and we should see that our expression is now evaluated to 6.

We've barely scratched the surface of debugging with VS Code, but we've done enough to see how we can use it to understand why our code isn't behaving as we think it should. Debugging is an incredibly complex topic and the best way to learn it is to do it. VS Code can make that task a lot easier, though. Let's summarize what we've covered in this chapter.

Summary

We started this chapter by looking at what an error actually is and covered some computer science that is applicable to most programming languages. We saw how PowerShell is different from many languages by having the concept of terminating and non-terminating errors, and how this is a feature of it being an interpreted language that sits on top of .NET.

Once we understood what errors are, we looked at different ways in which PowerShell can handle those errors using the $ErrorActionPreference variable and the -ErrorAction parameter.

We saw how we must turn errors into terminating errors so that we can use the most common way of trapping errors, the Try/Catch/Finally family of statements. We also learned how we can use those statements to provide custom error-handling routines.

Having seen how we work with errors, we learned how we can use a `Throw` statement to generate our own terminating errors when we encounter situations that are undesirable but don't naturally cause an error.

Having explored how we deal with errors, we looked at the art of debugging in the second half of the chapter. We started by looking at the concept of script instrumentation using `Write-Debug`, and how we can use it to generate insights into what our code is doing when we use the `-Debug` parameter to access the debug output stream.

We moved on to looking at how we can perform interactive debugging on our scripts using debugging cmdlets such as `Set-PSBreakPoint` to access the built-in PowerShell debugger. After seeing how difficult that is, we concluded the chapter by looking at a far more powerful and much easier way of interactively debugging our scripts using VS Code.

In the next chapter, we're going to be looking at how we can distribute our code so that others can use it in a flexible fashion, by turning our scripts into modules. Can't wait!

Exercises

1. In terms of running a script, what is the main difference between terminating and non-terminating errors?

2. How can we access detailed information about errors?

3. What is the purpose of the `-ErrorActionPreference` variable in PowerShell?

4. What is the purpose of the `Write-Error` cmdlet in PowerShell?

5. Why might we want to use a `Throw` statement?

6. How can we display debug messages in a script?

7. How can we write debug messages in a script, and who are we writing them for?

8. What is a breakpoint in PowerShell?

9. What is the purpose of the `stepOver` debugger command?

Further reading

- If debugging interests you, the best way to learn is by doing it. However, you can get a head start by reading *The Science of Debugging*, by Matt Telles and Yuan Hsieh:

  The Science of Debugging, Matt Telles and Yuan Hsieh, 2001, Coriolis Group

- There are some good docs on debugging PowerShell with VS Code that go into far more detail:

  - `https://devblogs.microsoft.com/scripting/debugging-powershell-script-in-visual-studio-code-part-1/`

- `https://devblogs.microsoft.com/scripting/debugging-powershell-script-in-visual-studio-code-part-2/`

- And here is a more general link about the VS Code debugger:

  `https://code.visualstudio.com/Docs/editor/debugging`

- This article has lots of interesting links, although some of them are a little old now:

  `https://learn.microsoft.com/en-us/powershell/scripting/dev-cross-plat/vscode/using-vscode?view=powershell-7.3`

11

Creating Our First Module

Most programming languages include the concept of a library – an object that contains code, documentation, programming objects such as classes, message templates, and a host of other things. These libraries extend what we can do with that language by helping us to use other people's code and reuse our own. In this chapter, we're going to explore PowerShell modules – a convenient way of distributing PowerShell code.

We'll start by briefly recapping how to work with modules and the cmdlets we use to do that. Then, we'll look at the components of a module. We'll learn how to write a module manually, before wrapping up with a brief look at using a module scaffolding application called **Plaster**.

The main topics we will cover in this chapter are as follows:

- Working with modules
- Writing a simple module
- Module manifests
- Using scaffolding tools such as Plaster

Working with modules

Back in *Chapter 2, Exploring PowerShell Cmdlets and Syntax*, we spent some time exploring how we can use modules to find new cmdlets. In this chapter, we'll be writing modules, but first, let's recap what we learned previously and place it in some sort of context.

Modules allow us to reuse and distribute code so that it can be easily automated by including the cmdlets that manipulate modules in our scripts. So, if we need a cmdlet from the PowerShell math module in our script, then we can programmatically import that module (or just the required cmdlet) and use it. We can do this in a predictable and controllable fashion, without user intervention.

270   Creating Our First Module

Modules fulfill three basic functions:

- **Configuring the environment**: They provide a repeatable custom work environment – for example, the PowerShell module for Exchange, as well as Exchange-specific cmdlets – configuring the PowerShell environment to work in a particular way with Exchange

- **Code reuse**: They provide libraries of functions that we or other people can use, such as the math module

- **Solution engineering**: Because modules can be nested inside other modules, whole groups of modules may be distributed to create an application for redistribution – this is common in Windows administration environments

We can find modules on the internet, in places such as GitHub, where they've been distributed with software, in a public repository such as the PowerShell Gallery or internal repositories in our workplace or school, or via friends and colleagues.

By installing the modules in standard locations, we can control access to them on a given machine, or we can add to the default list of places that PowerShell will search for modules. Let's start by looking at the common locations for modules on our client device.

Module locations

There are three default locations for modules. These are shown in the following table:

	Windows	**Linux**
System	None for PowerShell 7, but Windows PowerShell uses `C:\WINDOWS\system32\WindowsPowerShell\v1.0\Modules\`	`/opt/Microsoft/PowerShell/7/Modules`
AllUsers	• `C:\Program Files\PowerShell\Modules` • `C:\Program Files\PowerShell\7\Modules`	`/usr/local/share/PowerShell/Modules`
User	`C:\Users\<user name>\Documents\PowerShell\Modules`	`/home/<username>/.local/share/PowerShell/Modules`

Table 11.1 – Default module locations in Windows and Linux

The System location is reserved for Microsoft modules. The User location does not exist by default in Windows and will need to be created before it can be used. The AllUsers location was introduced in PowerShell v4 to provide a location for non-Microsoft modules that need to run under the system account. This also gives us a place to install modules for any user on the client to use. Modules downloaded from the PowerShell Gallery are placed here by default.

As we saw in *Chapter 2, Exploring PowerShell Cmdlets and Syntax*, we can add locations where we may install modules by manipulating the $ENV:PSModulePath variable. Locations should be separated by a semicolon (;) in Windows and a colon (:) in Linux, as shown here:

```
PS /home/nickp> $env:PSModulePath
/home/nickp/.local/share/powershell/Modules:/usr/local/share/
powershell/Modules:/opt/microsoft/powershell/7/Modules
```

Figure 11.1 – The $env:PSModulePath variable in Linux

We can make this listing tidier by calling the $env:PSModulePath -Split ":" variable, which will output each location on a separate line. Obviously, on a Windows client, the separator should be a semicolon (;). Paths often get added to this variable when installing applications.

Module autoloading

We can load modules automatically under certain circumstances. Modules in correctly named folders in the module paths defined in $env:PSModulePath are automatically discovered by PowerShell. We can do this by doing the following:

- Running a cmdlet from the module
- Using Get-Command for a cmdlet in the module
- Using Get-Help for a cmdlet in the module

Module autoloading is great for when we're working interactively in the shell, but we shouldn't rely on it in a script. The recommended way to load modules inside a script is with the using keyword, like this:

```
using module <module name>
```

Here's an example:

```
Using module ActiveDirectory
```

Note that some caveats on this are covered in the *Nested modules* section.

Importing modules

Autoloading modules is convenient, but it's not particularly controlled. For instance, it loads everything in the module, some of which we might not need, and we cannot control the version of the module that is loaded. It can also consume a lot of memory. Therefore, we might choose to manually import modules into a session using the `Import-Module` cmdlet, which gives us several options to control how and what we import:

- `-Name`: Use this to specify the name of the module to import. We can also include a path here if the module is not in the module path specified in `$ENV:PSModulePath`.

- `-Cmdlet`: This allows us to import a selection of cmdlets from an array of strings. Similar parameters, such as `-Alias`, `-Function`, and `-Variable`, have the expected effect.

- `-Force`: This forces a module to reload completely. By default, if a module is already loaded, then `Import-Module` does not reimport it. This is useful if we are developing a module and need to test it repeatedly.

- `-RequiredVersion`: Use this to specify the version of the module to be imported.

- `-Prefix`: This parameter adds a prefix to the nouns in cmdlets that are imported from the module, to prevent confusion with cmdlets that already exist in the session.

- `-NoClobber`: This prevents cmdlets from being imported if they have the same name as cmdlets that already exist in the session.

There are several other parameters, but we won't consider them here.

We can unload a module using the `Remove-Module` cmdlet. Why might we want to do that? Well, when we first import a module, we import all the nested modules that it requires as well. However, if we then use `Import-Module -Force` to reload the module, it only reloads the named module, not the nested modules. `Remove-Module` also removes the nested modules. In practice, of course, just starting a new session is often quicker and cleaner.

Very often, we'll see scripts on the internet using the `Import-Module` cmdlet to make module contents available inside a script. I do this too, despite it not being the recommended way of doing it; it just feels more readable to me. Microsoft recommends we do this with the `using` keyword, though. My doctor recommends I eat less salt; I tend to ignore that advice as well.

PowerShellGet

Microsoft has a module called `PowerShellGet` that includes a lot of resources for working with repositories and modules. This module is included in PowerShell 7. It allows us to work easily with the PowerShell Gallery so that we can find, register, and unregister other repositories, which allows us to find, install, and uninstall modules and scripts in repositories, as well as manipulate those modules and scripts. We covered the basic uses of `PowerShellGet` at some length in *Chapter 2, Exploring PowerShell Cmdlets and Syntax*.

From PowerShell 7.4 onwards, the PowerShellGet v2.2.5 module will be accompanied by version 3. The version 3 module is called `Microsoft.Powershell.PSResourceGet` and replaces the `Install-Module` and `Install-Script` cmdlets with the single `Install-PSResource` cmdlet, among many other changes. In PowerShell 7.4, the two modules will ship side by side, allowing any current resources that use `PowerShellGet` to continue working. However, no compatibility layer will be included, so scripts written for v2.2.5 and earlier won't work with version 3 unless we use the separate `CompatPowerShellGet` module that will be included in PowerShell 7.5.

Next, we'll learn how to create a module, but first, a word of caution. There is a PowerShell cmdlet called `New-Module`. This creates a very specific type of module – a **dynamic module**. Dynamic modules only exist in memory; they're not stored in files, and they are session-specific, so when the PowerShell session ends, the module is lost. We're not going to cover those modules or their uses in this chapter – they're quite advanced. We're not going to cover `New-Module`, either.

Writing a simple module

A module, at its most basic, is a script file containing functions, saved with a `.psm1` extension. That's it. That's the simplest possible module. Try it – save the following lines as a `.psm1` file, in a folder with the same name as the file, inside your `\users\<username>\documents\powershell\modules` folder (or the `home/<user>/.local/share/powershell/Modules` folder in Linux):

```
function Get-Square($a) {
    $result = $a * $a
    return $result
    }
```

It doesn't matter what you call the file, so long as the file and folder name are the same, and the folder is in the module path so that PowerShell can find it, like this:

Figure 11.2 – Saving a module in the module path correctly

Now, if we start a PowerShell session, we can type the following:

```
Import-Module <ModuleName>
```

PowerShell will load it. Once it is loaded, we can use the functions inside, like this:

```
PowerShell 7.3.6
PS C:\Users\nickp> Import-Module MyFirstModule
PS C:\Users\nickp> Get-Square 13
169
PS C:\Users\nickp>
```

Figure 11.3 – Using our first module

As you can see, the `Import-Module` cmdlet produces no output, but the function inside the module is available. If we run `Remove-Module`, the function disappears as well. Or does it?

Activity 1

Try running `Remove-Module` to get rid of the module we've just installed, and then running `Get-Square`. What happens? Why does this happen?

Before we look at ways to create modules, let's talk about the earliest method of building libraries in PowerShell – dot-sourcing.

A word of caution – dot-sourcing

In the very first version of PowerShell, there was only one way to include the functions in one script inside another: **dot-sourcing**. Let's try it. Write the following line in a new script and save it as `Dot-Source.ps1` in a suitable folder – I'm using `c:\temp\poshbook\ch11`:

```
Write-Message "dot source test"
```

It should be obvious that if we run this, it isn't going to work. There is no cmdlet called `Write-Message`, and the script doesn't define one. Let's create a `Write-Message` function in another script, and save it as `Write-Message.ps1`:

```
$text = "default message"
function Write-Message($text) {
    Write-Output "$text"
}
```

Now, let's go back to `Dot-Source.ps1` and add this line at the start:

```
. C:\temp\poshbook\ch11\Write-Message.ps1
```

Change the path to reflect the location where you saved `Write-Message.ps1`. Now, when we run `Dot-Source.ps1`, our message should be displayed, as shown here:

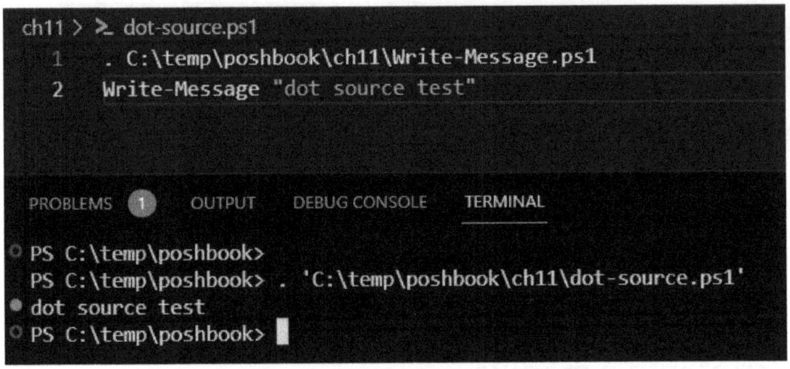

Figure 11.4 – Using dot-sourcing in a script

We can do this interactively as well, in a PowerShell session, just by dot-sourcing the script, as shown here:

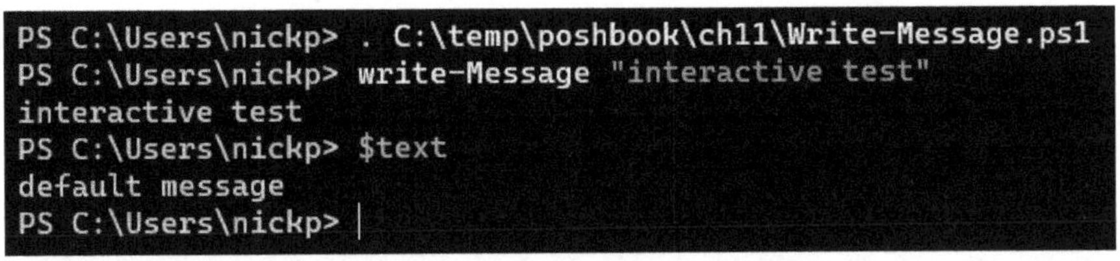

Figure 11.5 – Interactive dot-sourcing

So, if dot-sourcing is so straightforward, why should we bother with modules at all? The reason is the management problems that dot-sourcing introduces. When we dot-source a script, we bring the members of that script, as well as the variables and functions, into the parent scope. We can see this in the preceding screenshot; if we call the `$text` variable, then we get the `default message` string. Remember, the concept of scope was introduced to protect us from ambiguously written code; by dot-sourcing code, we remove that protection. When we interactively dot-sourced `Write-Message.ps1`, we brought a function into the global scope that we now have no easy way of removing. Any variables in that script outside the function would be brought in as well. If those variables are poorly named, they may conflict with important existing variables, leading to, as they say, hilarious consequences.

If we are unsure where a function has come from, we can use the `File` property on the object to check, like this:

```
${function:Write-Message}.File
```

This will give us the path of the file that contains that function. We can also remove it from a session with the `Remove-Item` cmdlet, as shown here:

```
PS C:\Users\nickp> ${function:Write-Message}.File
C:\temp\poshbook\ch11\Write-Message.ps1
PS C:\Users\nickp> Remove-Item function:Write-Message
PS C:\Users\nickp> ${function:Write-Message}.File
PS C:\Users\nickp>
```

Figure 11.6 – Finding the source of functions and removing them

Modules allow us to control what functions and variables are exported from our code, and to control those as a group. Let's see how we can turn an existing script into a module.

Turning a script into a module

As we saw at the start of this section, the basic process for turning a script into a module is to change the file extension from `.ps1` to `.psm1`. Let's do that now with the `Write-Message.ps1` script we wrote previously, and save a copy of it as `Write-Message.psm1`.

Now, we can open a new session and import our module into the session with the following command:

```
Import-Module C:\temp\poshbook\ch11\Write-Message.psm1
```

Let's take a look at this module in detail:

```
PS C:\Users\nickp> Import-Module C:\temp\poshbook\ch11\Write-Message.psm1
PS C:\Users\nickp> Get-Module Write-Message

ModuleType Version    PreRelease Name                               ExportedCommands
---------- -------    ---------- ----                               ----------------
Script     0.0                   Write-Message                      Write-Message

PS C:\Users\nickp> Get-Module Write-Message | Format-List

Name              : Write-Message
Path              : C:\temp\poshbook\ch11\Write-Message.psm1
Description       :
ModuleType        : Script
Version           : 0.0
PreRelease        :
NestedModules     : {}
ExportedFunctions : Write-Message
ExportedCmdLets   :
ExportedVariables :
ExportedAliases   :


PS C:\Users\nickp> Get-Command -Module Write-Message

CommandType     Name                                               Version    Source
-----------     ----                                               -------    ------
Function        Write-Message                                      0.0        Write-Message
```

Figure 11.7 – Details of the Write-Message module

In the first line, we imported the module. We used the full path because we haven't saved it in a location included in the module path. This is to prevent PowerShell from autoloading it. Now, let's run the following command:

```
Get-Module Write-Message
```

We'll see a script module, its location, and the exported command – that is, `Write-Module`. Now, let's run the following command:

```
Get-Module Write-Message | Format-List
```

We will see that only the function is exported, not the variable.

We can check the details of the `Write-Message` function with `Get-Command` and see that the source is the `Write-Message` module.

Let's try some other things with this module. Open the module file and add the following code:

```
function setMessage {
    Write-Output "$text"
}
```

Import the module again, using the `-Force` parameter to reload it. Now, we have two functions in our module. If we run `Get-Module` again, we'll see that they are both visible:

```
PS C:\Users\nickp> import-Module C:\temp\poshbook\ch11\Write-Message.psm1 -Force
PS C:\Users\nickp> Get-Module Write-Message | Format-List

Name              : Write-Message
Path              : C:\temp\poshbook\ch11\Write-Message.psm1
Description       :
ModuleType        : Script
Version           : 0.0
PreRelease        :
NestedModules     : {}
ExportedFunctions : {setMessage, Write-Message}
ExportedCmdlets   :
ExportedVariables :
ExportedAliases   :


PS C:\Users\nickp> setMessage
default message
```

Figure 11.8 – Multiple exports

As you can see, the `setMessage` cmdlet is available for us to use. What happens if we don't want that? The name we've used doesn't conform with cmdlet naming conventions and is generally one we'd use to signify a private function; something that we need to be available to the other functions within the module, but not something we want available for use outside those functions. We can control access using the `Export-ModuleMember` cmdlet. Add the following line to the bottom of `Write-Message.psm1`:

```
Export-ModuleMember -Function Write-Message
```

Then, import the module again with the `-Force` parameter. The results are shown in the following screenshot:

```
PS C:\Users\nickp> import-Module C:\temp\poshbook\ch11\Write-Message.psm1 -Force
PS C:\Users\nickp> get-module Write-Message | Format-List

Name              : Write-Message
Path              : C:\temp\poshbook\ch11\Write-Message.psm1
Description       :
ModuleType        : Script
Version           : 0.0
PreRelease        :
NestedModules     : {}
ExportedFunctions : Write-Message
ExportedCmdlets   :
ExportedVariables :
ExportedAliases   :


PS C:\Users\nickp> setMessage
setMessage: The term 'setMessage' is not recognized as a name of a cmdlet, function,
 script file, or executable program.Check the spelling of the name, or if a path was
 included, verify that the path is correct and try again.
PS C:\Users\nickp> |
```

Figure 11.9 – Controlling exported functions

Now, only the `Write-Message` function is exported, and when we try and run `setMessage`, this time, we get an error. We can also use `Export-ModuleMember` to export variables and aliases from the module, which aren't exported by default, like this:

```
Export-ModuleMember -variable $MyVariable
```

If we don't explicitly use `Export-ModuleMember`, all the functions in a module will be exported, but nothing other than functions.

In the introduction to this chapter, we mentioned one of the use cases for modules: building applications and solutions. To do this, we will often call a module from within another module – this is called nesting modules, and that's what we're going to look at next.

Nested modules

In *Chapter 9, Don't Repeat Yourself – Functions and Scriptblocks*, we looked at some functions for writing output to log files. It would be useful to write those functions in a module so that we could just call them when we needed them, rather than having to write them in every script we create. These are great examples of functions we would want to keep private, rather than export them for general use. Let's do this. Copy the `Write-Log.ps1` script we wrote previously to a module file called `Write-Log.psm1` in a suitable location. We'll need to edit the `.psm1` file to remove the following line:

```
Write-Log "Is this thing on?"
```

This is how my module file looks:

```
ch11 > ≥ write-log.psm1 > ⊘ function Remove-Log ()
  1    $LogFile = "c:\temp\MyLogFile" + $(Get-Date -UFormat "%Y-%m-%d_%H-%M-%S") + ".log"
       2 references
  2    Function Write-Log {
  3        Param (
  4            [string]$LogString
  5        )
  6        $stamp = (Get-Date).ToString("yyyy/m/dd HH:mm:ss")
  7        $LogMessage = "$stamp $Logstring"
  8        Add-Content $Logfile -Value $LogMessage
  9    }
 10
 11    # Write-Log "Is this thing on?"
 12
       0 references
 13    function Remove-Log {
 14        $limit = (Get-Date).AddDays(-7)
 15        Get-ChildItem -Path "C:\temp" -Include "MyLogFile*" -Recurse -Force |
 16        Where-Object {$_.CreationTime -lt $limit} |
 17        Remove-Item -Force
 18    }
```

Figure 11.10 – The Write-Log.psm1 module

As we can see, I've remarked line 11, rather than deleting it. We are left with two functions and a variable – that is, `Write-Log`, `Remove-Log`, and `$LogFile`.

We can now add a couple of lines to our `Write-Message.psm1` module so that we can call the `Write-Log` module and run one of the functions in it. Edit your `Write-Message` function, like this:

```
Import-Module "C:\temp\poshbook\ch11\write-log.psm1"
$text = "default message"
function Write-Message($text) {
    Write-Output "$text"
    Write-Log "$text"
```

```
}
function setMessage {
    Write-Output "$text"
}
```

I've added the first line to import the `Write-Log` module and the fifth line to call the `Write-Log` function from it. I've also removed the `Export-ModuleMember` line. Now, let's see what happens when we import the `Write-Message` module:

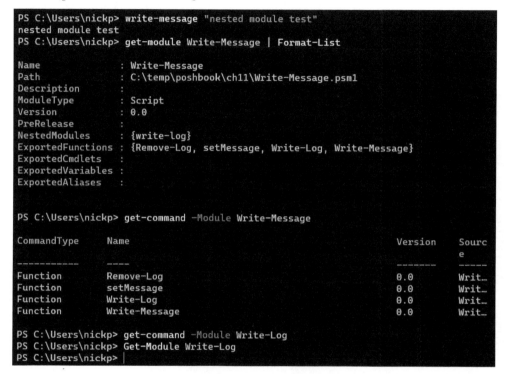

Figure 11.11 – Nested modules

As we can see, the module is imported as before and works as we expect. We can see from the output of `Get-Module` that there are four exported functions – two from `Write-Message` and two from `Write-Log` – and we can see that the `Write-Log` module is nested. When we attempt to access it with `Get-Command`, however, we don't see any loaded functions, and `Get-Module Write-Log` returns nothing. However, if we check the log file that was created, we'll see a message stating `nested module test`, so it is working.

This is because nested modules are only visible to the calling module, so we can't access `Write-Log` directly. However, because we removed the `Export-ModuleMember` line, all functions are exported, including the functions from nested modules; they appear as functions of the calling module. We'll be able to see the `Write-Log` module if we use `Get-Module -All`, though, and we can find the real location of the `Write-Log` function as before – that is, by calling the `File` property:

```
PS C:\Users\nickp> Get-Module -All

ModuleType Version    PreRelease Name                              ExportedComman
                                                                   ds
---------- -------    ---------- ----                              --------------
Binary     7.3.6.500             Microsoft.PowerShell.Commands.Mana… {Add-Content,…
Binary     7.3.6.500             Microsoft.PowerShell.Commands.Util… {Add-Member, …
Manifest   7.0.0.0              Microsoft.PowerShell.Management     {Add-Content,…
Binary     2.2.6.0              Microsoft.PowerShell.PSReadLine2    {Get-PSReadLi…
Manifest   7.0.0.0              Microsoft.PowerShell.Utility        {Add-Member, …
Script     2.2.6                PSReadLine                          {Get-PSReadLi…
Script     0.0                  write-log                           {Remove-Log, …
Script     0.0                  Write-Message                       {Remove-Log, …

PS C:\Users\nickp> ${function:Write-Log}.File
C:\temp\poshbook\ch11\write-log.psm1
```

Figure 11.12 – Finding nested modules

As we can see, the `Write-Log` function is defined in the `write-log.psm1` file.

Sometimes, we may not want nested modules to be hidden like this; if that's the case, then we can use the `-Global` parameter of `Import-Module`, like this:

```
Import-Module -Global "C:\temp\poshbook\ch11\write-log.psm1"
```

The `Write-Log` module will be imported at the same top level as the `Write-Message` module.

Now, let's look at some other types of modules, including binary and manifest modules.

More modules

You may have noticed that when we create a function in a module, we use it like a cmdlet, but it's still called a function. It will behave as a cmdlet, with parameters, help, members, and so on, but it's not a cmdlet. Consider the following:

```
PS C:\Users\nickp> Get-Command Write-Message

CommandType     Name                                              Version     Source
-----------     ----                                              -------     ------
Function        Write-Message                                     0.0         Write-Message

PS C:\Users\nickp> Get-Command Get-Service

CommandType     Name                                              Version     Source
-----------     ----                                              -------     ------
Cmdlet          Get-Service                                       7.0.0.0     Microsoft.PowerShell.Management
```

Figure 11.13 – Functions and cmdlets

As we can see, `Write-Message` is of the `Function` type, whereas the Microsoft `Get-Service` command is of the `Cmdlet` type.

To write custom cmdlets, we need to write a binary module. Remember that PowerShell is based on .NET and is an interpreted language, written in a compiled language, usually C#, in the same way that Python is an interpreted language written in C.

We're not going to cover writing modules in C# here, but we will discuss how they work and how they are used.

A binary module does not have a `.psm1` extension – it is a .NET assembly compiled from code such as C# and has a `.dll` extension. We can create it by writing our C# code within a `Here-String` declaration, a block of multi-line text inside the `@"       "@` construct, and then use the `Add-Type -OutputAssembly` cmdlet to compile it:

```
$code = @"
using System.Management.Automation;
namespace SendMessage
{
    [Cmdlet(VerbsCommunications.Send, "Message")]
    public class SendMessageCommand : Cmdlet
    {
        [Parameter(Mandatory = true)]
        public string Name { get; set; }
        protected override void ProcessRecord()
        {
            WriteObject(Name + " loves PowerShell!");
        }
    }
}
```

```
}
"@
Add-Type -TypeDefinition $Code -OutputAssembly  c:\temp\
MyBinaryModule.dll
```

Other than that, we can import it in the same way as a script module with Import-Module:

```
Import-Module c:\temp\MyBinaryModule.dll
```

If we were to run Get-Module on our fictional MyBinaryModule, we would see that ModuleType is Binary and that it has exported cmdlets, rather than exported functions.

The main difference between binary modules and script modules is that once they're loaded into a session, they can't be unloaded. If we need to make a change to a binary module we are writing, we will need to close PowerShell first.

We may also see PowerShell modules written in CDXML, an XML wrapper for Common Information Model commands. This used to be quite common for Windows administration modules, but it is largely deprecated now since modules written this way are slower to load and run than script modules due to the extra effort required to parse the XML into PowerShell, which then itself needs parsing. In the words of the official documentation, "*Avoid CDXML.*" Similarly, we may see references to PowerShell SnapIns. These are deprecated forms of Windows PowerShell that aren't supported in PowerShell 7, so we don't need to worry about them.

There's one more type of module for us to consider – the manifest module. A manifest module is a script or binary module that includes a module manifest. That's what we're going to look at in the next section.

Module manifests

The script modules we've been playing with so far are monolithic single files, either standalone or nested. That's fine for hobbyist use, but it's not great in a production environment, where we might want to split our functions into separate files and include version information and a whole bunch of other metadata and resources, such as XML formatting files or binaries. To organize a more complex module, we need a document that explains how it is to be loaded and implemented; this document is called a module manifest, and it is a hash table saved with a .psd1 extension. Let's have a look at an example. if we browse to the PowerShellGet module in C:\Program Files\PowerShell\7\ Modules (or /opt/microsoft/PowerShell/7/Modules in Linux), we will see the following files and folders:

> Local Disk (C:) > Program Files > PowerShell > 7 > Modules > PowerShellGet

Name ^	Date modified	Type	Size
DscResources	08/08/2023 08:27	File folder	
en-US	08/08/2023 08:28	File folder	
Modules	08/08/2023 08:27	File folder	
PowerShellGet.psd1	22/09/2020 22:41	Windows PowerSh...	24 KB
PSGet.Format.ps1xml	22/09/2020 22:41	PS1XML File	24 KB
PSGet.Resource.psd1	22/09/2020 22:41	Windows PowerSh...	58 KB
PSModule.psm1	22/09/2020 22:41	Windows PowerSh...	1,337 KB

Figure 11.14 – The PowerShellGet module

As we can see, there are four files and three folders. These folders contain several `.psm1` and `.psd1` files that define functions and manifests for nested modules. The main code for the module is in `PSModule.psm1`. `PSGet.Format.ps1xml` contains formatting information for displaying the output of functions. `PowerShellGet.psd1` is the module manifest. `PSGet.Resource.psd1` is a set of output strings for the module to use; we won't worry about it here. If we open the `PSModule.psm1` file, we will see it is written in PowerShell, not C#, so it is a script module. It's a big file, with a lot of functions defined in it. Let's take a look at the `PowerShellGet.psd1` file.

The first thing to note is that it is given the same name as the folder it's housed in. This is deliberate; if there is a manifest present in a module folder, it must have the same name as the folder; otherwise, the module won't load. Giving the same name to the `.psm1` file, in the absence of a manifest, allows PowerShell to easily find it for autoloading, but otherwise, this doesn't matter. It's different for manifests.

Let's open it up and look inside:

```
C: > Program Files > PowerShell > 7 > Modules > PowerShellGet > ≥ PowerShellGet.psd1
 1  @{
 2      RootModule          = 'PSModule.psm1'
 3      ModuleVersion       = '2.2.5'
 4      GUID                = '1d73a601-4a6c-43c5-ba3f-619b18bbb404'
 5      Author              = 'Microsoft Corporation'
 6      CompanyName         = 'Microsoft Corporation'
 7      Copyright           = '(c) Microsoft Corporation. All rights reserved.'
 8      Description         = 'PowerShell module with commands for discovering,
 9      PowerShellVersion   = '3.0'
10      FormatsToProcess    = 'PSGet.Format.ps1xml'
11  FunctionsToExport = @(
12      'Find-Command',
13      'Find-DSCResource',
14      'Find-Module',
15      'Find-RoleCapability',
16      'Find-Script',
```

Figure 11.15 – The PowerShellGet manifest

On line 1, we can see that this is a hash table from @{, and that everything after that takes the format of a key-value pair. As we can see, this is a long file with a lot of information in it; over 200 lines, although much of this is a big blob of text with the `ReleaseNotes` key.

A manifest consists of up to 37 different key-value pairs that may contain strings or arrays. We can add additional code to a manifest, including comparison and arithmetic operators, basic data types, and the `if` statement, but we're not going to cover that here; I've never needed to do it. Let's create a new manifest for ourselves and see what's in it.

In a suitable directory, create a folder called `ManifestModule`. Now, open a PowerShell session and type the following cmdlet:

```
New-ModuleManifest
```

At the prompt, supply the path and the name of the new manifest file, like this:

```
C:\temp\poshbook\ch11\ManifestModule\ManifestModule.psd1
```

That's it – this creates a new manifest file for a module called `ManifestModule`. Let's open it up in VS Code:

```
ch11 > ManifestModule > ≥ ManifestModule.psd1
 1    #
 2    # Module manifest for module 'ManifestModule'
 3    #
 4    # Generated by: nickp
 5    #
 6    # Generated on: 12/08/2023
 7    #
 8
 9    @{
10
11    # Script module or binary module file associated with this manifest.
12    # RootModule = ''
13
14    # Version number of this module.
15    ModuleVersion = '0.0.1'
16
17    # Supported PSEditions
18    # CompatiblePSEditions = @()
19
20    # ID used to uniquely identify this module
21    GUID = '4126717f-53c9-4275-8c65-c5234d0d858b'
22
```

Figure 11.16 – A basic module manifest

The first thing to notice is that some of the values have been generated for you. ModuleVersion is 0.0.1, there is an autogenerated GUID to ensure that this module can be differentiated from any other modules with the same name, and the Author, CompanyName, and Copyright keys are populated. Other than that, everything is empty and generally remarked out.

The keys in a manifest fall into three groups that cover the following aspects:

- **Production data**: Who wrote it, when, who for, and what sort of systems it will run on.

- **Module construction**: Broadly separated into what to load and what to export, these keys cover the loading of nested modules, formatting information, type information, and assemblies. They also define which functions, variables, and aliases are exported. RootModule defines the main module file that calls everything else – the main .psm1 file.

- **Module content**: These are lists of all the modules, files, and other assets that are included in the module. These keys are optional, but generally, they should be populated accurately.

We can populate the keys when we call the New-ModuleManifest cmdlet, by adding the key name as a parameter:

```
New-ModuleManifest -Path 'C:\temp\newmodule\newmodule.psd1'
-ModuleVersion '1.0.0'
```

The alternative is to edit the manifest file directly in a text editor or VS Code. If we edit it directly, there is always the possibility of mistyping something and breaking the file, so it's a good idea to test our edited manifest, like this:

```
Test-ModuleManifest -Path 'C:\temp\newmodule\newmodule.psd1'
```

We can see the results in the following figure:

```
PS C:\Users\nickp> Test-ModuleManifest 'C:\temp\poshbook\ch11\ManifestModule\ManifestModule.psd1'


ModuleType Version    PreRelease Name                               ExportedCommands
---------- -------    ---------- ----                               ----------------
Manifest   0.0.1                 ManifestModule

PS C:\Users\nickp>
```

Figure 11.17 – Testing a module manifest file

If the module's information is returned, then the file has been formatted correctly.

As we've seen, module construction can get complicated pretty quickly. Let's finish this chapter by taking a look at a tool that can make it very much easier – Plaster.

Using scaffolding tools such as Plaster

If we are working long-term on a module, or collaborating with other people, then it's a really good idea to use a framework that splits everything up into separate files and assets. This is where a scaffolding tool comes in. My choice of tool is Plaster, a module that was originally produced by Microsoft but is now maintained by PowerShell.Org, one of the most prolific online PowerShell communities.

Plaster uses a template file that consists of a manifest (similar to the module manifest) and a set of content files and directories. The template is written in XML and is highly customizable. The manifest has three sections:

- Metadata, which contains information about the template, such as its name, version, and author
- Parameters, which defines choices that the user can make about their module structure – what files and folders to create and include
- Content, which specifies the actions that Plaster will perform – copying files, modifying files, and checking that required modules are installed.

Let's start by installing the module from the PowerShell gallery. Type the following to download the module:

```
Install-Module Plaster
```

We may need to acknowledge that the PowerShell gallery is an untrusted repository. Now, let's import the module:

```
Import-Module Plaster
```

And that's it – we're ready to go. Let's see what we've got:

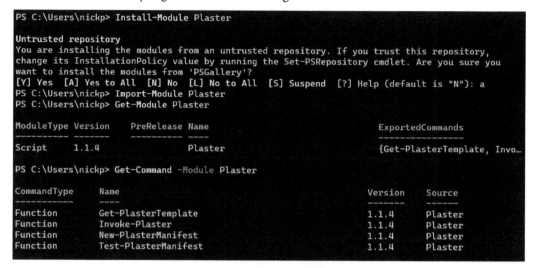

```
PS C:\Users\nickp> Install-Module Plaster

Untrusted repository
You are installing the modules from an untrusted repository. If you trust this repository,
change its InstallationPolicy value by running the Set-PSRepository cmdlet. Are you sure you
want to install the modules from 'PSGallery'?
[Y] Yes  [A] Yes to All  [N] No  [L] No to All  [S] Suspend  [?] Help (default is "N"): a
PS C:\Users\nickp> Import-Module Plaster
PS C:\Users\nickp> Get-Module Plaster

ModuleType Version       PreRelease Name                              ExportedCommands
---------- -------       ---------- ----                              ----------------
Script     1.1.4                    Plaster                           {Get-PlasterTemplate, Invo…

PS C:\Users\nickp> Get-Command -Module Plaster

CommandType     Name                                               Version    Source
-----------     ----                                               -------    ------
Function        Get-PlasterTemplate                                1.1.4      Plaster
Function        Invoke-Plaster                                     1.1.4      Plaster
Function        New-PlasterManifest                                1.1.4      Plaster
Function        Test-PlasterManifest                               1.1.4      Plaster
```

Figure 11.18 – Examining the Plaster module

As we can see, we've installed version 1.1.4 of the module, and we've got four new commands to play with:

- Get-PlasterTemplate: This lists the existing templates available for us to use. We can write or download templates as XML files. Only two are included, and the one we need is NewPowerShellScriptModule.

- Invoke-Plaster: This runs the Plaster scaffolding tool.

- New-PlasterManifest: This command creates a new manifest.

- Test-PlasterManifest: This command tests that the manifest is formatted correctly.

Let's run it and see what we get:

```
Get-PlasterTemplate
```

Then, copy the path for `NewPowerShellScriptModule`. Now, type the following:

```
Invoke-Plaster
```

You'll be asked for the path to the default template and then a destination path; this needs to be a folder, not a file.

You'll also be asked to provide the module's name and version, as well as whether you want to set VS Code as the default editor. Here's how it looked for me:

```
PS C:\Users\nickp> invoke-Plaster

cmdlet Invoke-Plaster at command pipeline position 1
Supply values for the following parameters:
TemplatePath: C:\Users\nickp\OneDrive\Documents\PowerShell\Modules\Plaster\1.1.4\Templates\NewPowerShellScriptModule
DestinationPath: c:\temp\poshbook\ch11\plaster
  ____  _           _
 |  _ \| | __ _ ___| |_ ___ _ __
 | |_) | |/ _` / __| __/ _ \ '__|
 |  __/| | (_| \__ \ ||  __/ |
 |_|   |_|\__,_|___/\__\___|_|
                                             v1.1.4
==================================================
Enter the name of the module: NewPlasterModule
Enter the version number of the module (0.0.1):
Select an editor for editor integration (or None):
[N] None  [C] Visual Studio Code  [?] Help (default is "C"): c
Destination path: C:\temp\poshbook\ch11\plaster

Scaffolding your PowerShell Module...

   Create NewPlasterModule.psd1
   Create NewPlasterModule.psm1
   Create test\NewPlasterModule.Tests.ps1
   Create .vscode\settings.json
   Create .vscode\tasks.json
  Missing The required module Pester (minimum version: 4.0.3) was not found.
          Without Pester, you will not be able to run the provided Pester test to validate your module manifest file.
          Without version 4.0.3, VS Code will not display Pester warnings and errors in the Problems panel.

Your new PowerShell module project 'NewPlasterModule' has been created.

A Pester test has been created to validate the module's manifest file.  Add additional tests to the test directory.
You can run the Pester tests in your project by executing the 'test' task.  Press Ctrl+P, then type 'task test'.

PS C:\Users\nickp>
```

Figure 11.19 – Invoking Plaster

As we can see, one of the required modules, Pester, is missing from my sandbox machine. Pester is a module that makes it a breeze to do unit testing and test-driven development, but it's a bit beyond the scope of this book.

Let's see what has been created in the destination path:

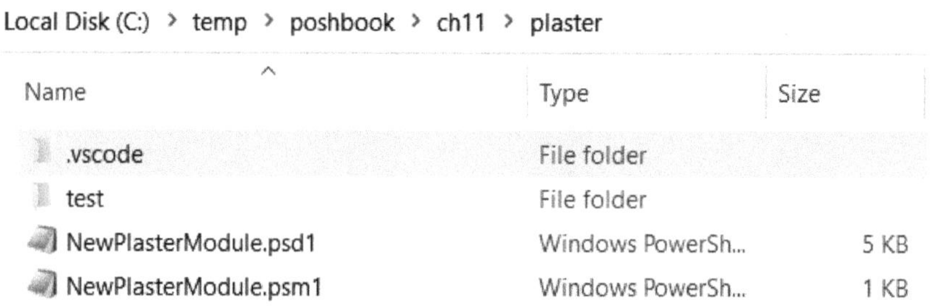

Figure 11.20 – A module created with the default Plaster template

As we can see, Plaster has created two files – a script module file and a module manifest file – a folder for test scripts, and a folder for VS Code settings.

The `NewPlasterModule.psm1` file looks like this:

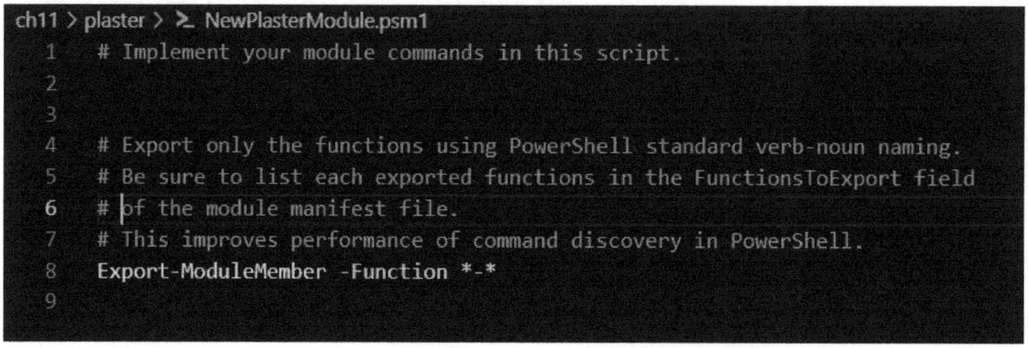

Figure 11.21 – A basic module file generated by Plaster

As we can see, it's very simple, but it includes a great trick – if the functions in the file are named with standard cmdlet naming conventions, such as `Verb-Noun`, then they will be exported. If they are not, like the `setMessage` function we wrote earlier in this chapter, then they will not be exported. Neat.

The beauty of Plaster is how extensible it is; it's easy to write templates to create folder structures for public and private functions and classes, and it can all be done in a repeatable way. To get some idea of how versatile Plaster is, have a look at Kevin Marquette's blog at `https://powershellexplained.com/2017-05-12-Powershell-Plaster-adventures-in/` and his GitHub page at `https://github.com/KevinMarquette/PlasterTemplates`. Have a play with his example templates.

That is as much as we're going to cover regarding Plaster – there are several other scaffolding modules available, so if you don't like Plaster, take a look at some of the others. That also wraps up this chapter; let's recap what we've done.

Summary

We started this chapter by reminding ourselves of what we learned in earlier chapters regarding modules and placing that into a more formal context. We looked at the standard module locations and how we can add locations by editing the $ENV:PSModulePath variable. We saw how PowerShell uses these locations to facilitate autoloading, and we saw how sometimes, we might not want that to happen. Then, we looked at how we can manually import modules and finished up our review by looking at the PowerShellGet module.

After, we started to write our own modules. We began by looking at the earliest method for importing code, known as dot-sourcing, and saw why that could be a bad idea. Then, we created our first module by writing a script and converting it. Next, we looked at how we can build applications by nesting modules, before discussing some other types of modules, such as binary modules.

Then, we looked at the most common complex module type – the manifest module. We saw how the manifest file controls what is loaded and exported, and how to write and test a manifest file. Finally, we looked at a tool that can make writing modules much simpler – Plaster.

In the next chapter, we are going to look at the security aspects of PowerShell, and how we can best go about making ourselves and our colleagues and users safe with such a powerful tool.

Exercises

Here are the exercises for this chapter:

1. How can you list all imported modules in the current PowerShell session?
2. What is the purpose of the -Global parameter when importing a module?
3. How do we import a module that isn't in a path specified in the $ENV:PSModulePath variable?
4. We want to import a module that contains functions that have the same name as cmdlets that already exist in our session. What are two ways we can get around this?
5. By default, all the functions of a module are exported. What are two ways we can control what functions are exported?
6. What is the purpose of the HelpInfoURI key in a module manifest?
7. What might be in a file with the .ps1xml extension?
8. If we load a module with the .dll extension, what sort of commands will we get?
9. Why don't we write CDXML modules?

Further reading

To learn more about the topics that were covered in this chapter, take a look at the following resources:

- `PowerShellGet` and its replacement:

    - `https://devblogs.microsoft.com/powershell/powershellget-in-powershell-7-4-updates/`

    - `https://learn.microsoft.com/en-us/powershell/module/microsoft.powershell.psresourceget/?view=powershellget-3.x`

    - `https://learn.microsoft.com/en-us/powershell/module/powershellget/?view=powershellget-2.x`

- Writing module manifests: `https://learn.microsoft.com/en-us/powershell/scripting/developer/module/how-to-write-a-powershell-module-manifest`

- Plaster: `https://powershellexplained.com/2017-05-12-Powershell-Plaster-adventures-in/#template-folder-and-file-structure`

12

Securing PowerShell

As we've seen, PowerShell is an incredibly powerful tool, and, to quote Uncle Ben, *"with great power comes great responsibility."* If you don't know who Uncle Ben is, ask your friendly neighborhood Spider-Man. PowerShell can wreak absolute havoc across a system or an organization. This damage can be deliberate, by someone setting out to cause damage, but it can just as easily be inadvertent.

We're going to start this chapter by looking at one of the features that makes PowerShell so powerful – PowerShell remoting. We'll continue by looking at how PowerShell protects against inadvertent mistakes, and then move on to the PowerShell features that protect us from deliberate attacks. We'll then look at the features PowerShell has that let us analyze what has happened on the machine through logging, before wrapping up with a look at the things we can do to make the code we write more secure. Because of PowerShell's history with Windows, many of these features are exclusive to Windows, or more fully developed in Windows. When this is the case, it will be acknowledged.

The main topics we will cover in this chapter are as follows:

- Why is security so important?
- Securing PowerShell against inadvertent mistakes
- Running PowerShell securely
- PowerShell logging
- Writing secure code

Why is security so important?

We've seen that PowerShell is powerful, but we haven't seen why it can be so dangerous. Everything we've done so far has required an interactive logon to the client we are using, which implies someone would need physical access to a device before attacking it. PowerShell, however, has the concept of **PowerShell remoting**, which allows us to log on to a remote device and run PowerShell code as if we were physically there. This is why it is such a powerful administration tool. We'll not cover much about remoting in this book, as it is very much an admin tool, but it's important to know the basics. Let's take a closer look.

A PowerShell remoting whistlestop tour

Many older cmdlets in Windows PowerShell have a -ComputerName parameter, which allows PowerShell to query a remote machine for information. The trouble with this parameter is that it relies on the credentials under which we are running our PowerShell session having the authorization to query the remote machine. If we're lucky, the cmdlet will have a -Credential parameter that we can use to supply alternate credentials. Quite often, we're not lucky; see the following screenshot.

```
Windows PowerShell
Copyright (C) Microsoft Corporation. All rights reserved.

Try the new cross-platform PowerShell https://aka.ms/pscore6

PS C:\Users\nickp> Get-Process -ComputerName localhost -credential $cred
Get-Process : A parameter cannot be found that matches parameter name 'credential'.
At line:1 char:37
+ Get-Process -ComputerName localhost -credential $cred
+                                     ~~~~~~~~~~~~
    + CategoryInfo          : InvalidArgument: (:) [Get-Process], ParameterBindingE
    + FullyQualifiedErrorId : NamedParameterNotFound,Microsoft.PowerShell.Commands.
```

Figure 12.1 – Get-Process does not feel lucky

As we can see, the Get-Process cmdlet has no -Credential parameter, so we just have to hope that our session credentials will work on the remote machine. If we don't have the right credential on our PowerShell session, we can't run Get-Process on a remote machine. Even if we do have the right credential, it's quite possible that a remote firewall will block the request. In PowerShell 7.2 and later, it doesn't have a -ComputerName parameter either.

To get around this, PowerShell remoting was developed for Windows PowerShell 3.0. It uses the **WinRM** (short for **Windows Remote Management**) protocol, which is part of Windows. WinRM runs over HTTP/S on ports 5985 (HTTP) and 5986 (HTTPS), which means it can be encrypted using SSL. In enterprise configurations, where Active Directory is used, the traffic is also encrypted, using Kerberos. Obviously, Linux machines don't include WinRM, so PowerShell 7.x helpfully includes support to run remote sessions over SSH. We'll cover that in more detail later in this chapter, in the *Running PowerShell securely* section. Let's have a look at how PowerShell remoting works in a Windows environment; we'll start by enabling PowerShell remoting. Note that I'm running this on a Windows 10 client, and I have created a new local user called Admin, with a password and administrator rights.

Enabling PowerShell remoting

By default, PowerShell remoting is enabled on all Windows servers. However, it's disabled on Windows clients. The easiest way to get it running is to use the Enable-PSRemoting cmdlet. This cmdlet does everything we need, from enabling the endpoints to creating the correct rules in Windows Firewall. This needs to be run from an elevated admin prompt. Take a look at the following screenshot:

```
PS C:\Users\nickp> Enable-PSRemoting -Force -SkipNetworkProfileCheck
WARNING: PowerShell remoting has been enabled only for PowerShell 6+ configurations and does
not affect Windows PowerShell remoting configurations. Run this cmdlet in Windows PowerShell
to affect all PowerShell remoting configurations.
WinRM is already set up to receive requests on this computer.
WinRM is already set up for remote management on this computer.
PS C:\Users\nickp>
```

Figure 12.2 – Enabling PowerShell remoting

As we can see, I've run `Enable-PSRemoting` with a couple of common parameters. The `-Force` parameter means we don't get asked whether we're sure we want to do this a bunch of times, and we've seen the parameter used this way before. The `-SkipNetworkProfileCheck` is an interesting one, however. Many people haven't configured their network profile on standalone clients, and the default is public. However, PowerShell remoting won't operate over a public network, by default. Using the `-SkipNetworkProfileCheck` bypasses the network profile check but creates a firewall rule that only allows remote sessions from the local subnet. This rule is easily edited, but it's probably better to set the network profile up correctly, or to not try running remote sessions over a public network.

Creating a session

Now we've got remoting set up on our client, let's create a session. We can do that with the `New-PSSession` cmdlet. I'm going to store my `Admin` user credentials in a variable called `$cred`, and then I'm going to run it like this:

```
New-PSSession -ComputerName localhost -Authentication Negotiate
-Credential $cred
```

And we can see the output we get here:

```
PS C:\Users\nickp> $cred = Get-Credential

PowerShell credential request
Enter your credentials.
User: admin
Password for user admin: *********

PS C:\Users\nickp> New-PSSession -ComputerName localhost -Authentication Negotiate -Credential $cred

 Id Name        Transport ComputerName  ComputerType    State    ConfigurationName      Av
                                                                                        ai
                                                                                        la
                                                                                        bi
                                                                                        li
                                                                                        ty
 -- ----        --------- ------------  ------------    -----    -----------------      --
  3 Runspace3   WSMan     localhost     RemoteMachine   Opened   Microsoft.PowerShell  …e
```

Figure 12.3 – Creating a new remoting session

This will create a persistent session that may be connected to and disconnected from as needed.

Joining and leaving a session

We can use the Enter-PSSession cmdlet to connect to a session like this:

```
Enter-PSSession -Name <session name>
```

The session we create is a PowerShell object (like everything else in PowerShell), and so we can also enter by passing the session through the pipeline:

```
Get-PSSession -Name <session name> | Enter-PSSession
```

This is how it looks on my machine:

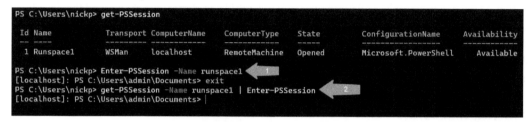

Figure 12.4 – Entering and leaving a remoting session

In the first command, I've called the session by name. In the second command, I've passed the session object to Enter-PSSession. I've left the session by using the exit keyword. Note that once I am in a session, the PowerShell prompt changes to reflect ComputerName of the client I am connected to and the remote working directory.

This is called a one-to-one remoting session. Once we're in this sort of session, it is the same as if we were directly connected to the remote machine. Only the PowerShell modules on the remote machine are available.

We can also enter an ad hoc session by not specifying an existing session when we use Enter-PSSession; instead, we specify a computer name and a credential like this:

```
Enter-PSSession -ComputerName <name> -Credential <credential>
```

As we can see here, creating a session this way means it ceases to exist when we exit it, rather than persisting:

```
PS C:\Users\nickp> Enter-PSSession -computerName localhost -Credential $cred
[localhost]: PS C:\Users\admin\Documents> exit
PS C:\Users\nickp> Get-PSSession
PS C:\Users\nickp>
```

Figure 12.5 – Ad hoc remoting

In the first command in the preceding screenshot, I'm creating an ad hoc session, which I then `exit`. As we can see, after I type `exit`, the session is no longer available, as shown in the last command, where I run the `Get-PSSession` cmdlet.

To remove persistent sessions, we can either pass the session name to `Remove-PSSession`, like this:

```
Remove-PSSession –Name <session name>
```

Alternatively, we pipe the session object:

```
Get-PSSession -Name <session name> | Remove-PSSession
```

If we run the preceding `Get-PSSession` cmdlet without specifying a session name, then all sessions will be removed.

One-to-many sessions

We can also run commands and scripts on multiple machines at once by using the `Invoke-Command` cmdlet, like this:

```
Invoke-Command -ComputerName <name 1>, <name 2> -ScriptBlock
{Get-Service}
```

This will run the commands or scripts in the scriptblock against the list of names specified in the `-ComputerName` parameter. This command uses PowerShell remoting the same as the previous `PSSession` cmdlets.

Being able to run commands on remote machines makes PowerShell an extremely useful administration tool, which unfortunately means that it is also a security risk. Let's look now at the ways we can help prevent PowerShell from causing problems.

Securing PowerShell against inadvertent mistakes

The first set of tools we'll look at are the ones that protect us from people doing things by accident. The most useful of these is a built-in execution policy that can be used to control how scripts can be run.

Execution policy

We encountered the execution policy feature back in *Chapter 8, Writing Our First Script – Turning Simple Cmdlets into Reusable Code*, and noted that we would cover it in more detail in this chapter. The execution policy is a safety feature that controls how we can run scripts, but only in a Windows environment. Don Jones (the Don!) has described the execution policy as intended to "...*slow down an uninformed user who is unintentionally trying to run an untrusted script.*" There is a lot of unintentionality in that sentence. The execution policy will present a few obstacles to an educated user who is deliberately trying to run a script. The best way to stop a user from running a potentially destructive script is to make sure that they don't have the permissions to carry out the commands in the script. I have seen customer environments where the number of domain admin accounts runs into the hundreds, many of them unused for years, but still enabled. These customers have much bigger problems than PowerShell's execution policy.

The execution policy has different levels of security and is applied at different scopes. The levels are determined by the script's origin, and whether it is signed with a code signing certificate from a trusted certificate authority; we'll discuss code signing certificates later in this chapter, in the *Signing scripts* section. Let's look at the levels first:

- `Restricted`: This is the default policy on Windows client computers and prevents the running of scripts, including formatting files and modules – any files with the `.ps1xml`, `.psm1`, or `.ps1` extensions. Individual commands may be run at the terminal, but that's it.

- `AllSigned`: This level allows scripts with a digital signature from a trusted publisher to be run; this includes scripts that were written on the computer. If it isn't signed, it can't run. If it is signed by an untrusted publisher, then PowerShell will prompt the user. Obviously, if a script is malicious and signed, then it can still be run.

- `RemoteSigned`: Scripts that originated elsewhere than the local machine need a digital signature, but scripts written on the local machine do not. Obviously, there are a number of clandestine ways around this that might involve opening Notepad and using copy and paste. This is the default policy for Windows server computers.

- `Default`: This sets the default policy. On a Windows client, the default policy is `Restricted`. On a Windows server, the default policy is `RemoteSigned`.

- `Undefined`: This removes any execution policy that is set on the current scope. If we use this on all scopes, then the resulting policy is the default policy, as previously mentioned.

- `Unrestricted`: This is the default policy on non-Windows computers. Unsigned files from anywhere can be run; users may get a warning when running scripts that didn't originate in the local network.

- `Bypass`: Nothing is blocked, and there are no warnings. Execution policy is ignored. This can be set by calling the `-ExecutionPolicy` parameter of the `pwsh.exe` program. We can see how this looks in the following figure:

```
C:\Users\nickp>pwsh.exe -ExecutionPolicy Bypass
PowerShell 7.3.6
PS C:\Users\nickp> Get-ExecutionPolicy -List

        Scope ExecutionPolicy
        ----- ---------------

MachinePolicy        Undefined
   UserPolicy        Undefined
      Process           Bypass
  CurrentUser       Restricted
 LocalMachine       Restricted

PS C:\Users\nickp> |
```

Figure 12.6 – Bypassing the execution policy

As we can see, the execution policy is only bypassed at the pwsh.exe process level but remains at the default for the other scopes. When this pwsh process ends, the execution policy bypass will lapse.

Let's consider the scopes at which we can apply execution policies next.

As we can see in *Figure 12.6*, there are five scopes at which we can apply an execution policy. Each one has a different precedence level. The MachinePolicy and UserPolicy scopes can only be set in Group Policy – a feature of Windows Active Directory. Group Policy is an enterprise application for controlling the configuration of users and machines centrally, and we're not going to worry too much about it here. There is a good introductory article on Group Policy here: https://techcommunity.microsoft.com/t5/ask-the-performance-team/the-basics-of-group-policies/ba-p/372404.

Scopes have an order of precedence, and a scope at a lower level will be overridden by a scope at a higher level. In descending order of precedence, the scopes are as follows:

- MachinePolicy: This scope is set using a group policy and applies to all users of a machine.

- UserPolicy: This scope is set by group policy and applies to the current user of a machine.

- Process: This scope refers to the current PowerShell session. There is no registry location for this; it is governed by the content of the $env:PSExecutionPolicyPreference variable. When the session is closed, the content of the variable is removed.

- CurrentUser: This only applies to the current user and is stored in the Windows registry, a database of machine settings.

- LocalMachine: This applies to all users on the machine and is also stored in the registry.

In *Figure 12.6*, we can see that the scopes are listed in order of precedence. Because the execution policy is Undefined at both the MachinePolicy and UserPolicy levels, the effective execution policy is Bypass, defined at the Process level.

The two cmdlets we can use with the execution policy are Get-ExecutionPolicy and Set-ExecutionPolicy, which we saw back in *Chapter 8, Writing Our First Script – Turning Simple Cmdlets into Reusable Code*. Let's briefly look at two other features of PowerShell that are intended to help prevent mistakes.

Other features

These features only protect against someone accidentally running a script. Firstly, PowerShell extensions such as .ps1 are associated with Notepad by default, rather than as executable files. This means that if someone double-clicks a script by accident, they will open it in Notepad, rather than run it. This is in contrast to earlier Windows script files such as batch files and Visual Basic script files, which would execute if clicked accidentally.

The other way we are protected against accidental execution is that PowerShell doesn't search the current folder for script files, so either a relative path or absolute path must be provided to run a script at the terminal prompt, like this:

```
PS C:\Users\nickp> C:\temp\poshbook\ch12\HelloWorld.ps1          1
hello world
PS C:\Users\nickp> cd C:\temp\poshbook\ch12          2
PS C:\temp\poshbook\ch12> HelloWorld          3
HelloWorld: The term 'HelloWorld' is not recognized as a name of a cmdlet, function,
 script file, or executable program.Check the spelling of the name, or if a path was
 included, verify that the path is correct and try again.

Suggestion [3,General]: The command HelloWorld was not found, but does exist in the
current location. PowerShell does not load commands from the current location by def
ault. If you trust this command, instead type: ".\HelloWorld". See "get-help about_C
ommand_Precedence" for more details.
PS C:\temp\poshbook\ch12> .\HelloWorld.ps1          4
hello world
PS C:\temp\poshbook\ch12> |
```

Figure 12.7 – Absolute and relative paths

In the first line, I've used an absolute path to call a script called HelloWorld.ps1, which outputs the line hello world. In the second line, I switch to the folder containing the script, and in the third line, I attempt to call it by using HelloWorld, which would work for a program Windows recognizes as an executable, such as a batch file, but doesn't for a PowerShell script. Note how PowerShell helpfully tells me what I was doing wrong. In the fourth line, I call it using a relative path by prefacing the full script name with .\, which is successful.

That used to be it for PowerShell security. Thankfully, in recent versions, lots of new features have been added that are more proactive. Let's explore how we can run PowerShell securely.

Running PowerShell securely

PowerShell has several features that actively increase the security of our environments. Let's start by looking at application control.

Application control

Application control solutions prevent unauthorized applications from running. There are third-party applications, such as Trellix, but Windows 10 and later come with two built-in applications – **Windows Defender Application Control** (**WDAC**) and AppLocker. These can be used to create policies that enforce a whitelist of applications that are allowed to execute and prevent anything else from running. AppLocker is no longer under development, so WDAC is recommended. These solutions are intended for an enterprise environment and allow for centralized control. I am not aware of any solutions that work with PowerShell on Linux or macOS. When PowerShell runs under a default WDAC policy, then trusted modules and scripts are granted more access than untrusted ones, using a feature called language modes.

Language modes

Language modes are used to control how scripts can run in a PowerShell environment that is subject to an Application Control policy. It's worth noting that there are lots of articles on the internet showing you how to set language modes using a variable; this is just for testing how code behaves under a particular mode and is not secure, as we'll shortly. The only way to use language modes to enforce security policies is through an application such as WDAC, according to Microsoft. There are three language modes:

- `FullLanguage`: This is the default when not running under an Application Control policy.

- `ConstrainedLanguage`: This prevents the creation and use of certain .NET types and restricts access to C# code from PowerShell. It also restricts access to features such as `ScheduledJob`. Many scripts will not run in constrained language mode; they will need to be signed, and the publishing authority will need to be added to the whitelist.

- `NoLanguage`: This disables PowerShell scripting completely. Only native commands and cmdlets can run. `New-Object` is also disabled.

We can check the language mode of our session by calling the $ExecutionContext. SessionState.LanguageMode variable, like this:

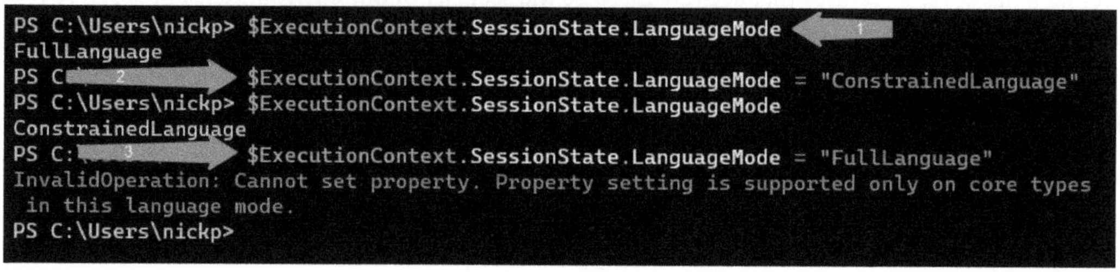

Figure 12.8 – Getting and setting the language mode

In the first line, I call the variable, and we can see that the language mode is set to FullLanguage. I then set the variable to ConstrainedLanguage; we can see that when I call the variable again, it is now set to ConstrainedLanguage. Unfortunately, when I try to set it back to FullLanguage in the third line, I can't, because we're in ConstrainedLanguage mode, and there is limited access to variables. The easiest way to get around this is to close the session and open a new one; the language mode will revert to FullLanguage. As we discussed previously, setting this variable does not make PowerShell secure.

Security servicing criteria

PowerShell is subject to Microsoft's Security Servicing Criteria for Windows, and so some features will receive security updates when vulnerabilities are detected. Unfortunately, those features that are included only operate on Windows, such as the execution policy and Application Control.

Software Bill of Materials

A **Software Bill of Materials** (**SBOM**) helps provide transparency, integrity, and identity to a piece of software by identifying each resource used in its creation, and it provides code signing and software identities that can be used to associate the software with known vulnerabilities. SBOMs are required by many governments as a response to the SolarWinds supply chain attack of 2020. This is applicable to both Windows and Linux/Mac.

Windows Antimalware Scan Interface support

PowerShell passes script blocks and .NET invocations to the Windows **Antimalware Scan Interface** (**AMSI**) API so that anti-malware applications, such as Windows Defender, can inspect them for malicious code. This is a Windows-only feature.

Secure Shell (SSH) remoting

The SSH protocol is a cryptographic protocol that supports secure network services over an unsecured network. It is cross-platform and works on both Windows and Linux/Mac systems. It relies on public key cryptography; we need to generate a key pair and pass the public key to the system we want to remote to. When we subsequently open a session, we specify the path to the private key on our machine, and SSH verifies that the public key on the remote machine is part of a pair with the local private key. At no point is the private key passed over the network. While setup is quite complex, using SSH once it is set up is very easy.

Just Enough Administration

Just Enough Administration (JEA) is another Windows-only security feature that allows us to delegate administration for things that may be managed by PowerShell, such as **Domain Name Service** (DNS), Active Directory, and applications such as Exchange. For instance, we may want someone to be able to monitor the processes on a machine but not start new ones. We can configure PowerShell endpoints that only have access to the commands that are needed for a particular task, such as `Get-Process`, using the principle of least privilege, and exclude everything else from running, meaning they would be unable to run `Start-Process`. We can also configure the endpoint to use virtual privileged accounts so that a user doesn't need to have an admin account at all to run the commands. This allows us to drastically reduce the number of users who have admin-privileged accounts.

As we've seen, nearly all of these features are only applicable to Windows environments. Luckily, everyone who uses Linux is entirely trustworthy. Let's look at the features that are available to us to understand what PowerShell has been used for – logging.

PowerShell logging

PowerShell has a number of ways to record what we do with it. In this section, we're going to look at three of them – over the shoulder logging, deep script block logging, and module logging.

Over the shoulder logging

PowerShell can record a transcript of a session, using the `Start-Transcript` and `Stop-Transcript` cmdlets. The transcript function will record everything that is displayed on the screen. This is useful for recording what we do and the output we get, and then sharing it with others.

We can set the path where the transcript is saved using the `-Path` parameter, and we add to an existing transcript with the `-Append` parameter, followed by the name and path of an existing transcript. The `-InvocationHeader` parameter logs the time each command was run. When we want to stop recording, we can use the `Stop-Transcript` cmdlet.

In older versions of PowerShell, we had to perform some magic to ensure that transcription was turned on, and even then, it would only log interactive sessions in the console, but that is no longer the case. We can turn on automatic transcription in Windows systems by either using Group Policy or by editing the `powershell.config.json` file in the `$pshome` location – `C:\Program Files\PowerShell\7` in Windows. Editing the config file works for both Windows and Linux/Mac, although you may need to create it first. To enable transcription, we would need to add the following JSON to the file:

```
{
    "Transcription": {
        "EnableTranscripting": true,
        "EnableInvocationHeader": true,
        "OutputDirectory": "c:\\Temp\\MyTranscriptPath"
    }
}
```

To stop transcription, delete the JSON entry.

The transcript contains a useful header that includes the account the session was run under, whether the session was using `RunAs` credentials, such as administrator, which version of PowerShell was used, and the process number. Let's take a look:

```
PS C:\Users\nickp> $transcript = Start-Transcript
PS C:\Users\nickp> get-content $transcript.Path -Head 19
**********************
PowerShell transcript start
Start time: 20230922112239
Username: DESKTOP-QBJB5QM\nickp
RunAs User: DESKTOP-QBJB5QM\nickp
Configuration Name:
Machine: DESKTOP-QBJB5QM (Microsoft Windows NT 10.0.19045.0)
Host Application: C:\Program Files\PowerShell\7\pwsh.dll
Process ID: 16684
PSVersion: 7.3.6
PSEdition: Core
GitCommitId: 7.3.6
OS: Microsoft Windows 10.0.19045
Platform: Win32NT
PSCompatibleVersions: 1.0, 2.0, 3.0, 4.0, 5.0, 5.1.10032.0, 6.0.0, 6.1.0, 6.2.0, 7.0.0, 7.1.0
, 7.2.0, 7.3.6
PSRemotingProtocolVersion: 2.3
SerializationVersion: 1.1.0.1
WSManStackVersion: 3.0
**********************
PS C:\Users\nickp> Get-Command *transcript*

CommandType     Name                                     Version    Source
-----------     ----                                     -------    ------
Cmdlet          Start-Transcript                         7.0.0.0    Microso…
Cmdlet          Stop-Transcript                          7.0.0.0    Microso…

PS C:\Users\nickp> Stop-Transcript
Transcript stopped, output file is C:\Users\nickp\OneDrive\Documents\PowerShell_transcript.DE
SKTOP-QBJB5QM.FILWUoJf.20230922112239.txt
```

Figure 12.9 – The transcript header

I've used Get-Content with the -Head parameter to call the first 19 lines of the transcript file, and we can see the information it contains. When I run Stop-Transcript, the name and path of the transcript file is displayed.

Over the shoulder logging is a very powerful tool for recording what is done with PowerShell, especially if transcripts are sent to a central shared location and then scanned by a **Security Information and Event Management (SIEM)** application. However, it doesn't capture everything. Let's look at the next technique, deep script block logging.

Deep script block logging

If we call a function or a script, the transcript will record that call, but it won't tell us anything about the contents of the function or script. This is where we need deep script block logging, which will record the contents of the script and other pertinent information to the logging system. In Windows, this is the PowerShellCore log, under **Applications and Services Logs** in **Event Viewer**, and it's the systemd log in Linux, under /var/log/journal.

We can enable deep script block logging via group policy on Windows, or through the config file if the machine we use is not in an Active Directory domain.

On my machine, I have edited the PowerShell.config.json file to include lines 4–16 in the following screenshot:

```json
{} powershell.config.json  ●

C: > Program Files > PowerShell > 7 > {} powershell.config.json > ...
   1   {"Microsoft.PowerShell:ExecutionPolicy":"Unrestricted",
   2   "WindowsPowerShellCompatibilityModuleDenyList":["PSScheduledJob","BestPractices","UpdateServices"],
   3
   4       "PowerShellPolicies": {
   5
   6           "ScriptBlockLogging": {
   7
   8               "EnableScriptBlockInvocationLogging": false,
   9
  10               "EnableScriptBlockLogging": true
  11
  12           }
  13
  14       },
  15
  16       "LogLevel": "verbose"
  17
  18   }
```

Figure 12.10 – Enabling deep script block logging in PowerShell

Remember that this is JSON, so it is really important to get the syntax correct. VS Code will underline any syntax errors. We will also need admin privileges to save the file.

Now, if I open a new session and call the `HelloWorld.ps1` script that we used at the start of this chapter, I can expect to see events appear in my event log, like this:

```
Event 4104, PowerShellCore

  General   Details

    Creating Scriptblock text (1 of 1):
    write-output "hello world"

    ScriptBlock ID: 2c60ba4c-16ed-4660-851d-bd709a4a646a
    Path: C:\temp\poshbook\ch12\HelloWorld.ps1


  Log Name:          PowerShellCore/Operational
  Source:            PowerShellCore            Logged:          26/09/2023 21:56:35
  Event ID:          4104                      Task Category:   Execute a Remote Command
  Level:             Verbose                   Keywords:        None
  User:              DESKTOP-QBJB5QM\nickp      Computer:        DESKTOP-QBJB5QM
  OpCode:            On create calls
  More Information:  Event Log Online Help
```

Figure 12.11 – Script block logging events in the event log

Remember that the `HelloWorld.ps1` script was a single line of code – `Write-Output "hello world"`. We can see that line clearly in the preceding event. We can also see the account it was run under, when it was run, and on what machine.

Module logging

The final type of logging we'll look at is module logging. This is similar to script block logging and tracks the modules that are being loaded and called in PowerShell. This can generate a lot of information quite quickly, so there is an option to only record specified modules. If we want to record all the modules, then we can use a wildcard (*) instead of an array of module names in the JSON we add to the config file. Again, if group policy is available, then we can use it to enable module logging.

There are other types of logging available, but they are quite specialized, such as protected event logging for events that may contain sensitive information, such as personal details. I've not needed to use them.

That wraps up the security features we're going to cover. Let's move on to the final section of this chapter and look at ways we can write secure code.

Writing secure code

Most code has security flaws; it is our job to make sure that the code we write is as secure as possible. In this section, we will look at some ways to write more secure PowerShell code. We'll look at how to store passwords our scripts might need, code signing scripts, and parameter validation.

Storing passwords securely

Quite often, we will write a script that contains commands that need to be run with a particular set of credentials. We saw how to store credentials in an XML file in *Chapter 6, PowerShell and Files – Reading, Writing, and Manipulating Data*. To recap, we can do it like this:

```
$cred = Get-Credential
$cred | Export-Clixml Credential.xml
```

The credential is then stored in an XML object. This object contains an encrypted standard string, which is the password that was entered encrypted with a reversible encryption, based on the account and machine that the string was encrypted on. Let's look at how this works.

I have a password that I want to save as a secure string:

```
$pwd = "ILovePowershell"
```

To turn it into a secure string, I use the ConvertTo-SecureString cmdlet:

```
$securepwd = $pwd | ConvertTo-SecureString -AsPlainText -Force
```

The password is now encrypted, as we can see if we try this:

```
$encryptedpwd = $securepwd | ConvertFrom-SecureString
write-host $encryptedpwd
```

Encryption, in this case, is based on the logged-on account and the machine, and the string cannot be decrypted by anyone other than the original user (or someone logged on as them) on the original machine. Let's see how it looks:

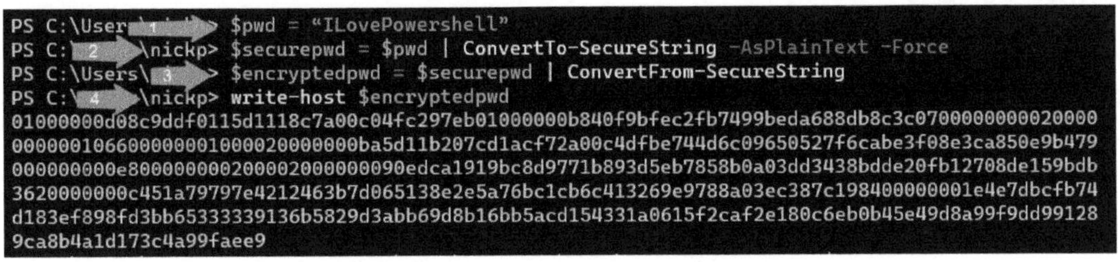

Figure 12.12 – Putting a password in a secure string

On line 1, I create a variable called $pwd that holds a string, ILovePowerShell. On line 2, I create a new variable, $securepwd, by piping $pwd to the ConvertTo-SecureString cmdlet, with the -AsPlainText parameter, and use the -Force parameter to suppress any prompts. On line 3, I convert the contents of $securepwd back from a secure string to text and store it in the $encryptedpwd variable. Finally, on line 4, I write the contents of the $encryptedpwd variable, and as we can see, it is now an encrypted string, not the original password.

$encryptedpwd can be stored in a file or in the registry, and it can be used to create a PSCredential object that can be passed to a cmdlet, using the Add-Content cmdlet:

```
PS C:\Users\       1       add-content C:\temp\poshbook\ch12\encryptedpwd.txt $encryptedpwd
PS C:    2       \nickp> $securepwd2 = (Get-Content C:\temp\poshbook\ch12\encryptedpwd.txt |
ConvertTo-SecureString)
PS C:\Users\r   3       $cred = New-Object System.Management.Automation.PSCredential ("User
Name",  $securepwd2)
PS C:   4       \nickp> $cred.GetNetworkCredential().Password
ILovePowershell    5
PS C:\Users\nickp>
```

Figure 12.13 – Adding a password to a PSCredential as a secure string

On line 1, I add the content of $encryptedpwd to a file, encryptedpwd.txt. On line 2, I add the contents of the file to a variable, $securepwd2, after converting it to a secure string. On line 3, I create a new PSCredential object with two values – a username string and the $securepwd2 variable. Finally, on line 4, I check the password property of the credential, and we can see it is ILovePowerShell, the string I originally started with, on line 5. In this way, we can store passwords securely in a file on a machine, and they can't be copied to another machine and decrypted. Of course, someone can remote into PowerShell on the machine and decrypt them, so it's not bulletproof.

So, what is the difference between a secure string and an encrypted string? An encrypted string is a plain text string that has been encrypted, as you can see if you look in the encryptedpwd.txt file. A secure string is an object of type System.Security.SecureString. They are two different types. Many PowerShell cmdlets will only accept passwords of type System.Security.SecureString, so it's important to understand which type is needed.

Signing scripts

Earlier in this chapter, we discussed execution policies and how they rely on scripts being signed to determine their trustworthiness. A digital signature does two things – it provides assurance that the script was signed by a trusted source and verifies that the script has not been edited after it was signed.

To sign a script, we need either a code-signing certificate from a trusted authority, such as VeriSign, that will be trusted by the majority of computers, a certificate from an Active Directory certificate authority that will be trusted by machines within that directory, or we can use a self-signed certificate that will only be trusted on the machine that was used to sign the script. Code-signing certificates are not cheap, and while there are a few companies that may be exploring such a thing, at the time of writing they're not generally available.

Once we have a code-signing certificate, we can use the `Set-AuthenticodeSignature` cmdlet to sign the script with our certificate. The signature includes a hash of the script, so any changes made after signing will break the signature and lead to the script not being trusted. This signing only works on Windows environments, much like the execution policy feature that makes use of it.

Parameter security

We saw in *Chapter 8, PowerShell and Files – Reading, Writing, and Manipulating Data*, that we can use accelerators to force a parameter to only accept a specific type of input. We can also use regular expressions to ensure that the input is in the right format, such as a date string or IP address. This code will test a parameter and only accept date strings in the DD/MM/YYYY format:

```
function Test-Date {
    param(
        [string]$date
    )
    if ($date -match "^(3[01]|[12][0-9]|0?[1-9])(\/|-)(1[0-2]|0?[1-
9])\2([0-9]{2})?[0-9]{2}$")
{
        return $true
    }
    else {
        return $false
    }
}
```

We can see how it looks in the following screenshot:

```
PS C:\Users\nickp> function Test-Date {
>>      param(
>>          [string]$date
>>      )
>>      if ($date -match "^(3[01]|[12][0-9]|0?[1-9])(\/|-)(1[0-2]|0?[1-9])\2([0-9]{2})?[
0-9]{2}$")
>> {
>>          return $true
>>      }
>>      else {
>>          return $false
>>      }
>> }
PS C:\Users\nickp> Test-Date 21/05/2023
True
PS C:\Users\nickp> Test-Date 21/13/2023
False
PS C:\Users\nickp>
```

Figure 12.14 – Validating parameter input

I've created a `Test-Date` function that uses a regular expression to test whether the input is a valid date or not. When I pass a valid date in the correct format, the function returns `True`. When I pass an invalid date, `21/13/2023`, it returns `False`. We could use that return value to stop a script from continuing, or to prompt for valid input.

The preceding instance is trivial, but it is possible for unvalidated parameters to be used for malicious code injection, where code is inserted into the parameter and then executed. Parameter validation can help prevent this.

That wraps up what we are going to cover in this chapter. Let's summarize what we've learned.

Summary

We started this chapter by looking at PowerShell remoting and saw how the feature can make PowerShell a security risk. We looked at how to create, join, and leave sessions and how to run expressions on multiple remote computers at once.

We then moved on to see how we could secure PowerShell against inadvertent mistakes and saw how the execution policy can *"…slow down an uninformed user who is unintentionally trying to run an untrusted script."* We also saw some of the other early security features, such as requiring an absolute or relative path for script execution.

We then looked at more modern security features, many of which only apply to Windows, such as Application Control and language modes. Unfortunately, the security features for Linux and macOS are still sadly lacking.

We looked at the different ways of recording what PowerShell is doing, with over the shoulder logging, script block logging, and module logging, and saw how to turn these features on and off and where to find the logs.

In the final section, we looked at three techniques for writing scripts more securely – storing passwords as encrypted strings, signing our scripts, and validating parameters.

That's it for this chapter, and for this part of the book, where we've looked at scripting and tooling. In the final part of the book, we'll be looking at how PowerShell works in three different environments – Windows, Linux/macOS, and ARM – finishing off with a chapter on using PowerShell with .NET, the underlying platform that PowerShell is built on. I'm looking forward to it.

Exercises

1. Which cmdlet is used to create a new PowerShell session for remote administration?
2. How can we use PowerShell remoting securely on Linux?
3. Which execution policy in PowerShell allows only signed scripts to run?
4. What is the purpose of the `-ExecutionPolicy Bypass` switch?
5. On Windows, what can be used to analyze and block known malicious scripts and configurations?
6. What is the purpose of the constrained language mode in PowerShell?
7. How can you restrict the use of specific cmdlets for a particular user in PowerShell on Windows?
8. What is script block logging in PowerShell, and why is it important for security?
9. What is the difference between a secure string and an encrypted string?

Further reading

- PowerShell remoting:

  `https://learn.microsoft.com/en-us/powershell/scripting/learn/ps101/08-powershell-remoting`

- Execution policies:

  `https://learn.microsoft.com/en-us/powershell/module/microsoft.powershell.core/about/about_execution_policies`

- Application Control:

  - `https://learn.microsoft.com/en-gb/Windows/security/application-security/application-control/Windows-defender-application-control/wdac`

  - `https://learn.microsoft.com/en-us/powershell/scripting/learn/application-control`

- Language modes:

  `https://learn.microsoft.com/en-us/powershell/module/microsoft.powershell.core/about/about_language_modes`

- Security Servicing Criteria:

  `https://www.microsoft.com/en-us/msrc/Windows-security-servicing-criteria`

- SBOM:

  `https://devblogs.microsoft.com/engineering-at-microsoft/generating-software-bills-of-materials-sboms-with-spdx-at-microsoft/`

- SSH:

  - `https://en.wikipedia.org/wiki/Secure_Shell`

  - `https://learn.microsoft.com/en-us/powershell/scripting/learn/remoting/ssh-remoting-in-powershell-core`

- JEA:

  `https://learn.microsoft.com/en-us/powershell/scripting/learn/remoting/jea/overview`

- A deep dive into PowerShell logging:

  `https://devblogs.microsoft.com/powershell/powershell-the-blue-team/`

- Logging on Windows

  `https://learn.microsoft.com/en-us/powershell/module/microsoft.powershell.core/about/about_logging_Windows`

- Logging on Linux and macOS

  `https://learn.microsoft.com/en-us/powershell/module/microsoft.powershell.core/about/about_logging_non-Windows`

Part 3: Using PowerShell

Now we understand how to use PowerShell 7, and how to write simple scripts and modules, it's time to learn how to use it on different platforms. One of the defining features of PowerShell 7 is that it is cross-platform. This section will detail how to use PowerShell with a variety of platforms. This part has the following chapters:

- *Chapter 13, Working with PowerShell 7 and Windows*

- *Chapter 14, PowerShell 7 for Linux and macOS*

- *Chapter 15, PowerShell 7 and the Raspberry Pi*

- *Chapter 16, Working with PowerShell and .NET*

13

Working with PowerShell 7 and Windows

Welcome to the final section of the book, where over the next four chapters we'll look at using PowerShell 7 in different environments. In this chapter, we'll be looking at the peculiarities of Windows-based systems, and the various workarounds that exist to allow us to use PowerShell 7 effectively. We'll also look at when we absolutely need to use native Windows PowerShell instead. It's important to remember that PowerShell 7 is an open source product and is subject to fast-paced change. The examples in this and subsequent chapters are true at the time of writing, but may not be true at the time of reading. Also; there are bugs. The PowerShell GitHub pages are a powerful source of information regarding recent changes, and also things that don't work the way they should: `https://github.com/PowerShell/PowerShell`.

As we covered in *Chapter 1, Introduction to PowerShell 7 – What It Is and How to Get It*, PowerShell 7.2 and later are built on the .NET 6 platform, the latest version of .NET Core. However, Windows PowerShell and many Windows applications are built using the .NET 4.5 framework, which is not open source, and contains much proprietary code. This has led to some incompatibilities, where things that work in Windows PowerShell won't work in PowerShell 7. We'll be covering them in this chapter, and then look at how we can use the **Common Information Model** (**CIM**) and **Windows Management Instrumentation** (**WMI**) to work with our Windows machines.

The main topics we will cover in this chapter are the following:

- Understanding PowerShell 7 and Windows PowerShell
- Exploring compatibility
- What doesn't work with PowerShell 7
- Managing machines with CIM and WMI

Understanding PowerShell 7 and Windows PowerShell

The key to understanding how we can use PowerShell 7 on Windows is to understand that PowerShell 7 is built on a fundamentally different platform; PowerShell 7 is built on an open source, stripped-down version of .NET, whereas Windows PowerShell is built on the full proprietary .NET Framework. This means that Windows PowerShell has a greater degree of native compatibility with the Windows operating system and many of the applications that run on it and can make use of elements of .NET Framework that are not accessible to PowerShell 7. Microsoft uses the terminology **Desktop edition** for PowerShell running on .NET Framework, and **Core edition** for PowerShell running on open source .NET.

In *Chapter 11, Creating Our First Module*, we learned that most PowerShell functionality comes from using extensible libraries called modules, and looked at how modules are put together. To run a command in a module, PowerShell must first load that module. Microsoft has done a pretty good job of rewriting the core PowerShell modules and the more heavily used ones, such as the Active Directory module, but not all modules are compatible with PowerShell 7; sometimes the authors haven't got around to it yet, but sometimes the incompatibility is because key functionality in the module relies on features of .NET Framework that just aren't in the open source .NET Core. If we attempt to load these incompatible modules, they will generally either cause an error or just not work. In the next section, we'll see how we can get around this. Sometimes, however, we will find that things just don't work, and we need to use Windows PowerShell. We'll examine some of those cases in the third section of this chapter.

Exploring compatibility

It's all very well saying that some modules aren't compatible with PowerShell 7, but how do we know which ones are OK to use, and what happens when they aren't? The good news is that most of this process is automated and transparent to the casual user; we need to know about it however so we can understand why bad things happen sometimes. To understand compatibility, we'll need to remember what we learned about modules and module manifests from *Chapter 11, Creating Our First Module*, and the section on PowerShell remoting that we did in the last chapter, *Chapter 12, Securing PowerShell*.

Which modules are compatible with PowerShell 7?

Let's have a look at some modules to see how we can tell whether they are compatible with PowerShell 7. Run this cmdlet in Windows PowerShell:

```
Get-Module | Format-Table -Auto -Wrap Name, CompatiblePSEditions,
Version
```

We should see something like the following output:

```
PS C:\Users\nickp> Get-Module | Format-Table Name, CompatiblePSEditions, Version

Name                                  CompatiblePSEditions Version
----                                  -------------------- -------
Microsoft.PowerShell.Management       {Desktop, Core}      3.1.0.0
Microsoft.PowerShell.Security         {Desktop}            3.0.0.0
Microsoft.PowerShell.Utility          {Desktop}            3.1.0.0
Microsoft.WSMan.Management            {Desktop}            3.0.0.0
PSReadline                            {}                   2.0.0
RemoteDesktop                         {}                   2.0.0.0
ServerManager                         {}                   2.0.0.0
```

Figure 13.1 – Uncovering compatible editions

We can see that we have seven modules loaded. Four of them have compatibility information; Microsoft.PowerShell.Management says it is compatible with Desktop and Core editions. Microsoft.Powershell.Utility, Microsoft.PowerShell.Security, and Microsoft. WSMan.Management are only compatible with the Desktop edition. We could have run the command in PowerShell 7, but of course then it would generally only show modules that were compatible with the Core edition.

Three of the modules have no compatibility information available; this may mean that they were written before PowerShell Core was released, and are therefore only compatible with the Desktop edition, or it may be that they are the wrong type of module to have compatibility information. Recall that there are four types of modules; script modules, manifest modules, binary modules, and dynamic modules. Manifest modules contain a manifest file with a .Psd1 extension. We can check what the type of the module is by running Get-Module <modulename>, like so:

```
PS C:\Users\nickp> Get-Module PSReadline

ModuleType Version   Name                              ExportedCommands
---------- -------   ----                              ----------------
Script     2.0.0     PSReadline                        {Get-PSReadLineKeyHandler,
```

Figure 13.2 – Checking the module type

In this case, we can see that PSReadline is a script module, and so doesn't have an associated manifest file that could contain compatibility information.

So, what can we do when we need some functionality, but the module isn't listed as compatible with PowerShell 7? We have three choices:

- Find a compatible version

- Load it anyway

- Use Compatibility mode

Let's take a look at these methods.

Finding a compatible version

The Microsoft.PowerShell.Utility module shown previously in *Figure 13.1* is really useful; for a start, it provides the ConvertTo-* cmdlets. We know that these work in PowerShell 7, because we've been using them throughout the book. Look at the following figure:

```
PS C:\Users\nickp> Get-Module | Format-Table Name, CompatiblePSEditions, Version

Name                             CompatiblePSEditions Version
----                             -------------------- -------
Microsoft.PowerShell.Management  {Core}               7.0.0.0
Microsoft.PowerShell.Utility     {Core}               7.0.0.0
PSReadLine                       {}                   2.2.6
```

Figure 13.3 – Microsoft.PowerShell.Utility in PowerShell 7

As we can see, the Microsoft.PowerShell.Utility module is loaded in our PowerShell 7 session. How is that? Check the version numbers shown in the different screenshots. PowerShell 7 loads Microsoft.PowerShell.Utility 7.0.0.0, whereas Windows PowerShell loads Microsoft.PowerShell.Utility 3.1.0.0. Different versions of core PowerShell modules have been supplied with PowerShell 7, and are installed in C:\program files\powershell\7\ Modules. Some third-party modules will have specific versions that are compatible with PowerShell 7, even if the one we currently have is not, and it's worth checking on the repository if this is the case. For instance, in the PowerShell gallery, we can include the search term Tags:"core" to find modules that are compatible with PowerShell 7, like this:

Figure 13.4 – Searching the PowerShell gallery for a module that is compatible

As you can see, I've included two search terms; the first is the string databases and the second is Tags:"core". This has found me a module for manipulating databases that will run on PowerShell 7. Let's see what we can do if there is no compatible version.

Loading it anyway

If we don't find a version of the module compatible with PowerShell 7, we can attempt to load it anyway. This might work, although quite often the module will load but then not work as expected when we come to use it. I include this method as a last resort and a sort of warning; there are articles on the internet that recommend doing this. Personally, I wouldn't.

That said, how do you load a module that doesn't have a compatible version? We can use the

-SkipEditionCheck parameter of Import-Module like this:

```
PS C:\Users\nickp> Import-Module RemoteDesktop -SkipEditionCheck
Add-Type: (35,16): error CS0012: The type 'Enum' is defined in an assembly that is
not referenced. You must add a reference to
assembly 'mscorlib, Version=4.0.0.0, Culture=neutral, PublicKeyToken=b77a5c561934e0
89'.          public CertificateRole
Role { get; private set; }                                    ^
Add-Type: (44,29): error CS0012: The type 'Enum' is defined in an assembly that is
not referenced. You must add a reference to
assembly 'mscorlib, Version=4.0.0.0, Culture=neutral, PublicKeyToken=b77a5c561934e0
89'.
CertificateRole role,                                         ^
Add-Type: Cannot add type. Compilation errors occurred.
ParserError: Attribute argument must be a constant or a script block.
Import-Module: The module to process 'DeploymentProperties.psm1', listed in field '
NestedModules' of module manifest 'C:\WINDOWS\system32\WindowsPowerShell\v1.0\Modul
es\RemoteDesktop\RemoteDesktop.psd1' was not processed because no valid module was
found in any module directory.
PS C:\Users\nickp>
```

Figure 13.5 – Forcing a module to load

In this example, I've used the -SkipEditionCheck parameter to try to force PowerShell 7 to load the RemoteDesktop module in a PowerShell 7 session with admin privileges. As we can see, this hasn't worked very well. The problem is that with some modules it does work, while with others it doesn't, but it doesn't produce an error like RemoteDesktop does. So, what is the right way to do this? We use Compatibility mode.

Using Compatibility mode

Using Compatibility mode in recent versions of PowerShell 7 is easy. Just import the module you want to load, like this:

```
Import-Module RemoteDesktop
```

As we can see in the following figure, something magical happens:

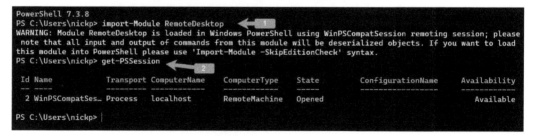

Figure 13.6 – Using Compatibility mode

In the first command, all I've done is use `Import-Module` with no parameters. PowerShell checks for a compatible module, and when it doesn't find one it creates a remote session to run Windows PowerShell in the background. The module is loaded into this remote session, which is running on the local machine. It warns us that this is what it has done. In the second command, I check what remote sessions are running, and we can see that there is a session called `WinPSCompatSession` created. We saw remote sessions in *Chapter 12, Securing PowerShell*. In that chapter, though, we explicitly created the sessions. The `WinPSCompatSession` is an example of implicit remoting.

There are two important things to remember about Compatibility mode. The first important thing is that `WinPSCompatSession` is running Windows PowerShell, not PowerShell 7. Look at this:

Figure 13.7 – Demonstrating the PowerShell version running in WinPSCompatSession

In the first command, I'm putting `WinPSCompatSession` into a variable called `$session` so I can easily use it. On the second line, I pass the `$session` variable to `Invoke-Command` and call the `PSVersion` property of the `$PSVersionTable` automatic variable from within that session. We can see from the result that the session is running PowerShell version 5.1 – Windows PowerShell. In the third command, I get the same information for the local terminal session, where I'm running PowerShell 7.3.8.

The second important thing is that this is a remote session, and therefore behaves differently to directly running commands. The most important difference is that the output has been deserialized, which we can see in the warning in *Figure 13.6*. Recall that the output of a command is a PowerShell object. To pass a PowerShell object from a remote computer to the local computer, the object is converted to CliXML (the specialized form of XML that PowerShell uses to serialize objects) on the remote end of the session, and then converted back to a PowerShell object at the local end. This has implications for what we can do with the object, as it now has different methods and properties. Let's see what this looks like:

```
PS C:\Users\nickp> Get-WmiObject win32_bios | gm


   TypeName: System.Management.ManagementObject#root\cimv2\Win32_BIOS

Name                        MemberType     Definition
----                        ----------     ----------
PSComputerName              AliasProperty  PSComputerName = __SERVER
BiosCharacteristics         Property       uint16[] BiosCharacteristics {get;set;}
BIOSVersion                 Property       string[] BIOSVersion {get;set;}
BuildNumber                 Property       string BuildNumber {get;set;}

PS C:\Users\nickp> Invoke-Command -Session $session -ScriptBlock {Get-WmiObject win32_bios} | gm

   TypeName: Deserialized.System.Management.ManagementObject#root\cimv2\Win32_BIOS

Name                 MemberType     Definition
----                 ----------     ----------
GetType              Method         type GetType()
ToString             Method         string ToString(), string ToString(string format, System.
PSComputerName       NoteProperty   string PSComputerName=localhost
PSShowComputerName   NoteProperty   bool PSShowComputerName=True
```

Figure 13.8 – Deserialized objects

In the top pane I am using Windows PowerShell to run the Get-WmiObject win32_bios
| gm command to get the TypeName and members of the object that the Get-WmiObject
command generates: System.Management.ManagementObject. Note it has no methods,
and PSComputerName is an AliasProperty, so if we call PSComputerName, we actually
get the value of the __SERVER property.

In the lower pane, I am using PowerShell 7 to run Get-WmiObject inside the WinPSCompatSession
session using Invoke-Command, and then getting the members of the returned object. As we can see,
this is now a Deserialized.System.Management.ManagementObject, and the methods
and properties are subtly changed. For example, PSComputerName is now a NoteProperty that
contains a string: PSComputerName=localhost.

Now, this is fairly easy to remember when we are explicitly using Invoke-Command. We know that
what we get back is running in a remote session and will be a deserialized object. However, because this
can happen transparently in the background, it is easy to accidentally load a module in Compatibility
mode, and then be surprised that the objects we are working with aren't behaving quite the way we
expect them to. Some administrators like to prevent implicit imports in PowerShell compatibility by
editing the powershell.config.json file to include the JSON line:

```
"DisableImplicitWinCompat" : "true"
```

This doesn't disable Compatibility mode altogether, however, it just makes us more mindful of when we
are using it. We can still explicitly use Compatibility mode by adding the -UseWindowsPowerShell
parameter of the Import-Module cmdlet, like this:

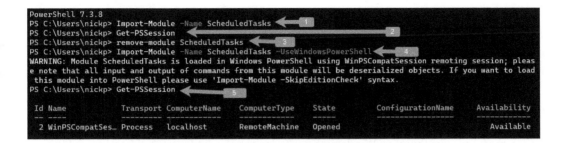

Figure 13.9 – Explicitly using PowerShell Compatibility

In the command on the first line, I import the `ScheduledTasks` module as normal, with no parameters. In the second line, I test for the presence of the compatibility session – as we can see, no remote session has been opened. In the third line, I remove the module, and in the fourth line I reload it, this time adding the `-UseWindowsPowershell` parameter. In the fifth line, I again test for the compatibility session, and there it is.

We can also prevent specific modules from loading in Compatibility mode altogether by editing the deny list in the `powershell.config.json` file:

```
"WindowsPowerShellCompatibilityModuleDenyList":  [
    "PSScheduledJob","BestPractices","UpdateServices"
]
```

If we try and load a module on that list, then we will see an error similar to the following:

```
PS C:\Users\nickp> Import-Module -Name PSScheduledJob
Import-Module: Module 'PSScheduledJob' is blocked from loading using Windows PowerShell compatibility
feature by a 'WindowsPowerShellCompatibilityModuleDenyList' setting in PowerShell configuration file.
```

Figure 13.10 – No, you can't load the PSScheduledJob module

It's important to understand the limitations of Compatibility mode. There are four main ones:

- It only works on local computers – you can't call Compatibility mode while already in a remote session on another machine

- It requires Windows PowerShell 5.1 to be installed on the local machine – older machines might still have only Windows PowerShell 3.0 or 4.0 installed

- It returns deserialized objects based on values – not live objects that can be manipulated

- There can be only one compatibility session running on a machine at any one time, so all modules that use Compatibility will share a runspace

It's also important to remember that this area of PowerShell 7 is one that lots of people are actively working on, and each new version of PowerShell is better than the last, and each new version of Windows is more compatible with PowerShell 7. Lots of the instructions and tutorials on the internet date very quickly, and so will this chapter.

What doesn't work with PowerShell 7

However, there are some things on Windows that just don't work with PowerShell 7 and aren't likely to either. In this section we'll cover a few of them, which will set us up nicely for the final section of the chapter, *Managing machines with CIM and WMI.*

The `-ComputerName` parameter had been ported from Windows PowerShell to PowerShell 7; unfortunately, some of the protocols and models that this parameter uses in Windows are not compatible with PowerShell 7, and so the parameter didn't work. In the most recent releases of PowerShell 7, such as 7.3, the parameter has finally been removed from the non-working cmdlets. For people moving from Windows PowerShell to PowerShell 7, however, it can still cause confusion. The workaround is to use `Invoke-Command` instead.

Some important administration modules like `UpdateServices` for managing **Windows Server Update Services** (**WSUS**) won't work in Compatibility mode as they rely on manipulating the objects that are returned through their methods, which don't survive the deserialization process.

Windows Management Instrumentation (**WMI**) commands aren't included in PowerShell 7, as Microsoft has been trying to deprecate them since PowerShell 3.0, preferring people to use the more lightweight CIM commands. They remain popular, however, and many people still use WMI over CIM. We'll be discussing these CIM commands and how to use them in the next section, as it is an important topic.

Managing machines with CIM and WMI

CIM and WMI are related technologies for managing local and remote machines. In this section, we will look at the basics of each and discuss their similarities and differences.

Introduction to CIM and WMI

CIM and WMI are based on the **Web-Based Enterprise Management** (**WBEM**) standard introduced by the **Distributed Management Task Force** (**DMTF**) in 1996. WMI is Microsoft's implementation of a set of tools based on WBEM, released in 1998, and CIM is an open standard from the DMTF that defines how the entities in an environment are represented and related. It was released in 1999. In a Windows environment, CIM uses elements of WMI but uses a different set of protocols to access them; WMI uses the **Distributed Common Object Model** (**DCOM**) protocol, which is proprietary, and CIM uses the **Web Services for Management** (**WS-MAN**) protocol over HTTP, which we saw in *Chapter 12, Securing PowerShell.*

Both technologies link to a common repository – the WMI repository, which we'll look at shortly. This repository holds information about the type of objects we might want to manage, such as printers, clients, network adapters, and so on, and instances of those objects.

The PowerShell CIM commands allow us to connect to local and remote machines via WS-MAN to the **Windows Remote Management (WinRM)** endpoint that we use for remote sessions. We can do this either as an ad hoc connection or via a CIM session, similar to remoting.

WMI only supports ad hoc connections over DCOM. This means WinRM doesn't need to be enabled on the remote machine.

Why CIM is better than WMI

CIM is slightly newer, but crucially uses an open connection protocol – WS-MAN. This requires a pair of static network ports to be available on machines and any devices in the network. DCOM uses the **Remote Procedure Call (RPC)** protocol, which relies heavily on ephemeral TCP/IP ports; it's much easier to run WS-MAN over a network than it is to run DCOM because of this difference. There are lots of other reasons why WS-MAN is better than DCOM, but the biggest stumbling block in my experience is DCOM's requirement for ephemeral ports.

Microsoft has been trying since PowerShell 3.0 in 2012 to deprecate the WMI cmdlets and persuade people to use the CIM cmdlets instead, as CIM uses a lighter protocol with less of a network footprint; RPC has many disadvantages, and I've spent a good chunk of my career identifying and fixing problems that have resulted from RPC. However, plenty of people still use the WMI cmdlets, and there are lots of popular scripts available on the internet that use them.

The WMI cmdlets are not available within PowerShell 7, but we will see many workarounds on the internet involving `Invoke-Command` that enable us to use them via Compatibility mode.

Commands that use CIM and WMI

The WMI repository is huge and confusing, as we shall see. Therefore, it's better, where possible, to use a dedicated cmdlet rather than a CIM or WMI cmdlet. What does that look like? For instance, we might use `Get-CimInstance Win32_Printer` to query the printers on a machine, but it's quicker and more intuitive to use the `Get-Printer` cmdlet, demonstrated as follows:

```
PS C:\Users\nickp> Get-CimInstance Win32_Printer | Where-Object {$_.Name -like 'HPF*'}

Name              ShareName         SystemName      PrinterState    PrinterStatus    Location
----              ---------         ----------      ------------    -------------    --------
HPFA1D7F (HP EN…                    DESKTOP-QBJB5QM 0               3                http://[fe80::…

PS C:\Users\nickp> Get-Printer | Where-Object {$_.Name -like 'HPF*'}

Name                            ComputerName      Type      DriverName              PortName
----                            ------------      ----      ----------              --------
HPFA1D7F (HP ENVY 4500 series)                    Local     HP ENVY 4500 Series Clas… IP6_1c852…
```

Figure 13.11 – Looking for printers

Both commands are looking for the HP printer on my local machine. They both use CIM to query the WMI repository. Arguably, the second command is easier to run and remember, and is generally faster too. Get-Printer supports the -ComputerName parameter for remote machines and even supports using CIM sessions. Before digging around for hours to work out how to do something using a CIM cmdlet, check there isn't already a handy pre-written cmdlet that does what we want. Of course, Get-Printer is a Windows PowerShell cmdlet, and therefore we need to be running on a Windows client and use Compatibility.

Repository

The WMI repository is a hierarchical database – a tree structure. At the top level are namespaces – essentially containers. Namespaces contain classes. A class represents a type of object, such as a printer, and contains instances of that type of object. Each instance of a class has the same set of properties and methods as other instances of a class – although they may not all be populated or enabled. There is a class called __NAMESPACE, with two underscores (_), that contains namespaces, so a namespace may contain other namespaces as well.

The root namespace is called, unimaginatively, root. We can see the contents of this with the following command:

```
Get-CimClass -Namespace 'Root' | Select-Object -First 10
```

And we can see the instances of the __NAMESPACE class with the following:

```
Get-CimInstance -Namespace 'Root' -ClassName __NAMESPACE
```

The contents of the namespaces and classes may vary on each machine, as hardware and software will create their own namespaces and classes when installed. The important namespace for most people though is root/CIMV2, shown in the following figure.

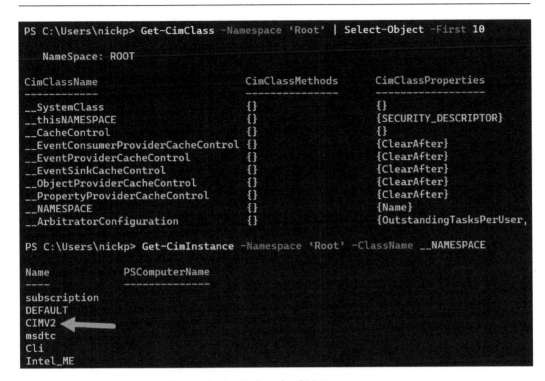

```
PS C:\Users\nickp> Get-CimClass -Namespace 'Root' | Select-Object -First 10

   NameSpace: ROOT

CimClassName                              CimClassMethods          CimClassProperties
------------                              ---------------          ------------------
__SystemClass                            {}                       {}
__thisNAMESPACE                          {}                       {SECURITY_DESCRIPTOR}
__CacheControl                           {}                       {}
__EventConsumerProviderCacheControl      {}                       {ClearAfter}
__EventProviderCacheControl              {}                       {ClearAfter}
__EventSinkCacheControl                  {}                       {ClearAfter}
__ObjectProviderCacheControl             {}                       {ClearAfter}
__PropertyProviderCacheControl           {}                       {ClearAfter}
__NAMESPACE                              {}                       {Name}
__ArbitratorConfiguration                {}                       {OutstandingTasksPerUser,

PS C:\Users\nickp> Get-CimInstance -Namespace 'Root' -ClassName __NAMESPACE

Name                  PSComputerName
----                  --------------
subscription
DEFAULT
CIMV2
msdtc
Cli
Intel_ME
```

Figure 13.12 – Finding the CIMV2 namespace

In the first command, I'm listing out the first 10 returned classes in the root namespace. There are 75 classes in the root namespace on my client so I'm only listing the first 10 – this number will likely differ on yours. In the second command, I'm listing the instances of the __NAMESPACE class on my machine – again, there is quite a large number, and yours may be different. The CIMV2 namespace is highlighted.

The CIMV2 namespace contains the Microsoft Windows classes. We can use Get-CimClass to list them out, but there are over 1,200 classes in this namespace on my machine; most of them called either MSFT_* or Win32_*. With so many classes, we can see that finding things in the repository can be a challenge. Microsoft has done a reasonable job of documenting the contents of the root/CIMV2 namespace online, but the contents of other namespaces are typically not well documented, and finding out what things do and how to use them can be a bit of an exercise.

In *Figure 13.11*, we used the Get-CimInstance Win32_Printer command, without specifying a namespace – this is because PowerShell has the CIMV2 namespace set as the default, so that we don't have to add the -Namespace 'root/CIMV2' parameter to every command.

Querying data

We use CIM and WMI for two main tasks – finding out information and changing things, frequently on large numbers of machines at once. Let's start by looking at how we can find things out. We've already seen two CIM cmdlets that we can use; Get-CimClass and Get-CimInstance.

Get-CimClass

This cmdlet gets a list of the CIM classes in a specified namespace, or in the default namespace if no namespace is given. There are a few parameters for this cmdlet:

- -ClassName: This allows us to either specify a class, or provide a partial class name when we're looking for a specific class; e.g., Get-CimClass -ClassName *disk* will get all the classes in CIMV2 with the word disk in the name.

- -Namespace: This allows us to specify a namespace other than root/CIMV2.

- -ComputerName: This parameter allows us to specify a machine other than the local machine. We can use an FQDN, a NetBIOS name, or an IP address.

- -MethodName: This parameter allows us to search for classes that have a particular method. For example, Get-CimClass -MethodName 'term*' will return the Win32_Process class, which has a Terminate method. No prizes for guessing what that method does.

- -PropertyName: Similar to the -MethodName parameter, this allows us to search for classes with a particular property.

- -QualifierName: Qualifiers are like tags that are applied to classes. There is no standard list (a bit like tags), but they can sometimes be quite useful. For instance, we can use Get-CimClass -QualifierName 'deprecated' to retrieve a list of classes that are being phased out, and probably shouldn't be used in a script.

- -Amended: This parameter gets amended information – usually information that changes depending on the locale of the machine. Localizable information is often presented numerically and requires a lookup to be translated into the local language – this parameter will do that.

- -OperationTimeoutSec: If we are running the command against a remote computer, it's possible that the machine is unresponsive or not even switched on. This allows us to specify a timeout other than the default network timeout set for the local machine, which is by default 3 minutes. If we were querying 1,000 machines, and 10% of them are switched off or not connected to the network, this allows us to complete the command in less than 5 hours.

- -CimSession: This allows us to run the command in a pre-existing CIM session. More on CIM sessions shortly.

Let's take a look at Get-CimInstance next.

Get-CimInstance

This cmdlet gets the instances of a given CIM class – again, the default namespace is root/CIMV2. It has many of the same parameters as `Get-CimClass`, with a few differences. Let's take a look:

- `-CimSession`: Same as for `Get-CimClass`.

- `-ClassName`: Same as for `Get-CimClass`.

- `-ComputerName`: Same as for `Get-CimClass`.

- `-Filter`: Allows us to specify a filter string to only get certain instances. For instance, `Get-CimInstance -Classname Win32_Printer -Filter "Name like 'HP%'"` will find the HP printer on my machine. Note that we must use **Windows Query Language (WQL)** or **Cassandra Query Language (CQL)**.

- `-KeyOnly`: Returns only the key properties of an instance, rather than all the properties.

- `-Namespace`: Same as for `Get-CimClass`.

- `-OperationTimeoutSec`: Same as for `Get-CimClass`.

- `-Property`: Unlike `Get-CimClass`, this doesn't search for instances with a given property; remember, all instances of a class have the same properties and methods. Notice it is `-Property`, not `-PropertyName`. We can use this parameter to retrieve a list of specified properties, rather than all the properties of an instance.

- `-Query`: Allows us to specify a query string written in WQL or CQL. For example, `Get-CimInstance -Query "SELECT * from Win32_Printer WHERE name LIKE 'HP%'"` will find my HP printer, again.

- `-QueryDialect`: Specifies the dialect the query is written in. The default is WQL, so we would generally only use this parameter if we were supplying a query written in CQL.

- `-Shallow`: By default, `Get-CimInstance` returns all instances of a class, and instances of any child classes. This parameter prevents any results from child classes being returned.

We can see that both these cmdlets have a `-ComputerName` parameter for working with remote machines. Each time we use this parameter, we create and then remove an ad hoc CIM session. If we have a bunch of commands to run against a remote machine then we can create a persistent CIM session in the same way as we can create a persistent PowerShell remoting session. Let's see how we can do this.

CIM sessions

There are four cmdlets for manipulating CIM sessions – `New-CimSession`, `Get-CimSession`, `Remove-CimSession`, and `New-CimSessionOption`. They behave in a very similar way to the PowerShell remoting cmdlets, and `Get-CimSession` and `Remove-CimSession` do exactly what you would expect. Note that CIM sessions work best in an Active Directory domain environment that uses Kerberos, which is the default authentication scheme. If this isn't available, then the remote machines will need to be added to the TrustedHosts exception list in WinRM. Let's take a quick look at how `New-CimSession` works.

The cmdlet has the following parameters:

- `-Authentication`: Which authentication scheme we want to use. This will depend on the environment we are working in. Kerberos is the best option for a domain environment.
- `-CertificateThumbprint`: If we are working in a certificate-based authentication scheme, then we will need to provide the details of our certificate.
- `-ComputerName`: The name of the remote computer we want to work on. If not given, then a CIM session to the local machine over DCOM is created. WSMan is used for remote computers.
- `-Credential`: Again, depending on the authentication scheme we are working with, we might need to give a credential object.
- `-Name`: We can assign a friendly name to the session to make it easier to work with.
- `-OperationTimeoutSec`: This is the same as for `Get-CimClass`.
- `-Port`: We can specify a particular TCP port if our network is restricted, but this isn't recommended.
- `-SessionOption`: This allows us to set advanced options for the session by creating a `SessionOption` object with `New-CimSessionOption`.
- `-SkipTestConnection`: This stops the cmdlet testing the session connectivity before creating it.

There are a number of advanced options covering the use of proxy servers and controlling how we work with different authentication schemes. These can all be set with the `New-CimSessionOption` cmdlet, but we're not going to go into them here.

Let's see how this all works in the following figure:

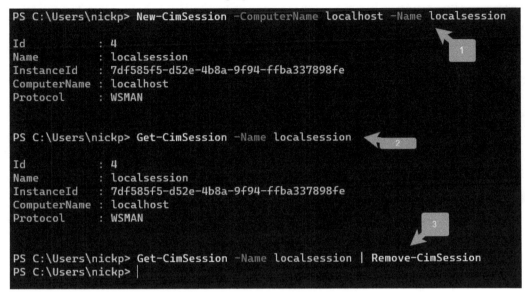

Figure 13.13 – Working with CIM sessions

In the first command, I create a new CIM session on the local machine and give it a friendly name, `localsession`. In the second command, I get the details of my session using the friendly name; notice this is using WSMan, not DCOM, even though it's the local machine. That's because I specified the local machine with the `-ComputerName` parameter, so the cmdlet automatically uses a WSMan session. Neat, huh? In the final command, I remove the session.

So, that's the cmdlets we can use to get information about classes and instances. In the next section, we'll look at how we can manipulate the properties of instances and use their methods.

Making changes

We can use the CIM cmdlets to manipulate the objects in the WMI repository as well; we can change their properties (sometimes) or use their methods. Let's start with changing properties.

Changing properties

Let's run the following command:

```
Get-CimInstance Win32_Printer | Where-Object {$_.Name -like 'HP*'} |
gm
```

Then we will see all the methods and properties of an HP printer installed on our local client. If we don't have an HP printer installed, then we'll get an error, but we can change the search string to match the sort of printer we might have; for instance `'can*'` will find Canon printers. Note that the properties are followed by a string that looks like {get;set;}. If it only reads {get;} then it is not writable. Let's see how changing a writable property looks:

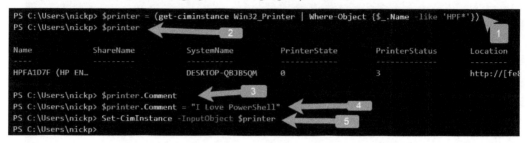

Figure 13.14 – Changing the properties with Set-CimInstance

In the first command, I'm creating a variable called `$printer` and putting my HP printer in it. In the second command, I'm calling the variable, just to check the right thing is in there. It is.

In the third command, I'm checking the current value of the Comment property of the `$printer` variable – we can see it's empty. In the fourth command, I'm changing the property of the variable to I Love PowerShell.

The fifth command is the important bit – I'm taking the contents of the variable, and now I'm writing them back to the instance in the WMI repository with the Set-CimInstance cmdlet. The variable contains a WMI object so I'm using the -InputObject parameter of the cmdlet. Has it worked? Let's take a look.

Figure 13.15 – My printer has an opinion

Of course it worked. Phew. If we look at the list of properties on a printer object, we can see that the majority of them are not writable. For instance, there is a `Default` property, but it's not writable, and we can't set it with `Set-CimInstance`. In the next section, we'll look at a cmdlet that could do it, `Invoke-CimMethod`.

Discovering methods

We know that objects have properties and methods, and that includes the objects in the WMI repository. We've looked at the properties, seen how to get them, and how to set them. Now we're going to look at the methods those objects may have. Here, we're going to see just why working with the WMI repository is sometimes such a pain.

Our first problem is knowing the name of the class we want, and we saw how to do that in the preceding section on querying data. Once we know the name of the class, we need to understand what methods are available. The `Get-CimClass` cmdlet doesn't discover all the methods by default, unlike the `Get-WmiObject` cmdlet, so we have to use something like the following command:

```
Get-CimClass -Class Win32_Printer | Select-Object -ExpandProperty
CimClassMethods
```

This will expose the full set of methods. Once we've got our method, of course, we need to know how to use it. Because WMI isn't part of PowerShell, the PowerShell documentation won't help us. Most of the time, we can find out what we need to know from the Microsoft website, here:

https://learn.microsoft.com/en-us/windows/win32/cimwin32prov/cimwin32-wmi-providers

However, it takes a bit of searching, and quite often the examples are given in Visual Basic, not PowerShell. Let's see how we might do it.

In the next section, we're going to see how to start and stop a process, so let's use the `Win32_Process` documentation, here:

https://learn.microsoft.com/en-us/windows/win32/cimwin32prov/win32-process

We can see if we scroll down that there is a *Methods* section. The most likely method there is `Create`. If we click on the link, we can see that the `Create` method has a `CommandLine` parameter. Let's see how that might work.

Invoking methods

Now we have our method, and a likely parameter for that method, let's give it a try. First of all, we'll need our `Invoke-CimMethod` cmdlet. This cmdlet has the following parameters, many of which work in ways we should now be familiar with:

- `-ClassName`: Same as for `Get-CimClass`.

- `-CimClass`: We can use this parameter to specify a WMI class instead of the `-ClassName` parameter. We need to pass it a WMI class object, however, via a variable, instead of a string.

- `-CimSession`: Same as for `Get-CimClass`.

- `-Namespace`: Same as for `Get-CimClass`.

- `-ComputerName`: Same as for `Get-CimClass`.

- `-MethodName`: This is a mandatory parameter that accepts a string; the name of the method.

- `-Arguments`: Here, we specify the parameters we are passing to the method, as an `iDictionary` hash table, like this: `-Arguments @{ ParameterName = 'value'}`.

- `-OperationTimeoutSeconds`: Same as for `Get-CimClass`.

- `-Query` and `-QueryDialect`: Same as for `Get-CimInstance`.

Let's start the Notepad program; we may want to close any running instances of Notepad, especially if we're working on Windows 11. First, we'll use the `Invoke-CimMethod` cmdlet. We'll need the class name, `Win32_Process`, the method name, `Create()`, and the argument. We'll use `CommandLine = 'notepad.exe'`, as `notepad.exe` is in the PATH environmental variable, so shouldn't need a location:

```
Invoke-CimMethod -ClassName Win32_Process -MethodName Create
-Arguments @{CommandLine = 'notepad.exe'}'}
```

And it looks like this:

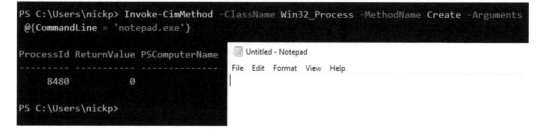

Figure 13.16 – Invoking a method

We can see the return value (0) indicates success, and we get the `ProcessId` of the new Notepad process we've created. Note that this command may create the process in the background; we don't see the Notepad window suddenly appear, but we'll see it on the taskbar.

Activities

1. How could we close the `notepad.exe` process we just started with PowerShell?

2. How can we set a printer as the default with PowerShell? Hint: we can't use the Windows PowerShell `Set-Printer` cmdlet.

That's all we're going to cover here. Just remember that properties and methods are not well documented, and that quite often there will be a PowerShell cmdlet specifically written for our purpose, either as part of PowerShell 7 or Windows PowerShell. Let's summarize this chapter.

Summary

We started the final section of the book in this chapter on using PowerShell in different environments. We've started with the Windows environment, arguably the environment in which PowerShell is most effective. However, we saw there are some important differences between PowerShell 7 and Windows PowerShell.

We saw that PowerShell 7 can't necessarily use modules written for Windows PowerShell, and we looked at three ways of coping with that; finding an equivalent module for PowerShell 7, loading the module anyway, or using Compatibility mode.

While most of the time Compatibility mode is used transparently, we looked at how it works, and some cases where we might want to limit how it is used. However, it is incredibly useful, and we saw that it is getting better all the time.

We moved on to look at some stuff that just doesn't work with PowerShell 7, and why. Generally, this is related to older modules that are no longer worth rewriting to be compatible with PowerShell 7.

We then looked at one of the most useful ways to use PowerShell 7 on a Windows machine: using CIM to manipulate the WMI repository. We took some time to understand the WMI repository, then moved on to how we can get the properties of objects there to understand the environment on both our local machine and remote machines.

The final section looked at how to manipulate the properties of objects in the WMI repository, and then looked at how we can call the methods on those objects to affect the wider computing environment.

That's it for this chapter. In the next chapter, we're going to look at how we can use PowerShell 7 on Linux and macOS machines.

Exercises

1. What type of modules have compatibility information?

2. Why might a module have no compatibility information?

3. We've run `Get-PSSession`, and we can see that there is a remote session called `WinPSCompatSession` running on the localhost machine. What version of PowerShell is it running?

4. What sort of objects do we get back from commands run in the `WinPSCompatSession`?

5. Our local admin has disabled implicit Windows compatibility on our machine. How can we still import modules in Compatibility mode?

6. What CIM class contains instances of namespaces?

7. What is the purpose of the `-OperationTimeoutSecs` parameter on the `Get-CimInstance` cmdlet?

8. What cmdlet would we use to change the properties of a WMI object?

9. How do we pass method parameters to `Invoke-CimMethod` and what format do they need to be in?

Further reading

- *.NET Framework*:

  https://en.wikipedia.org/wiki/.NET_Framework

- *Module compatibility*:

  https://learn.microsoft.com/en-us/powershell/gallery/concepts/module-psedition-support

- *PowerShell editions*:

  https://learn.microsoft.com/en-us/powershell/module/microsoft.powershell.core/about/about_powershell_editions

- *Differences in PowerShell 7*:

  https://learn.microsoft.com/en-us/powershell/scripting/whats-new/differences-from-windows-powershell

- *Web-Based Enterprise Management*:

  https://en.wikipedia.org/wiki/Web-Based_Enterprise_Management

- *Common Information Model*:

  https://en.wikipedia.org/wiki/Common_Information_Model_(computing)

- *WSMan*:

  https://en.wikipedia.org/wiki/WS-Management

- *Windows Management Instrumentation*:

  https://en.wikipedia.org/wiki/Windows_Management_Instrumentation

- *Distributed Component Object Model*:

  https://en.wikipedia.org/wiki/Distributed_Component_Object_Model

- *Migrating from Windows PowerShell 5.1 to PowerShell 7.x*:

  https://learn.microsoft.com/en-us/powershell/scripting/whats-new/migrating-from-windows-powershell-51-to-powershell-7

- *About Windows PowerShell Compatibility*:

  https://learn.microsoft.com/en-us/powershell/module/microsoft.powershell.core/about/about_windows_powershell_compatibility

- *PowerShell 7 module compatibility*:

  https://learn.microsoft.com/en-us/powershell/scripting/whats-new/module-compatibility

- *Modules with compatible PowerShell editions*:

  https://learn.microsoft.com/en-us/powershell/gallery/concepts/module-psedition-support

- *About PowerShell editions*:

  https://learn.microsoft.com/en-us/powershell/module/microsoft.powershell.core/about/about_powershell_editions

- *Implicit remoting*:

  https://devblogs.microsoft.com/scripting/remoting-the-implicit-way/

- *Getting WMI objects with Get-CimInstance*:

  https://learn.microsoft.com/en-us/powershell/scripting/samples/getting-wmi-objects--get-ciminstance-?view=powershell-7.4

- *Using PowerShell CIM cmdlets to explore WMI classes*:

  https://devblogs.microsoft.com/scripting/using-powershell-cim-cmdlets-to-explore-wmi-classes/

14

PowerShell 7 for Linux and macOS

It is commonly said that Linux is the most popular operating system for servers, and while this is true, it doesn't acknowledge that there are nearly as many types of Linux as there are actual servers. Whereas Windows and macOS are closely engineered and maintained by companies that are concerned that everybody should be running homogenous, secure, and often forcibly updated code, the Linux world is far more unrestricted, with a multiplicity of free, open source, and often barely maintained variations that seem to hang around on servers for years or sometimes decades. In this chapter, we're going to look at how we can use PowerShell on some of the more common varieties of Linux; in our case, Ubuntu and CentOS, a free version of **Red Hat Enterprise Linux (RHEL)**.

We're going to start by looking at how we can get access to a Linux machine to practice on; without that, this chapter would be pretty boring. Once we've got a machine, we will look at three different ways of installing PowerShell, using package managers and direct download.

After that, we'll install VS Code and see how to set it up on CentOS 7 before going on to look at some of the main differences we will see running PowerShell on Linux rather than Windows.

We will look at one of the most common ways of using PowerShell on Linux: remote sessions over the **Secure Shell (SSH)** protocol. This is important and is easily the most common way I see people logging in to Linux machines.

Finally, we'll take a quick look at how easy it is to install PowerShell and VS Code on macOS using the free open source package manager, Homebrew.

The main topics we will cover in this chapter are the following:

- Installing PowerShell 7
- Installing VS Code
- Running PowerShell on Linux

- Remoting with OpenSSH
- PowerShell for macOS

Technical requirements

Unless we already have a client running some form of Linux, we'll need a Linux device to work on. There's a really easy way to get one and a slightly harder way to get one. I've done both on my machine to get the screenshots for this chapter, providing a Ubuntu server (with no graphical interface) and a CentOS desktop client.

The Ubuntu server is very easy to install:

1. Go to **Control Panel | Programs and Features | Turn Windows features on and off** and make sure the checkbox for **Windows Subsystem for Linux** is checked, like this:

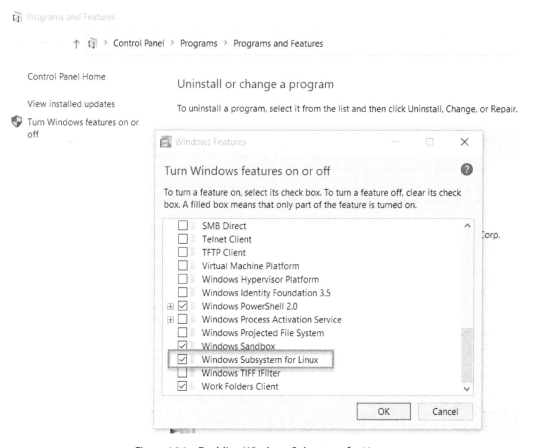

Figure 14.1 – Enabling Windows Subsystem for Linux

Windows Subsystem for Linux is displayed inside the red box.

2. Once **Windows Subsystem for Linux (WSL)** is enabled, reboot, go to the Microsoft Store (`https://apps.microsoft.com`), and select a Linux application. I'm using the latest version of Ubuntu – 22.04:

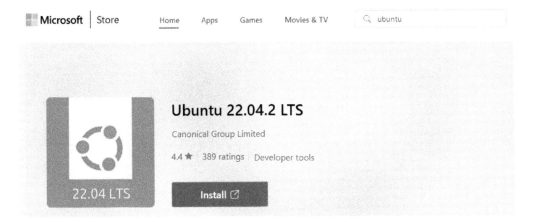

Figure 14.2 – An Ubuntu app on the Microsoft Store

All I've done here is search for Ubuntu in the search box and select the most recent app.

3. Click on **Install**, and a Microsoft Store window will open; click on **Get**, and once the app is downloaded, the button will change to **Open**:

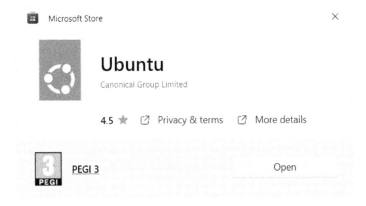

Figure 14.3 – The Microsoft Store app

4. Click **Open**, and a terminal window will open, with a message saying `Installing, this may take a few minutes....` After a few minutes, we'll be asked to create a username and then input a password twice, and that's it. We now have a Ubuntu server running inside WSL on Windows:

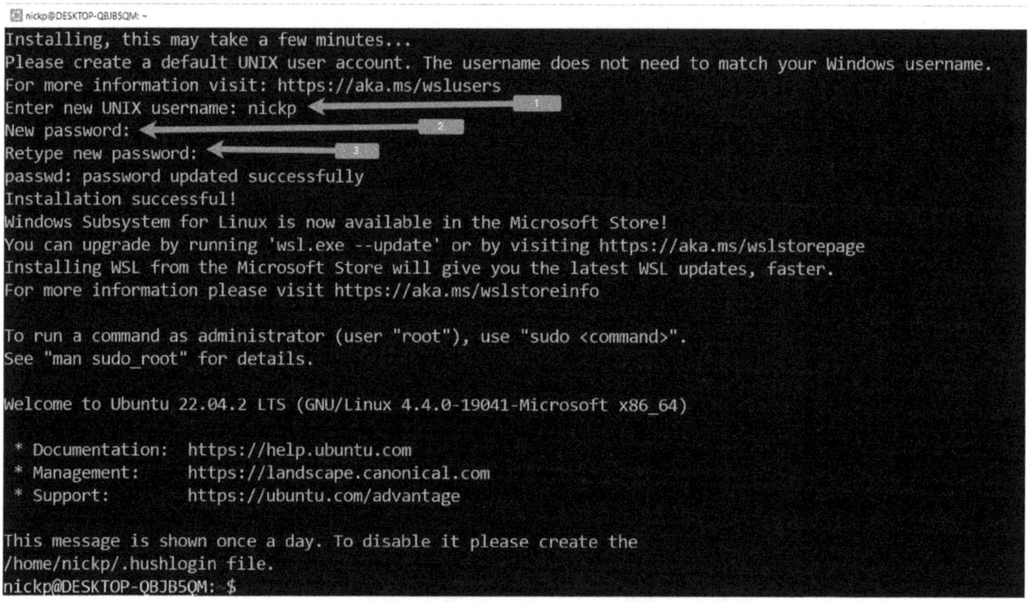

Figure 14.4 – Ubuntu on WSL

In the first line, I've created a new username, `nickp` (imaginative), and in the second and third, I've input the new password. Ubuntu hides the password when you type, but unlike Windows, it doesn't do it by displaying dots or asterisks. It just displays... nothing.

And that's it – our Ubuntu environment is ready to have PowerShell installed.

> **Note**
>
> These instructions are for Windows 10 Pro build 19045. Different platforms such as Windows 11 or Windows Server may have different instructions for installing WSL. Also, this is WSL. There is another version called WSL2 for later operating systems.

I've also installed CentOS into Oracle VirtualBox; it would work just as well from the Microsoft Store, but I want a separate machine with a GUI we can use for this chapter.

Instructions for installing VirtualBox are available here:

`https://www.virtualbox.org/manual/UserManual.html#installation`

It's pretty straightforward.

Once VirtualBox is installed, we'll need to download a CentOS image from here:

`http://isoredirect.centos.org/centos/7/isos`

And we need to create a VM to install it on. There are good instructions for that here: `https://www.linuxfordevices.com/tutorials/centos/centos-on-virtualbox`.

I've installed CentOS 7 with a GNOME desktop GUI so that we can have a look at how to install PowerShell on older operating systems; I find that a lot of the Linux systems I work with are getting on a bit. I'm still using Ubuntu 12.04 in some places. Precise Pangolin was a great name for an operating system, but really, we should all be on Jammy Jellyfish – at least for the sake of security.

Finally, to follow the section on macOS, we'll need a Mac of some description. I'm an absolute cheapskate, so I've borrowed a MacBook from my friend Paul that's running OS 13, Ventura, which is pretty recent. Thanks, Paul.

Now we've covered the sort of environment we'll need and how to install it, let's look at installing PowerShell.

Installing PowerShell 7

Somewhat perversely, I find that installing PowerShell on Linux is probably easier than installing it on Windows, despite PowerShell being developed for Windows. Microsoft publishes good scripts that we can use for the supported versions of Linux; note, though, that there are very few supported flavors: RHEL, Ubuntu, Alpine, and Debian.

This doesn't mean we can't install PowerShell on other versions, only that Microsoft doesn't provide any support for us. Microsoft only supports specific recent versions as well. Because of the rate at which both operating systems change, it's worth making sure that our versions of PowerShell and Linux are on the supportability matrix; otherwise, we may get unexpected results, as we will see when we look at installing on CentOS.

Let's start with Ubuntu, which I've got running in WSL on my Windows 10 client.

Installing PowerShell on Ubuntu 22.04

In this section, we are going to install PowerShell 7.4 on Ubuntu 22.04. Ubuntu is running inside WSL on my Windows 10 client, but it will work just as well on a VM or a physical machine. There are detailed alternative instructions here: `https://learn.microsoft.com/en-us/powershell/scripting/install/install-ubuntu`.

Let's have a go. We're going to run the commands shown next:

1. In the first line, we are updating the local packages with the latest versions from the default repositories. This is good practice before installing any software on Linux. We use the sudo command to tell Linux that we want to use administrator privileges, or root privileges, to run the command. Obviously, to do that, we need to actually have those privileges, and we will be asked to input our account password to confirm that before we can run the command:

```
sudo apt-get update
```

2. In the second line, we're installing some prerequisite packages:

```
sudo apt-get install -y wget apt-transport-https software-
properties-common
```

3. In the third line, we are grabbing the exact version of the operating system and then using that in the fourth line:

```
source /etc/os-release
```

4. We use wget to download the correct repository package for our operating system. This is the Linux package repository for Microsoft products, abbreviated **PMC** (short for **packages.microsoft.com**):

```
wget -q https://packages.microsoft.com/config/ubuntu/$VERSION_
ID/packages-microsoft-prod.deb
```

5. In the fifth line, we're registering PMC with dpkg, the Ubuntu package management system:

```
sudo dpkg -i packages-microsoft-prod.deb
```

6. In the sixth line, we're deleting the key file for security:

```
rm packages-microsoft-prod.deb
```

7. In the seventh line, we're running sudo apt-get update again to make sure we've got the latest list of packages for the new repository:

```
sudo apt-get update
```

8. Finally, in the eighth line, we're installing PowerShell:

```
sudo apt-get install -y powershell
```

Linux is quite chatty, and we'll see 60 or 70 lines of output as we type the preceding commands, but the process is very straightforward and works well.

To start PowerShell, we simply type pwsh, and we will be taken to a PowerShell prompt, as in the following screenshot:

```
nickp@DESKTOP-QBJB5QM:~$ pwsh
PowerShell 7.4.0
PS /home/nickp> $PSVersionTable

Name                            Value
----                            -----
PSVersion                       7.4.0
PSEdition                       Core
GitCommitId                     7.4.0
OS                              Ubuntu 22.04.2 LTS
Platform                        Unix
PSCompatibleVersions            {1.0, 2.0, 3.0, 4.0…}
PSRemotingProtocolVersion       2.3
SerializationVersion            1.1.0.1
WSManStackVersion               3.0

PS /home/nickp> exit
nickp@DESKTOP-QBJB5QM:~$
```

Figure 14.5 – Starting PowerShell on Ubuntu

In the preceding screenshot, I started PowerShell with pwsh. Once PowerShell started, I called the $PSVersionTable automatic variable to get some information about the environment, including the version of PowerShell, the edition, and which operating system is running. I closed PowerShell by typing exit. If I'd wanted to keep PowerShell running in the background, I could have typed bash and gone to a Bash prompt instead. As we can see, we get the same color coding on Linux that we see on Windows, which helps to keep the experience consistent across platforms.

It's good to know that tab completion works in Linux as well. One of the things that trips me up most often with Linux is capitalization; PowerShell on Windows has made me lazy. Therefore, being able to use tabs to complete paths is really useful. Note that PowerShell itself is not case-sensitive on Linux; get-process works just as well as Get-Process.

Let's look now at installing PowerShell on CentOS.

Installing PowerShell on CentOS 8 and 9

Installing the latest version of PowerShell on recent versions of CentOS, CentOS 8, or CentOS 9 (and also RHEL and Fedora) is very similar to installing it on Ubuntu, but using the `yum` package manager for RHEL 8 or the `dnf` package manager for RHEL 9; if anything, it's even easier. Do note, however, that Microsoft only officially supports PowerShell on RHEL, not on CentOS or Fedora. We're going to run the commands shown next:

1. In the first line, we're using the `curl` application rather than `wget` to fetch PCM:

    ```
    curl -ssl -O https://packages.microsoft.com/config/rhel/8/
    packages-microsoft-prod.rpm
    ```

2. In the second line, we're registering the repository with `rpm`, the package manager:

    ```
    sudo rpm -i packages-microsoft-prod.rpm
    ```

3. In the third line, we're removing the key files, again:

    ```
    rm packages-microsoft-prod.rpm
    ```

4. In the fourth line, we're updating the package lists now we've registered the new repository:

    ```
    sudo dnf update
    ```

5. In the final line, we are installing PowerShell. The `-y` switch at the end specifies that we are answering `yes` to all questions. We can start PowerShell using `pwsh`, again, just like on Ubuntu:

    ```
    sudo dnf install powershell -y
    ```

> **Troubleshooting tip**
>
> If this doesn't work, there's a pretty good chance that it's the proxy settings. There are at least three different places in CentOS where we might find the proxy settings. For `yum`, it's `/etc/yum.conf`. For `dnf`, it's `/etc/dnf/dnf.conf`.

What happens if we want to use PowerShell on an older version, though? We must install a specific older version of PowerShell.

For RHEL 7 (and, therefore, CentOS 7), the last definitely good version of PowerShell was 7.2. Early releases of 7.3 work, but later releases don't, as they rely on Linux libraries that aren't compatible with CentOS 7. What we see if we try to install a recent version of PowerShell are error messages such as this:

```
GLIBCXX_3.4.21 not found (required by pwsh)
```

The answer here is to install PowerShell 7.2. Let's see how we do that.

Installing PowerShell on CentOS 7

Installing by direct download is really easy on CentOS; it's one line:

```
sudo yum install https://github.com/PowerShell/PowerShell/releases/
download/v7.2.17/powershell-7.2.17-1.rh.x86_64.rpm
```

All we're doing here is using yum, the package manager on CentOS 7, to fetch and install a package from a URL. The trick here is knowing the URL of the package you need to download, though. All the packages are maintained on GitHub by Microsoft, here: https://github.com/PowerShell/PowerShell/releases/.

To download a release, click on the link in the name of the package (in our case, **v7.2.17 Release of PowerShell**) and scroll down to the **Assets** section on the next page. Click on the package we need, powershell-7.2.17-1.rh.x86_64.rpm, and copy the hyperlink: https://github.com/PowerShell/PowerShell/releases/download/v7.2.17/powershell-7.2.17-1.rh.x86_64.rpm.

Once we have that, we pass it to sudo yum install, like this:

```
[nick@localhost ~]$ sudo yum install https://github.com/PowerShell/PowerShell/releases/
download/v7.2.17/powershell-7.2.17-1.rh.x86_64.rpm
Loaded plugins: fastestmirror, langpacks
powershell-7.2.17-1.rh.x86_64.rpm                              |  65 MB  00:00:16
Examining /var/tmp/yum-root-94S0jo/powershell-7.2.17-1.rh.x86_64.rpm: powershell-7.2.17
-1.rh.x86_64
Marking /var/tmp/yum-root-94S0jo/powershell-7.2.17-1.rh.x86_64.rpm to be installed
Resolving Dependencies
--> Running transaction check
---> Package powershell.x86_64 0:7.2.17-1.rh will be installed
--> Finished Dependency Resolution

Dependencies Resolved

================================================================================
 Package        Arch        Version        Repository                      Size
================================================================================
Installing:
 powershell     x86_64      7.2.17-1.rh    /powershell-7.2.17-1.rh.x86_64  165 M

Transaction Summary
================================================================================
Install  1 Package
```

Figure 14.6 – Installing PowerShell on CentOS 7 using a direct download

In the first line, I've run the direct download command, as shown previously. The rest of the screen output is chat from the operating system, telling us what it is doing. There are quite a few more lines of this before we finally get to run PowerShell. It's a very easy way to install PowerShell; the downside is that we don't register the Microsoft repository.

That is pretty much all we're going to cover on installing PowerShell on Linux; we've covered representatives of the two main families of Linux, Ubuntu and CentOS, and we've looked at how we can install different versions of PowerShell. Let's look now at how we can install VS Code on Linux. We'll be using my CentOS system because that has a GUI.

Installing VS Code

Installing VS Code on Linux is straightforward. On recent Ubuntu machines, we can use `snapd`, a package management system for Ubuntu, like this:

```
sudo snap install --classic code
```

And that's it. On RHEL and CentOS machines, we may need to enable `snapd` first, before we can use it to install code.

We're going to run the commands shown next:

1. In the first line, we are installing the `snapd` package:

    ```
    sudo yum install snapd
    ```

    Note: For CentOS 7, we will also need to run the following command:

    ```
    sudo yum install epel-release
    ```

2. In the second line, we're enabling the network socket that `snap` uses:

    ```
    sudo systemctl enable --now snapd.socket
    ```

3. In the third line, we're creating a symbolic link that maps /snap to /var/lib/snapd/snap:

    ```
    sudo ln -s /var/lib/snapd/snap /snap
    ```

4. Finally, we need to log out and log back in, or reboot the machine, to make sure that everything is updated.

We're now ready to use `snap` to install VS Code, as before. The big advantage of using `snap` is that it will keep VS Code updated in the background.

We can also install VS Code manually if we don't have access to `snap`. We can do it like this on CentOS 7:

```
sudo rpm --import  https://packages.microsoft.com/keys/microsoft.asc
```

This will register the Microsoft GPG encryption keys with `rpm`, the CentOS 7 package manager. Next, type the following:

```
sudo nano /etc/yum.repos.d/vscode.repo
```

This will create an empty text file called `vscode.repo`. We need to add some lines to this file and save it, so type this:

```
[code]
name=Visual Studio Code
baseurl=https://packages.microsoft.com/yumrepos/vscode
enabled=1
gpgcheck=1
gpgkey=https://packages.microsoft.com/keys/microsoft.asc
```

Press *Ctrl* and *X* to exit, and answer y when prompted to save the file.

The `vscode.repo` file should look like this:

Figure 14.7 – The vscode.repo file in nano

When we create the file, it is empty, and we must type in the code and then save and exit.

Finally, to install VS Code, type the following:

```
sudo yum install code
```

That's it. We can start VS Code by typing code at the terminal prompt. VS Code works exactly the same way in Linux as it does in Windows. Refer to the *Configuring VS Code for PowerShell* section of *Chapter 5, PowerShell Control Flow – Conditionals and Loops*.

Now we've got everything installed, let's look at how we can use PowerShell on Linux.

Running PowerShell on Linux

Mostly, PowerShell works exactly the same on Linux as it does on Windows, but obviously, there are some differences between the two underlying operating systems that we need to be aware of and subsequently understand how PowerShell handles them.

Case sensitivity is the obvious one; while get-content works as well as Get-Content on Linux, get-content ./myfile.txt doesn't work if the file is called MyFile.txt; see the following screenshot:

```
PS /home/nickp> get-content MyFile.txt
welcome to my file
PS /home/nickp> get-content myfile.txt
Get-Content: Cannot find path '/home/nickp/myfile.txt' because it does not exist.
PS /home/nickp>
```

Figure 14.8 – The importance of capitalization

As you can see, if the capitalization of the path or filename is incorrect, then PowerShell can't find the file. The best way I have found to compensate for this is to use tab completion as much as possible, as tab completion ignores capitalization, so typing myfi and pressing *Tab* will find a file called MyFile.txt.

The filesystems are different, also. Linux doesn't use letters to distinguish drives and uses forward slashes (/) instead of backslashes (\). PowerShell recognizes both as a file path separator, so there is no functional difference between Get-Content ./MyFile.txt and Get-Content .\MyFile.txt:

```
PS /home/nickp> Get-Content ./MyFile.txt
welcome to my file
PS /home/nickp> Get-Content .\MyFile.txt
welcome to my file
```

Figure 14.9 – Versatile path separators

As you can see, we get the contents of the file whichever file path separator we choose. This makes writing cross-platform scripts easier.

I have made my views on aliases known already, and it appears my furious letter writing has paid off, because PowerShell 7 on Linux no longer includes common aliases such as `ls`, although they persist when running PowerShell 7 on Windows. Instead, PowerShell now calls the Bash command, like this:

```
nickp@DESKTOP-QBJB5QM: $ ls
MyFile.txt  packages-microsoft-prod.deb
nickp@DESKTOP-QBJB5QM: $ pwsh
PowerShell 7.4.0
PS /home/nickp> ls
MyFile.txt  packages-microsoft-prod.deb
PS /home/nickp> Get-ChildItem

    Directory: /home/nickp

UnixMode          User Group        LastWriteTime        Size Name
--------          ---- -----        -------------        ---- ----
-rw-r--r--        nickp nickp        11/29/2023 11:45       19 MyFile.txt
-rw-r--r--        nickp nickp        10/25/2022 18:40     3692 packages-microsoft-prod.deb
```

Figure 14.10 – Fewer aliases in PowerShell 7 on Linux

We can see the difference between running `ls` in Bash and PowerShell in the preceding screenshot. The output is the same, but we don't get the color coding we get when running in Bash. By contrast, we get a completely different type of output when we run `Get-ChildItem`. Compare this to the behavior on Windows, where `ls` is an alias for `Get-ChildItem`. Other Linux commands that are no longer aliased include `cp`, `mv`, `rm`, `cat`, `man`, `mount`, and `ps`.

Running as an administrator is different on Linux, as well. People familiar with Linux will be used to running commands with the `sudo` prefix to run the command as root. This won't work in PowerShell. Instead, we must start PowerShell with `sudo`, like this:

```
sudo pwsh
```

This will give us a new PowerShell session running with root privileges.

Given that one of the big attractions of running PowerShell on Linux (and macOS, and ARM) is that we can start to write cross-platform scripts, how do we know which platform our script is running on? Easy – we test the automatic variables. There are three automatic variables called `$IsWindows`, `$IsLinux`, and `$IsMacOS`, which return either `true` or `false`, depending on the operating system. We can use these variables to write `if` statements in our scripts that alter behavior depending on the environment.

> **Activity – Writing a cross-platform script**
>
> Given what we've learned previously, write a cross-platform script that will run on both Windows and Linux and return five running processes with the highest current CPU usage. Output the processes in descending order to a text file with a name that includes the name of the computer it was run on.
>
> We can get the name of the computer in Windows with `$env:computername`, and in Linux by typing `hostname`.

Of course, much of the time, we won't actually be running commands and scripts directly on a Linux machine; most of the time, we will want to remote into it. In the next section, we'll look at the recommended way of remoting into Linux machines.

Remoting with OpenSSH

We saw in *Chapter 12*, *Securing PowerShell*, that remoting was a powerful way to establish a connection with a machine and take control. When we looked at remoting in that chapter, we explored remoting over the **Windows Remote Management** (**WinRM**) protocol on other Windows machines. We mentioned that we could also use SSH to establish remote sessions. Linux does not support the WinRM protocol, so we must use SSH to remotely administer it.

OpenSSH is an open source SSH toolset that is almost ubiquitous on Linux and other Unix machines. Since 2018, it has been available for Windows and makes managing heterogeneous environments much easier. It can be a bit tricky to set up, but once it is working, it makes remoting very easy. Let's take a look.

Checking that PowerShell has OpenSSH support

The first thing to check is that our version of PowerShell 7 has got OpenSSH support; if we've downloaded and installed it from GitHub, then we should be OK, but first, let's check using the following command:

```
(Get-Command New-PSSession).ParameterSets.Name
```

If we see parameter sets called `SSHHost` and `SSHHostHashParam`, then we are good to go. If not, then we should download a recent version of PowerShell 7 from GitHub.

Installing OpenSSH on Windows

We only need to install OpenSSH on Windows if we are going to want to remote into that Windows machine. If we're going to remote from it to other machines, then we can skip installing it; PowerShell already has a working SSH client that will allow us to connect to Linux machines using PowerShell remoting.

If we decide we want to install an OpenSSH server, then we first need to check if we are running on a viable version of Windows and that we have the correct rights. Start an elevated administrator PowerShell session, and type the following:

```
(New-Object Security.Principal.WindowsPrincipal([Security.Principal.
WindowsIdentity]::GetCurrent())).IsInRole([Security.Principal.
WindowsBuiltInRole]::Administrator)
Winver.exe
```

This is what I get on my machine:

Figure 14.11 – Checking OpenSSH prerequisites on Windows

As we can see, my rights test returns `True`, so I do have the correct rights, and when I run `winver.exe`, the pop-up window shows I am running Windows 10 22H2, more recent than the minimum version of Windows 10 1809. We're ready to install. In the elevated prompt we've just used, type the following:

```
Get-WindowsCapability -Online | Where-Object {$_.Name -like
'OpenSSH*'} | Add-WindowsCapability -Online
```

This will install OpenSSH. We also need to start the `sshd` service and set it to automatically start up:

```
Start-Service sshd
Set-Service sshd -StartupType Automatic
```

Finally, we need to configure `sshd` to allow PowerShell to use it. Open `notepad.exe` as an administrator (right-click and choose **Run as Administrator**), and then open the `C:\ProgramData\ssh\sshd_config` file, add the following lines above the last entry in the file, and save the file:

```
PasswordAuthentication yes
PubkeyAuthentication yes
Subsystem powershell c:/progra~1/powershell/7/pwsh.exe -sshs -nologo
```

The `-nologo` parameter isn't needed if we're using PowerShell 7.4 or later. Be careful not to save the file as `sshd_config.txt`.

> **Warning!**
>
> Wait! What's that `c:/progra~1/powershell/7/pwsh.exe` path all about? Working with non-Microsoft open source software on Windows can be frustrating at times. OpenSSH is an example. It doesn't understand paths with a space in them, even if the path is enclosed in single or double quotes, and so we have to use something called 8.3 format, which is the short filename format that we used to use with older Microsoft operating systems.
>
> Unfortunately, it's even more complicated. Some releases of OpenSSH don't like that format either; when we add the PowerShell subsystem into the `sshd_config` file, the `sshd` service refuses to start. The answer here is to side-load another copy of PowerShell into a directory with no spaces and no names longer than eight characters. To get mine to work, I downloaded the PowerShell 7.4 ZIP file from the PowerShell GitHub pages, unblocked it by right-clicking on the downloaded file, selecting **Properties**, and checking the **Unblock** checkbox, and then extracted the contents to a suitable directory; in my case, I used `c:\scratch\pwsh`. I then added this line to `sshd_config`:
>
> ```
> Subsystem powershell c:/scratch/pwsh/pwsh.exe -sshs
> ```
>
> And now, the `sshd` service will start normally.

Finally, restart the service with the following command:

```
Restart-Service sshd
```

And that's it. Our Windows machine is ready to receive PowerShell remoting over OpenSSH.

Installing OpenSSH on Linux

Now, we have to configure OpenSSH on Linux. We're going to use my CentOS 7 machine, which already has OpenSSH installed, but if we wanted to install it on an Ubuntu machine, we'd need to install it first with the following command:

```
sudo apt install openssh-client
sudo apt install openssh-server
```

Once OpenSSH is installed, we need to edit the `sshd_config` file at `/etc/ssh`. To do this, we need to start our text editor with `sudo`:

```
sudo nano /etc/ssh/sshd_config
```

We need to add the following lines:

```
PasswordAuthentication yes
PubkeyAuthentication yes
Subsystem powershell /usr/bin/pwsh -sshs -nologo
```

Then, we save the file. Next, we need to restart the sshd service:

```
sudo systemctl restart sshd
```

And then, we set it to start automatically:

```
sudo systemctl enable sshd
```

And that's us set up for remoting. Note that the final command may throw an error if it is already enabled.

Running remote sessions

Using remote sessions over SSH is just as easy as using them over WinRM, which we saw in *Chapter 12*, *Securing PowerShell*. We start out by creating a session object:

```
$session = New-PSSession -HostName <name of remote computer> -UserName
<username>
```

Notice that we're using the -HostName parameter, not the -ComputerName parameter. This tells PowerShell to create an SSH session, not a WinRM one. We'll be asked to input the user's password, and then the session object is created. We can then use the variable containing the session object to start a remote session:

```
Enter-PSSession -Session $session
```

We'll see the prompt change to reflect the machine that we are remoting into, and we are straight into a PowerShell session on that machine. To leave the session, we can just type exit and return to the local machine. This is how it looks in practice:

```
PS C:\Users\nickp> $session = New-PSSession -HostName 192.168.56.101 -UserName nick          1
nick@192.168.56.101's password:          2
PS C:\Users\nickp> $session          3

 Id Name          Transport ComputerName    ComputerType    State    ConfigurationName    Availability
 -- ----          --------- ------------    ------------    -----    -----------------    ------------
  8 Runspace7     SSH       192.168.56.101  RemoteMachine   Opened   DefaultShell         Available

PS C:\Users\nickp> Enter-PSSession -Session $session          4
[nick@192.168.56.101]: PS /home/nick> Get-Process *shell*          5

NPM(K)    PM(M)      WS(M)     CPU(s)     Id  SI ProcessName
------    -----      -----     ------     --  -- -----------
     0     0.00     185.12     112.04   5297 …00 gnome-shell
     0     0.00      12.52       0.22   5518 …33 gnome-shell-calendar-server

[nick@192.168.56.101]: PS /home/nick> hostname          6
localhost.localdomain
[nick@192.168.56.101]: PS /home/nick> $IsLinux          7
True
[nick@192.168.56.101]: PS /home/nick> exit          8
PS C:\Users\nickp>
```

Figure 14.12 – SSH remoting into a Linux server

The numbering in the preceding screenshot is explained as follows:

1. In *line 1*, I'm creating a new session object and storing it in a variable. I'm passing the IP address of the remote machine because I haven't set up name resolution. I'm also passing the username of a user on the remote machine who has the right to log in.

2. In *line 2*, I am asked for the remote user's password; once it is provided, the session object is created.

3. In *line 3*, I'm calling the `$session` variable, and the properties of the new session are displayed.

4. In *line 4*, I'm passing the `$session` variable to `Enter-PSSession`, and I'm entering a remote session.

5. In *line 5*, we can see that the prompt has changed to `[nick@192.168.56.101]: PS /home/nick>`, which tells us I'm in a PowerShell session on the machine at `192.168.56.101` and I'm logged in as `nick`. The working directory is `/home/nick`. I'm running the `Get-Process` PowerShell cmdlet, looking for processes containing the `shell` string, and I get two gnome processes returned. This is definitely Linux – my CentOS 7 GUI box, to be precise. If we run it on Ubuntu, we may not see any processes at all if there is no GUI installed.

6. In *line 6*, I run the `hostname` Bash command, and the name of the remote system is returned: `localhost.localdomain`.

7. In *line 7*, just so there is no doubt, we can see that the value of the `$IsLinux` automatic variable is `True`.

8. Finally, on *line 8*, I type `exit` and am returned to my local PowerShell session running on Windows.

The trouble is, I've used a username and password combination here, and many Linux machines will be set up to use key-based authentication. Let's take a look at how we can set that up.

Authentication

Key-based authentication is a more secure way of using SSH for PowerShell remoting. It also makes it easier to automate scripts, as once it is set up, no one needs to manually enter a password. Let's look at how we can get it working.

PowerShell 7 includes a utility called `Ssh-keygen` that we can use to create a public/private key pair that we can use to authenticate ourselves to the remote machine. We can use it like this:

```
Ssh-keygen -t Ed25519
```

We're asking PowerShell to generate a key pair using the Ed21559 algorithm, which is quite modern. Older systems may require that we use the RSA algorithm instead. We will be asked for a path to save the files to; it's best to accept the default one by just pressing *Enter*. We will also be asked to enter a passphrase; again, this is optional, and we can just press *Enter* twice to save the files with no passphrase.

Now, we can save the public key onto the Linux machine in the `.ssh` directory of the user we want to log in with. PowerShell has another utility called `scp` that we can use to copy the file across (note that we might need to create a .ssh directory first):

```
scp c:\Users\<username>\.ssh\id_ed25519.pub <user>@<remote_host>:~/.
ssh/authorized_keys
```

I'm using `scp` with two parameters here – the first is the path to the file we've created, and the second is the path we want it copied to. We'll be asked to provide the password for the remote user again, but that's the last time we'll need to do that. Now, when we log in as that user, we will pass a hash of our private key on the local machine that pairs with the hash of the public key on the remote machine, and we will be recognized as the remote user. This is how it looks on my machine:

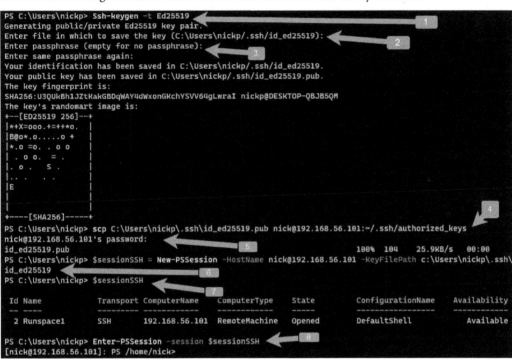

Figure 14.13 – Setting up key-based authentication

In the preceding screenshot, I've run the commands needed to set up key-based authentication:

1. In *line 1*, I am running `Ssh-keygen` to create my key pair.

2. In *line 2*, I'm accepting the default path by pressing *Enter*.

3. In *line 3*, I'm setting a blank passphrase by pressing *Enter* twice.

4. In *line 4*, I'm using `scp` to copy the public key across to the user `.ssh` directory on the remote machine.

5. In *line 5*, I'm providing the password – hopefully for the last time ever.

6. In *line 6*, I am storing a new session object in a variable called `$sessionSSH`. Notice that I am not providing a password, but I am providing the path to the private key in the `-KeyFilePath` parameter.

7. In *line 7*, I'm calling the variable to check the properties.

8. In *line 8*, I am entering the session using the `$sessionSSH` variable.

9. In the final line, we can see that the prompt has changed to reflect that I am working in a remote session.

There's an awful lot more to using SSH, but that is enough to get us started. Let's move on to the final section of this chapter: *PowerShell for macOS*.

PowerShell for macOS

macOS is very similar to Linux; both operating systems are based on elements of Unix, and many Linux programs can run on macOS without modifying the source code. The differences we will focus on here are how we install PowerShell and VS Code. I've used a friend's MacBook, which is running Ventura (macOS 13). If anything, installing on macOS is even easier than installing on Linux.

Installing Homebrew on macOS

Homebrew is a free open source package manager that works on Linux and macOS, but mostly we see it on macOS. It's very easy to install and use, and it's what we're going to use to install PowerShell and VS Code on macOS. It's a one-line installation. Open the terminal and type the following:

```
/bin/bash -c "$(curl -fsSL https://raw.githubusercontent.com/Homebrew/
install/HEAD/install.sh)"
```

We're passing a `curl` command to the `bash` shell here to download and run a Bash script from a URL. We'll probably be asked to provide our password. macOS is just as chatty as Linux, but after a few minutes, we should see a message saying `Installation successful!`. Now, we're ready to install PowerShell.

Installing PowerShell on macOS

Once we've got Homebrew installed, everything else is easy. To install PowerShell, we type the following:

```
brew install powershell/tap/powershell
```

And that's it. We can start PowerShell by typing `pwsh` in the terminal. This is how it looks on Paul's machine:

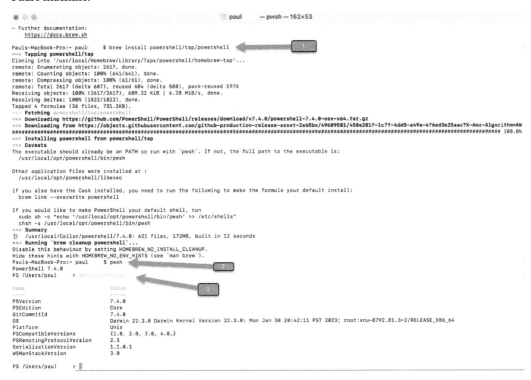

Figure 14.14 – Installing PowerShell on macOS

In *line 1*, I'm installing PowerShell using Homebrew. In *line 2*, I'm starting PowerShell with `pwsh`, and in *line 3*, I'm calling `$PSVersionTable` to check what we've got.

We'll need to keep PowerShell updated. We can do that with these two lines:

```
brew update
brew upgrade powershell
```

The first line updates the Homebrew database, and the second upgrades PowerShell based on the most recent information.

Finally, to uninstall PowerShell, we can just type the following:

```
brew uninstall --cask powershell
```

However, I've no idea why we would want to do that. Let's look at installing VS Code next.

Installing VS Code on macOS

We can use Homebrew to download and install VS Code using the following command, which updates the latest files for Homebrew:

```
brew update
```

This installs the `cask` repository if it's not already present:

```
brew tap caskroom/cask
```

This searches for VS Code in the repository:

```
brew cask search visual-studio-code
```

And this line installs it:

```
brew cask install visual-studio-code
```

We can use the launcher application to start VS Code, or we can add it to the PATH variable with this `cat` command:

```
cat << EOF >> ~/.bash_profile
# Add Visual Studio Code (code)
export PATH="\$PATH:/Applications/Visual Studio Code.app/Contents/
Resources/app/bin"
EOF
```

We can also install it by downloading it directly from `https://code.visualstudio.com/` and double-clicking the downloaded file.

We can uninstall VS Code by running the following:

```
brew cask uninstall visual-studio-code
```

But I bet we won't want to.

That's it for this chapter. Let's review what we've learned.

Summary

In this chapter, we saw that there is no standard way to install PowerShell and VS Code. We saw how to use package managers to install PowerShell 7 on Ubuntu and RHEL, and then used the direct download method to install on an older version of Linux: CentOS 7.

After that, we looked at how we can install VS Code on Linux, with a practical example on CentOS 7, again.

We looked at a number of ways PowerShell on Linux differs from running PowerShell on Windows, including the filesystem, capitalization, and the use of aliases.

We spent some time on an important topic: how we can remote into Linux machines using SSH. The use of Linux as a desktop is rare, and the majority of work carried out on Linux machines is over remote sessions on SSH, whether that is with PowerShell or directly into a Bash terminal.

Finally, we had a quick tour of ways of installing PowerShell and VS Code on macOS. We saw that it was very easy to both install and uninstall these applications using the free open source package manager, Homebrew.

In the next chapter, we're going to look at running PowerShell on a different processor, ARM, and the associated operating system, Raspbian.

Exercises

1. Where would we go to get support installing PowerShell on Kali Linux?

2. Which command are we calling when we type `ls` into a PowerShell session on Linux?

3. Which file path separator does PowerShell use on Linux?

4. How could we easily tell if we were working on a macOS machine?

5. How would we run a PowerShell script with root privileges in Linux?

6. Which cmdlet and parameter would we use to create a new remote session to a Linux machine?

7. Which cmdlet and parameter would we use to avoid having to send a password across the network?

8. What does `scp` do?

9. What is Ed25519?

Further reading

- *Install PowerShell on Linux*:

  ```
  https://learn.microsoft.com/en-us/powershell/scripting/install/
  installing-powershell-on-linux
  ```

- *Installing PowerShell on Ubuntu*:

  ```
  https://learn.microsoft.com/en-us/powershell/scripting/install/
  install-ubuntu
  ```

- *Installing PowerShell on Red Hat Enterprise Linux (RHEL)*:

  ```
  https://learn.microsoft.com/en-us/powershell/scripting/install/
  install-rhel
  ```

- *Installing PowerShell on macOS*:

  https://learn.microsoft.com/en-us/powershell/scripting/install/installing-powershell-on-macos

- *Running Visual Studio Code on macOS*:

  https://code.visualstudio.com/docs/setup/mac

- *PowerShell remoting over SSH*:

  https://learn.microsoft.com/en-us/powershell/scripting/learn/remoting/ssh-remoting-in-powershell

- *Get started with OpenSSH for Windows*:

  https://learn.microsoft.com/en-us/windows-server/administration/openssh/openssh_install_firstuse?tabs=gui

- *OpenSSH Server configuration for Windows Server and Windows*:

  https://learn.microsoft.com/en-us/windows-server/administration/openssh/openssh_server_configuration

15
PowerShell 7 and the Raspberry Pi

This is one of the chapters I've looked forward to writing the most. I've got a house full of Raspberry Pis (and Arduinos, micro:bits, and ESP32s…). I use them to teach coding to school kids (and adults), as well as to run adblockers, media centers, wildlife cameras, and horticultural systems. I've got one with buttons that randomly selects episodes of my favorite radio shows and plays them (called the Shendomizer). Mostly, I program them with Python, but PowerShell is also an option. We can even install a stripped-down version of Windows 10 on them, but we won't cover that in this book. Instead, we'll look at how to install PowerShell 7 and **Visual Studio (VS)** Code, how to connect remotely to a headless Pi over Wi-Fi using SSH with both PowerShell and VS Code, the default module for working with PowerShell on the Raspberry Pi, and finish up by creating a script to accomplish the first steps in physical computing: getting an LED to blink on and off.

The main topics we'll cover in this chapter are as follows:

- Introduction to the Raspberry Pi
- Installing PowerShell and VS Code
- Connecting remotely to the Pi
- Running PowerShell on Raspberry Pi OS
- Simple physical computing

Technical requirements

For this chapter, we will need a Raspberry Pi with a power supply, screen, keyboard and mouse, and the requisite cables. Some of this chapter has been written on the Pi 400, which is a handy version of the Pi that's installed on a keyboard with everything we need except a monitor. Other parts have been written using a Raspberry Pi 3 single-board computer.

Note that a Pi Zero or Pi Pico will not work. They use a different ARM chip version, so the architecture won't work with .NET.

For simple automation, we'll need the following:

- A breadboard

- An LED

- A 300-400 Ohm resistor (but 250-500 will work)

- Two male-to-female jumper cables

Introduction to the Raspberry Pi

The Raspberry Pi is a small, affordable, and versatile single-board computer developed by the Raspberry Pi Foundation in the UK. Its primary goal was to promote the teaching of basic computer science in schools and developing countries. However, its accessibility, low cost, and ease of use have made it incredibly popular among hobbyists, educators, and professionals for various applications, from learning programming to building complex projects.

It's designed to be a blank slate, allowing users to understand the basics of hardware and software interactions. This computer is essentially a tiny, self-contained PC that can be used for many of the same tasks we might use a desktop or laptop PC for, such as browsing the internet, word processing, and playing games. Moreover, its **general-purpose input/output (GPIO)** pins enable it to interact with external hardware, making it ideal for electronics projects and **Internet of Things (IoT)** applications.

Over the years, several models of the Raspberry Pi have been released, each improving on its predecessor. The latest model is the Raspberry Pi 4 Model B. This model has a 64-bit quad-core ARM Cortex-A72 CPU, offering processing speeds of up to 1.5 GHz. It comes in variants that have 2 GB, 4 GB, or 8 GB of LPDDR4-3200 SDRAM. For connectivity, it includes Gigabit Ethernet, Bluetooth 5.0, and dual-band Wi-Fi (2.4G Hz and 5.0 GHz). It also has two USB 3.0 ports, two USB 2.0 ports, two micro HDMI ports supporting up to 4K resolution, and a USB-C port for power.

The Raspberry Pi can run various **operating systems (OSs)**, with Raspberry Pi OS (formerly Raspbian) being the most popular. This Debian-based OS is optimized for the Raspberry Pi hardware and comes pre-loaded with essential tools, programming languages, and applications. Users can also install different flavors of Linux and even a version of Windows 10 IoT Core. The OS can be installed by flashing an image to a MicroSD card.

For programming, Python is the most commonly used language due to its simplicity and power. However, the Raspberry Pi supports numerous other languages, such as JavaScript, PHP, C++, Java, and, most importantly for us, PowerShell 7. Its versatility makes it a valuable tool for software development, especially in IoT and embedded systems.

The Raspberry Pi's range of use cases is vast. In education, it's used to teach programming, computer science fundamentals, and even hardware design. Hobbyists use it for projects such as retro gaming consoles, media centers, and home automation systems. In professional settings, it serves as a cost-effective tool for prototyping, data collection, and automation. We can also use it for parallel computing; an example of this is the OctaPi project run by GCHQ in the UK. Some institutions even use it as a supercomputer; the Los Alamos National Laboratory built a 750-node high-performance computer out of Pis.

The Raspberry Pi ecosystem has expanded over the years since its release in 2012. There are three separate series: the Pi, the Pi Zero, developed as a lightweight and even cheaper alternative that can be dedicated to a single project and left to run (I have several Pi Zero wildlife cameras running on rechargeable batteries), and the Pi Pico, an alternative to the popular Arduino single chipboard. PowerShell 7 will only run on the full-fat Pi, not the Pi Zero or Pico. These smaller alternatives run on ARMv6 chip designs; .NET, and therefore PowerShell 7, requires an ARMv7 or ARMv8 chip, as found in the Pi 2, 3, and 4. This is partly because the ARMv6 is lower-powered, but also because nobody wants to be designing for old hardware, do they?

Right. Shall we get on and install PowerShell on a Pi?

Installing PowerShell 7 and VS Code

Raspberry Pi OS is a Linux distro based on Debian, the same as Ubuntu, so the Ubuntu instructions we followed in *Chapter 14, PowerShell 7 for Linux and macOS*, will work, but there's an even easier way to do it.

Installing PowerShell

If we go to the *Community support for PowerShell on Linux* page at `https://learn.microsoft.com/en-us/powershell/scripting/install/community-support`, we'll find a very handy script that will install PowerShell for us, as shown in the following screenshot:

```sh
sh                                                            Copy

####################################
# Prerequisites

# Update package lists
sudo apt-get update

# Install dependencies
sudo apt-get install jq libssl1.1 libunwind8 -y

####################################
# Download and extract PowerShell
```

Figure 15.1 – The Raspberry Pi OS install script

If we click the **Copy** button in the top-right corner of the script box, then we can simply open a terminal window on the Raspberry Pi and right-click to paste it into the terminal, as shown here:

Figure 15.2 – Installing PowerShell by pasting the script into the terminal

Once we've pasted it, all we have to do is press *Enter* on the line highlighted in the preceding screenshot, at which point the script will work through, install, and then start PowerShell.

Of course, that may be prone to errors, so we might want to actually create a script, check that it's right, and then execute it. To do this, from the terminal prompt, type the following:

```
nano
```

This will open the nano text editor. Paste the script into nano, as shown here:

```
  GNU nano 7.2                              ./installPosh.sh *
###################################
# Prerequisites


# Update package lists
sudo apt-get update

# Install dependencies
sudo apt-get install jq libssl1.1 libunwind8 -y

####################################
# Download and extract PowerShell

# Grab the latest tar.gz
bits=$(getconf LONG_BIT)
release=$(curl -sL https://api.github.com/repos/PowerShell/PowerShell/releases/latest)
package=$(echo $release | jq -r ".assets[].browser_download_url" | grep "linux-arm${bits}.tar.gz")
wget $package

# Make folder to put powershell
mkdir ~/powershell

# Unpack the tar.gz file
tar -xvf "./${package##*/}" -C ~/powershell

# Start PowerShell
Save modified buffer?
 Y Yes
 N No                    ^C Cancel
```

Figure 15.3 – Creating a PowerShell install script in nano

Check that you've pasted it correctly, and then save it by pressing *Ctrl* + *X*, typing *Y* when asked to save it, and then typing a suitable filename – I've called mine `installPosh.sh`. Once we've returned to the terminal prompt, we can run the script by typing the following:

```
sudo bash ./installPosh.sh
```

Again, we'll be taken straight to PowerShell. Now, let's look at installing VS Code.

Installing VS Code

Getting VS Code onto our Pi is even easier. VS Code is included in the official repositories for Raspberry Pi OS, so we don't need to manually download files or set up alternative repositories – we can just open the terminal and type the following:

```
sudo apt-get update
sudo apt install code
```

Once we've done this, after a few minutes, VS Code will appear on our machine alongside a lot of chatter:

Figure 15.4 – Installing and starting VS Code on the Raspberry Pi

We can either type `code` in the terminal, or we can find it in the **Programming** subsection of the applications menu by clicking on the raspberry icon in the top-left corner.

Now, let's look at the most common way I use the Raspberry Pi: remotely.

Connecting remotely to the Pi

While it's quite common to see the Raspberry Pi used as a PC in educational settings, it's more likely that we'll want to use it as a server of some sort, and therefore connect to it remotely, rather than set it up with its own monitor, mouse and keyboard. This is called **headless** mode, and it's what we're going to look at next.

Working with a headless Pi

To use a headless Pi, we'll need to set it up so that we have a way of connecting it to the network and accessing it remotely. We're going to configure a new Pi (or just rebuild the old one) to access a wireless network, and we're going to use SSH for access, which we saw in *Chapter 14, PowerShell 7 for Linux and macOS*. We can set up both of these things with the Raspberry Pi Imager tool on the Pi website at `https://www.raspberrypi.com/software/`. Note that a lot of documentation on the internet suggests that we might want to create and edit a file called `wpa_supplicant.conf`. This is true for older versions of Raspberry Pi OS and Raspbian, but recent versions won't use it.

Download the appropriate version of the installer for the OS we are going to run it from – in my case, Windows – and install it.

When we run it, we may experience an OpenGL error if we haven't kept our graphics drivers up to date, so make sure that the latest drivers are installed.

We will also need a microSD card ready to be imaged.

When we open the imager tool, we'll be asked what device we want to install on, what OS we want, and what storage we are going to use, as shown here:

Figure 15.5 – The Raspberry Pi Imager tool

In my case, I'm installing on a Raspberry Pi 4, I want the latest 64-bit OS, and I would like the image to be written to the SDHC card in my laptop. When we click **NEXT**, we'll be asked if we'd like to apply OS customization settings. Yes. Yes, we would. Click **Edit Settings**; we'll see the **OS Customisation** dialog box open on the **GENERAL** tab, as shown here:

Figure 15.6 – Customizing our Raspberry Pi OS

In the preceding screenshot, I have set my hostname, the username and password I want to use on the Pi, and, most importantly, I've configured the wireless LAN settings to automatically connect to the Wi-Fi network I want to use, ShedWifi, which is the Wi-Fi network in my shed. Now, we need to switch to the **SERVICES** tab to enable SSH. By default, when we click on **Enable SSH**, it will select **Use password authentication**. I'm sticking with that, but we could configure it to **Allow public-key authentication only**. If we click **Save**, we will be warned that all the data on our destination SDHC card will be overwritten and asked to confirm this. Once we do, after a few minutes, we'll get a **Write Successful** popup telling us that we can remove the SDHC card. Let's do just that – put it in the Pi and power it up. The **SERVICES** tab is shown in the following screenshot:

Figure 15.7 – The Raspberry Pi Imager SERVICES tab

Once the Pi has booted up, we should be able to see it on the network if our client is on the same subnet. To test this, in a PowerShell session on our client, type the following:

```
Test-NetConnection <pi hostname> -InformationLevel Detailed
```

We should see the IPv6 and IPv4 addresses, as well as a lot of other information:

```
PS C:\Users\nickp> Test-NetConnection "poshpi" -InformationLevel Detailed

ComputerName           : poshpi
RemoteAddress          : fe80::a14:5ca5:c2b4:d30e%19
NameResolutionResults  : fe80::a14:5ca5:c2b4:d30e%19
                         192.168.68.136
InterfaceAlias         : Wi-Fi
SourceAddress          : fe80::6b81:78a:4831:2420%19
NetRoute (NextHop)     : ::
PingSucceeded          : True
PingReplyDetails (RTT) : 2 ms
```

Figure 15.8 – Confirming the presence of my Pi

As we can see, my Pi has got its IP addresses, as expected, and I can now connect to it.

Let's try it out.

Connecting to the Pi with PowerShell

In the PowerShell session on the client, type the following:

```
ssh <pi hostname>
```

Alternatively, you can type the following if your usernames are different on the client and the host:

```
Ssh <username>@<hostname>
```

The following screenshot shows what the process looks like:

```
PS C:\Users\nickp> ssh poshpi
The authenticity of host 'poshpi (fe80.:a14:5ca5:c2b4:d30e%19)' can't be established.
ECDSA key fingerprint is SHA256:vtSTilgRFD1vIVZpV+Kdlzth8ed6FVdCOgp5OMZBBIs.
Are you sure you want to continue connecting (yes/no/[fingerprint])? yes
Warning: Permanently added 'poshpi' (ECDSA) to the list of known hosts.
nickp@poshpi's password:
Linux poshpi 6.1.0-rpi7-rpi-v8   SMP PREEMPT Debian 1:6.1.63-1+rpt1 (2023-11-24) aarch64

The programs included with the Debian GNU/Linux system are free software;
the exact distribution terms for each program are described in the
individual files in /usr/share/doc/*/copyright.

Debian GNU/Linux comes with ABSOLUTELY NO WARRANTY, to the extent
permitted by applicable law.
Last login: Wed Jan  3 21:07:16 2024 from fe80::6b81:78a:4831:2420%wlan0
nickp@poshpi:~ $
```

Figure 15.9 – Using SSH to connect to the Pi

On line 1, we started an SSH session to the Pi with the `ssh poshpi` command.

On line 2, we were prompted to agree to connect since the authenticity of the Pi can't be determined. We're probably OK to type `yes` here; note that typing `Y` on its own won't work.

On line 3, we're asked to input the password for the user – in my case, this is `nickp`.

On line 4, we're presented with the bash prompt from the Pi – that is, `nickp@poshpi.local:~ $`.

Now, we need to install PowerShell. We can do that in the same way we did it earlier – that is, by copying the contents of the Microsoft script into the command line or creating a bash script with it in nano. Once it's finished, we can start PowerShell with the following command:

```
~/powershell/pwsh
```

Alternatively, we can create a **symbolic link (symlink)**, like this:

```
sudo ln -s ~/powershell/pwsh /usr/bin/pwsh
```

Then, all we need to type in the future is pwsh, like so:

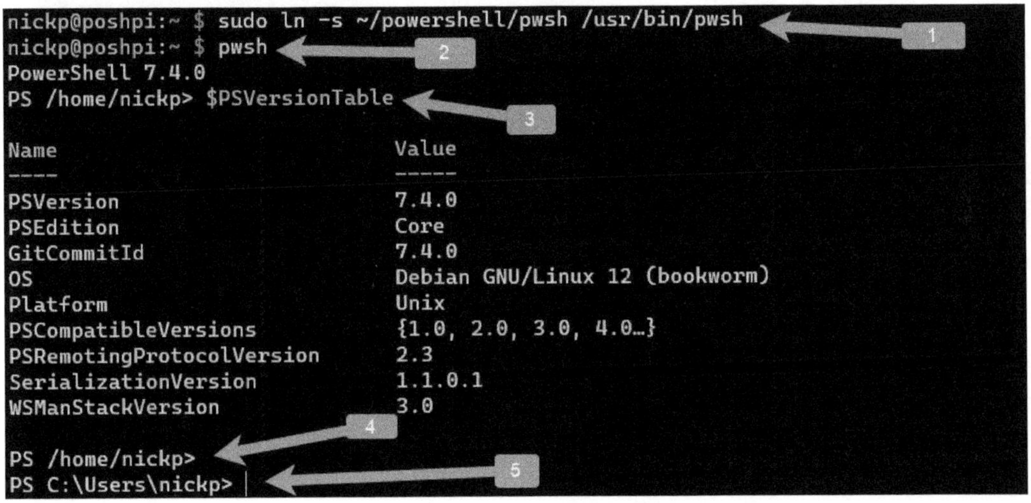

Figure 15.10 – Setting up a symlink to run PowerShell

On line 1, we created a symlink, while on line 2, we started PowerShell.

On line 3, we're running PowerShell on Linux via the PS /home/nickp> prompt; we can call the $PSVersionTable variable to see what version of PowerShell we're running.

Finally, on line 4, we used *Ctrl + Break* to drop out of the SSH session and go back to the PowerShell session running on the Windows client – PS C:\users\nickp> – on line 5. We can also use *Ctrl + D* to log out of the session.

Great! Let's look at another way to connect to our headless Pi: with VS Code.

Connecting to the Pi with VS Code

This method will work with any machine we want to connect to with SSH, including Linux. We're going to use a VS Code extension called **Remote - SSH**. Open VS Code on the client, click the extensions icon on the left sidebar (this looks like a stack of boxes), then type Remote-SSH in the search bar, as shown here:

Figure 15.11 – Installing the Remote – SSH extension

Once you've found the extension, click on it, then click **Install** in the center pane, as shown in the preceding screenshot.

Once we've done this, we've have a desktop icon in the left-hand sidebar. We can click on that to open the **Remote Explorer** window and set up an SSH connection to the Pi. We'll be asked to choose what sort of remote we want – a remote machine or a WSL target. We want a remote machine, so select that, and then click on **SSH**:

Figure 15.12 – Selecting SSH

Click on the + icon on the right-hand side, then enter `ssh <username>@<hostname>`. In my case, I typed the following and pressed *Enter*:

```
ssh nickp@poshpi
```

Next, we'll be asked to choose an SSH config file to update. I'm updating my personal file, `C:\Users\nickp\.ssh\config`. Then, we'll see a message box telling us **Host added!**. In the **REMOTE EXPLORER** area, click the refresh icon next to **REMOTES (TUNNELS/SSH)**, as highlighted in green in *Figure 15.13*; we should see our new host appear in the **SSH** subsection with two icons next to it – one to open the host in the existing window, which is depicted with an arrow, and another to open in a new window, as highlighted in red. Click the *Connect in a New Window* icon:

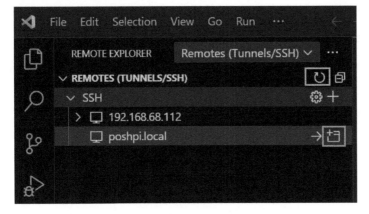

Figure 15.13 – Opening a connection to the Pi

Next, we'll be asked to select the platform of the remote host; it's Linux. We'll also need to enter the password. Once we've done that, we'll need to wait a minute or two while everything gets set up and dismiss a message window or two. Finally, we'll have a new window connected to our Pi; we know this because in the bottom-left corner is a box saying **SSH: <hostname>**. Everything we do in this window is happening on the Pi. Cool, eh? This means that instead of writing our scripts on our client and transferring them to the Pi, we can write them directly to the Pi from VS Code.

So, that's us ready to go. We can use PowerShell in the same way we've been doing throughout this book on the Pi, but that's not really what I use the Raspberry Pi for. Next, we'll look at how we can use PowerShell on the Pi.

Running PowerShell on Raspberry Pi OS

The beauty of the Raspberry Pi is just how many ways you can connect it to the outside world, from joystick controllers to cameras to sensors to motors to… ooh… *everything*. In this chapter, we're going to look at using GPIO pins to make an LED blink, but first, we need to learn how we can interact with the GPIO. There are two options, neither of them particularly well supported. The better option is to install a new OS: Windows 10 IoT Core. That would take a chapter or two in itself, and it doesn't really address the topic of running PowerShell on Raspberry Pi OS. The other way is to use the PowerShell IoT module. This hasn't been updated since about 2020 and doesn't appear to work with later versions of the Pi 4B, but it works reasonably well on older ones, and we can live in hope that it will be updated at some point. I'm going to take advantage of a Pi 3B I've got in my drawer.

Installing the IoT module

We're working with hardware here, so we need to start PowerShell with root privileges by typing the following:

```
sudo pwsh
```

Once we're in PowerShell, we can install the module as we usually do:

```
Install-Module Microsoft.powershell.iot
```

Finally, we'll probably want to clone the repository from GitHub so that we have access to the examples. We can do this with the following command:

```
git clone https://github.com/PowerShell/PowerShell-IoT.git
```

This will install all the code in the GitHub repository into a new folder below our chosen folder:

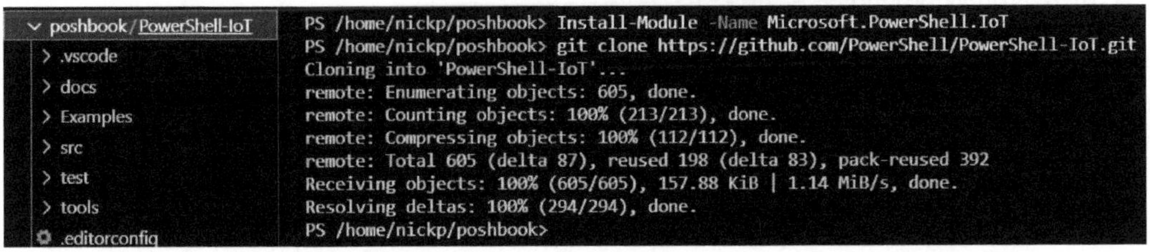

Figure 15.14 – Installing the PowerShell IoT module and cloning the GitHub repository

This gives us access to all the example modules in the `Examples` folder. This includes some interesting tools that we can use with various sensors, such as the BME280 environmental sensor.

The next step is to import the module and check that it's working:

```
Import-Module Microsoft.PowerShell.IoT
Get-GpioPin 15
```

And with a bit of luck, we'll see something similar to the following:

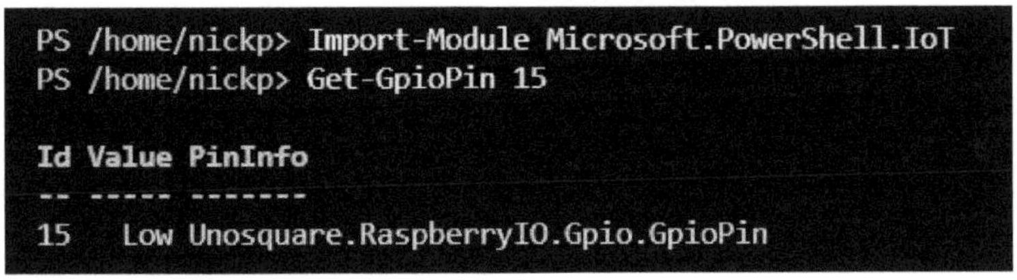

Figure 15.15 – Importing the module and checking the voltage on a given GPIO pin

Shall we explore the cmdlets we get in this module?

Exploring the IoT module

Inside the IoT module, there are six cmdlets for working with the three I/O interfaces on the Pi: simple GPIO, I2C, and **Synchronous Peripheral Interface** (**SPI**). Confusingly, all three interfaces use the GPIO pins. This can sometimes make it difficult to choose which pins we wish to use for what purpose:

- Simple GPIO reads or sets the voltage on a specific GPIO pin with a pair of cmdlets called `Get-GpioPin` and `Set-GpioPin`. We'll be using this shortly.

- I2C uses the **Inter-Integrated Circuit** (**I2C**) protocol developed by Philips, which allows our Pi (the controller) to communicate with multiple peripheral devices. Because we can have multiple devices, as well as `Get-I2CRegister` and `Set-I2CRegister`, there is also a `Get-I2CDevice` cmdlet.

- Finally, there is the SPI. This is quite complex, and we're not going to cover it in this book. There is only one cmdlet: `Send-SPIData`.

Let's take a closer look at the five cmdlets we're going to use the most. The helpfiles for these cmdlets can be found in the `/home/<username>/PowerShell-IoT/docs/help/` folder, but let's cover their basic uses here:

- `Get-GpioPin`: This cmdlet gets the voltage from a specified GPIO pin. There are three parameters:

    - `-Id`, which takes an Int32 value and specifies which GPIO pin we want to look at.

    - `-PullMode`, which may be set to `Off`, `PullDown`, or `PullUp`, and may be needed with some chipsets, but not the Pi. The default value is `Null`.

    - A `-Raw` switch, which returns a value of `High` or `Low`.

- `Set-GpioPin`: This cmdlet sets the voltage on a specified pin to `High` or `Low`. It has three parameters:

    - `-Id`, which takes an `Int32` value and specifies the pin.

    - `-Value`, which takes either `High` or `Low`.

    - `-PassThru`, which, by default, results in the cmdlet returning nothing. If we want it to return a PowerShell object confirming that the value was set, then we can use this parameter.

- `Get-I2CDevice`: This cmdlet creates an I2C device object with a friendly name that we can then use with the `*-I2Cregister` cmdlets. It has two parameters:

    - `-Id`, which takes an `Int32` value and specifies the address of the device

    - `-FriendlyName`, which we use to assign a string to the device

- `Get-I2Cregister`: This cmdlet gets the value held in a register on a particular device. There are four parameters:

    - `-Device`, which takes an I2C device object

    - `-Register`, which takes a `Uint16` value that specifies the register on the device we want to read

    - `-Raw`, which returns the value stored in the register, rather than an `I2CdeviceRegisterData` object

    - `-Bytecount`, which takes a byte value and specifies the number of bytes expected in the data

- `Set-I2Cregister`: This cmdlet sets the register value on a device. There are four parameters:

  - `-Device`, which takes an I2C device object.

  - `-Register`, which takes a `Uint16` value that specifies the register on the device we want to set.

  - `-Data`, a value in bytes to be written to the register.

  - `-PassThru`, which, by default, results in the cmdlet returning nothing. If we want it to return a PowerShell object confirming that the value was set, then we can use this parameter.

And that's it. The best way to see how they work is to get on and play with them.

Simple physical computing

Physical computing on the Raspberry Pi uses the GPIO pins on the right of the board, as shown here:

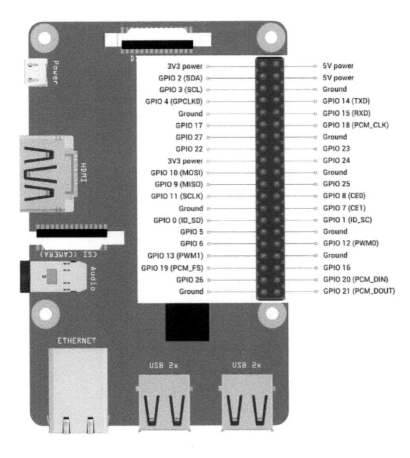

Figure 15.16 – The GPIO pins of the Raspberry Pi

The important things to remember are that the ground pins are negative and the voltage pins, 3V3 and 5V, are positive and always on. While the GPIO pins may have secondary specialist purposes, they are the ones we can turn on and off – they will deliver a positive current.

When we're learning a new programming language, we start with the simplest possible program – *Hello World*:

```
Write-Output "Hello World"
```

In Python, we can write the following:

```
print("Hello World")
```

Physical computing is slightly different – we write a program to make an LED blink on and off. It doesn't seem to matter what the platform is; this is where we start. For instance, the program to get an Arduino to blink an LED is written in C and looks like this:

```
void setup() {
    pinMode(LED_BUILTIN, OUTPUT);
}
void loop() {
  digitalWrite(LED_BUILTIN, HIGH);
  delay(1000);
  digitalWrite(LED_BUILTIN, LOW);
  delay(1000);
}
```

void setup() initializes the onboard LED as an output and runs once each time the Arduino is reset. The void loop() command sets up a loop that runs continuously while the Arduino is switched on (void just tells the Arduino not to produce an output). The digitalwrite() commands set the voltage to the output as HIGH (on) or LOW (off). This looks pretty similar on the Raspberry Pi in Python:

```
From RPi.gpio import LED
Red_led = LED(17)
Red_led.blink(on_time=1, off_time=1)
```

Let's try it in PowerShell. First, we'll need to set up our hardware according to the following diagram:

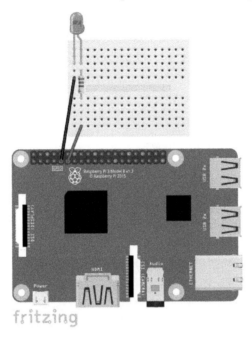

Figure 15.17 – How to set up the components

The LED will have two legs on it, one longer than the other. The longer leg needs to be connected to the positive side of the circuit, and the shorter leg needs to be on the negative or ground side. The current the Pi sends is too high for the LED, so we need to use a resistor of around 300-400 Ohms to drop it slightly. More than 1K Ohms will possibly stop the LED from lighting, and less than 200 risks burning it out, if it's cheap. The breadboard sockets are connected in columns of five, so the resistor spans two columns here.

Now, we need to write some PowerShell code to turn the LED on and off. Let's connect to the Pi using VS Code SSH remoting and open a new document. Call it `blink.ps1`.

Let's start by importing the IoT module:

```
Import-Module Microsoft.PowerShell.IoT
```

Now, we're going to need a loop that always runs:

```
While ($true) {
}
```

In this loop, we're going to need to turn the LED on and off using `Set-GpioPin`. If you followed the preceding diagram, you should be using pin 17.

We'll also need to use `Start-Sleep` to wait between each command; otherwise, we'll blow the LED up:

```
Import-Module Microsoft.PowerShell.IoT
while ($true) {
    Set-GpioPin -Id 17 -Value "High"
    Write-Host "LED on"
    Start-Sleep 1
    Set-GpioPin -Id 17 -Value "Low"
    Write-Host "LED off"
    Start-Sleep 1
}
```

I've added a couple of output lines here so that I can reasonably demonstrate this without using a YouTube link. Running it looks like this in VS Code:

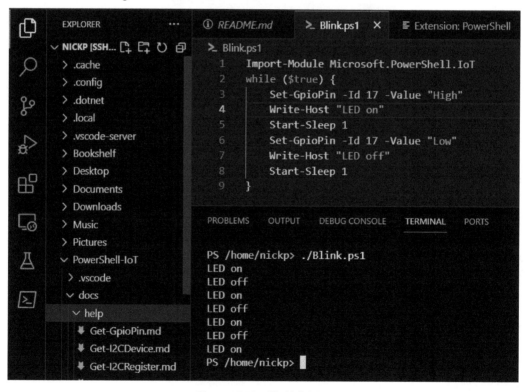

Figure 15.18 – Blinkin' LEDs

As we can see, the LED's state changes once a second; this will continue until the script is stopped manually. We can see how it compares to the programs we saw for the Arduino, in C, and the Python program.

There's also an example LED module in the `Examples` folder – it's well worth taking a look to see how they've done it in there.

That about wraps it up for this chapter. Let's summarize what we've learned.

Summary

We started this chapter by taking a quick look at the Raspberry Pi, including what it does, what it was designed to do, and how people use it. We looked at the different series; the main B series single board computers, the Zero mini version, and the Pico single chip board. We learned that we can only install PowerShell on the B series since the architecture of the chip is wrong on the Zero and Pico series.

Next, we looked at different ways of installing PowerShell on the Pi using a script provided by Microsoft. Then, we saw how easy it is to install VS Code on the Pi since it is included in the official Raspberry Pi repositories.

While there are Raspberry Pi models that are suitable as desktop PC replacements, most people will use the Raspberry Pi without a screen or mouse – that is, in headless mode. We looked at how to set up a Raspberry Pi in headless mode, and then how to connect to it from PowerShell with SSH, before going on to look at a convenient way to work directly on the Pi with VS Code.

Then, we discussed one of the most popular use cases for the Pi: physical computing. This is where we interact with sensors and objects in the physical world. We looked at the Microsoft module for interacting with the GPIO on the Raspberry Pi and finished up with a script that can be used to make an LED blink on and off.

That's it for the environments we're going to look at. In the next and final chapter, we're going to look at how we can access the .NET system that PowerShell is built on and look at what our next steps could be.

Questions

1. Why can't we install PowerShell on the Raspberry Pi Zero or Pico?
2. Where is the SSH configuration stored for VS Code on a Windows machine?
3. What is the PowerShell cmdlet for testing network connectivity to another device from the Raspberry Pi?
4. How do you create an SSH connection to a headless Pi from PowerShell?
5. We've saved our install script as `Install.sh`. How do we run it?
6. Why might we want to create a symlink to the `pwsh` executable?

7. How might we create a symlink to pwsh?

8. How would we get a value of High or Low from a GPIO pin?

9. What sort of OS is Raspberry Pi OS?

Further reading

- OctaPi cluster computer: https://projects.Raspberrypi.org/en/projects/build-an-octapi

- Oracle's 1050-node Pi supercomputer: https://blogs.oracle.com/developers/post/building-the-worlds-largest-Raspberry-pi-cluster

- Community support for PowerShell on Linux: https://learn.microsoft.com/en-us/powershell/scripting/install/community-support

- PowerShell on ARM processors: https://learn.microsoft.com/en-us/powershell/scripting/install/powershell-on-arm

- VS Code on the Pi: https://code.visualstudio.com/docs/setup/raspberry-pi

- VS Code remote SSH: https://code.visualstudio.com/docs/remote/ssh-tutorial

- PowerShell IoT module on GitHub: https://github.com/PowerShell/PowerShell-IoT

- An overview of Windows for IoT: https://learn.microsoft.com/en-us/windows/iot/product-family/windows-iot

- Windows 10 IoT Core on Raspberry Pi:

  - https://cdn-learn.adafruit.com/downloads/pdf/getting-started-with-windows-iot-on-raspberry-pi.pdf

  - https://devblogs.microsoft.com/premier-developer/getting-started-with-windows-10-iot-core-raspberry-pi-3b/

- Raspberry Pi Configuration documentation: https://www.raspberrypi.com/documentation/computers/configuration.html

- I2C overview:

  - https://en.wikipedia.org/wiki/I%C2%B2C

  - https://learn.sparkfun.com/tutorials/i2c/all

- SPI overview: https://learn.sparkfun.com/tutorials/serial-peripheral-interface-spi/all

16
Working with PowerShell and .NET

Here we are then, the last chapter. We're going to look at the product that PowerShell 7 is built on, .NET, and how we can use it to expand the range of things we can do in PowerShell. Note that this chapter can't be anything more than a whistlestop tour; .NET is a huge subject, and there are many, many more books written for it than there are for PowerShell. PowerShell is just one application written on .NET, and it only touches a subset of the things that we can do with .NET. That being said, let's have a look at how it works and some of the exciting things we can use it for.

The main topics we will cover in this chapter are as follows:

- Exploring .NET
- The components of .NET
- Working with .NET in PowerShell
- Using .NET

Exploring .NET

.NET (**dot-net**) is a software framework. It's free and open source and can be used to write web applications, command-line applications, and applications that run in a **Graphical User Interface (GUI)**. It is based on the proprietary coded .NET Framework, which is the software framework that the Windows operating system uses. It can be used with a range of programming languages, including C#, F#, and Visual Basic .NET. Let's unpack all that, shall we?

Software frameworks explained

A software framework is a tool for constructing applications. Some frameworks are written for specific purposes and specific languages; AngularJS is a framework for developing the frontends of web applications in JavaScript. PhaserJS is a game development framework, again for JavaScript. While frameworks contain many libraries, they differ from libraries in that libraries provide tools for our code that we can use in any way we like; with a framework, we need to work within the structure. The basics of an application are provided; we need to provide the specifics.

.NET implements a **Common Language Infrastructure** (**CLI**) that allows different high-level languages (such as C#) to be used on multiple operating system platforms, without needing to be rewritten for each architecture; this is how PowerShell 7 can work on Intel and ARM processors. By installing the correct version of .NET, our PowerShell code can then run anywhere.

A .NET component called **CoreFX** houses the .NET libraries of classes, interfaces, and value types in a **Framework Class Library**. .NET provides more than just libraries, though. .NET applications run in a virtual machine called **CoreCLR**, in the same way that Java applications run inside the Java Virtual Machine.

Common language infrastructure

The CLI is an open technical standard developed by Microsoft and is largely only found in variations of .NET, although there is an open development platform called **Mono** that uses it as well. The CLI specifies five things:

- **Common Type System** (**CTS**) – the set of types that can be accessed by programming languages using the framework.

- **Metadata**, which is used to describe the program structure.

- **Common Language Specification** (**CLS**) – rules for using the framework.

- **Virtual Execution System** (**VES**) – this loads and executes applications. It uses metadata to run code generated in compliant languages at runtime, compiling them into a platform-agnostic **Common Intermediate Language** (**CIL**), which is then compiled to a platform-specific machine language in real time. In .NET, the VES is implemented in the CoreCLR component.

- **Standard libraries**, which provide common functions, such as accessing networks and files.

Let's look at the CoreCLR component.

Common language runtime – CoreCLR

CoreCLR provides a common language runtime, which is a layer that sits between the application and the operating system. It is similar in principle to the PowerShell program; .NET applications need .NET to be running on the machine to interpret the application code as machine code. This means PowerShell needs .NET to be running, as PowerShell is a .NET application.

However, CoreCLR doesn't just provide a runtime. It also includes additional services such as memory management (allocating portions of virtual memory to applications), garbage collection (recovering unused memory that is no longer needed), and thread management. This means that when we use .NET to write applications, we don't need to worry about memory leaks or memory addressing errors, as all that is handled for us by CoreCLR.

Happily, we don't need to know much about how CoreCLR works to use .NET with PowerShell. Most of what we are interested in is held in the libraries – CoreFX.

Framework Class Library – CoreFX

CoreFX contains the class libraries that .NET uses, which include types, functions, and classes. All the PowerShell data types, for instance, are a subset of the available .NET types. We've seen this already; in *Chapter 4, PowerShell Variables and Data Structures*, we saw that changing the contents of a PowerShell array was resource-intensive because each time we change an array, we create a new one and delete the old one. We saw that one of the solutions to this was to use a .NET type that is not available natively inside PowerShell, ArrayList, like this:

```
$ArrayList = [System.Collections.ArrayList]@()
1..10000 | ForEach-Object { $Null = $ArrayList.Add($_) }
```

We use the [System.Collections.ArrayList] full .NET type to set the array as ArrayList. Sometimes, working with .NET really is that easy.

.NET history

.NET Framework was first released in 2002 and was intended to create Windows applications. It introduced the Microsoft concept of **managed code**, code that would only interact with the CLI. Managed code could be more tightly controlled, both in terms of resource use and security, and it was also less prone to causing system crashes – the dreaded Blue Screen of Death – because it only touched the CLR, not the underlying operating system. In time, many of Microsoft's most popular applications, such as Microsoft Exchange Server, were written in managed code and required .NET Framework to run. .NET Framework will only run on Windows and contains many Windows-specific features.

In 2014, Microsoft released .NET Core, an open source, cross-platform implementation of the CLI. This shared many features of .NET Framework but not all of them, and similarly, it contained many features that were not implemented in .NET Framework, notably the ability to run on different operating systems. In 2022, Microsoft released a new version of .NET Core, simply called .NET 5; the intention was that .NET would eventually overtake .NET Framework. As happened with PowerShell and Windows PowerShell, in practice, both versions now exist side by side. The latest release of .NET Framework, at the time of writing, is version 4.8.1 in August 2022, whereas .NET is released annually, around November; the latest version is .NET 8.0, released in November 2023.

So, what can we use .NET for? Let's take a look.

The uses of .NET

.NET Framework was developed to create Windows applications – while we can use it for command-line programs, it includes the **Windows Presentation Foundation** (**WPF**) framework, ASP.NET (for internet applications), and Windows Forms for graphical applications.

The current iteration of .NET includes libraries for cloud-native applications and serverless functions on Azure, cross-platform desktop applications and games, mobile apps using .NET **Multi Application User Interface** (**MAUI**), machine learning applications with ML.NET, and Internet of Things applications with .NET IoT.

The most mature libraries, however, are for Windows, and they include libraries for Windows Desktop apps with WPF, Windows Forms, and the **Universal Windows Platform** (**UWP**) and Windows services libraries that allow us to run applications as services.

It would be easy to write a whole series of books on .NET, and many people have. However, we are mostly interested in how we can use .NET with PowerShell. We are going to focus on the .NET libraries and how we can access their contents from PowerShell, accessing in turn the APIs we wish to work with. Let's start by looking at the structure of the .NET libraries.

The components of .NET

Before we can start using the .NET libraries, we need to understand how they are structured. **Members** (properties, methods, etc.) are contained inside **types**, which in turn are contained in **namespaces**. This is **logical type containment**. There is also **physical type containment**. These logical structures are physically held in **assemblies**. We've already seen many of these components in PowerShell. Let's start with assemblies.

Assemblies

Assemblies are collections of types and the resources needed to support them. They can be either **static**, loaded from a file, or **dynamic**, existing solely in memory. PowerShell will load a number of default assemblies at startup, and then, as we import modules, that list will expand. We can see the list of assemblies we have loaded with the following:

```
[System.AppDomain]::CurrentDomain.GetAssemblies()
```

That will output a table like this:

```
PS C:\Users\nickp> [system.AppDomain]::currentdomain.GetAssemblies()

GAC     Version      Location
---     -------      --------
False   v4.0.30319   C:\Program Files\PowerShell\7\System.Private.CoreLib.dll
False   v4.0.30319   C:\Program Files\PowerShell\7\pwsh.dll
False   v4.0.30319   C:\Program Files\PowerShell\7\System.Runtime.dll
False   v4.0.30319   C:\Program Files\PowerShell\7\Microsoft.PowerShell.ConsoleHost.dll
False   v4.0.30319   C:\Program Files\PowerShell\7\System.Management.Automation.dll
False   v4.0.30319   C:\Program Files\PowerShell\7\System.Threading.Thread.dll
False   v4.0.30319   C:\Program Files\PowerShell\7\System.Runtime.InteropServices.dll
```

Figure 16.1 – Enumerating assemblies

We can see the version and the location of the files that these static assemblies are stored in. There is another column, GAC, which refers to the **Global Assembly Cache**; this is a storage area for assembly files that can be used by any .NET Framework application. Unfortunately, it only works in .NET Framework, so PowerShell 7 doesn't reference it; all assemblies loaded in PowerShell 7 will show a GAC value of False. We can use assemblies that are usually stored in the GAC by installing them with NuGet, the .NET package manager; we just can't access them from the GAC. We can also see that the assemblies are .dll files, which we talked about when discussing binary modules in *Chapter 11, Creating Our First Module*, and we also saw that binary modules are a type of .NET assembly. We can think of loading .NET assemblies as similar to loading binary modules. PowerShell loads a set of default assemblies when it starts, and these assemblies define the types that are available to us. To access other types, we need to load further assemblies.

Types

We first encountered types in *Chapter 4, PowerShell Variables and Data Structures*. The PowerShell types are a subset of the types found in .NET. We used a .NET type earlier in the chapter when we created an ArrayList object. Types are enclosed in square brackets.

> **Type versus class**
>
> In type theory, a type is an abstract concept, whereas a class is a set of instructions to create an object of a given type. An object is of a certain type – for example, a string or an imaginary bike. A class is an implementation of the type. An object is an instance of the class. For instance, we could have multiple different classes of an imaginary bike that would all be of type Imaginary. Bike, but they could all have different features – for example, ape hanger handlebars or drop handlebars. We could then create many instances of each class (i.e., objects) – in this case, imaginary bikes.
>
> In practice, classes are user-defined in PowerShell, whereas types are provided by .NET – except, of course, where that isn't true.

Enumerations

An enumeration is a list of constant values. While we haven't discussed them before, we have certainly used them. In *Chapter 10, Error Handling – Oh No! It's Gone Wrong!*, we saw the `$ErrorActionPreference` automatic variable and how, by changing the value of the variable, we could control how PowerShell handles errors temporarily. We can check the type of the `$ErrorActionPreference` variable by calling the variable `GetType()` method, and we can see that it is a `System.Enum` type in the following screenshot:

```
PS C:\Users\nickp> $ErrorActionPreference.GetType()

IsPublic IsSerial Name                                                BaseType
-------- -------- ----                                                --------
True     True     ActionPreference                                    System.Enum

PS C:\Users\nickp> $ErrorActionPreference.GetType().GetEnumValues()
SilentlyContinue
Stop
Continue
Inquire
Ignore
Suspend
Break
```

Figure 16.2 – How can I set thee? Let me count the ways

We can list out the list of possible values with the `GetEnumValues()` method, and we can see the familiar list of possible values. `$ErrorActionPreference` can only have those values, and we can't change them.

Classes

A class is a logical definition of an object that defines the properties and methods of the object – a recipe. It is an implementation of a type. Back in *Chapter 4, PowerShell Variables and Data Structures*, we created three objects of type `Imaginary.Bike`, by creating the objects and their properties and labeling them as `Imaginary.Bike`. We could also have defined a class of objects called `Imaginary.Bike` with the same properties and methods, using a **constructor** to create actual instances of the class. We use classes when we want to be able to create objects easily and repeatably.

Namespaces

Namespaces are analogous to folders in a filesystem; we saw namespaces used in this context in *Chapter 13, Working With PowerShell 7 and Windows*, when we discussed CIM classes. Most PowerShell types and functions are found in the `System.Management.Automation` namespace. When we interact with the filesystem, we use the System.IO namespace. We don't need to write System when we refer to a namespace in PowerShell, as the System namespace is automatically searched; Management.Automation is functionally the same as System.Management.Automation. Unfortunately, we need to specify the namespace of any type that isn't immediately in the System namespace, like this:

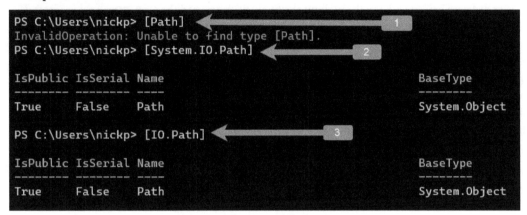

Figure 16.3 – Accessing namespaces

The Path type defines the file path of an object and is in the System.IO namespace. If we try to reference it without specifying the namespace in line 1, we get an error. In line 2, we specify the full namespace, but in line 3, we can see that we don't need to specify the System portion of the namespace, as it is implied.

We can also use the using keyword to load the namespace, like this:

```
using namespace System.IO
```

After running this, we can call the Path type without specifying the namespace, like this:

```
PS C:\Users\nickp> using namespace System.IO
PS C:\Users\nickp> [Path]

IsPublic IsSerial Name                                     BaseType
-------- -------- ----                                     --------
True     False    Path                                     System.Object
```

Figure 16.4 – The using keyword in action

We saw the using keyword in *Chapter 11, Creating Our First Module*, where we learned it was the recommended way of loading modules inside a script. As we can see, we can also use it to load namespaces and assemblies. Unfortunately, in the console, only the most recent using statement is applied, so if we access another namespace with it in the current session, we will lose access to the System.IO namespace. Scripts allow multiple using statements, written at the start of the script;

they can only be preceded by comments. We can load multiple namespaces in the console by using semicolons (;) to separate the using statements.

Members

Types and classes have members; throughout the book, we have used the Get-Member command to examine the properties and methods available on objects, and we've seen that objects are instances of a specific type. .NET types have a member we have not seen before, the constructor. Constructors provide ways of instantiating objects of the given class and take the same name as the class. They don't appear when we run Get-Member against the class and can't be directly called. Constructors may have parameters that we can use to populate the data members of the new object, or they may not; the object is created with a set of null value properties. Constructors may have overloads, where different sets of arguments can be passed when constructing the object. Most .NET classes have an automatic constructor called new(), which is a static method added by PowerShell.

Let's look at an example. The [string] type is immutable; when we change a string, we destroy the old string and create a new one. If we need the string to change frequently, this can cause a performance problem, much the same as the issue we have seen with arrays. There is a class in .NET that defines mutable strings that get around this problem; it's called the StringBuilder class, and objects of this class are of type System.Text.Stringbuilder. If we create a new StringBuilder object with the default automatic constructor, we get an object with three properties, Capacity, MaxCapacity, and Length, in characters. If we call the new() method without the brackets, then we can see a list of the possible overloads:

```
PS C:\Users\nickp> [System.Text.StringBuilder]::new

OverloadDefinitions
-------------------
System.Text.StringBuilder new()
System.Text.StringBuilder new(int capacity)
System.Text.StringBuilder new(string value)
System.Text.StringBuilder new(string value, int capacity)
System.Text.StringBuilder new(string value, int startIndex, int length, int capacity)
System.Text.StringBuilder new(int capacity, int maxCapacity)
```

Figure 16.5 – The overloads of the StringBuilder class

As we can see, we can pass different combinations of arguments to the new() method to construct StringBuilder objects with different properties. Let's try it. Type the following:

```
$string1 = ([System.Text.StringBuilder]::new(32))
$string2 = ([System.Text.StringBuilder]::new('32'))
```

Now, if we call $string1 and $string2, we can see that $string1 is empty and has a capacity of 32. $string2 has a length of 2 and a capacity of 16. That's because we called the overload new (int capacity) for $string1 and the overload new(string value) for $string2.

We can use the ToString() method to see the contents, like this:

```
$string1.tostring()
$string2.tostring()
```

$string1 is empty, and $string2 contains the '32' string. If we use the GetType() method, we can see that both are StringBuilder objects. If we pipe them to the Get-Member cmdlet, we can also see that the new() method isn't listed because it's a constructor.

Versioning

An assembly is a .dll file that contains metadata called the assembly manifest, which lists the contents of the file, as well as the name and the version of the file. The concept of strong names was introduced in .NET; a strong name consists of the name of the module, the version, and also a cryptographic hash that validates the file author. When .NET programs are linked to a strong named assembly, then the name, version, and hash of the file must match the linked strong name. If we simply replace the .dll file with a later version, then the program will fail to load it. This leads to different versions of .dll that have the same version number to prevent introducing breaking changes. Great.

There are many other components, but these are the things we most need to be aware of when working with .NET and PowerShell. Let's look now at how PowerShell makes use of .NET.

Working with .NET in PowerShell

In this section, we are going to look at some of the details of how PowerShell accesses .NET libraries. We'll look at the default assemblies, how PowerShell finds types, and another way of creating objects.

> **Why bother?**
>
> PowerShell and C# are part of the .NET family and thus work well together, as they are based on the same .NET foundation. They share many features, such as classes and libraries. We can call C# inside PowerShell by using Add-Type, allowing us to compile and run the C# code when we run the PowerShell script. This lets us take advantage of the simplicity and ease of PowerShell, but we have C# available whenever we need it, without having to write an entire program.

PowerShell assemblies

We saw at the start of the chapter that we could list the loaded assemblies with the statement:

```
[System.AppDomain]::CurrentDomain.GetAssemblies()
```

`AppDomain` is a class that encapsulates and isolates the execution environment; it's a bit like `PSSession` but even more secure; each instance of `PSSession` shares a set of assemblies, whereas each instance of `AppDomain` loads its own assemblies. `CurrentDomain` gets the current execution environment. The double colon (`::`) represents the C# namespace alias operator; we need to use it to access a member of an aliased namespace, and it goes between two identifiers. Let's run the statement again, like this:

```
[System.AppDomain]::CurrentDomain.GetAssemblies() | select FullName
```

Then, we can see a list of the strong names of the assemblies we've loaded:

```
PS C:\Users\nickp> [System.AppDomain]::CurrentDomain.GetAssemblies() | select FullName

FullName
--------
System.Private.CoreLib, Version=7.0.0.0, Culture=neutral, PublicKeyToken=7cec85d7bea7798e
pwsh, Version=7.3.10.500, Culture=neutral, PublicKeyToken=31bf3856ad364e35
System.Runtime, Version=7.0.0.0, Culture=neutral, PublicKeyToken=b03f5f7f11d50a3a
Microsoft.PowerShell.ConsoleHost, Version=7.3.10.500, Culture=neutral, PublicKeyToken=31bf3856ad364e35
```

Figure 16.6 – Default assemblies and their strong names

Note that each strong name contains a short name, a version, a culture identifier, and the cryptographic key that identifies the author.

Dynamic assembly loading

Automatic loading works for compiled programs such as `pwsh.exe`, but it relies on the required assembly list in the executable. We can add required assemblies to a module manifest as well, in the `RequiredAssemblies` element. If we need to load non-default assemblies when writing scripts, we can use the preceding `using` keyword, the `Add-Type` cmdlet, or even the `Import-Module` cmdlet if the assembly is in a `.dll` file.

The `Add-Type` cmdlet has five parameter sets; three of them are for defining new types, but we can also use it to import assemblies from a named path, or to just import the types we need from the assembly, such as the following:

```
Add-Type -AssemblyName PresentationCore,PresentationFramework
```

This will add the assemblies required to call simple Windows GUI elements from within PowerShell.

Once we've imported (or created) our new type, we can create instances of types with the `New-Object` cmdlet.

Creating instances of types

The New-Object cmdlet creates an instance of a type. Either the type must exist inside the PowerShell default assemblies, or we must import it first with Add-Type. New-Object is easy to use. All we need to provide is TypeName and a list of arguments that matches one of the available overloads. For instance, one of the overloads on the StringBuilder type allows a string to define the value of the new object, and an integer to define the initial capacity. Note that it takes a string value, (System.Text.String.Builder), not a namespace and namespace alias qualifier ([System.Text.StringBuilder]::), so we can do this:

```
$loveit = (New-Object -TypeName System.Text.StringBuilder
-ArgumentList "i love powershell", 128)
```

That will create a variable called $loveit that contains the "i love PowerShell" string and has an initial capacity of 128 characters:

```
PS C:\Users\nickp> $loveit = (New-Object -TypeName System.Text.StringBuilder -ArgumentList "i love powershell", 128)
PS C:\Users\nickp> $loveit

Capacity MaxCapacity Length
-------- ----------- ------
     128  2147483647     17

PS C:\Users\nickp> $loveit.ToString()
i love powershell
```

Figure 16.7 – Loving it

We can see in the preceding screenshot that the initial capacity is 128, whereas we would expect it to be 17, the length of the string, if we had just passed a string value. Note that we have to understand the required arguments for the overload we wish to use as a constructor – in this instance, "i love powershell" and 128. For instance, if we supply two strings, we will get an error.

An alternative is to use the -Property parameter, which accepts a hashtable of property names and the required values. We'll see how to use that in the next section, but note that if you misspell a property, PowerShell will simply add the misspelled property to the object, rather than tell you that you have it wrong.

Let's try a couple of examples to get a feel for how we can use .NET with PowerShell.

Using .NET

We'll try two examples in this section – an alternative way of getting an action to fire, such as a script, and how we can call Windows GUI elements from PowerShell.

An alternative to the Task Scheduler

In this example, we're going to create a timer object and then use the Register-Event cmdlet to fire an action at regular intervals.

First, let's make a timer:

```
$timer = (New-Object -TypeName System.Timers.Timer -Property @{
AutoReset = $true
Interval = 5000
Enabled = $true
}
)
```

Now, we need to register the event and define an action:

```
Register-ObjectEvent -InputObject $timer -EventName Elapsed
-SourceIdentifier Test -Action {Write-Host "hello"}
```

Now, let's start the timer going with the following:

```
$timer.start()
```

Then, we should see the hello string appear on the screen, every five seconds, until we type the following:

```
$timer.stop()
```

This is how it looks on my machine:

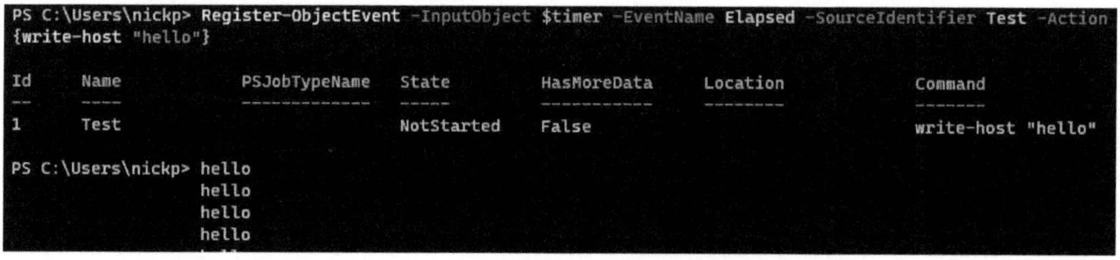

Figure 16.8 – hello

We can see the command firing every time the timer reaches 5,000 milliseconds. Cool, eh?

Let's try creating a GUI message box.

Creating GUI objects

This example will create a pop-up message box in Windows with a pair of yes/no buttons. The value of the pressed button is recorded in the PowerShell session:

```
Add-Type -AssemblyName PresentationCore,PresentationFramework
$Button = [System.Windows.MessageBoxButton]::YesNo
$Title = "PowerShell for Everyone"
```

```
$Body = "Do you love PowerShell?"
$Icon = [System.Windows.MessageBoxImage]::Warning
[System.Windows.MessageBox]::Show($Body,$Title,$Button,$Icon)
```

We could use this in conjunction with the preceding timer object to display a message box, allowing people to cancel a long-running script. This is how it looks on my machine:

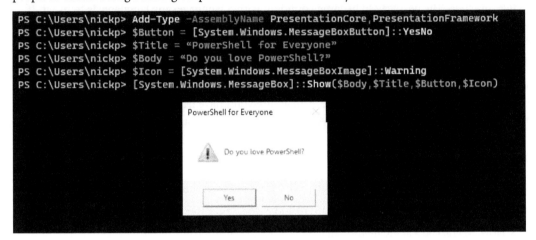

Figure 16.9 – Of course you do

Note that the default answer is **Yes**. We could also use the response to set parameters, add an event, or trigger a conditional statement.

Let's summarize what we've seen in this chapter.

Summary

We started out by understanding what .NET is – a software framework. We learned that it is based on the Common Language Infrastructure and is similar to .NET Framework in Windows, but it is not the same. We saw that it includes its own runtime, CoreCLR, and a set of libraries, CoreFX. We learned about the relationship between .NET and .NET Framework and how they co-exist. We saw that .NET can be used for many things, including machine learning and Internet of Things applications, but is mostly used for Azure and Windows.

We went through the components of .NET, and we understood how they are related to each other and are represented in PowerShell. We saw the constructor member, a special type of method for instantiating objects, and understood why versioning is frequently confusing.

We then looked at the specifics of how we access .NET libraries from PowerShell, learned about dynamic loading, and then saw how to use the New-Object cmdlet to create instances of classes.

Finally, we worked through two examples of things we can do using .NET – creating an event timer and a Windows message box.

What's next? Well, it depends. If you want to learn more about PowerShell, then there are great books such as *Mastering PowerShell Scripting* by Chris Dent from Packt, or the absolute bible, *Windows PowerShell in Action* by Bruce Payette et al. Whichever you choose, what you need to do is practice, practice, practice. The best way to become confident with a language, any language, is to use it. If you are interested in .NET, then PowerShell is a good start, but sooner or later, you will want to use a compiled language with it, such as C#. While it's technically possible to write a machine learning application in PowerShell, I think it would be a lot easier to do it with C#.

That's it. That's the end of the book. Thank you for sticking with it alongside me; I hope you enjoyed reading it as much as I enjoyed writing it. I can assure you I have learned a lot in the process, and hopefully, so have you. I hope you've enjoyed my company as much as I've enjoyed yours.

Exercises

1. How do you create a new instance of a .NET class in PowerShell?

2. What command in PowerShell is used to add a .NET assembly to the session?

3. How do you call a static method of a .NET class in PowerShell?

4. In PowerShell, how can you access a static property of a .NET class?

5. How can you invoke a .NET constructor with parameters in PowerShell?

6. What is the PowerShell cmdlet to load a .NET assembly from a file?

7. How can you determine the .NET type of an object in PowerShell?

8. In PowerShell, how do you list all the methods of a .NET object?

9. What is the syntax to invoke an instance method of a .NET object in PowerShell?

10. How do you access an instance property of a .NET object in PowerShell?

Further reading

- What is .NET?: https://dotnet.microsoft.com/en-us/learn/dotnet/what-is-dotnet

- The Microsoft .NET documentation: https://learn.microsoft.com/en-us/dotnet/core/introduction

- The original .NET documentation; surprisingly useful: https://learn.microsoft.com/en-us/previous-versions/tn-archive/bb496996(v=technet.10)

- The System.Management.Automation namespace: https://learn.microsoft.com/en-gb/dotnet/api/system.management.automation

- Classes: `https://learn.microsoft.com/en-us/powershell/module/microsoft.powershell.core/about/about_classes`

- Constructors: `https://learn.microsoft.com/en-us/powershell/module/microsoft.powershell.core/about/about_classes_constructors`

- The StringBuilder class: `https://learn.microsoft.com/en-gb/dotnet/api/system.text.stringbuilder`

- Add-Type: `https://learn.microsoft.com/en-us/powershell/module/microsoft.powershell.utility/add-type`

- New-Object: `https://learn.microsoft.com/en-us/powershell/module/microsoft.powershell.utility/new-object`

- The Timer class: `https://learn.microsoft.com/en-us/dotnet/api/system.timers.timer`

- Register-ObjectEvent: `https://learn.microsoft.com/en-us/powershell/module/microsoft.powershell.utility/register-objectevent`

- PowerShell Eventing: `https://devblogs.microsoft.com/powershell/powershell-eventing-quickstart/`

- Learn C#: `https://dotnet.microsoft.com/en-us/learn/csharp`

Answers to Activities and Exercises

Chapter 1

Activities

1. You can use ADD_FILE_CONTEXT_MENU_RUNPOWERSHELL, like this:

    ```
    msiexec.exe /package c:\Users\WDAGUtilityAccount\Downloads\
    PowerShell-7.2.1-win-x64.msi /quiet REGISTER_MANIFEST=1 USE_MU=1
    ENABLE_MU=1 ADD_FILE_CONTEXT_MENU_RUNPOWERSHELL=1
    ```

2. By using kill(). Charming, right? CloseMainWindow() might work for a graphical process, and Close() will ask politely, but kill() should do it. Note that sometimes it won't, for instance, if the process you are trying to kill is running with higher privileges than the account you are running PowerShell with.

    You can use it like this. Here's my list of pwsh processes:

    ```
    PS C:\Users\PARLOWN> get-process pwsh

    NPM(K)    PM(M)    WS(M)    CPU(s)      Id  SI ProcessName
    ------    -----    -----    ------      --  -- -----------
        76    67.16    53.02     82.44     220   1 pwsh
        71    53.03    50.43    103.00    4052   1 pwsh
       107    83.99    93.69  1,098.06   24972   1 pwsh
       146   345.03   156.86     72.11   36556   1 pwsh
    ```

    Figure A.1 – Some PowerShell processes

Let's get rid of 4052:

```
PS C:\Users\PARLOWN> (get-process -id 4052).kill()
PS C:\Users\PARLOWN> get-process pwsh

NPM(K)    PM(M)     WS(M)     CPU(s)        Id  SI ProcessName
------    -----     -----     ------        --  -- -----------
    76    67.16     53.02      82.44       220   1 pwsh
   106    83.96     93.68   1,098.36     24972   1 pwsh
   147   345.05    158.06      72.27     36556   1 pwsh
```

Figure A.2 – Fewer PowerShell processes

Exercises

1. Input Get-Random.

2. Input Get-Random -Minimum 1 -Maximum 11.

3. Input Get-ChildItem -Path <folderpath>.

4. Input Get-ChildItem -Path <folderpath> -Recurse.

5. Input New-Item -Path <folder path> -Name <item name> -ItemType.

6. Directory.

7. Input Get-Uptime.

8. Input Out-File.

9. Store a username and password for use later in the shell or in a script.

10. This cmdlet converts the output of a previous cmdlet or pipeline to HTML, which can then be displayed in a web browser. Note that you might need to save it as a file using out-file as well, or it will just display the HTML code in the shell.

Chapter 2

Activities

1. New creates a new object. For instance, New-Item C:\foo\bar.txt will create an empty text file called bar.txt in the C:\foo directory. Add will add things to the existing object, so Add-Content C:\foo\bar.txt "PowerShell rocks my world" will add that string to the previously empty text file.

2. Just specify the -InputObject parameter like this: Get-Random -InputObject 20.

3. Use the -Prefix parameter. This is particularly useful when using remote sessions.

Exercises

1. Get-Content is correct. This is a bit of a trick question, as the *Approved Verbs for PowerShell Commands* web page says that Get should be reserved for getting information *about* an object, not its contents. Nonetheless, Get-Content is right, as we are getting the contents of a file and reserving it for future use *as an object*, as opposed to reading data from a remote resource such as a web page. Read-Host is an example of a cmdlet that reads things—in this case, information from the shell.

2. You should see the words alive alive printed on the screen. This is because oh is an alias for Out-Host, which takes an object—in this case, the string alive alive—and prints it to the default host, usually the screen.

3. Get-ChildItem has two parameter sets. The parameter that determines which set you use is -LiteralPath.

4. *.exe is being passed to the -filter parameter. If you look at the help file, you can see that -filter is a positional parameter with a position of 1, so the second value without a specified parameter will be understood as a filter argument.

5. No. the -Filter parameter only takes a single argument. If you want this cmdlet to run, then Get-ChildItem c:\foo* -include *.exe, *.txt will work.

6. Find-module *aws* will find lots of official modules for working with AWS, provided by Amazon.

7. At the time of writing, there aren't any on the PowerShell Gallery, but there are some on GitHub. I'm not sure how official they are, though. Be wary.

8. Holding the *Ctrl* key and scrolling the mouse wheel is the easiest temporary way of doing it. *Ctrl* and + (plus) or *Ctrl* and - (minus) will also do it. To change it permanently, open **Settings**, click on the profile you wish to change, and go into the **Appearance** subsection.

Chapter 3

Activities

1. We can combine -first, -last, and -skip to do this, like so:

    ```
    1,2,3,4,5,6,7,8 | Select-Object -last 2 -First 3 -skip 1
    ```

    If we read the help file carefully, we will see that the -skip parameter will skip from the start, unless it is combined with -last. However, it is not positional, so if we specify both the -first and -last parameters, -skip will always skip from the start of the array; it doesn't matter where we put it in the cmdlet:

```
PS /home/nickp> 1,2,3,4,5,6,7,8 | Select-Object -last 2 -skip 1 -first 3
2
3
4
7
8
```

Figure A.3 – Output when we use first, last, and skip

2. This is because `-contains` doesn't support wildcards. The value must match exactly, except that it is not case sensitive.

3. `Get-Command -ParameterName filter` will do this for us. If you run it, you will see that there are lots of them. Most of them make use of the same `filter` block syntax we've been looking at in this chapter.

Exercises

1. `Get-Date | Select-Object DayOfWeek`

   First, we need to know how to get today's date; `Get-Command` will let us find the `Get-Date` cmdlet. Next, we need to use `Get-Member` to see the properties of the object that `Get-Date` produces. Finally, we need to use `Select-Object` to just show the `DayOfWeek` property – **Day** returns the day of the month.

2. `Get-Process | Select-Object name, cpu, path`

   `path` isn't a property that is displayed when we run `Get-Process`, so we will need to use `Get-Member` to find it.

3. `Get-Process | select-object name, cpu, path | sort-object path -descending`

   Simple.

4. `Get-Process | Where-Object cpu -gt 5 | select-object name, path | sort-object path -descending`

   The tricky bit here is remembering that `Where-Object` needs to come early. Remember, *filter left*.

5. It's best to make use of the filtering properties of a cmdlet rather than passing everything through the pipeline to `Where-Object`, so the following code is the most efficient way:

   ```
   Get-ChildItem -File -Attributes ReadOnly
   ```

   However, the following will also work:

   ```
   Get-childitem -file | where {$_.isreadonly -eq 'true'}
   ```

6. This is a bit of a trick question; we could use `ForEach-Object` here, like this:

```
Get-ChildItem -File | ForEach-Object -Process {$_.Name +
$_.length}
```

However, the output is horrible. It's far better to do something like this:

```
Get-ChildItem -File | Select-Object name, length
```

These days, it's quite rare that there isn't a better alternative to using `ForEach-Object` interactively.

7. `Get-Process (Get-Content ./processes.txt)`

`Get-Content` is the cmdlet you need, and we'll be covering this in *Chapter 6, PowerShell and Files – Reading, Writing, and Manipulating Data*. You will remember from the work we have done earlier in this chapter that the `-Name` parameter for `Get-Process` doesn't accept objects `ByValue`, only `ByProcessName`, so we can't use `Get-Content` to grab the list of names. Instead, we must use parentheses and feed them directly to the `-Name` parameter.

8. It won't run like that; although the `-computername` parameter accepts a `system.string` object, it does so `ByPropertyName`, not `ByValue`. The correct way to run this is as follows:

```
Stop-Computer 'bobscomputer'
```

This will pass the string to the parameter correctly.

Unfortunately, this cmdlet is seriously deficient on Linux and macOS – it's just a wrapper for the `shutdown` command and can't work against remote machines. Hopefully, you followed the instructions not to try it, as it will ignore the `bobscomputer` string and shut down your local machine if you don't include the `-WhatIf` parameter.

Chapter 4

Activities

1. It's all about memory. As we mentioned, the stack has limited space, and value-type objects are held in the stack. Therefore, it makes sense to conserve memory as much as possible while being transparent to the human writing the code. `[Int64]` type objects take up twice as much space on the stack as `[Int32]` type objects.

2. `MyString` has been told to take the contents of `MyVariable`, the integer `42`, and treat it as a string. We can subsequently put an integer in `MyString`, because we didn't constrain it in any way when we created it.

   Doing it the other way around, with `[string] $MyOtherString`, constrains `MyOtherString` to only be able to contain strings.

Exercises

1. There's a space in there – spaces aren't allowed. If we really must use a space in the variable name, then we must enclose it in curly braces – {My Variable}, which is arguably more work than using a variable name that doesn't include a space.

2. System.Management.Automation.PSVariable, PSVariable, or even Variable.

3. Use the preference variable $ErrorView. By default, it is set to ConciseView, a shorter, reader-friendly message containing just the error. This was introduced in PowerShell 7.0 and replaced a slightly more oblique format. This old format can still be seen by setting $ErrorView to NormalView. Interestingly, the PowerShell documentation lists $ErrorView as both a preference and an automatic variable – I suspect this is wrong; I think it's a preference variable.

4. $Null will do this. $Null is different from 0 and is still a value; it's just an empty value.

5. We can use the CompareTo() method. This will give us three possible outputs: 0 if the integers are the same, -1 if the first integer is smaller than the second, or 1 if it is larger. Try the following:

```
$x = 42
$y = 23
$y.CompareTo($x)
```

This sort of thing will come in handy in the next chapter, *Chapter 5, PowerShell Control Flow – Conditionals and Loops*, where we will be looking at conditional statements.

6. It's a System.Array object or array.

7. MyString.ToCharArray() will output each char as an element of an array on a separate line.PowerShell Variables and Data Structures 34

8. Because we are only using single quote marks, the output will be My Name is $MyName. If we want the variable to be expanded, we must use double quotes.

9. This is the TypeName of an ordered hashtable, and we can create it using the [ordered] accelerator. Remember, this goes on the right-hand side of the statement, not the left, like so:

```
$OrderedHash = [ordered]@{a=10;b=20;c=30}
```

Chapter 5

Activities

1. Because the switch is 7 `{ Write-Output 'contains 7' }`, which is looking for an integer. The line it is searching is a string, and so contains no integers. If we replaced the 7 in the `switch` statement with `'*7'`, making it a string, then it would work.

2. It's because we're executing the increment statement before we write the output. Switching the two statements around would demonstrate that the scriptblock doesn't execute when the condition isn't met.

Exercises

1. None. The statement only produces output if $x is larger than 4. There is no `else` statement here to produce alternative output. This is a true conditional statement, rather than a conditional that provides alternate flows.

2. `$x = 4 ; IF ($x -gt 4) {Write-Host '$x is larger than 4'}Else {Write-Host '$x is not larger than 4'}`

3. `$x = 4 ; IF ($x -gt 4) {Write-Host '$x is larger than 4'}elseif ($x -lt 4) {Write-Host '$x is smaller than 4'} Else {Write-Host '$x is 4'}`

4. `$x = 4 ; ($x -gt 4) ? (Write-Host '$x is larger than 4') : (Write-Host '$x is not larger than 4')`

5. Because `foreach` is after a pipe character, there is only a single statement here, and `foreach` is interpreted as an alias of `ForEach-Object`, so the syntax is wrong. We can make it right by replacing the pipe character with a semicolon. This separates it into two statements, and `foreach` is correctly interpreted:

   ```
   $processes = Get-process ; foreach ($process in $processes)
   {$process.name}
   ```

6. `number = 0 ; Do {$number ++ ; Write-Host "Number is $number"} While (!($number -eq 5))` will work. We'll see that construction using the not operator alias (`!`) to reverse a statement quite often.

7. t's missing the iterator. This will work: `for ($i = 0 ; $i -lt 5 ; $i ++) {Write-Host $i}`.

8. `switch` statements. Using them outside loops and `switch` statements can lead to unpredictable outcomes.

9. There are a few ways to do this; any that work are right, but my solution involves substituting a `for` loop instead of the existing `while` loop to implement the counter. I've also added an extra `elseif` statement to handle a winning condition, like this:

```
 Brucie2.ps1 > ...
 1   [int]$Hidden = Get-Random -Minimum 1 -Maximum 101
 2   Write-Host "Let's play the Brucie Game! Guess the hidden number between 1 and 100.
 3   give me a number below"
 4   $guess = 0
 5   for ($i = 0; $i -lt 10; $i++) {
 6       $guess = [int] (Read-Host)
 7       If ($guess -eq $hidden) {
 8           Write-Host "You Win" ; break
 9       } elseif ($guess -lt $hidden) {
10           Write-Host "Higher!"
11       } elseif ( $guess -gt $hidden) {
12           Write-Host "Lower!"
13       }
14   }
15   Write-Host "Game Over"
16   |
```

Figure A.4 – Guess limited Brucie

There are lots of ways of writing this on the internet – I've chosen this way just to use concepts that we've covered in this chapter.

Chapter 6

Activity

This is just one way of doing it. If you got something different that worked, well done. That's the right way – one of them, anyway. According to *Exercises in Programming Style*, there are at least 41 others:

```
$TheTrial = Get-Content -Path .\thetrial.txt -Raw
$StopWords = Get-Content -Path .\stopwords.txt -Raw
$TrialWords = $TheTrial.Split(" ", "`t", "`n", ",","`"","." , [System.
StringSplitOptions]::RemoveEmptyEntries)
$Words = [System.Collections.ArrayList]@()
Foreach ($Word in $TrialWords) {
$LWord = $Word.ToLower()
```

```
if (!($StopWords.Contains($LWord))) {
$Words.Add($Word)
}
}
$Grouped = ($Words | Group-Object | Sort-Object Count)
$Grouped[-1 .. -10]
```

Here it is running:

```
wordcount.ps1 > ...
1    $TheTrial = Get-Content -Path .\thetrial.txt -Raw
2    $StopWords = Get-Content -Path .\stopwords.txt -Raw
3    $TrialWords = $TheTrial.Split(" ", "`t", "`n", ",","`"","."., [System.StringSplitOptions]::RemoveEmptyEntries)
4
5    $Words = [System.Collections.ArrayList]@()
6
7    Foreach ($Word in $TrialWords) {
8        $LWord = $Word.ToLower()
9        if (!($StopWords.Contains($LWord))) {
10           $Words.Add($Word)
11       }
12   }
13   $Grouped = ($Words | Group-Object | Sort-Object Count)
14   $Grouped[-1 .. -10]
15
```

PROBLEMS   OUTPUT   DEBUG CONSOLE   **TERMINAL**   JUPYTER

```
Count Name          Group
----- ----          -----
  191 door          {door, door, door, door…}
  169 lawyer        {lawyer, lawyer, lawyer, lawyer…}
  141 court         {court, court, court, court…}
  132 looked        {looked, looked, looked, looked…}
  121 painter       {painter, painter, painter, painter…}
  103 people        {people, people, people, people…}
   95 Trial         {Trial, TRIAL, trial, trial…}
   85 judge         {judge, judge, judge, judge…}
   84 Leni          {Leni, Leni, Leni, Leni…}
   78 Uncle         {Uncle, uncle, uncle, uncle…}
```

Figure A.5 – The ten most frequent words in an English translation of The Trial

Let's step through it quickly:

- Lines 1 and 2 bring our two files into PowerShell using Get-Content, in Raw format as single strings.

- Line 3 adds some extra delimiters and removes empty strings. I don't expect you to know about the string split options, so I gave you this in the hint.

- Line 5 creates an empty array list to hold interesting words; if we used a PowerShell array, this would be painfully slow.

- Line 7 starts a Foreach loop to step through each word in $TrialWords.

- Line 8 creates a variable and casts each word to lowercase into it each time the loop repeats.

- Line 9 starts an `if` statement matching the condition "`$Lword` is not in `$StopWords`." Note we are using the `-Contains` method, which matches substrings in a single string, so it is searching the `$StopWords` string for substrings that match `$LWord`.

- Line 10 adds `$Word` to the `$Words` array list if the condition is true.

- Line 13 groups and sorts the words in `$Words`.

- Line 14 returns the 10 most frequent words, in descending order.

Exercises

1. `Get-Childitem -Path C:\Temp -File | Format-Wide -Column 3`

2. `Get-Process | Format-Wide -column 5 | Where-Object id -gt 100`

   It will produce no output. Remember, **Format Right**. The correct code should be as follows:

   `Get-Process | Where-Object id -gt 100 | Format-Wide -column 5`

3. `"I love PowerShell" | Out-File -Path Q3.txt`

4. `"Sooo much" | Out-File -Path Q3.txt -Append`

5. `Get-ChildItem | Export-Csv -Path items.csv -Delimiter ";"`

6. `(Get-ChildItem Function:).count`

7. `Get-Content Q3.txt -Delimiter " "` Or `(Get-Content Q3.txt).Split(" ")`

8. `Import-Csv -Path items.csv -Delimiter ";"`

   We will get an array of `PSCustomObjects`.

9. `Import-Clixml: Element 'Objs' with namespace name 'http:// schemas. microsoft.com/powershell/2004/04' was not found.`

   The XML file we are trying to import wasn't formatted correctly for the cmdlet or it isn't a PowerShell object.

Chapter 7

Activity

Here is my solution:

```
ch7 > ≳ astros.ps1 > ...
  1   #task 1 - getting information about the astronauts
  2   $astronauts = (Invoke-RestMethod "http://api.open-notify.org/astros.json")
  3
  4   #task 2 - displaying the information as a web page
  5   $params = @{
  6       Title = 'Astronauts on the ISS'
  7       Body = 'These are the Astronauts on the ISS (some of them are Cosmonauts)'
  8       CssUri = 'Style.css'
  9       Property = 'name'
 10       PostContent = 'Image credit; NASA/Paolo Nespoli'
 11   }
 12   $astronauts.people |
 13   Where-Object {$_.craft -like "ISS"} |
 14   ConvertTo-Html @params |
 15   Out-File C:\temp\poshbook\ch7\astros.html
 16
```

Figure A.6 – One solution

Line 2 grabs the data in JSON format from the API and puts it in a variable. If we look at the $astronauts variable, we can see it has two key-value pairs, message and people. people contains an array of JSON objects, which themselves have two key-value pairs; name and craft. We can see this in the following figure:

```
PS C:\Users\nickp> $astronauts = (Invoke-RestMethod "http://api.open-notify.org/astros.json")
PS C:\Users\nickp> $astronauts

message people
------- ------
success {@{name=Sergey Prokopyev; craft=ISS}, @{name=Dmitry Petelin; craft=ISS}, @{name=Frank Rubio;
```

Figure A.7 – Getting the JSON data

So, we know the data we need are in the $astronauts.people.name key-value pair. All we need to do now is display it in a pleasing manner. We covered how to use ConvertTo-Html in *Chapter 6, PowerShell and Files – Reading, Writing, and Manipulating Data*, and this is the way I've chosen.

On line 5, we set up a $params hashtable so we can splat all the parameters we need. I've chosen to include a CSS stylesheet that displays a lovely image, but that's not necessary. This is my CSS:

```
Table {
color: white;
text-align: left;
background-color: black;
}
Body {
background-image: url("iss.jpg");
background-size: cover;
background-repeat: no-repeat;
background-color: black;
font-family: 'Trebuchet MS';
color: yellow;
}
```

Finally, the magic happens on line 12. We feed the values we are interested in into ConvertTo-Html via the pipeline and then use Out-File to write the HTML to a file. We can then open this file in the browser of our choosing.

Hopefully, this has shown you how easy it is to obtain, manipulate, and display data using an API.

Exercises

1. `Invoke-WebRequest -Uri 'https://httpbin.org/delete' -Method Delete`

2. We use the `-SessionVariable` parameter in the first request (usually a login request) to supply a string, and then, in subsequent requests, we supply the session variable as a variable using the `-WebSession` parameter.

3. We can use the `-SkipCertificateCheck` parameter, but we should only do this if we're really sure that the site is valid and not malicious.

4. The mistake we made is in encoding the token before supplying it via the header. Encode the token to supply it as a parameter and keep it in plain text for headers. This means that supplying it as a parameter is slightly more secure, but not all services will accept it that way.

5. WebSocket APIs are usually stateful. This means information about the requestor is persisted through multiple requests; this makes it more complicated to use, as we need to persist session information, and susceptible to network conditions.

6. There are lots of ways to do this, but the most straightforward is probably this:

    ```
    Invoke-RestMethod 'http://api.open-notify.org/iss-now.json' |
    Format-List iss_position
    ```

7. This will get just the count: (Invoke-RestMethod 'http://universities. hipolabs.com/search?country=United+kingdom').name | Where-Object {$_ -like '*x*'} | Measure | select -Property 'count'.

    I get 8, but this is subject to change.

8. We can either pass it a long string describing the custom schema using the -Schema parameter, or we can pass it a file location using -SchemaFile. You're right! This isn't in the chapter. You hopefully read the help file to get the answer.

Chapter 8

Activities

1. The easy way to do this is to create an $Output variable in the Param() block, and pass that as a parameter to the Out-File cmdlet in the script, like this:

    ```
    [CmdletBinding()]
    Param(
    $City = "London",
    $Output = "c:\temp\poshbook\ch8\WeatherData.html"
    )
    $headers = @{"key" = "<Key>"}
    $uri = "https://api.weatherapi.com/v1/current.
    json?q=$($City)&aqi=no"
    $response = Invoke-RestMethod -Uri $uri -Method GET -Headers
    $headers
    $response | Convertto-Html | Out-File $Output
    ```

    The trouble with that is if we want to change the filename, we need to type both the filename and the path each time. It's likely that we will want to change the filename far more often than we want to change the path. Let's separate out the path and the filename like this:

```
ch8 > ≥ weatherdata.ps1 > …
  1    [CmdletBinding()]
  2    Param(
  3    $City = "London",
  4    $OutputFile = "WeatherData.html",
  5    $OutputPath = "C:\temp\poshbook\ch8"
  6    )
  7
  8    $Output = "$($OutputPath)\$($OutputFile)"
  9
 10    $headers = @{"key" = "                              "}
 11
 12    $uri = "https://api.weatherapi.com/v1/current.json?q=$($City)&aqi=no"
 13
 14    $response = Invoke-RestMethod -Uri $uri -Method GET -Headers $headers
 15
 16    $response | Convertto-Html | Out-File $Output
 17
```

Figure A.8 – Separating the filename and file path

Now, we can just pass a different filename when we want to, and a different path if we want to, without having to type out the whole thing each time.

2. From the help file of a cmdlet that has a parameter that takes multiple strings, we can see that the attribute contains an empty pair of square brackets, like this: [string[]]. That part is easy enough. We also need to process each element of the array that is then passed to the -City parameter. To do that, we'll need a foreach loop as well, wrapped around the working part of the script.

Finally, we'll need some way of sending each city's data to a separate output file. I've chosen to do that by passing the $item variable from the foreach loop. Here's my solution. Yours may look different, but if it works, that's great.

```
1    [CmdletBinding()]
2    Param(
3    [string[]]$City = "London",
4    $OutputFile = "WeatherData.html",
5    $OutputPath = "C:\temp\poshbook\ch8",
6    $KeyFile = "key.txt"
7    )
8
9    foreach ($item in $City) {
10
11       $Output = "$($OutputPath)\$($item)_$($OutputFile)"
12
13       $key = Get-Content $KeyFile
14
15       $headers = @{"key" = "$key"}
16
17       $uri = "https://api.weatherapi.com/v1/current.json?q=$($item)&aqi=no"
18
19       $response = Invoke-RestMethod -Uri $uri -Method GET -Headers $headers
20
21       $response | Convertto-Html | Out-File $Output
22   }
23
```

Figure A.9 – Processing multiple cities

In line 3, I've added the [string[]] attribute to the -City parameter to allow it to take multiple strings.

I've opened a foreach loop on line 9 and closed it on line 22. The lines in between will now be repeated for each $item in the array of strings held in the $City parameter. I've also indented the lines in between to make it easier to read.

I've changed line 17 so that it uses the $item variable (the current city) rather than the array in $City because that would cause an error – the API only accepts a single string at a time.

Finally, I've changed line 11 so that it sends each output to a file that includes the name of the city.

3. Here's my example. Yours may differ but, hopefully, you've included warnings about needing the API key in advance:

```
<#
.SYNOPSIS
Gathers weather data for a number of cities and stores the API
output.
.DESCRIPTION
This cmdlet will gather the current weather data from a number
of cities from
```

```
the API endpoint at https://api.weatherapi.com and outputs the
responses to a
set of named HTML files stored in the specified directory.
The -City parameter takes an array of strings, either explicitly
or via the
pipeline (ByValue).
The -OutputFile parameter takes a single string specifying the
filename and
suffix. This filename will be prefixed by the string provided in
the -City
parameter, eg. London_WeatherData.html
The -OutptPath parameter specifies a location for the output
file.
The -Key parameter specifies a txt file that contains the key
from
weatherapi.com
.NOTES
This script requires a personal API key from https://weatherapi.
com
The output path will need to exist before running the script
.LINK
No link, sorry.
.EXAMPLE
.\weatherdata.ps1 -City london,paris
This will generate two html files; one for London and one for
Paris
#>
```

Exercises

1. This might be because of a few settings, but let's imagine it is the simplest; the execution policy is correct for you, but not for them. This implies that the CurrentUser policy is restricting them.

   Using the following should do it if the script was written on the local machine, or if we have signed it with a code-signing certificate on another machine:

   ```
   Set-ExecutionPolicy -ExecutionPolicy RemoteSigned -Scope
   CurrentUser
   ```

   If that's not the case, then we'd need to set the execution policy to Unrestricted.

2. The -Maximum parameter. I'm not aware of any *Dungeons and Dragons* dice that start at a number other than 1 (except for the d100, but we'll come to that in a question shortly).

3. Well, there are a few ways we could do it, but hopefully, you've come up with something like this:

   ```
   [CmdletBinding()]
   param(
   ```

```
$Sides = 20
)
get-random -minimum 1 -Maximum $Sides
```

You don't need to have the `CmdletBinding()` attribute in there, but I always put it in.

4. It should be an integer, and we'd specify it with the `[int]` attribute:

```
[int]$Sides = 20
```

5. So, if we read the link, we can see that we can assign the `ValidateSet` attribute to a parameter and pass it an array of legal values, which looks like this:

```
[CmdletBinding()]
param(
[ValidateSet(4,6,8,10,12,20)]
[int]$Sides = 20
)
get-random -minimum 1 -Maximum $Sides
```

6. To do this, we're going to need a loop and to specify the number of times we run the loop with a parameter, then add the output of each loop to a running total. It might look like this:

```
[CmdletBinding()]
param(
[ValidateSet(4,6,8,10,12,20)]
[int]$Sides = 20,
[int]$Dice
)
$total = 0
while ($Dice -gt 0) {
$result = (Get-Random -Minimum 1 -Maximum $Sides)
$Dice -= 1
$total += $result
write-output "die says $result"
}
Write-Output "The total is $total"
```

7. This is because there is no default value assigned for `$Dice`. We could assign it a default, but it might be better to make it a mandatory parameter by adding `[Parameter(Mandatory)]` like this:

```
param(
[ValidateSet(4,6,8,10,12,20)]
[int]$Sides = 20,
[Parameter(Mandatory)]
```

```
[int]$Dice
)
```

8. We could make both parameters mandatory and include a `HelpMessage` attribute that explains what to put for each parameter.

9. So, the first thing to do is to add the value of `100` to the `ValidateSet` attribute of the `$sides` parameter.

    Once that's done, we need to treat the value of `100` differently, so we can't just add it to the loop. I've used an `if` and an `else` statement. Here's my resulting script:

```
1   [CmdletBinding()]
2   param(
3       [ValidateSet(4,6,8,10,12,20,100)]
4       [int]$Sides = 20,
5       [Parameter(Mandatory, HelpMessage = "How many dice are you rolling?")]
6       [int]$Dice
7   )
8   $total = 0
9   if ($Sides = 100) {
10      $result100 = 10 * (Get-Random -Minimum 0 -Maximum 9)
11      $result10  = (Get-Random -Minimum 0 -Maximum 9)
12      $total = $result100 + $result10 + 1
13  }
14  else {
15      while ($Dice -gt 0) {
16      $result = (get-random -minimum 1 -Maximum $Sides)
17      $Dice -= 1
18      $total += $result
19      write-output "die says $result"
20      }
21  }
22  Write-Output "the total is $total"
```

Figure A.10 – My level 15 paladin will crush your chaotic evil cleric

Remember, there are lots of ways to do this; if your code is completely different to mine but it works, that's fine.

Chapter 9

Activities

1. Nothing, because our parameter is not written to accept pipeline input. As we discovered in *Chapter 8, Writing Our First Script – Turning Simple Cmdlets into Reusable Code*, to allow a parameter to accept pipeline input, we must add a parameter argument, like this:

```
ch9 > ≥ basicfunction.ps1 > ...
      1 reference
   7  function Get-RoughRoot {
   8      param (
   9          [Parameter(ValueFromPipeline)]
  10          $number
  11      )
  12      process {
  13          $start = 1
  14          while (($start * $start) -le $number)  {
  15              $result = $start
  16              $start += 1
  17              }
  18      $result
  19          }
  20  }
  21
  22  785692, 3492858  |  Get-RoughRoot |
```

Figure A.11 – Accepting values from the pipeline

On line 9, we've added a ValueFromPipeline argument to the parameter, which allows it to accept values from the pipeline. We've also enclosed the function in a process block, opening on line 12 and closing on line 20; if we don't have a process block, then the function will only act on the last value in the pipeline.

2. Because Get-Random only accepts one positional parameter, -Maximum. If we run it as previously, then the maximum will be set as 15, and the cmdlet has no idea what to do with the 20 value. Similarly, Get-Fifteen20 15 -maximum 20 won't work because the -Maximum parameter is already filled by the named value, 20, so it doesn't know what to do with the 15 value. Get-Fifteen20 -minimum 15 20 will work, however.

3.   There are lots of ways to do this, as always. My method is as follows:

```
function Remove-Log {
$limit = (Get-Date).AddDays(-7)
Get-ChildItem -Path "C:\temp" -Include "MyLogFile*" -Recurse
-Force |
Where-Object {$_.CreationTime -lt $limit} |
Remove-Item -Force
}
```

I've created a function called Remove-Log that I can call in my script. I've created a variable called $limit that gets a date seven days less than when it is run. I then get all the items in the C:\temp directory that start with the string MyLogFile, using a wildcard. I've then filtered the list using Where-Object to select only the files older than my $limit date. Finally, I've piped that to Remove-Item with the -Force parameter to suppress any confirmations.

Exercises

1.   Avoid Hasty Abstractions – it's a software engineering principle that encourages us to only create an abstraction, such as a function, when we know we will need it and we know exactly what we need it to do.

2.   Because dot sourcing causes whatever it is calling to be run in the local, or parent, scope rather than the appropriate child scope.

3.   Because just calling the variable will produce the code in the scriptblock; it won't run it. We need to use the invoke() method, the call operator, or the Invoke-Command cmdlet. What we shouldn't do is dot source it without careful consideration.

4.   The ValidatePattern validation attribute should do it, but we'd need to use a regular expression. Ugh! Hopefully, you looked this up in the help file mentioned in the *Further reading* section.

5.   Because filters expect pipeline input, and we haven't supplied any. However, 365 | get-square would work.

6.   We're preventing the $number variable from being accessed from another scope.

7.   A function is named, whereas a scriptblock is anonymous.

8.   We're trying to feed a value through the pipeline, but there's no parameter that accepts pipeline input. We need to either make it an advanced function and create a parameter that accepts pipeline input, or we need to use $Args.

9.   We will write the function as follows:

```
Function get-root ($a) {
<what goes here?>
}
```

Probably the easiest way is to use this line:

```
[math]::Sqrt($a)
```

We can use it like this:

```
PS C:\Users\nickp> Function get-root($a) {
>> [math]::Sqrt($a)
>> }
PS C:\Users\nickp> get-root 453466
673.398841697846
PS C:\Users\nickp>
```

Figure A.12 – Getting a root the easy way

Chapter 10

Activities

1. The -ErrorAction parameter will override the $ErrorActionPreference variable, and the nosuchfile string will cause a terminating error. Because it's a terminating error, the cmdlet will not process bar.txt.

2. Because if there is an error, then the error object is put into the pipeline, replacing the string that caused the error.

Exercises

1. Terminating errors stop the script altogether. Non-terminating errors may stop the script from doing the current step, but PowerShell will move the script on to the next step.

2. Either with the Get-Error cmdlet, which displays the most recent error object, or with the $Error variable. This has an array of all the error objects created during a session up to a default maximum of 256.

3. The -ErrorActionPreference variable allows us to set the default error action preference for all cmdlets and scripts running in a specific PowerShell session. It determines whether errors should be displayed, ignored, or handled in a specific way.

4. The Write-Error cmdlet allows us to manually generate and display custom non-terminating error messages within a script. It is useful when we want to explicitly signal an error condition to the user or the calling code.

5. To generate a terminating error that can be handled by a try/catch statement pair.

6. By either using the -Debug parameter with a cmdlet or advanced script or by setting the $DebugPreference variable to Continue; the default is SilentlyContinue.

7. By using the `Write-Debug` cmdlet in the script. Debug messages are for people who write code; error messages are for people who use code. As such, a debug message should include detailed information about what is going on in the script at that point, possibly including variable values and step counts.

8. A breakpoint is a marker set in the script to pause its execution at a specific line or condition. It allows us to inspect the state of the script and variables at that point. A break point in tennis is quite different.

9. It executes the current line of a script and moves on to the next line but treats whole functions as a single line. So, if the next line of code is a function, or we are currently in a function, then the whole function call will complete, rather than moving on to the next line in the function.

Chapter 11

Activity

Try running `Remove-Module` to get rid of the module we've just installed, and then running `Get-Square`. What happens? Why does this happen?

The `Get-Square` cmdlet is still available. This is because we saved the module in the module path correctly; this means that PowerShell will autoload the module when we call a function in the module. We can see it working in the following screenshot:

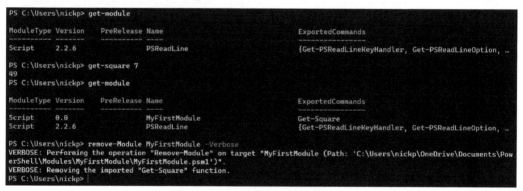

Figure A.13 – Autoloading with PowerShell

In the first line, I list the loaded modules. Then, I run `Get-Square 7`, which autoloads `MyFirstModule`. After that, I confirm that's what happened by running `Get-Module` again. We can see that `Remove-Module` removes the `Get-Square` cmdlet by running it with the `-Verbose` switch in the last line.

Exercises

1. `Get-Module`

2. It imports a module into the global scope. Note that when we import a module from the command prompt, it is already imported into the global scope – we use this when we're importing a module from inside another module; a nested module.

3. We need to give the full path to the module in the -Name parameter of `Import-Module`.

4. Either use the -NoClobber parameter if they are not functions we want to use or use the -Prefix parameter if they are.

5. Either with the `Export-ModuleMembers` cmdlet in the module file or with a module manifest.

6. It provides a link to the online documentation for the module, allowing the help to be updated.

7. In the context of a module, it might be either formatting information for function or cmdlet output, or it might be custom type information.

8. We'll get cmdlets; a `.dll` extension signifies a binary module, so the commands inside it will be of the `Cmdlet` type. Script modules contain commands of the `Function` type.

9. Because they are slow. The CDXML gets parsed to a PowerShell script, which then has to be interpreted.

Chapter 12

Exercises

1. `New-PSSession` creates a persistent session, but an ad hoc session can be created with `Enter- PSSession`.

2. By using SSH.

3. The `AllSigned` execution policy only allows scripts signed by a trusted publisher to run.

4. The -ExecutionPolicy Bypass switch is used to temporarily bypass an execution policy when running a script.

5. PowerShell AMSI.

6. The constrained language mode is used to restrict access to dangerous cmdlets and scripting features in PowerShell.

7. By using JEA.

8. Script block logging records the content of script blocks executed in PowerShell, providing visibility into potentially malicious actions. It records the contents in the `PowerShellCore` operational event log in Windows and in the systemd log in Linux.

9.   A secure string is a PowerShell object of type System.Security.SecureString, and an encrypted string is a string object that has been encrypted with a key so that it cannot be read in a file.

Chapter 13

Activities

1.   We could write a fairly complicated cmdlet with Invoke-CimMethod, but that isn't the best way to do it. Instead, we should use the cmdlet specifically written for this purpose, Stop-Process, with the ProcessId of the notepad process:

```
Stop-Process -Id 8480
```

2.   We can use Invoke-CimMethod like this:

```
PS C:\Users\nickp> $printer = (get-ciminstance Win32_Printer | Where-Object {$_.Name -like 'HPF*'})
PS C:\Users\nickp> Invoke-CimMethod -InputObject $printer -MethodName SetDefaultPrinter

ReturnValue PSComputerName
----------- --------------
          0
```

Figure A.14 – Setting a default printer with CIM commands

In the first command, I put the printer object into a variable, then I used that variable as the input object for Invoke-CimMethod and invoked the SetDefaultPrinter method. The return value of 0 indicates success.

Note that the SetDefaultPrinter method doesn't appear on the $printer variable. Unfortunately, we need to read the documentation to discover this method:

- https://learn.microsoft.com/en-us/windows/win32/cimwin32prov/win32-printer-methods

- https://learn.microsoft.com/en-us/windows/win32/cimwin32prov/setdefaultprinter-method-in-class-win32-printer

Exercises

1. Manifest modules.

2. It may have been written before PowerShell Core was released, the author may not have included compatibility information in the manifest, or it may not be a manifest module.

3. Windows PowerShell 5.1.

4. Deserialized ones.

5. Use the -UseWindowsPowershell parameter.

6. __NAMESPACE

7. It allows us to specify a different timeout when querying remote machines, as the default is 3 minutes per machine.

8. Possibly we could use Set-CimInstance, but because many properties are not writable, we more likely will use Invoke-CimMethod.

9. We pass them as an iDictionary hash table to the -Arguments parameter.

Chapter 14

Activity

Because PowerShell is very forgiving about file path separators, the only bit of code that needs to be different depending on the platform is how we get the name of the machine. Everything else is straightforward. Here's my solution; yours could be very different and still achieve the task:

```
if ($IsWindows) {
$computername = $env:COMPUTERNAME
}
elseif ($IsLinux) {
$computername = (hostname)
}
Get-Process |
Sort-Object -Property CPU -Descending |
Select-Object -First 5 |
Out-File "$($computername)_processes.txt"
```

Because we need to use different ways to get the machine name, those two lines are within if statements. Everything else works the same on Linux and Windows, so it's very straightforward. This is how it looks running on my CentOS box:

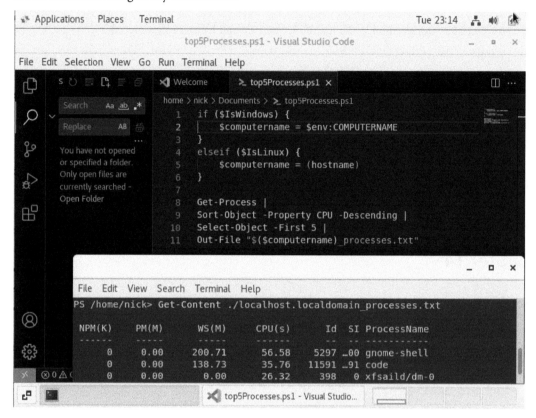

Figure A.15 – Running a cross-platform script on CentOS

As we can see, it works just fine. The script would be better for some error checking; for instance, what if both automatic variables are false?

Exercises

1. The internet. As with most Linux distributions, Kali Linux is not supported by Microsoft.

2. Trick question. We are actually calling the `ls` Bash command on Linux. When we type it on Windows, we are calling `Get-ChildItem` via the `ls` alias.

3. Either \ or /. It doesn't matter, thankfully. This means it's a lot easier to write cross-platform scripts.

4. By calling the `$IsMacOS` variable. If it returns `true`, then we are running on macOS.

5. By starting PowerShell with the `sudo pwsh` command. There is no way to elevate privilege during a PowerShell session.

6. `New-PSSession` with the `-HostName` parameter.

7. `New-PSSession` and the `-KeyFilePath` parameter.

8. It's a file transfer program that is included in the PowerShell 7 packages.

9. Ed25519 is a recent, more secure encryption algorithm for digital signatures based on public/private keys.

Chapter 15

Answers

1. Because the Zero and Pico use an ARMv6 chip architecture, which isn't compatible with .NET since it requires ARMv7 or ARMv8.

2. Either `C:\Users\<username>\.sshconfig` or `C:\ProgramData\ssh\ssh_config`.

3. `Test-NetConnection`

4. `ssh <username>@<hostname>`

5. `sudo bash ./install.sh`

6. Because it's a pain typing ~/powershell/pwsh.

7. `sudo ln -s ~/powershell/pwsh /usr/bin/pwsh`

8. Use the `-Raw` switch parameter with the `Get-GpioPin` cmdlet.

9. Debian Linux, similar to Ubuntu.

Chapter 16

Exercises

1. `$object = New-Object -TypeName Namespace.ClassName`

2. `Add-Type -AssemblyName "AssemblyName"`

3. `[Namespace.ClassName]::MethodName()`

4. `[Namespace.ClassName]::PropertyName`

5. `$object = New-Object -TypeName Namespace.ClassName -ArgumentList (arg1, arg2, ...)`

6. `Add-Type -Path "Path\To\Assembly.dll"`

7. `Using $object.GetType()`

8. `$object | Get-Member -MemberType Method`

9. `$object.MethodName()`

10. `$object.PropertyName`

Index

Symbols

$ErrorActionPreference variable 248, 249
$uri variable 201
-City parameter 204
-ErrorAction parameter 249
-Full parameter 207
-Joke parameter 207
.msi file
  PowerShell 7, installing from 8-11
.NET 385
  alternative, to Task Scheduler 395, 396
  Common Language Infrastructure
    (CLI) 386
  CoreCLR 387
  CoreFX 387
  GUI objects, creating 396, 397
  history 387
  software framework 386
  uses 388
.NET, components 388
  assemblies 388, 389
  classes 390
  enumerations 390
  members 392
  namespaces 390, 391
  types 389
  versioning 393
.NET exceptions
  versus PowerShell exceptions 247
.NET, in PowerShell
  dynamic assembly loading 394
  instances of types, creating 395
  PowerShell assemblies 394
  working with 393
.NET MAUI 388
.zip file
  PowerShell 7, installing from 12-14

A

absolute path 300
adding 89
administrator privileges
  PowerShell, running with 18, 19
advanced function 221
Alias attribute 230
aliases, types
  abbreviations 29
  synonyms 29
APIs, types
  REST APIs 176
  RPC APIs 175

SOAP APIs 176

WebSocket APIs 176

application control 301

Application Programming Interfaces (APIs)

types 175

used, for communicating between
    client and server 174, 175

argument completion attributes 230

arrays 92-95

copying 98

performance 97

properties and methods 95

arrays, properties and methods

Clear method 95, 96

Count 95

ForEach method 95, 96

Length 95

Rank 95

Where method 95, 96

assemblies 388

dynamic assemblies 388

static assemblies 388, 389

assembly manifest 393

automatic variables 81, 82

automation

principles 197

Avoid Hasty Abstraction (AHA) 219

B

basic syntax 62

begin statement 223

Boolean operators 62

Boolean-type variable 86

break statement 133

ByPropertyName parameter binding 71

ByValue parameter binding 69, 70

C

cardinal rules, of troubleshooting 255

Cassandra Query Language (CQL) 329

CentOS 8

PowerShell 7, installing on 346, 347

CentOS 9

PowerShell 7, installing on 346, 347

char type 88

CIM cmdlets

methods, discovering 333

methods, invoking 334, 335

properties, modifying 331, 333

CIM sessions 330, 331

cmdlet, parameters 330

CIMWin32 WMI Providers

reference link 333

classes 390

clean statement 223

CmdletBinding attribute 201, 228

cmdlet pipeline

values, identifying and modifying 200

code debugging

exploring 255

logic errors 255

script instrumentation 256-259

syntax errors 255

code repetition, into function

turning 220, 221

command-lets (cmdlets) 28, 53

aliases 29, 30

debugging 259-262

exploring 35

modules, finding 35-39

PowerShell Gallery 40, 41

structure, exploring 28

syntax 30-35

comment-based help 210
  rules 210
Common Information Model (CIM) 324
  repository 326, 327
  used, for commands 325
  versus Windows Management
    Instrumentation (WMI) 325
Common Intermediate Language (CIL) 386
Common Language Infrastructure
    (CLI) 386
  Common Language Specification (CLS) 386
  Common Type System (CTS) 386
  metadata 386
  standard libraries 386
  Virtual Execution System (VES) 386
Common Language Infrastructure
    XML (Clixml) 149, 150
comparison operators 60-62
compatibility
  exploring 316
Compatibility mode
  limitations 323
  using 320-322
compatible version
  searching 318, 319
compensatory principle 197
complementarity principle 197
concatenating 89
conditional control flow
  elseif statement 121, 122
  else statement 120, 121
  if statement 118-120
  switch statement 123-126
  ternary operator 123
conditionals 109
constructor 390
continue statement 133, 134

ConvertFrom-Json 182-184
ConvertTo- cmdlets
  using 146
ConvertTo-Csv cmdlet 147, 148
ConvertTo-Html cmdlet 151, 152
ConvertTo-Json 184-187
ConvertTo-Xml 149
CoreCLR 386, 387
CoreFX 386, 387
Create, Read, Update, and
    Delete (CRUD) 177
cross-platform script
  writing 352
CSV 147
  ConvertTo-Csv cmdlet 147, 148
  Export-Csv cmdlet 148, 149
curl 12

D

data
  querying 328
declarative languages 220
deep script block logging 305, 306
default format 142
default formatting view 142
default property set 142
Desired State Configuration (DSC) 4
Distributed Common Object
    Model (DCOM) 324
Distributed Management Task
    Force (DMTF) 324
Domain Name Service (DNS) 303
Don't Repeat Yourself (DRY) principle 217
do until loop statement 128-130
do while loop statement 128-130
dynamic module 273

dynamic parameters **228**
dynamic typing **88**
  versus static typing 88, 89

E

elseif statement **121, 122**
else statement **120, 121**
end statement **223**
End-User License Agreement (EULA) **111**
enumeration **390**
enum type **187**
en-US culture **22**
error **244-246**
  catching 250
  creating 253, 254
  non-terminating 246-248
  terminating 246-248
  Try/Catch/Finally statement 250-253
error actions **248**
  $ErrorActionPreference variable 248, 249
  -ErrorAction parameter 249
execution policy **298, 299**
Export- cmdlets
  using 146
Export-Csv cmdlet **148, 149**
eXtensible Markup Language (XML) **149**
  ConvertTo-Xml 149
  Export-Clixml 149, 150
Extreme Programming (XP) **219**

F

files
  Get-Content cmdlet 156
  handling 152
  Import-Clixml cmdlet 158-160
  Import- cmdlets 156
  Import-Csv cmdlet 157
  Item- cmdlets 154, 155
  PSDrives 153, 154
  PSProviders 153, 154
  working with 155
filters
  using 231
filter scripts **62**
foreach loop statement **126-128**
for loop statement **130-132**
Format-List **143**
Format-Table **144**
formatting **142, 143**
  Format-List 143
  Format-Table 144
  Format-Wide cmdlet 144
  gotchas 144
Format-Wide cmdlet **144**
Framework Class Library **386**
function
  behaviors 225
  code repetition, turning into 220, 221
  creating 222-225
functional module **220**
functional programming **220**
functions parameters **225**
  attributes 228
  filters 231
  types 225
functions parameters, attributes
  Alias attribute 230
  argument completion attributes 230
  CmdletBinding attribute 228
  HelpMessage argument 230
  Mandatory argument 229
  ParameterSetName argument 229
  Position argument 229
  SupportsWildcards attribute 230

validation attributes 231

ValueFromPipeline argument 230

ValueFromPipelineByPropertyName argument 230

ValueFromRemainingArguments argument 230

functions parameters, types

dynamic parameters 228

named parameters 225, 226

positional parameters 226-228

switch parameters 226

G

game, in PowerShell

writing 135-138

general-purpose input/output (GPIO) 364

Get-CimClass 328

Get-CimInstance 329

Get-Command cmdlet 20, 21

Get-Content cmdlet 156

Get-Help cmdlet 21, 22

about files 23

Get-Help Get-Process 22

Get-Help command 19

Get-Member cmdlet 23-25

Global Assembly Cache 389

Graphical User Interface (GUI) 385

Group Policy

reference link 299

H

hashtable 102-104

ordered hashtables 104, 105

headless mode 368

headless Pi

working with 369-372

heap 86

HelpMessage argument 230

Homebrew

installing, on macOS 358

HTML 150

ConvertTo-Html cmdlet 151, 152

Hypertext Transfer Protocol (HTTP)

authentication 172-174

Forms information, visibility in PowerShell 7 170-172

working with 166-170

I

if statement 118-120

imperative languages 220

Import-Clixml cmdlet 158-160

Import- cmdlets 156

Import-Csv cmdlet 157

integer types 87

Integrated Development Environments (IDEs) 109, 110

Integrated Scripting Environment (ISE) 110

Inter-Integrated Circuit (I2C) 377

International Space Station 188, 189

Internet Information Server (IIS) 176

Internet of Things (IoT) 364

Invoke-RestMethod cmdlet 177-180

IoT module

exploring 377-379

installing 376, 377

J

JavaScript Object Notation (JSON) 49, 174
  ConvertFrom-Json 182-184
  ConvertTo-Json 184-187
  Test-Json cmdlet 187, 188
  working with 180-182
Just Enough Administration (JEA) 303

L

lambdas 237, 238
language modes 301, 302
last-in, first-out (LIFO) 265
left-over principle 197
Linux
  OpenSSH, installing on 354
  PowerShell 7, running on 350-352
  VS Code, installing on 110
logic errors 255
Long Term Support (LTS) 9

M

macOS
  Homebrew, installing on 358
  PowerShell for 358
  PowerShell, installing on 358, 359
  VS Code, installing on 111, 360
managed code 387
Mandatory argument 229
members 392
methods
  discovering 333
  invoking 334, 335
module logging 306
module manifest 283-287
  groups 286

modules 316
  autoloading 271
  dot-sourcing 274-276
  function, creating 282, 283
  functions 270
  importing 272
  locations 270, 271
  PowerShellGet 272, 273
  script, turning into 276-278
  working with 269, 270
  writing 273, 274
modules, compatible with PowerShell 7 316, 317
  Compatibility mode, using 320-324
  compatible version, finding 318, 319
  module, forcing to load 319, 320
  options 318
Monad 5
Mono 386
MSI package, installing from command line
  reference link 11

N

named parameters 225, 226
namespace identifiers (NIDs) 168
namespaces 390, 391
namespace-specific string (NSS) 168
Natural Language Processing 162
nested modules 279-281
New-Module 273
non-terminating error 246-248

O

objects 54, 55, 68
  enumerating 67, 68
  filtering 60

parallel enumeration 68

selecting 55

selecting, with Select-Object 56, 57

selecting, with Sort-Object 57-60

sorting 55

object types

exploring 83, 84

redux 84, 85

one-dimensional 95

one-to-many sessions 297

one-to-one remoting session 296

OpenSSH

installing, on Linux 354

installing, on Windows 352-354

key-based authentication 356-358

remote sessions, running 355, 356

remoting with 352

OpenSSH support

PowerShell7, checking has 352

operating systems (OSs) 51

ordered hashtables 104, 105

over the shoulder logging 303, 304

P

packages.microsoft.com (PMC) 344

parameters 30

creating 201-204

making, mandatory 204

switching 207, 208

type, specifying 204

values, obtaining from pipeline 205, 206

working with 201

ParameterSetName argument 229

parameter sets 35

parameters, types

common parameters 34

mandatory parameters 34

mandatory positional parameters 34

optional parameters 34

optional positional parameters 34

switch parameters 34

parentheses 72

parenthetical commands 72

physical computing 379-383

pipeline 51, 53

troubleshooting 72-74

pipeline character 24

pipeline parameter binding 69

pipeline tracing 72

Plaster 269

scaffolding tools, using such as 287-291

positional parameters 226-228

Position argument 229

PowerShell 4, 293

for macOS 358

installing, on macOS 358, 359

installing, on Pi 365, 367

running, on Raspberry Pi OS 376

running, with administrator
    privileges 18, 19

streams 52

used, for connecting to
    Raspberry Pi 372-374

VS Code, configuring 113-117

Windows Terminal, installing from
    Microsoft Store 44-49

Windows Terminal, using 44

working with 43

PowerShell 7 5, 316

autocomplete feature 19

checking, has OpenSSH support 352

Forms information, visibility in 170-172

installing 343

installing, as .NET Global tool 15

installing, from Microsoft Store 15

installing, from .msi file 8-11

installing, from .zip file 12-14

installing, on CentOS 7 347, 348

installing, on CentOS 8 and 9 346

installing, on Ubuntu 22.04 343, 345

installing, with winget 14, 15

obtaining 7, 8

running 16-18

running, on Linux 350-352

scripting languages, versus system
    programming languages 6, 7

usage, considerations 324

used for 6

versus Windows PowerShell 5

PowerShell, concept of scope 232

child scope 233

parent scope 233

scope modifiers 234, 235

types 232, 233

PowerShell control flow

conditional control flow 117, 118

PowerShell Core 10

PowerShell debugger commands 261, 262

PowerShell exceptions

versus .NET exceptions 247

PowerShell Gallery 40, 41

reference link 42

repositories 42

sources 42, 43

PowerShellGet 272, 273

PowerShell logging 303

deep script block logging 305, 306

module logging 306

over the shoulder logging 303, 304

PowerShell remoting 293, 294

enabling 294

PowerShell variables 77, 78

casting 89-91

MyVariable is not $MyVariable 78, 79

types 81

variable, naming 80, 81

PowerShell variable, types

automatic variables 81, 82

preference variables 82, 83

Practical 365 site

URL 198

preference variables 81-83

primitive types 86

procedural programming 220

Process class

reference link 25

process statement 223

properties 84

modifying 331, 333

providers 153

PSBreakpoint cmdlets 259

Python Package Index (PyPI) 39

R

Raspberry Pi 364, 365

connecting, with PowerShell 372-374

connecting, with VS Code 374-376

remotely, connecting to 368

Raspberry Pi OS 364

PowerShell, running on 376

real numbers 87

Red Hat Enterprise Linux (RHEL) 339

reference types

array 92, 93

hashtable 102-104

navigating 91

splatting 106

string 98-101

relative path 300
Remote Procedure Call (RPC) 175, 325
Remote - SSH 374
REST APIs 176
   Invoke-RestMethod cmdlet 177-180
   working with 176, 177
return keyword
   using 225

S

sandbox 15
scaffolding tools
   using, such as Plaster 287-291
scope 81, 217
   repetition, consideration 218, 219
scriptblocks 62, 217
   executing 235-237
   exploring 235
   lambdas 237, 238
scripting 196
   writing, significance 197
scripting languages
   versus system programming languages 6, 7
script instrumentation 256-259
scripts
   comment-based help 210, 211
   comment blocks 209, 210
   comments 208
   help, providing 208
   obtaining 197, 198
   parameter help messages 213, 214
   running 198
   Write-Verbose cmdlet 212, 213
   writing 198-200
   writing, significance 196

secure code, writing 307
   parameter security 309, 310
   passwords, storing securely 307, 308
   scripts, signing 308
Secure Shell (SSH) protocol 339
   remoting 303
security
   significance 293
Security Information and Event
      Management (SIEM) 305
Security Servicing Criteria 302
Select-Object
   using 56, 57
session
   creating 295
   joining 296
   leaving 297
Session ID (SI) 59
Shendomizer 363
Simple Object Access Protocol
      (SOAP) APIs 176
Software Bill of Materials (SBOM) 302
Software Development Kit (SDK) 15
Sort-Object
   used, for sorting objects 57-60
splatting 106
stack 86
standard error (stderr) 52
standard input (stdin) 52
standard output (stdout) 52
standard streams 52
stateful 175
stateless 175
static typing 88
   versus dynamic typing 88, 89
stop words 162

strings 98-101
    single and double quote marks 101, 102
SupportsWildcards attribute 230
switch parameters 226
switch statement 123-126
symbolic link (symlink) 373
Synchronous Peripheral Interface (SPI) 377
syntax errors 255
System Center Configuration
    Manager (SCCM) 11
system programming languages
    versus scripting languages 6, 7

T

Tab-Separated Values (TSV) file 148
Term Frequency 160
terminating error 246-248
ternary operator 123
Test-Json cmdlet 187, 188
text file
    frequent words, measuring 160-163
    writing 145, 146
Try/Catch/Finally statement 250-253
type-Promiscuous 88
types 389

U

Ubuntu 22.04
    PowerShell 7, installing on 343, 345
Ubuntu server
    installing 340-342
UI cultures 148
Uniform Resource Identifier (URI) 168

Uniform Resource Locator (URL) 168
Uniform Resource Name (URN) 168
Universal Windows Platform (UWP) 388
User Account Control (UAC) 18
user-created variables 81
UTF-8 with no Byte Order Mark
    (utf8NoBOM) 156

V

validation attributes 231
ValueFromPipeline argument 230
ValueFromPipelineByPropertyName
    argument 230
ValueFromRemainingArguments
    argument 230
values
    identifying and modifying 200
value types
    Boolean-type variable 86
    char type 88
    discovering 86
    integer types 87
    real numbers 87
versioning 393
VS Code 110
    configuring, for PowerShell 113-117
    debugging with 262-265
    installing 110, 348-350
    installing, on Linux 110, 111
    installing, on macOS 111, 360
    installing, on Raspberry Pi 368
    installing, on Windows 111, 112
    used, for connecting to
        Raspberry Pi 374-376

W

Weather API Service
personal key, obtaining 199
web applications 176
layers 176
**Web-Based Enterprise Management
(WBEM) 324**
**Web Services for Management
(WS-MAN) 324**
WebSocket APIs 176
Where-Object
advanced syntax 62, 63
advanced syntax, multiple filters 63-65
filter optimization 66
while loop statement 130
Win32_Process class
reference link 333
Windows 112
OpenSSH, installing on 352-354
VS Code, installing on 111, 112
**Windows Antimalware Scan
Interface (AMSI) API 302**
**Windows Defender Application
Control (WDAC) 301**
**Windows Management
Instrumentation (WMI) 324**
repository 326, 327
used, for commands 325
versus Common Information
Model (CIM) 325

Windows Package Manager 14
Windows PowerShell 5, 316
versus PowerShell 7 5
**Windows Presentation Foundation
(WPF) framework 388**
Windows Query Language (WQL) 329
**Windows Remote Management
(WinRM) 294, 325, 352**
Windows Sandbox 15
reference link 8
**Windows Server Update Services
(WSUS) 11, 324**
Windows Subsystem for Linux (WSL) 341
Windows Terminal
installing, from Microsoft Store 44-49
using 44
winget 14
reference link 15
used, for installing PowerShell 7 14, 15
Working Set (WS) 59
Write-Log.psm1 279
Write-Verbose cmdlet 212, 213

Y

You Aren't Gonna Need It (YAGNI) 219

packtpub.com

Subscribe to our online digital library for full access to over 7,000 books and videos, as well as industry leading tools to help you plan your personal development and advance your career. For more information, please visit our website.

Why subscribe?

- Spend less time learning and more time coding with practical eBooks and Videos from over 4,000 industry professionals

- Improve your learning with Skill Plans built especially for you

- Get a free eBook or video every month

- Fully searchable for easy access to vital information

- Copy and paste, print, and bookmark content

Did you know that Packt offers eBook versions of every book published, with PDF and ePub files available? You can upgrade to the eBook version at packtpub.com and as a print book customer, you are entitled to a discount on the eBook copy. Get in touch with us at customercare@packtpub.com for more details.

At www.packtpub.com, you can also read a collection of free technical articles, sign up for a range of free newsletters, and receive exclusive discounts and offers on Packt books and eBooks.

Other Books You May Enjoy

If you enjoyed this book, you may be interested in these other books by Packt:

PowerShell Automation and Scripting for Cybersecurity

Miriam C. Wiesner

ISBN: 978-1-80056-637-8

- Leverage PowerShell, its mitigation techniques, and detect attacks
- Fortify your environment and systems against threats
- Get unique insights into event logs and IDs in relation to PowerShell and detect attacks
- Configure PSRemoting and learn about risks, bypasses, and best practices
- Use PowerShell for system access, exploitation, and hijacking
- Red and blue team introduction to Active Directory and Azure AD security
- Discover PowerShell security measures for attacks that go deeper than simple commands
- Explore JEA to restrict what commands can be executed

Okta Administration Up and Running

HenkJan de Vries, Lovisa Stenbäcken Stjernlöf

ISBN: 978-1-83763-745-4

- Get a clear overview of Okta's advanced features
- Integrate Okta with directories and applications using hands-on instructions
- Get practical recommendations on managing policies for SSO, MFA, and lifecycle management
- Discover how to manage groups and group rules for Joiner, Mover, Leaver events in Okta using examples
- Manage your Okta tenants using APIs and oversee API access with Okta
- Set up and manage your organization's Okta environment, ensuring a secure IAM practice
- Find out how to extend your Okta experience with Workflows and ASA

Packt is searching for authors like you

If you're interested in becoming an author for Packt, please visit `authors.packtpub.com` and apply today. We have worked with thousands of developers and tech professionals, just like you, to help them share their insight with the global tech community. You can make a general application, apply for a specific hot topic that we are recruiting an author for, or submit your own idea.

Share your thoughts

Now you've finished *PowerShell 7 Workshop*, we'd love to hear your thoughts! Scan the QR code below to go straight to the Amazon review page for this book and share your feedback or leave a review on the site that you purchased it from.

`https://packt.link/r/1801812985`

Your review is important to us and the tech community and will help us make sure we're delivering excellent quality content.

Download a free PDF copy of this book

Thanks for purchasing this book!

Do you like to read on the go but are unable to carry your print books everywhere?

Is your eBook purchase not compatible with the device of your choice?

Don't worry, now with every Packt book you get a DRM-free PDF version of that book at no cost.

Read anywhere, any place, on any device. Search, copy, and paste code from your favorite technical books directly into your application.

The perks don't stop there, you can get exclusive access to discounts, newsletters, and great free content in your inbox daily

Follow these simple steps to get the benefits:

1. Scan the QR code or visit the link below

https://packt.link/free-ebook/9781801812986

2. Submit your proof of purchase
3. That's it! We'll send your free PDF and other benefits to your email directly

Milton Keynes UK
Ingram Content Group UK Ltd.
UKHW051159220224
438165UK00008B/191

9 781801 81298